APODICTIC TREATISES
ON THE PROCESSION
OF THE HOLY SPIRIT

APODICTIC TREATISES ON THE PROCESSION OF THE HOLY SPIRIT

Our Father Among the Saints
Gregory Palamas
Archbishop of Thessaloniki

Introduction & Translation
Fr. Christopher C. Moody

Assistant Translator & Editor
Gregory Heers

Uncut Mountain Press

APODICTIC TREATISES ON THE PROCESSION OF THE HOLY SPIRIT

© 2022

Uncut Mountain Press

uncutmountainpress.com

Front Cover Artwork: George Weis
Front Cover Image and frontspiece: Saint Gregory Palamas, Vatopedi Monastery, Mt. Athos

The Greek version of the Treatises is taken from series, The Greek-speaking Fathers of the Church (ΕΠΕ).

Special thanks to Elder Paisios of St. Anthony's Orthodox Monastery, Florence, AZ, for the initial encouragement to undertake this project and to Monk Iakovos of St. Anne's Skete for the initial draft translation.

Scriptural quotations are primarily taken from the King James Version. The translator has emended some quotations to better reflect the original Greek text. Citations from the Psalms are primarily taken from *The Psalter According to the Seventy, translated from the Septuagint Version of the Old Testament* by the Holy Transfiguration Monastery, Brookline, MA.

Library of Congress Cataloging-in-Publication Data

Saint Gregory Palamas, 1296-1359 AD.
   Apodictic Treatises On the Procession of the Holy Spirit — 1st ed.
   Translated by Fr. Christopher C. Moody and Gregory Heers
   Edited by Gregory Heers

ISBN: 978-1-63941-009-5

I. Orthodox Christian
II. Theology

"...εἰς τὸ Πνεῦμα τὸ Ἅγιον,
τὸ Κύριον, τὸ Ζωοποιόν,
τὸ ἐκ τοῦ Πατρὸς ἐκπορευόμενον..."

"... in the Holy Spirit,
the Lord, the Giver of life,
Who **proceedeth from the Father**..."

ΤΟΥ
ΕΝ ΑΓΙΟΙΣ ΠΑΤΡΟΣ
ΗΜΩΝ ΓΡΗΓΟΡΙΟΥ ΑΡΧΙ-
επισκόπȣ Θεσσαλονίκης λόγοι ἀπο-
δεικτικοὶ δύο.

FLOREAT IN ÆTERNVM

Χριστός μοι μόνος εἴη δόξα κ̀ νίκη.

Contents

Τὸ Σύμβολον τῆς Πίστεως - The Symbol of Faith
From a 16th-century Horologion, St. Catherine's Monastery, Mt. Sinai

καὶ ἀπελθόντας εἰς τὸ κολασις· καὶ και
θεζόμενον ἐκ δεξιῶν τοῦ προ καὶ
πάλιν ἐρχόμενον μετὰ δόξης κρῖ
ναι ζῶντας καὶ νεκροῦς· οὗ τῆς βασι
λείας οὐκ ἔσται τέλος· Καὶ εἰς τὸ πν̅
τὸ ἅγιον τὸ κν̅ τὸ ζωοποιόν· τὸ ἐκ τῆ
πρ̅ς ἐκπορευόμενον· τὸ σὺν πρὶ καὶ
ϊῶ σὺν προσκυνούμενον καὶ συνδο
ξαζόμενον· τὸ λαλῆσαν διὰ τῶν πρω
φητῶν· Εἰς μίαν ἁγίαν καθολικὴν
καὶ ἀποστολικὴν δὲ κλησίαν ὁ μο λογῶ
ἓν βάπτισμα εἰς ἄφεσιν ἁμῶν τῶν
προσδοκῶ δ ἀνάστασιν νεκρῶν· καὶ ζω
ὴν τοῦ μέλλοντος αἰῶνος ἀμην· †

τὸ τρισα· σταῦρον τοῖς· αυτο η μων·
ἅγιν ιλαβα· ὁ τι οὗ ϊσρ̅ν Πατρὸς η τη
δοῦλ ὁ μμαθ ιος ἐρχέται ἐν τῶ μέσω
τῆς νυκτος· καὶ μακάριος ὁ δοῦλος
ὁ μαγγι ὁν γρηγοροῦντα· ἀνάξιος δὲ

"...Καὶ εἰς τὸ Πνεῦμα τὸ Ἅγιον, τὸ Κύριον, τὸ Ζωοποιόν, τὸ ἐκ
τοῦ Πατρὸς ἐκπορευόμενον,..."

INTRODUCTION
to the Edition of 1981

SAINT GREGORY PALAMAS: EARLY LIFE AND WORK[1]

by Panagiotis Christou

By the time Saint Gregory Palamas appeared on the spiritual scene, the Roman Empire[2] had already completed the life-span of more than one thousand three hundred years. It had lived longer than any other empire in the world. This giant organism, giant not so much for its expansiveness as for the endurance of its ethos, which had diligently guarded, transformed, and transmitted the seeds of human civilization, which Hellenism had produced with such dexterity, as well as the flame of Christian faith and love, although old by now, had nevertheless not been deadened. Despite the savage beatings which it continually received from its innumerable enemies throughout all the centuries from the time of its constitution, it refused to bow the knee. It remained as the only fortress wherein all the spiritual goods of civilization were being preserved and cultivated with all safety. But it likewise was a wall behind which Western Europe was living securely.

Of course, its decline had already begun in the twelfth century, but the vitality of Romanía facilitated its continuation for another two hundred and fifty years. The vitality of Orthodoxy in these years goes hand in hand with the Hellenism's strength for resistance. Orthodox theology is renewed and enlivened, while the attempt to subjugate her to Franco-Latin Rome finds intense resistance from theological thought.

Saint Gregory Palamas, having experienced all these difficulties,

contributed in his own way to the struggles of the race and to the preservation of the autonomy of the Orthodox Church more than anyone else in his age, and thus occupied one of most significant positions amongst protagonists in the formulation of the spiritual teaching of Christianity.

The parents of Gregory, Constantine and Kalloni (or Kali, meaning 'belle'), were inspired by a spirit of holiness and temperance, even though the circles in which they lived demanded a worldly mentality. Coming from Anatolia, as is noted in the biography of their son,[3] they had settled down in Constantinople shortly after their marriage and probably had children there. It appears that the national troubles had driven them there, since shortly aforetime the Ottomans had begun to devastate the East. Being wealthy and of noble lineage, they did manage to bring to the capital substantial assets, which would allow them to live comfortably.

Constantine's exceptional ethos led Emperor Andronikos Palaiologos the Second, who was called the Elder, to choose him to be the teacher of his grandson and successor, who was subsequently Emperor Andronikos the Third, also called the Younger. But he also went further than this: appreciating his virtues, he made him his friend and offered him a seat in the Senate. In this capacity, Constantine become a counselor of the state but also a defender of the wronged, as he demonstrated on many occasions. He, however, was not one of those men that have a passion for political matters. He was so dedicated to God that, during the meetings of the Senate before the emperor, he gave himself over to silent prayer.[4] He liked to associate with monks experienced in spiritual practice, especially Phocas, and he would often visit the monasteries that existed inside and outside of the city. Sometimes he would also include his children in such visits, in order to initiate them into the spiritual life. The natural end of such tendencies was that shortly before his death he was tonsured a monk. His spouse Kalloni was to do the same much later.

The couple had at least five children, which, as far as we know, all followed the monastic life, three boys and two girls. Gregory was the first in order and was the teacher of the others. He was born

in 1296.[5] The emperor strengthened the orphaned family and in particular Gregory, who was of the same age as his royal grandson Andronikos. Gregory finished his studies of philosophy and rhetoric early with such success that he was admired by all the scholars of Constantinople. Then he attendned courses in natural physics and logic with similar success, with the Aristotelian literary corpus as the basis. The degree of his performance in them is testified by the words of Theodore Metochites, the rector of the university of Constantinople: after the conclusion of the graduation speech before the emperor, the officials, the professors, and the scholars of the city, in which Gregory developed a topic from the logic of Aristotle with such adroitness and completeness, the rector shouted with amazement that even Aristotle himself would have praised him exceedingly, if he were present and had heard him: "καὶ Ἀριστοτέλης αὐτὸς εἴγε περιὼν παρῆν, ἐπήνεσεν ἄν". Gregory was compelled to recount this incident himself in a letter of his many decades later,[6] when he came into conflict with partisans of the Renaissance who unjustly challenged his possession of a comprehensive education.[7]

His Spiritual Training (AGOGE)

From that time on, Gregory was given over to the study of ascetic literature and interaction with esteemed teachers of spiritual training, and he applied himself to the ascetic practice, to the great disappointment of the emperor, who had intended him for high political offices. Among his spiritual teachers Theoleptos was noteworthy, a chosen member of the Athonite Republic at the start, who afterward became Metropolitan of Philadelphia but was compelled to remain in Constantinople due to the circumstances of the war.[8] Gregory was taught by him sacred nepsis and noetic prayer, which he assuredly already knew from his conversations with his father and his father's interlocutors. At twenty years of age, having refused the offer of an elevated office by the emperor, he decided to go to labor ascetically on Mount Athos with his brothers, Makarios and Theodosios, abandoning his earthly goods. In the fall of 1316, having passed through Thrace, they came to

Chalkidiki, with Thessaloniki (far left) and the peninsula of Mt. Athos (far right).

Mount Papikion,[9] which is found on the borders of Thrace with Macedonia, and judged it good to spend the winter there close to eminent ascetics. Gregory now experienced the first of his troubles in which his struggles and the political circumstances were about to incessantly involve him. Groups of Messalian monks were settled near the mountain, apparently Bogomils, many of which visited him, seeking to influence him favorably toward their dyarchic and anti-liturgical sentiments. When they had broken off the visits, because they saw that the results would be the opposite of what they pursued, he himself began to visit them personally. Indeed, one of the leaders of their community and many members were converted by his arguments. Because of this, the heretics unsuccessfully tried to kill him by poisoning.

Philotheos Kokkinos[10] attaches great significance to this incident, because he wishes to stop the mouths of those that later accused Saint Gregory of friendliness and inclination toward these heretics. Indeed, Barlaam accused the hesychast monks of Mount Athos as Messalians, and the second triad of his writings was entitled *Against the Messalians*. Akindynos, the sometime friend of Saint Gregory, says that the latter had come into contact with Bogomils in Thessaloniki, while later Nicephorus Gregoras would assert that Saint Gregory and his friends fled from Mount Athos in 1325 so as to escape being condemned for Messalianism.[11] All these assertions are complete retaliatory fabrications and invoke the persistence of the Hesychasts in noetic prayer in an unfounded comparison with the Euchitism of the Messalians (who were also called Euchites). The incident above demonstrates the absence of any connection to this heresy.

In the spring of the following year (1317), Saint Gregory arrived with his brethren at the "Athos they longed for", and he himself settled down in the Lavra of Vatopedi near the experienced monk Nikodemos, a man brave and admirable in ascetic practice as well as in theory, at whose hands he also received his monastic tonsure. After the course of three years (1317-1320), as soon as his elder died, Saint Gregory moved to the renowned Lavra of Athanasius, where he was warmly received by the monks, who from his reputation already knew of his virtue. He served there in obedience for three years working in the refectory and serving as a chanter (1320-1323), after which he was again overcome by his love for solitude and *hesychia*.

So, next he settled down in the secluded location known as Glossia, situated on the eastern slope of Athos and now called Provata. Glossia had been previously honored by the ascetic sweat of Nikephoros the Italiote, instructor of the hesychastic method, and of Theoleptos, teacher of Saint Gregory; now a multitude of holy men were living there, including great spiritual guides such as Kallistos, who subsequently became patriarch, another Kallistos (Katafygiotis), and Elias Seliotas.

The Turkish pirates, who were at that time continually multiplying and perpetrating savage raiding incursions on the Greek

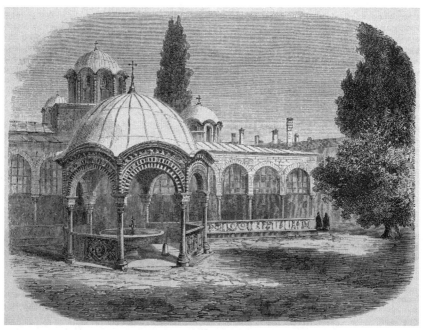

Great Lavra, Mt. Athos.

coasts, became especially dangerous for the fathers of Mount Athos and mainly for the ascetics found outside the walls, in the desert. Because of this, after living for two years in Glossia (1323-1325), Saint Gregory departed with other fellow ascetics (twelve in all) for Thessaloniki. Their first thought was to depart for the Holy City, Jerusalem, so as to venerate the Passion and Resurrection of the Lord and to rest there for life, being certainly ignorant of the fact that the situation there was no better as far as the barbarian incursions were concerned. But after a vision, in which Saint Demetrios appeared to Saint Gregory and demanded him for himself, they decided to settle in a place near Thessaloniki and chose a mountain next to Veria (Berea), where they settled in 1326, once Saint Gregory (who was by then thirty years of age) had been ordained a priest.

He lived there in solitude in his cell five days of the week, while on Saturday and the Lord's Day he made an appearance to administer the sacred services, for association with the fellow monks, and for teaching. Multitudes of monks and laymen from the surrounding area came to him at that time for spiritual refreshment from his conversation and radiance.

At this time, having been informed by a letter from his sisters about the death of his beloved mother Kalloni, he was forced to make a visit to Constantinople to strengthen them. They, however, placed him before a dilemma: either to remain in the capital so as to be close to them, or to take them with him. His commitments obliged him to choose the second solution. He settled his sisters in a monastery within the city of Berea, while he returned to the mountain; yet before much time had passed the eldest of them, Epicharis, reposed.

THE BEGINNING OF HIS SPIRITUAL WRITING

Five years after his settlement at the skete at Veria (1326-1331), the situation in the area also became uncertain. The invasion of the Serbs under Stephen Dushan, the lootings and enslavements, forced him to return to Athos, probably followed by his companions. He arrived at the Great Lavra, where his brothers enthusiastically received him; nevertheless, he did not wish to live inside the monastery but chose a cell in a neighboring area, the "phrontistery of Savas the divine", to make the area a source of *hesychia*. At this time, his teaching shifts focus from the ethos to dogma, following a commandment which he received in a vision. Under the cover of a light sleep, he thought that he was holding in his hand a vessel full of milk, which suddenly swelled and began to gush forth, while at the same time it was being changed into flavorful wine, giving off a pleasant aroma. An illustrious man appeared, who verbally rebuked him: "Why do you not give from this divine drink, which gushes forth in a marvelous manner, but let it be spilled in vain?" Saint Gregory realized that the meaning of the vision was that he had to give to his words elevated and dogmatic content, and so he began to write. His first composition was the *Life of Peter the Athonite*.

His fame and leadership abilities were to temporarily cost him the loss of *hesychia*. By the vote of the Protos of Mount Athos and of the synaxis, he was appointed abbot of the monastery of Esphigmenou and accepted this responsible administrative position with the understanding that it was temporary and was for the purpose of taking care of exigent problems, as it appears. Simple

Esphigmenou Monastery, Mt. Athos

in manners, free in opinion, pleasant in his sermons, strict on the slothful, forgiving to the repentant, he managed this monastery with skill, despite the internal difficulties. He was not able to remain in this position permanently and fled it very soon, perhaps out of the necessity to engage in dogmatic struggles and out of the displeasure which his strict monastic reformative actions provoked. He was probably appointed as abbot of the monastery in the middle of 1333, remained in the position for about a year, and returned to his old eremitic cell near the Lavra in 1334. From there he was to be called to an even wider field of action, which, in time, revealed him as a leading figure of Orthodoxy.

Shortly before this time, around 1330, the philosopher monk Barlaam came to Greece from Calabria. He belonged to the ethnically Greek-speaking Roman community of southern Italy, (which still exists despite the political adventures of the region), and had received a Greek education. He now wanted to become acquainted with his ancestral homeland, in which had lived the philosophers whom he admired, Plato and Aristotle, and in which his fellow-Orthodox were also living. He felt much national pride, and he probably thought it an easy thing to effect a revival of the

old glory of Romanía and a complete renaissance of letters and sciences, in which he himself would be a protagonist.

The Grand Domestic John Kantakouzenos, a patron of the Renaissance in Romanía at the time, supported the newcomer and gave to him a professorship at the university of Constantinople. His lectures on philosophical, theological, and natural subjects provoked the deepest impression, while his compositions found wide circulation. His success exacerbated his tendency to think highly of himself and nourished his passion to humiliate all who were practicing the same art as himself, which even his friends admit: "For when you first came to the Great City [Constantinople]," says Akindynos to him, "you took in all things great effort to prove the City devoid of all learning."[12] Who knows what frustrations he must have experienced in his homeland once, for which he was now coming here to satisfy his wounded ambition, seeking power and glory? In any case, a result of his behaviour was that in a short time he made enemies of the most famous scholars of Romanía, of whom Nicephorus Gregoras was chief, and for that reason the climate there became unbearable for him, and he was forced to settle in Thessaloniki.

The discussions which took place in the reign of Andronikos the Third, with the aim of the union of the Churches, in the years 1333 and 1334, were what first brought the two men of letters, Saint Gregory and Barlaam, into contact. Both of them composed polemical works against the Franco-Latins of Rome, but each started off from a different starting point. Barlaam considered meaningless the demand of the Latins, viz. that the Holy Spirit proceeds also from the Son, since God (according to the words of both Dionysius the Areopagite and others) is incomprehensible.

At the same time, Saint Gregory wrote the *Apodictic Treatises on the Procession of the Holy Spirit*, whose title alone shows Saint Gregory's opposition to the direction of Barlaam. In contrast to the latter's agnosticism, Saint Gregory speaks of an "apodictic" treatise.[13] It was natural for him to come into conflict with Barlaam, who on one occasion egotistically exploded and said characteristically, "I will humiliate the man!"

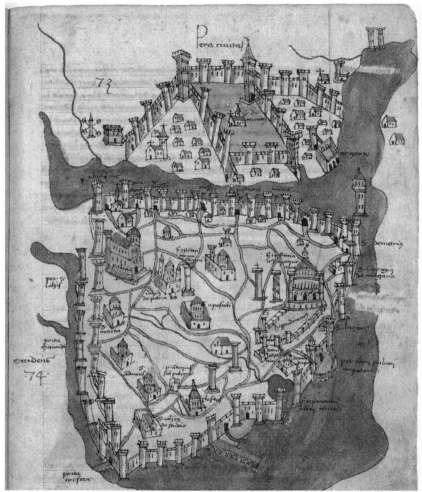

Ancient map of Constantinople from a book by Cristoforo Buondelmonti (1475)

Date and Occasion of the Treatises

During the years of 1333-1334, discussions were held in Constantinople concerning the union of the Churches between the representatives of the Pope and the Patriarchate. The head of the Orthodox delegation, Barlaam the Calabrian, while supporting the eastern view, employed in both his oral conversations and his written essays the paradoxical reasoning that the claim of the Latins (viz. that the Spirit proceeds also from the Son) is not found

on logic, since the divine is incomprehensible and unprovable [*anapodicton*]. Since apparently this position, being in harmony with the physiological presuppositions of Barlaam, undermined the foundations of Orthodox dogma, Saint Gregory composed works of his own.

1) *Apodictic Treatises on the Procession of the Holy Spirit.*

Following a direction opposite to that of Barlaam, he emphasizes that there is proof [*apodeixis*] in the case of God, but it is different from the logical constructions of men and is founded on faith, enlightenment, and Tradition. Afterward, on the basis of ancient writings, he explicates the dogma concerning the procession from the Father and the pouring forth through (or from) the Son. These two treatises were written in 1335 and are among the first works of Saint Gregory.

2) *Counter-Epigraphs*

These were directed at the Epigraphs of Bekkos. The Latin-minded Patriarch had made a philological anthology of passages from the Fathers in order to show that the Latin dogma is in harmony with the patristic teaching, which Saint Gregory refutes with this work. They had been composed at this time along with the previous, but in all likelihood they were revised around 1340, because he also classifies Akindynos with the "irreverent" Barlaam.

CONTENTS

The entire work is preceded by a characteristic introduction, wherein the "subtle serpent and source of vice" is presented as a base that acquires from time to time countless new heads, the heads of those that follow his counsels which lead to perdition, and as having appeared once again on the occasion of the discussions with the Latins. Next comes a prayer on behalf of the author, that he may theologise in a manner well-pleasing to God,[14] while at the end of the work another prayer is given, asking for the manifestation of God, that all may come to know his glory.[15]

The first treatise is divided into forty-two chapters, recapitulated at the end in forty-two short paragraphs. This division, which is

owed to the author's own pen, was not also extended to the second treatise, evidently because the work was snatched away too soon by Joseph.[16] As he states at the beginning of the second treatise, in the first the author attempts to clarify the Orthodox mindset, scarcely implying the objections of the Latins.[17]

The entire subject of the procession of the Holy Spirit is examined from two sides: first, whether it was permitted for the Latins to add "and from the Son", and whether this teaching is well-founded. The first problem is simple. The "Symbol free from false belief" of Nicaea and Constantinople can be laid down as the basis for all argumentation, which was composed by the chosen Fathers that gathered there, both eastern and western, and which they handed down to posterity complete and not accepting any addition or change. So there is no room for any debate regarding the addition, while the dialogues with the Latins will become possible and fruitful only if they cast it away. "Thus, it was most just not to deem you worthy even of conversation as long as you add to the sacred Symbol. Now, after you have cast out your addition, then one should inquire whether the Holy Spirit is also from the Son or not also from the Son."[18]

The second problem is initially interpretational. The Latins were claiming that, while the Symbol says that the Spirit proceeds "from the Father", yet it does not say "only from the Father"; therefore we may suppose that the Symbol silently accepts the procession from the Son as well. Through a multitude of passages Saint Gregory proves that, just as the "only" is not added with reference to the begetting of the Son from the Father and yet it is always implied, so also with the procession of the Spirit, although the "only" is not noted, it is always implied.[19] "Nearly every theological tongue" proclaims that the Spirit proceeds only from the Father.[20]

To support his view the author then resorts to the theological presuppositions regarding the Holy Trinity. The Latins were confusing the hypostatic with the natural attributes, i.e. the three hypostases with the nature of God. By confusing the energies (ἐνεργήματα) of the entire divine nature, such as the creative energy, with the hypostatic properties, such as the processional property,

they were attributing the latter not only to the hypostasis of the
Father but also to that of the Son, or rather to the entire divinity,
just as creation is indeed attributed to the entire divinity. Of course,
this confusion flows from older monarchianistic perceptions,[21] which
used to be dominant in Rome and which cost the whole Church so
many struggles. Unlike the easterners, the westerners at that time
did not distinguish between the essence and hypostasis, and it was
unwillingly that they accepted the solution of the Cappadocians,
which came after the council of 362 in Alexandria and according
to which God has one essence and exists in three hypostases; the
westerners instead preferred the term "person".

The Alexandrian theologians, who had originally been in
agreement with the western view, after 362 turned to the eastern
one, although they retained traces of their older views. Saint
Gregory interprets the phrase of St. Cyril of Alexandria, "the Spirit
that is poured forth essentially from both, that is, from the Father
through the Son,"[22] as agreeing with his own views.

It was mainly the Cappadocian theologians that established
the eastern position by introducing the term "cause" into the
intratrinitarian relationships. The cause refers exclusively to the
Father.[23] Saint Photius used the distinction between nature and
hypostasis in his argumentation regarding procession.[24] Saint
Gregory considers the Latins' claims unreasonable. If, according
to them, the Spirit proceeds directly from the Son and indirectly
from the father, they they must either accept two causes and two
caused or they must identify the two causes, that, the hypostasis of
the Son with that of the Father, in which case they will end up at the
old heresy of patripassianism.[25] If natural and hypostatic attributes
considered identical, then the Spirit will proceed not only "and from
the Son" but from Himself as well, in which case the proceeding
Spirit will be other than the originating Spirit, and we shall end up
with a tetrad instead of a Trinity.[26] Besides, the self-contradictory
claims of the Latins are found to lead to the acceptance of an
absolute prioritization (ἱεράρχησις) of the persons of the Holy Trinity,
resulting in the acceptance of the views of Eunomius.[27] The Holy
Trinity, however, is not subject to order: It is beyond order. There

is an order only in the manifestation of the three persons to the world.[28]

Saint Gregory does not reject the term "through the Son," and he is ready to accept procession "from the Son" (*Filioque*), if interpreted in Orthodox manner. While according to the confession of Dionysius he accepts one "fount of divinity" and "divinity-generating divinity",[29] whence proceeds the Spirit, he also accepts a double progression or pouring-forth of the Spirit, which can by concession be also called a procession. In other words, the Spirit, proceeding eternally from the Father, rests upon the Son and is poured forth by the two of them, "from both", onto the worthy ones.[30] This view, seeds of which may be found in a passage of Saint Gregory of Nyssa quoted by the author,[31] had already been developed in the thirteenth century by Gregory the Cypriot.[32]

In the second treatise the author analyses and refutes in detail the proposals of the Latins, as he also states in his preamble.[33] The western church, he says, being the largest, has suffered the same thing that happens to the largest of animals, the elephant, who, once he falls, cannot arise. Yet if this church should ask for help, he goes on to say, we all are ready and willing to stretch out a helping hand of salvation.[34]

The correct interpretation [by St. Gregory] of the passages brought forth by the Latins strengthens the view regarding a distinction between the origin of the hypostasis of the Spirit, which proceeds from the father, and His pouring-forth from the Father and from the Son. He goes to great lengths to establish such an interpretation of the following and other passages: "He breathed upon them and said, 'Receive ye Holy Spirit'",[35] "God sent forth the Spirit of His Son in our hearts crying, Abba, Father."[36]

At the end of the second treatise we find seeds of a teaching later developed systematically, the teaching regarding the difference between essence and energies, which allows us on the one hand to attribute the existential progression of the Spirit to the Father, while attributing the revelatory or energetic progression to the Son: "on the one hand the Spirit has His existential progression from the Father before all the ages, while on the other hand, since He exists

Latin Trinity Diagram, 13th c.

in the Son from eternity, He came forth from Him in order to be manifested, for us and after us, according to the revelatory and not the existential procession."[37]

NOTES

[1] Translated with modifications from Panagiotes Chrestou, Γρηγορίου τοῦ Παλαμᾶ Ἅπαντα τὰ Ἔργα, vol. 1, ed. Eleftherios Meretakis, Greek-speaking Fathers of the Church (ΕΠΕ) no. 51 (Thessaloniki: *Paterikai Ekdoseis "Gregorios Palamas"*, 1961), pp. 8-16, 34.

[2] In this translation all instances of "Byzantine Empire" and "Byzantium" have been replaced by "Roman Empire" and "Romanía" respectively so as to more accurately reflect historical reality. The "Byzantines" never called themselves "Byzantines" but "Romans", and "Byzantium" was a literary name for their capital city, never for their country, which they called "Romanía". For this see Anthony Kaldellis, *Romanland: Ethnicity and Empire in Byzantium* (Cambridge, MA, and London: The Belknap Press of Harvard University Press, 2019).

[3] Philotheos Kokkinos, *Encomium to Gregory Palamas* (PG 151:553). John Kantakouzenos, *History* 2, 39, publ. in Bonn, I, 545.

[4] Philotheos, *Encomium* (PG 151:555).

[5] This is gathered from the otherwise known year of his death (1359), when he was 63 years old.

[6] *Against Gregoras* I.

[7] He was called "ignorant and uneducated" by Barlaam, *First Epistle to Palamas*, in Schiro, *Barlaam Calabro, Epistole Greche*, Palermo 1954, o. 253; "illiterate" by Nicephorus Gregoras, *History* 30, 20, publ. in Bonn, III, 282; "not even known the first principles of philosophy" by Akindynos, *Epistle to Anonymous*, Loenertz, in ΕΕΒΣ 27 (Athens 1957) 106.

[8] Theoleptos's see was under Turkish occupation. —ED.

[9] St. Kyriakidis, "Τὸ Παπίκιον Ὄρος", Athens 36 (1923) 219-225.

[10] *Encomium* (PG 151:562).

[11] *History* 14, 7, Bonn, 719.

[12] Akindynos, *Epistles*, Cod. Ambros. 290, f. 67.

[13] Apodictic: from the Greek ἀποδείκνυμι, "to show by argument, prove, demonstrate."

[14] First Apodictic Treatise, preamble.

[15] Second Apodictic Treatise, 83.

[16] Joseph Kalothetos, a friend, disciple, and fellow-struggler of Saint Gregory Palamas; he died some time after 1355. —ED.

[17] Second Apodictic Treatise, 1.

[18] First Apodictic Treatise, 4.

[19] Ibid., 2 *et sequentia*; 20 *et alibi*.

[20] Ibid., 5.

[21] Monarchianism was a heretical theological movement that arose within the Church in the second and third centuries, consisting of a set of beliefs that emphasized God as being one, to the detriment of the doctrine of the Holy Trinity. —ED.

[22] *Regarding the Worship in Spirit*, PG 68, 148A.

[23] St. Basil the Great, *Letter 38*, 4, PG 32, 39D. See J. Meyendorff, "La Procession du Saint-Esprit chez les Pères orientaux", in *Russie et Chrétienté* 1950, p. 167.

[24] *Mystagogy of the Holy Spirit*, 6, PG 102, 288B.

[25] First Apodictic Treatise, 7; 22. Patripassianism is a kind of modalism, the heretical idea that there is only one God (one person, one hypostasis) appearing in three different ways ("modes"). The term literally means "the passion or

suffering of the Father": if, acording to modalism, the three persons (Father, Son, and Spirit) are actually one and the same, then the Father Himself would have suffered on the Cross as Son. —ED.

[26] Ibid., 15.

[27] See for instance the First Apodictic Treatise, 36. —ED.

[28] Ibid., 32 *et sequentia.*

[29] St. Dionysius, *On the Divine Names* 2, 5, PG 3, 641D. 2, 7, PG 3, 645B.

[30] First Apodictic Treatise, 29.

[31] *Great Catechetical Homily* 2, PG 45, 17B "We have learned the Spirit which accompanies the Word" ("πνεῦμα μεμαθηκότες θεοῦ τὸ συμπαρομαρτοῦν τῷ λόγῳ"). Cf. St. John of Damascus, *Exact Exposition of the Orthodox Faith* 1, 7, PG 94, 805AB.

[32] *On the Procession of the Holy Spirit*, PG 142, 274 *et sequentia.*

[33] Second Apodictic Treatise, 1.

[34] Ibid., 2.

[35] John 20:22.

[36] Gal. 4:6.

[37] Second Apodictic treatise, 77.

ΤΟΥ ΕΝ ΑΓΙΟΙΣ ΠΑΤΡΟΣ
ΗΜΩΝ ΓΡΗΓΟΡΙΟΥ ΑΡΧΙΕ-
ΠΙΣΚΟΠΟΥ ΘΕΣΣΑΛΟΝΙΚΗΣ
λόγος ἀποδεικτικὸς πρῶτος.

Αλιν ὁ δεινὸς καὶ ἀρχέκακος ὄφις τὴν ἑαυτοῦ κεφαλὴν καθ᾽ ἡμῶν ἀνερείπων, ὑποψιθυρίζει τὰ τῆς ἀληθείας ἀντίθετα. μᾶλλον δὲ τὴν μὲν κεφαλὴν τῷ τοῦ Χριστοῦ σταυρῷ συντριβείς, τῶν δὲ κατὰ γενεὰς πειθομένων ταῖς ἀπολαύσαις ὑπο-
θήκαις αὐτοῦ, κεφαλὴν ἑαυτῷ ποιούμενος ἕκαστον, καὶ οὕτω πολλὰς ἀντὶ μιᾶς κατὰ τὴν Ὕδραν κεφαλὰς ἀναδοὺς, δι᾽ αὐτῶν ἀδικίαν εἰς τὸ ὕψος λαλῶν οὐκ ἀνίησιν. οὕτως Ἄρειος, οὕτως Ἀπολιναρίους, οὕτως Εὐνομίους καὶ Μακεδονίους, οὕτω πλείους ἑτέρους προσαρμοσάμενος τῷ αὐτοῦ προσρώπῳ ὁλκῷ, διὰ τῆς ἐκείνων γλώσσης τὸν οἰκεῖον κατὰ τῆς ἱερᾶς
Ἐκκλησίας ἐπαφῆκεν ἰόν. ἀντ᾽ ὀλίγων ἰδίων, τοῖς ἐκείνων λόγοις ἀρξάμενος, καὶ ἐπιπείρας τούτοις τῇ τῆς εὐσεβείας ἀρχῇ τῇ τῆ ρίζῃ νεαρῶς καλὸν πεφυκότος φυτῶ, καὶ καρποῖς ὡραιοτάτοις βρίθοντος, οὐ μὴν τούτῳ καὶ λυμήνασθαι ἴσχυσε. καὶ γὰρ ὑπ᾽ αὐτῶν τῶν δειχθέντων αὖθις συνετρίβη τὰς μύλας, ὑπὸ τῶν ὡς ἀληθῶς κεφαλὴν ἑαυτῶν ποιησαμένων Χριστόν. οὗτος τοίνυν ὁ νοητὸς καὶ διὰ τοῦτο μᾶλλον ἐπάρατος ὄφις. τὸ πρῶτον καὶ μέσον καὶ τελευταῖον κακόν. ὁ πονηρὸς, καὶ τὴν χαμερπῆ καὶ γηΐνην πονηρείαν ἀεὶ σιτούμενος. ὁ τῆς ἔχθρας (διαλάδη τῆς εἰπόντος) θαυμετρητὴς ἀκάματος. ὁ πρὸς πᾶσαν θεοστυγῆ δόξαν πραγματικώτατος σοφιστής, καὶ ἀμηχάνως εὐμήχανος, μηδαμῶς ἐπιλελησμένος τῆς οἰκείας κακολογίας διὰ τῶν αὐτῶν πειθαίων Λατίνων, ἀεὶ τὰς

HISTORICAL NOTE
on the Edition of 1627

THE HISTORICAL CIRCUMSTANCES SURROUNDING
THE FIRST PRINTING OF THE TEXT

by Gregory Heers

Johannes Gutenberg, inventor of the printing press, printed his first, short text in 1450 and his 42-line Bible in 1455. His invention had reached Italy by 1465, France by 1470, and England by 1476. The first book to be printed entirely in the Greek language was Constantine Lascaris's *Grammar*, in Milan in 1476. Nevertheless, the Patriarchate of Constantinople did not acquire a printing press until 1627, when, with the blessing of Patriarch Cyril Lucaris and the permission of the Ottoman authorities, the Orthodox monk Nikodemos Metaxas bought and brought a press and all the necessary equipment from London, where he had studied this art. The first book to be printed was a treatise by Lucaris himself against the Jews, followed by a series of anti-Latin publications. One of these publications was a volume containing (among other things) the two Apodictic Treatises on the Procession of the Holy Spirit by Saint Gregory Palamas. This was the first ever appearance of this work in print, almost three centuries after the time of its composition. The introduction to this volume, a translation of which is given in the following pages, was written by the publisher, Nikodemos Metaxas himself, as is evident from his mention of the dangers which he faced while preparing the publication. (For the other works also published in this volume, see the footnotes on the "Introduction of the Edition of 1627".)

The Jesuits, however, who had developed extensive proselytizing activity in the Ottoman Empire by taking advantage of the poverty and illiteracy of the Orthodox people, were enraged by what they perceived as an enormous threat to their own pursuits, knowing all too well how much the press had contributed and was contributing to the spread of anti-Latin thought in the Protestant Reformation. When Metaxas showed no interest in their flatteries or their bribes, the Jesuits attempted to intimidate him by calling him a Lutheran and a heretic and accusing him of treason against the Sublime Porte. In fact, Metaxas was advised to take care lest he be assassinated (to which he alludes in his introduction), wherefore he even begged the English ambassador (whom he knew from his stay in London) to let him spend the nights in the embassy; but from his publications he was not deterred.

Finally, the Jesuits resorted to slander, saying all manner of evil against Metaxas and his press and falsely accusing him of publishing treacherous, blasphemous, and revolutionary material against the Ottoman religion and authority. Heeding their cries, the Grand Vizier sent a hundred and fifty Janissaries who broke into Metaxas's house on the 6th of January 1628, the feast of Theophany, vandalizing the press and confiscating books and manuscripts. Although Metaxas was soon found innocent of the charges levelled against him, the damage had already been done: broken to pieces, the printing press was no longer functional, having been in operation for barely more than six months.

Nevertheless, divine justice was not slow to manifest itself, and in March of that same year, as a result of the complaints of Lucaris and for disturbing the common peace with their unfounded slander, the Jesuits were shackled and shipped off to the island of Chios in the middle of the night. As for the Patriarchate, it would not have another printing press until 1798, 170 years later, when a new press was acquired by Patriarch Saint Gregory V, who showed particular interest in the education of the enslaved Orthodox and who was to meet a martyr's death in 1821.

ΤΟΙΣ ΑΓΙΩΤΑΤΟΙΣ ΚΑΙ
ΜΑΚΑΡΙΩΤΑΤΟΙΣ ΤΕΣΣΑΡΣΙ
ΠΑΤΡΙΑΡΧΑΙΣ ΤΗΣ ΚΑΘΟΛΙΚΗΣ ΚΑΙ

ἀποστολικῆς τῦ Χριστῦ Ἐκκλησίας, τῆς Ἀνατολικῆς
καὶ φωταυγῦς, Κυρίλλω Κωνσαντινυπόλεως. Γερα-
σίμω Ἀλεξανδρείας. Ἀθανασίω Ἀντιοχείας· Θεοφάνη Ἱεροσολύμων. τοῖς τῶ ἀποστόλων διαδόχοις, κ τῆς ἀληθείας ὑπερμάχοις.
τοῖς ὡς ἐκλεκτὰ σκεύη βαστάζουσι τὸ γλυκύτατον ὄνομα
τῦ Κυρίυ ἡμῶν Ἰησῦ Χριστῦ ἐναντίον ἐθνῶν κ
τυράννων, πᾶσαν ὑποταγὴν καὶ εὐπεί-
θειαν, ἐν αὐτῷ Χριστῷ τῷ
Θεῷ ἡμῶν:

Ἰ καὶ ἄμαχος ἡ ἀλήθεια (μακαριώτατοι καὶ
θεοσεβέστατοι ἀρχιποίμενες τῆς τῦ Χριστῦ λο-
γικῆς ποίμνης) καὶ ἀήττητον, ὡς ἐκ Θεῦ τὸ
κράτος ἔχυσα, καὶ μηδέποτε τῷ ψεύδει ὑπο-
κύπτυσα (κἂν πολλοὶ καὶ μεγάλοι ὦσιν οἱ ἐκεί-
νυ ὑπερασπισταὶ, ἀλλ᾿ οὐδὲν ἧττον αὕτη τύτυ
περιγίνεται καὶ κατακρατεῖ, ὡς καταγελάστυς καὶ ὑτιλαγεῖς ὑποφαί-
νεσθαι, τὺς ταύτη ἀντικειμένυς) ὅμως ὐ ἐκ τῦτο περὶ ὀλίγυ ποιη-
τέον, τὸ ταύτης μέχρι θανάτυ ὑπερασπίζεσθαι. Οὕτω γὰρ ἂν τὸ
δόκιμον ἡμῶν, καὶ ἡ πρὸς τἀγαθὸν ἔφεσις (ὁ περὶ τῶν ἄλλων τὸ λογι-
κὸν τῆς ἀλογίας διίστησιν) ἀειδήλως φανῆ, καὶ ὑπὲρ τῦ Θεῦ ἐ

A 2

ἡμῶν

INTRODUCTION
to the Edition of 1627[1]

by Monk Nikodemos Metaxas

To the most holy and most blessed four Patriarchs of the Catholic and Apostolic Church of Christ, the Eastern and luminous one: Cyril of Constantinople, Gerasimus of Alexandria, Athanasius of Antioch, Theophanes of Jerusalem, the successors of the Apostles and champions of the Truth, those who like chosen vessels bear the sweetest name of our Lord Jesus Christ against nations and tyrants: we pledge all submission and obedience, in Him, Christ our God.

Although truth is an invincible and unconquerable thing (most blessed and most God-fearing arch-pastors of Christ's rational flock), since it has its might from God and does never succumb to falsehood (even if the defenders of the latter be many and great, yet nonetheless truth overcomes and prevails over it, so that her opponents appear ridiculous and worthless), yet this does not mean that it is a small matter to defend it to the death. For in this way your trustworthiness and your desire for the good (which more than other things sets apart the rational from irrationality) and your fervent zeal for God may become clearly apparent.

For it would seem shameful if purchased slaves were to exhibit so much zeal for their own masters as to undergo for their sake not simply difficulties but even death itself, if this be at all needed, even though they gain nothing else besides the necessities of life, and perhaps also bodily freedom (even if this is rare), from their masters; while we, on the other hand, are unwilling to be zealous for the Lord God of hosts[2], from whom we have life, and from whom we

look for the permament good things with the hope that makes not ashamed.[3]

This is what convinced me, most holy and most reverend masters, to take up such a work on my shoulders; and also no less the present misfortune of our own race moved me to uncommon compassion. For that which was formerly admired of all and prided itself in many graces has been brought down to such a level of misfortune as to become an object of sneering and jesting for those far and those near; or rather, to speak truth more plainly, for those that do not understand the unsearchable abyss of the judgements of God. For, those excited by the the world's delights have forgotten that strait and narrow is the way which leadeth unto the eternal kingdom[4] and that all those that are in Christ must be persecuted and suffer many painful things,[5] not only from those outside but even from those inside the bridal chamber, so that (alas!) the arrows be from the members of one's own household. For just as, when the hedge is removed, a vineyard becomes henceforth accessible to all the wasting beasts,[6] so also with us as well: now that the imperial office has departed along with higher education, we lie exposed to be troden down by all the beasts.

But thanks be to the Almighty, who has sent the famine of hearing the word of the Lord, according to the divine oracle,[7] but spares the famished and still perserves furnishers of grain for us, although very few, yet adequate to suffice a people and to catapult the thieves of the good seed, or the sowers of tares,[8] somewhere far from the divine field. So, what was said of Egypt is more fitting to be said nowadays in the case of Hellas: Hellas does not bear many children, but when she does bear, she bears a great one.[9] Nevertheless, although the hardships of the race are an object of care for all that have ever so little a share in divine fear, and each one is willing to contribute and help in the way possible for him, yet for no one else is it so great a care, I think, as it is for you, "to whom hosts are entrusted, and upon whom rest so many cares."[10]

For to each one of the other shepherds of souls a certain individual country has been entrusted for pastoral care; but upon you, the four patriarchs (that is to say, the four evangelists), the entire

care of the catholic Church has been laid. For just as in the creation of the world in the beginning the creator was neither satisfied with one of the world's constituent elements, nor produced more than four, so also in the building of the Church, neither does He appear to have used one and only evangelist, nor was He in need of more than four; so also in the governance and direction thereof, neither did He entrust the entire care of the Christians to one and only man, nor again did he chose more than the four of you.

Therefore I myself am convinced that I am acting very wisely in addressing this sacred book to you, the four apostolic successors and defenders of the Christian body. For just as, when a light is set aloft on a candlestick,[11] the entire house is illumined by its rays, so also, once this fire-breathing book has first gone over onto your highest thrones as onto highest candlesticks, it will thence send out its rays to every part of the Church; and it will completely enlighten the pious while burning up every chaffy and rotten dogma.

It seems to me that in so doing I have imitated the best of gardeners; for when they need to water the garden, in the beginning they bring the water up onto a high place by means of some narrow pipes, so as thence to be able to convey it very easily to all the garden-beds. Therefore I also, by my own power, which is small and narrow, thought to lead up onto you, as onto lofty cisterns of the gifts of the all-holy Spirit, the book that will refresh many molten hearts; so that, as it were, it may henceforth be possible to carry it around with much ease wherever you deem fit. For the service it can provide is not small but more than great and salvific, both for those that tread the straight path and for those that have already wandered away from it. For the first, it will be like weapons of defense, keeping afar off every device and deceit of the adversaries, or as a sort of arrows sent out and confounding them that contrive a crooked thing against the truth, while for those that have inclined to the left it will be a guiding hand calling them toward the right side, even if only a fraction of them were to come to anchor at truth; for the good is not in the abundance, but in the good is the abundance tried before God.[12]

So then (my most divine masters), I have already done what falls

to me, not only taking no care for expense and labour, but making short mention even of the dangers that have hung over me; for I know that to this end was I made, that God be glorified in me. Thus, even if it be needful for me to undergo the inevitable, very willingly will I submit to this.[13] Yet yours it would be, and dependent upon your pastoral authority, to see to it that these here best parts of sacred theology be dispersed in every part of the catholic Church, parts which defenders of the truth and advocates of the just have collected and joined together, who are listed here according to the time in which they flourished.

So, there is the divinely sounding Nilus[14] and the sacred Gregory, the divine presidents of Thessalonica and radiant lights of the entire world, whereafter comes the fervent zealot of piety who shone forth for us as a new Elias, George Scholarius,[15] who, by the providence of God, served as the first patriarch of Constantine's city after its capture. Then there is Barlaam the wisest,[16] and the discourse of one anonymous.[17] Thereafter come some epistles of him who shone from bright Crete and enlightened the entire inhabited world, that Meletius Pegas,[18] whose sound has manifestly run across every part of the world,[19] whom Thy Reverence succeeded in Alexandria, most God-fearing master (for our discourse must be turned toward Thy Highness, since the occasion demanded it), although the Lord of all, taking thought for the race of Christians, moved thee to Constantinople, so that thou mightest emit thy rays farther, seeing that thou art standing on a higher candlestick. So who is ignorant of the wisest Cyril's name? And in what land or city has fame not zealously spread it abroad? Well, following after him is Maximos Margunios,[20] whose glory in both philosophy and theology and in every rational art and science all Europe knows, and especially Germany, which takes pride in many sciences and to which most of his epistles are manifestly written, all of them full of much knowledge. Seventh is Gabriel Severus from Monemvasia,[21] who, by the guidance of the all-holy Spirit, was appointed true bishop of Philadelphia and who was the first to establish a church of the Orthodox in renowned Venice. His work has been written in the common and vulgar tongue, at the request of those there, so as to

be easily comprehensible to all Hellenes of the present. The last one here is George Koressios from famous Chios,[22] still alive by the grace of God and arraying himself against the adversaries.

It would be your work, most divine masters, to make these things known to all Orthodox Christians, thus offering, as it were, a spiritual sacrifice unto God. May He grant unto all men enlightenment of knowledge and piety, so that together with us they may piously glorify one essence of divinity known in three hypostases, and may know one origin and one cause thereof, the unoriginate Father alone; and know the Son and the Holy Spirit having subsistence from the paternal hypostasis, beginninglessly and eternally, so as to be co-beginningless with the origin and co-eternal since they are of the same essence as it; and may they recognize one universal head of the catholic body of the Church, the Lord Jesus Christ, the God-man, the highest and greatest hierarch; in whom I wish that you fare well, most reverend masters, overwhelming your enemies and those that in any way oppose your true teaching, having them under your feet forever. Amen.

This was written by a lowly but faithful and Orthodox slave of yours, of the four most holy and most blessed patriarchs and unbroken pillars of the catholic Church.

---

[1] The edition of 1627 included in a single volume Saint Gregory's two Apodictic Treatises as well as a number of other anti-Latin works. This was the first instance in which these treatises appeared in print. What follows is the introduction of the publisher, addressed to the four Patriarchs of the Orthodox Church.

[2] Cf. 1 Kings 19:10, 14.

[3] Cf. Rom. 5:5.

[4] Cf. Matthew 7:14.

[5] Cf. John 15:20, Acts 14:22.

[6] Cf. Psalm 79:9-14.

[7] Amos 8:11.

[8] Cf. Matthew 13:24, 25.

[9] Cf. St. Symeon the Metaphrastes, "Life of Saint Patapius" in the *Eclogion*.

[10] Homer, *Iliad* 2.25.

[11] Matthew 5:15.

[12] A twist on the ancient proverb, "οὐκ ἐν τῷ πολλῷ τὸ εὖ, ἀλλ᾽ ἐν τῷ εὖ τὸ πολύ", which can be more freely rendered as "Quality is not in quantity, but quantity is in quality."

[13] This is a reference to the threats that Metaxas received from the Jesuits; see the "Historical Circumstances" above.

[14] Nilus Cabasilas, "On the Causes of the Ecclesiastical Division," "On the Authority of the Pope," a few relevant selections from his other writings.

[15] Also known as Gennadius, author of "The Treatise Entitled 'Refuge of the Orthodox.'"

[16] Barlaam (not the Calabrian), "On the Authority of the Pope", followed by "On the Fire of Purgatory," which has no attribution.

[17] Anonymous, "The Discourse of a Greek and Some Cardinals from Elder Rome" (only the beginining).

[18] Meletius Pegas, "Concerning the Authority of the Pope."
[19] Cf. Psalm 18:4.

[20] Maximos Margunios, "A Manual Regarding the Procession of the All-Holy Spirit in the Form of an Epistle", and "A Dialogue between a Greek and a Latin, That Is, an Orthodox and a Latin."

[21] Gabriel Severus, "Exposition Against Those That Ignorantly Claim and Lawlessly Teach That We, the Authentic and Orthodox Children of the Eastern Church, Are Schismatics from the Holy and Catholic Church," "On the Second Difference between the Eastern Church and the Roman One, That Is, on the Authority of the Pope," "On the Third Difference between the Eastern Church and the Roman One, That Is, on the Material of the Leavened and Unleavened," "On the Fourth Difference between the Eastern Church and the Roman One, That Is, on the Fire of Purgatory," "On the Fourth Difference between the Eastern Church and the Roman One, That Is, on the Blessedness of the Saints."

[22] George Koressios, "A Conversation with One of the Friars."

INTRODUCTION
by the Translator

THE FILIOQUE DEFINED AND DEVELOPMENTAL INFLUENCES
by Fr. Christopher C. Moody

THE FILIOQUE DEFINED

The Apostle Paul employed the metaphor of the olive tree, in his description of the Church of the Old Testament.[1] The Jewish believers partook of the fatness, a symbol of the spiritual richness of the promises, by the Abrahamic covenant. In the New Testament, which is the fulfillment of the paternal economy, the promise is expanded to the world and thus Gentiles are heirs, as well, of the root and fatness of the olive tree.[2] This is echoed again by the Apostle in his letter to the Galatians: "for ye are all the children of God by faith in Christ Jesus. For as many of you as have been baptized into Christ have put on Christ. There is neither Jew nor Greek, there is neither bond nor free, there is neither male nor female: for ye are all one in Christ Jesus. And if ye be Christ's, then are ye Abraham's seed, and heirs according to the promise."[3] As it is faith which grafts us into this tree and allows us to partake of the promise, departure from the Faith potentially cuts us off from the inheritance of the covenant.[4] This is the significance of heresy, and particularly of the *filioque*, the subject of these treatises. Consequently, in formalizing what had existentially been true, the schism of 1054 left the Church in Rome, which had visibly embraced heresy, formally separated from this olive tree.

The question is, why was this error accepted in Rome? In tracing the etiology of the schism between the Orthodox Catholic Church

and the Church in Rome, we need to carefully discern that there was a confluence of certain ideas and influences whose weight so bore down on the branch of the Latins, as it were, that it severed this preeminent branch from the trunk. This schism, after all, did not occur *in vacuo*. Before we examine these causes, we need to define exactly what is the *filioque*, leaving aside questions of justification for the insertion into the creed or polemics against it.

Traditional Orthodox Christian Nicene theology asserts that the Father is eternally the Cause of the existence of the Son and the Holy Spirit. The Son is "Light of Light, true God of true God, Begotten not made." The Father of lights not only begets the Son, Who is Light of Light, but causes the procession of the Spirit, Who, as well, is Light of Light, and true God, thus echoing the brother of God, who said, "every good gift is from above, and cometh down from the Father of lights"[5].

The Nicene Constantinopolitan Creed of 381 fully articulated the deity of the Holy Spirit, amplifying the Nicene Creed of 325. The text, quoting the biblical passage John 15:26, states, "We believe... in the Holy Spirit, the Lord, the Giver of life, Who proceedeth from the Father, Who with the Father and the Son together is worshipped and glorified..."

Yet within the Latin Church, after the creedal phrase "Who proceedeth from the Father", the phrase "and the Son", which is "*filioque*" in Latin, was inserted. What exactly does the Latin Church mean by this? As defined by the Catechism of the Catholic Church,

> "...The Western tradition expresses first the consubstantial communion between Father and Son, by saying that the Spirit proceeds from the Father and the Son (*filioque*). It says this, 'legitimately and with good reason', for the eternal order of the divine persons in their consubstantial communion implies that the Father, as "the principle without principle', *is the first origin of the Spirit, but also that as Father of the only Son, he is, with the Son, the single principle from which the Holy Spirit proceeds.* This legitimate complementarity, provided it does not become rigid, does not affect the identity of faith in the reality of the same mystery confessed."[6]

The Holy Spirit coming from the Father and Son, detail of the Boulbon Altarpiece of the Chapelle Saint-Marcellin, Boulbon, Provence, southern France (c. 1450).

For the Orthodox Christian, the statement that the Son assumes a secondary causality in the procession of the Spirit is an alien thought, and heretical. We can charitably say this formulation was adopted in defense against Arianism, which denied the divinity of the Son. In defending the deity of the Son of God, Latin theologians reasoned the Son must be able to generate divinity, as well as the Father, in order for Him to be equal with God.

The Theological Impetus for the Filioque: Defense Against Arianism

A concise summary of the *filioque* as a defense against Arianism is given in the statement of the United States Council of Catholic Bishops, "*The Filioque: A Church Dividing Issue?: An Agreed Statement*".

> "The earliest use of *Filioque* language in a credal context is in the profession of faith formulated for the Visigoth King Reccared at the local Council of Toledo in 589. This regional council anathematized those who did not accept the decrees of the first four Ecumenical Councils (canon 11), as well as those who did not profess that the Holy Spirit proceeds from the Father and the Son (canon 3). It appears that the Spanish

bishops and King Reccared believed at that time that the Greek equivalent of *Filioque* was part of the original creed of Constantinople, and apparently understood that its purpose was to oppose Arianism by affirming the intimate relationship of the Father and Son. On Reccared's orders, the Creed began to be recited during the Eucharist, in imitation of the Eastern practice. From Spain, the use of the Creed with the *Filioque* spread throughout Gaul."[7]

Certain understandings of trinitarian relations were advanced by the towering personage of Augustine of Hippo. His creative thought was a further impetus in the development of the *filioque*.

THE THEOLOGICAL INFLUENCE OF SAINT AUGUSTINE

Augustine's theological reflections on the Trinity and numerous other dogmas shaped the trajectory of Latin theology. His speculations on the interior relations of the Trinity, which were adoptions of psychological models of human relations, became normative in the West. Book 9 of his *De Trinitate* details the two psychological models he imported. In chapter 3, he introduces the triad of lover, beloved and love. He analogously identified the Father, Son and All Holy Spirit with these attributes. Thus the Father as Lover, loves the beloved Son by His love, the Holy Spirit. Eventually, this hypostasizing of a shared attribute, love, reduced the Spirit to be the product of the divine will.[8] In chapter 4, he introduces the triad of mind, knowledge, and love.[9] The human psychological acts correspond to the interior relations of the Trinity. The Father is analogously the Mind which knows Itself, conceiving the Word, corresponding with the begetting of the Son. The Mind, having known Itself, loves Itself by Its knowledge, which corresponds to the procession of the Spirit by the Father and the Son. The trajectory of this thought continues even until Aquinas, the architect of Scholasticism, who enshrined these Augustinian conceptions. A cursory reading of Aquinas, in his discussion about the procession of the All-Holy Spirit, betrays he was constrained to explain the

filioque as necessary due to this inner human psychology.[10]

THE THEOLOGICAL INFLUENCE OF
ARISTOTELIAN METAPHYSICS: ACTUS PURUS

As Latin theology interacted with Aristotelian philosophy, it wedded theology to philosophy, and in so doing adopted a different metaphysic than traditional Orthodox theology. While the employment of philosophical terms is necessary, as demonstrated by conciliar definitions, there appears to be a more than subordinate role afforded to philosophy within Catholic Dogma. As a case in point, the Aristotelian metaphysic affirms that being is an act. Thus when applied to God, He is pure being, or, *actus purus*. This does not allow potentiality in God. Therefore, this metaphysic, while ostensibly safeguarding the immutability of God, does not fully allow the biblical revelation that Christians participate in the energy, or glory of God. Lastly, there is an inference from *actus purus*. The trinitarian relations will be mirrored exactly in the economic Trinity, so that the economic Trinity reflects their internal eternal relations.[11]

THE THEOLOGICAL INFLUENCE OF PAPAL PRIMACY

Without exhaustively recounting the history of the insertion of the *filioque* clause into the Creed, we briefly note that in 1014, Pope Benedict VIII officially inserted the *filioque* into the Creed. The Council of Florence (the last session of which was held in 1439, some one hundred years after these treatises) legitimized the *filioque's* insertion on the basis that the Pope possessed authority and churches were to be subjected to him, a position aptly expressed in Ivan Ostroumoff's *History of the Council of Florence*. Having detailed the proceedings of the Council, the chronicler states,

> Explaining the circumstances under which the Church
> of Rome was obliged to make this addition to the Creed,
> Andrew said, that the Pope and a council of Western Fathers
> had determined to include this addition in the Creed, as a

refutation of the false opinions circulated by the historians
that the Holy Ghost does not proceed from eternity. This
happened, Andrew said, before the Sixth Ecumenical
Council. But history makes no mention of any such council
or council decree. On the contrary, it is well known that even
in the ninth century Pope Leo III forbade any such additions
to the Creed, and even had the Nicene Constantinopolitan
Creed engraved on two silver tablets in Greek and Latin and
without any addition. Lastly, to prove the right of the Latin
church or of her head, the Pope, to make this addition of
explanatory expressions, as the Latins called them, Andrew
referred to Saint Cyril of Alexandria in whose works he
purposed to find very plain allusions to the Pope's authority
for doing so: but at the same time Andrew took good care not
to quote St Cyril's own expressions. Cardinal Julian in his turn
offered Pope Agatho's epistle read in the Sixth Ecumenical
Council, in which the Pope says that all Orthodox councils
and church teachers always followed the doctrine of the
Church of Rome[12]

Later in this treatise, St Gregory argues that, on account of the
sanctity of the Fathers of the Ecumenical Councils who forbade
any addition to the Creed,we need not take into consideration the
primacy of the Pope regarding this matter.[13] Nonetheless, this is at
the heart of why discussions cannot proceed any further, for there
is an epistemological divide. In analyzing the thematic composition
of these two treatises, and the subsequent nine treatises comprising
the *Triads*, we may note they touch upon an epistemological theme.
The treatises *On the Procession of the Holy Spirit* provide the correct
understanding of what we can know of the Spirit's existence, while
the *Triads* initiate us into the experience and knowledge of Him.
It is not too bold to state that at the heart of the *filioque* there is
an epistemological controversy. To rephrase the question, is truth
preserved in the fullness of the faithful who universally experience
by participation in the energy of God, the Holy Spirit? Or is it found
through the particular, the Pope, and by means of ratiocination?

THE SINGLE CAUSE IS THE CAUSE OF THE TRINITY

In the Second Treatise, Saint Gregory emphasizes that the Old Testament presented God to the Jews as a monad, that is, the singular source of being, the great "I AM" who revealed Himself to Moses at the burning bush.[14] This revelation was inchoate and thus the New Testament revelation of the Son and Spirit reveals that God is not just one, but three in one. The monad out of its fecundity did not stop at a dyad but at a trinity. The Father is timelessly the Source, and simultaneously begets the Son and spirates the Spirit. The Father, as the source of the existence for the Son and Spirit, is also their point of reference, or *anaphora*. There is thus a projection from the source, and paradoxically, both Persons, without flux or distance or interposition, timelessly refer back to that source.

The best way to explain this is to resort to the geometric illustration of an isosceles triangle which Gregory will use in order to show that the Son cannot in any way be the Source of the divinity. The essential definition of an equilateral triangle highlights three essential features in the definition of the generation and procession of the Persons. By definition, in an equilateral triangle, the three end-points must be immediately related to one another, there must simultaneously be three points, and the points thus can be traced back immediately to the initial point. Therefore, if we postulate each Person of the Trinity to be one of the equidistant points in the triangle, then we can immediately see that each point is necessarily related to one another. Analogously, the Father, Son, and Spirit are immediately related to one another.

This word "immediately", *amesos*, is critical for understanding the wrong solution, as Gregory calls it, of the *filioque*. An immediate relation is one that is not mediated, meaning one that does not have the interposition of something else. Since each Person is related to the other immediately, the *filioque*, by interposing the Son, destroys the immediacy of the relationship. A consequence of placing the Son between the Spirit and the Father is that it places the Spirit in a relationship analogous to the relationship created beings enjoy with the Father. Creation is from the Father and through the Son, and

does not relate to God immediately, but in a mediated manner, by the mediation of the Son. Inasmuch as the *filioque* asserts the Spirit is also from the Son, similar to the creation, it ranks the Spirit with the creature.

Secondly, the illustration discloses that the three points must coexist. This analogously indicates that the Persons are *omou*, simultaneous. In contrast, the *filioque*, by having the Spirit exist through the Son necessarily means He is not coexistent, but derives existence from the Son.

Lastly, the two end-points can equally be traced back to the initial point. By analogy, both Persons have their reference, their *anaphora*, back to the Source, literally their point of origin, the Father.

THE SINGLE CAUSE UNIFIES THE ALL-HOLY TRINITY

Saint Gregory, following Saint Gregory Nazianzen, affirms that God is one in three for one reason: the Father. As the Source of being, He is the causal unity who directly relates to the Son and the Spirit, bestowing existence immediately and simultaneously to Both. The causality of the Father ensures the unity of the divinity. If two causes were present, there would be two different gods. Saint Gregory argues that if there were two causes God would be a dyad, consisting of the Father and Son coalesced into one and the Spirit spirated from them. This might seem pedantic, but why is it that only one cause must be in the Trinity? Because cause, *aitia*, is what gives existence to the effect, to the caused (*aitiaton*). Existence (*huparxis*) is literally the state of being under a principle (*hupo archen*), which implies dependency and contingency. If the Son was not from the Father directly, He would not be integrally one with the Father but a "part". If the Spirit did not proceed from the Father directly, He would be created, like creation.[15] For precisely this reason, the Spirit cannot be "through" or "from" the Son, for His dependence and existence from God would be reduced to the status of a creature. This explains the utter insistence Saint Gregory Nazianzus had on the *monarchia*, the monarchy or the single origin, in his trinitarian theology. This monarchy of the Father, then, is what differentiates

Christians from polytheists and Pagans.

THE SINGLE CAUSE IS INCOMMUNICABLE

We may understand the *filioque* to be a case of predicating to the universal what belongs to the particular . In other words, it is a confusion of the essential, that is, the shared attributes, with incommunicable characteristics, or *idiomata*, which define each Person. The primary definition which Gregory will quote to elucidate this is John Damascene's,

> We furthermore know and confess that God is one, that is to say, one substance, and that He is both understood to be and is in three Persons, I mean the Father and the Son and the Holy Ghost, and that the Father and the Son and the Holy Ghost are one in all things save in being unbegotten, in being begotten, in being proceeding[16].

The incommunicability of these three properties is what safeguards the Persons of the Trinity. Naturally, then, if the property to generate divinity belongs to only the Father, predicating it to the Son destroys the distinction between Father and Son. Furthermore, the Spirit, since the property is not communicated to Him, is logically severed from the Trinity. Saint Gregory will argue that if we predicate the ability to generate divinity to the Son, then the Spirit is severed from the Trinity, inasmuch as the ability to generate divinity is not commonly predicated to the Spirit. A tetrad will then result.

THE SINGLE CAUSE IS MIRRORED IN
THE HESYCHASTIC MODE OF EXISTENCE

At the risk of broaching an all too important topic too briefly, ideas have significance and eventually become first principles for action. The Orthodox dogma of the simultaneous and similar (to use Saint Gregory's description) generation of the Son and spiration of the Spirit from the Father alone is the dogmatic basis, albeit

implicit and not fully described, of hesychasm. The simultaneous begetting of the Son and the procession of the Spirit and their reference to their Source, the Father, is analogous to the practice of hesychasm, or sacred stillness. This ascetical discipline of the Church, in the essence of its practice, reflects the relations of the Holy Trinity in four significant ways. First, the intellect, analogous to the Father, has two powers of the soul; its *logos*, or rationality, corresponding to the Son, and its *pneuma*, its love, corresponding to the Spirit. Secondly, in the human act of knowing and loving, the powers of the soul are energized simultaneously and together, interpenetrated and inseparable, as with the trinitarian relations. Thirdly, the energies of the soul refer back to their source together, thus they bring the soul into a single form, *moneides*, and more importantly, bring it into a *theiodes* (deiform) state. In the Trinity, the direct and immediate reference of the Son and the Spirit to the Father preserves the formless form of God. The hesychast will find himself unconsciously withdrawing his thought and desire, retreating into himself. Fourthly, as man is bodily constituted, the physical posture of hesychasm reflects the circular position to the center of our being; it reflects this reality. Using the other analogy used elsewhere by the Fathers of the tripartite soul constituted as reason, the appetitive, and incensive power, the same holds true, as well. As from that perspective the hesychastic collects his anger and desire and returns their energies back to the heart.

This return to ourselves, to the inner man, as Saint Gregory will say in his defense of the hesychasts, is also called gathering ourselves. When we gather ourselves, *sunagoumen*, Saint Gregory says the soul turns to itself. The entirety of the soul makes a conversion, an *epistrophe*, which is an orientation back to our source, to our self, which mirrors the Son and Spirit returning directly and immediately to the Father together.

The *filioque*, however, when analyzed from the perspective of the analogy of intellect, reason, and desire, results in a different perspective on spirituality. In the first place, there is not a parity between knowledge and love. Love proceeds through *logos*, born by logic. Secondly, this creates a schism between our power of love

and its direct connect to its source. Lastly, on a deeper level, as these powers are not viewed typically energetically, the dynamic energetic sense of spirituality becomes replaced with a dry logic or belief.

The discussions about trinitarian relations and the analysis of the *filioque* are not meant to be burdensome exercises in scholasticism, but a dogmatic reality which practically points us to union with God in our very being. In so doing, we are retracing the image of God in ourselves by prayer and restoring the ancient beauty.

NOTES

[1] Cf. Rom. 11:16-23.

[2] Cf. Eph. 3:1-12.

[3] Gal. 3:26-29.

[4] Gal. 5:19-21.

[5] James. 1:17.

[6] Catechism of the Catholic Church: Revised in Accordance with the Official Latin Text Promulgated by Pope John Paul II. Ottawa: Canadian Conference of Catholic Bishops, 2006. 248.

[7] North American Orthodox-Catholic Consultation, "The Filioque: A Church Dividing Issue?: An Agreed Statement", United States Conference of Catholic Bishops, accessed February 15, 2021, The Filioque: A Church Dividing Issue?: An Agreed Statement. Accessed September 8, 2019. HTTP://WWW.USCCB.ORG/ BELIEFS-AND-TEACHINGS/ECUMENICAL-AND-INTERRELIGIOUS/ECUMENICAL/ORTHODOX/ FILIOQUE-CHURCH-DIVIDING-ISSUE-ENGLISH.CFM.

[8] Compare the statement, "In God there are two notional acts, notional knowing... through which the Father generates the Son, *and notional willing (love) through which the Father and the Son breathe the Holy Ghost.* The notional and the essential acts are factually identical; they are only virtually different". In Ott, Ludwig, Patrick Lynch, and James Bastible. *Fundamentals of Catholic Dogma.* Oil City, PA: Baronius Press, 2018, 70.

[9] Augustine, Saint. 1990. *De Trinitate, Book 9.* Edited by Phillip Schaff. Hendrickson. October. Accessed September 11, 2019. HTTP://WWW.NEWADVENT. ORG/FATHERS/130109.HTML

[10] Compare Aquinas, Summa Question 27; article 4; objection 3: "I answer that, the procession of love in God ought not to be called generation. In evidence whereof we must consider that the intellect and the will differ in this respect, that the intellect is made actual by the object understood residing according to its own likeness in the intellect; whereas the will is made actual, not by any similitude of the object willed within it, but by its having a certain inclination to the thing willed. Thus the procession of the intellect is by way of similitude, and is called

generation, because every generator begets its own like; whereas the procession of the will is not by way of similitude, but rather by way of impulse and movement towards an object. So what proceeds in God by way of love, does not proceed as begotten, or as son, but proceeds rather as spirit; which name expresses a certain vital movement and impulse, accordingly as anyone is described as moved or impelled by love to perform an action". Thomas Aquinas, "Question 27. the Procession of the Divine Persons," accessed February 15, 2021, HTTPS://WWW. NEWADVENT.ORG/SUMMA/1027.HTM.

[11] A Fokin, "St Augustine's Doctrine of the Trinity in the Light of Orthodox Triadology of the Fourth Century.," ed. M Stewart, *Studies in Philosophy and Religion* 24 (2003).

[12] Ivan N. Ostroumov, "The History of the Council of Florence: Transl. from the Russian, Basil Popoff," in *The History of the Council of Florence: Transl. from the Russian by Basil Popoff* (Boston: Holy Transfiguration Monastery, 1971), pp. 77-78.

[13] See First Treatise, section 4.

[14] Ex.3:14.

[15] See First Treatise, section 38, first paragraph; cf. Second Treatise, section 38, second paragraph, below.

[16] John, & Jr, C. F. (2015). Writings. In *Saint John of Damascus Writings* (p. 167). Washington, DC: Ex Fontibus Company.

The Holy Temple dedicated to the Saint in his bishopric, Thessaloniki, where his holy relics are treasured.

FIRST APODICTIC TREATISE
ON THE PROCESSION
OF THE HOLY SPIRIT

ΛΟΓΟΣ
ΠΡΩΤΟΣ

ΠΡΟΛΟΓΟΣ

Πάλιν ὁ δεινός καί ἀρχέκακος ὄφις, τήν ἑαυτοῦ κεφαλήν καθ' ἡμῶν διαίρων, ὑποψιθυρίζει τά τῆς ἀληθείας ἀντίθετα. Μᾶλλον δέ τήν μέν κεφαλήν τῷ τοῦ Χριστοῦ σταυρῷ συντριβείς, τῶν δέ κατά γενεάς πειθομένων ταῖς ἀπολουμέναις ὑποθήκαις αὐτοῦ κεφαλήν ἑαυτοῦ ποιούμενος ἕκαστον καί οὕτω πολλάς ἀντί μιᾶς κατά τήν ὕδραν ἀναδούς κεφαλάς, δι' αὐτῶν ἀδικίαν εἰς τό ὕψος λαλῶν οὐκ ἀνίησιν. Οὕτως Ἀρείους, οὕτως Ἀπολιναρίους, οὕτως Εὐνομίους καί Μακεδονίους, οὕτω πλείστους ἑτέρους προσαρμοσάμενος τῷ αὐτοῦ προσφύντας ὁλκῷ, διά τῆς ἐκείνων γλώττης τόν οἰκεῖον κατά τῆς ἱερᾶς Ἐκκλησίας ἐπαφῆκεν ἰόν, ἀντ' ὀδόντων ἰδίων τοῖς ἐκείνων λόγοις χρησάμενος καί περιπείρας τούτους τῇ τῆς εὐσεβείας ἀρχῇ, οἷόν τινι ῥίζῃ νεαρῶς καλόν τεθηλότος φυτοῦ καί καρποῖς ὡραιοτάτοις βρίθοντος, οὐ μήν τούτῳ καί λυμήνασθαι ἴσχυσε· καί γάρ ὑπ' αὐτῶν τῶν δηχθέντων αὖθις συνετρίβη τάς μύλας, ὑπό τῶν ὡς ἀληθῶς κεφαλήν ἑαυτῶν ποιησαμένων Χριστόν.

Οὗτος τοίνυν ὁ νοητός καί διά τοῦτο μᾶλλον ἐπάρατος ὄφις, τό πρῶτον καί μέσον καί τελευταῖον κακόν, ὁ πονηρός καί τήν χαμερπῆ καί γηΐνην πονηρίαν ἀεί σιτούμενος, ὁ τῆς πτέρνης, δηλαδή τῆς ἀπάτης, ἐπιτηρητής ἀκάματος, ὁ πρός πᾶσαν θεοστυγῆ δόξαν πορμώτατος σοφιστής καί ἀμηχάνως εὐμήχανος, μηδαμῶς ἐπιλελησμένος τῆς οἰκίας κακοτεχνίας, διά τῶν αὐτῷ πειθηνίων Λατίνων περί Θεοῦ καινάς εἰσφέρει φωνάς, μικράν μέν δοκούσας

TREATISE ONE

PREAMBLE

Once again the subtle[1] serpent and source of vice[2] rears his own head against us, whispering things opposite to the truth. Or rather, since he has been crushed in his head by the Cross of Christ,[3] he makes those who obey his destructive counsels in every generation each take the place of his own head, and similar to a hydra he has sprouted many heads instead of the one, relentlessly speaking utter unrighteousness through them.[4] Thus he attached to his coiled body the Arians,[5] thus the Apollinarians, thus the Eunomians[6] and Macedonians[7], thus the host of many others who ran to him, spewing his venom through their speech against the sacred Church. In lieu of fangs, he has used their words and sunk them into the source of piety, as into the root of a plant that had youthfully grown virtue, burdened with the best of fruit; yet he was not able to utterly lay waste to it.[8] For, his fangs were in turn shattered by those who had been bitten by him, meaning, by those who have truly made Christ their own Head.[9]

Accordingly, this serpent, which is noetic and, because of this, all the more accursed,[10] the first, middle, and final evil, the wicked one, always feeding off of serpentine and earthly wickedness, the vigilant stalker, tirelessly looking out for the heel,[11] that is to say, deception, the sophist, most resourceful and incomparably ingenious in every opinion obnoxious to God, not having at all forgotten his own evil art, introduces, through the Latins which were obedient to him, innovative expressions concerning God. While these innovations

ἔχειν ὑπαλλαγήν, μεγάλων δέ κακῶν ἀφορμάς καί πολλά καί δεινά φερούσας, τῆς εὐσεβείας ἔκφυλά τε καί ἄτοπα, καί τοῖς πᾶσι φανερῶς δεικνύσας, ὡς οὐ μικρόν ἐν τοῖς περί Θεοῦ τό παραμικρόν. Εἰ γάρ ἐφ' ἑκάστου τῶν καθ' ἡμᾶς ὄντων ἑνός ἀτόπου τήν ἀρχήν δοθέντος πολλά τά ἄτοπα γίνεται, πῶς οὐ μᾶλλον ἐπί τῆς κοινῆς ἁπάντων ἀρχῆς καί τῶν κατ' αὐτήν οἷον ἀναποδείκτων ἀρχῶν ἑνός ἀήθους δοθέντος οὐκ εὐσεβῶς πολλά γενήσεται παρά τοῦτο τά ἀτοπήματα;

Πρός ἅ καί φανερῶς τό Λατίνων γένος ἐκπεπτώκασιν ἄν, εἰ μή παρ' ἡμῶν ἀντιλεγόντων τῇ καινοφωνίᾳ τοῦ δόγματος τῆς κακοδοξίας τό πλεῖστον περιῃρεῖτο. Καί γάρ ἐπί τοσοῦτόν ἔστιν ὅτε συστέλλονται ὡς καί διανοίας ἡμῖν εἶναι τῆς αὐτῆς λέγειν, διαφωνοῦντας τοῖς ῥήμασι, σφῶν αὐτῶν ὑπ' ἀπορίας καταψευδόμενοι. Ἡμῶν γάρ οὐχί καί ἐκ τῆς ὑποστάσεως τοῦ Υἱοῦ λεγόντων εἶναι τήν τοῦ ἁγίου Πνεύματος ὕπαρξιν, ἐκείνων δέ καί ἐκ τῆς τοῦ Υἱοῦ, τῶν ἀδυνάτων εἰς μίαν ἀμφοτέρους συνάγεσθαι ἔννοιαν· εἰς γάρ ὁ μονογενής καί μία ἡ τοῦ Πνεύματος ὕπαρξίς ἐστιν. Ἡ γοῦν ἀπόφασις τῇ καταφάσει ἀεί ἀντίκειται καί ἀεί ψευδής ἡ ἑτέρα, εἰ ἀληθής ἡ ἑτέρα· καί τό αὐτό περί τοῦ αὐτοῦ καταφῆσαι καί ἀποφῆσαι σύν ἀληθείᾳ οὐκ ἔνι.

Ἀλλ' ὡς μέν ἡμῖν οὐ λέγουσι μόνον ἀλλά καί φρονοῦσι τά ἐναντία, οὐδείς οἶμαι τῶν εὖ φρονούντων καί μη ὁμοφρονούντων ἐκείνοις ἀντερεῖ. Ὡς δε οὐχ ἡμῖν μόνον, ἀλλά καί αὐτῷ τῷ τῆς ἀληθείας ἀντιδογματίζουσι λόγῳ, ὅς παρ' ἡμῖν ἀμείωτος καί ἀναυξής καί τό πᾶν ἀμεταποίητος διαπεφύλακται, πάντες μέν ὑμεῖς καί χωρίς ἀποδείξεως ἀκριβῶς ἴστε, το τῶν εὐσεβούντων λέγω πλήρωμα. Δειχθήσεται δέ ὅμως, Θεοῦ διδόντος, καί διά τοῦδε τοῦ λόγου, ὡς ἄν καί «πᾶν στόμα» το ἀντιλέγον «φραγῇ», καί προς μίαν ὁμολογίαν στηριχθῇ το ἀμφίρροπον.

seem to make but a small change, they actually create the occasion for many evils and bring in many things that are subtle, foreign to piety, and logically absurd. In doing this he clearly displayed to all that even the smallest thing is not small in matters concerning God. For if, with each of our arguments, when one fallacious thing has initially been premised many absurdities ensue, how can it not be that, when one uncustomary premise has been made in relation to the common principle of all and to the indemonstrable first principles,[12] from this more absurdities will not irreverently ensue?

Into these adsurdities the race of the Latins would have also fallen manifestly, had we not stripped away the greatest part of the cacodoxy by contradicting this novel dogma. Indeed, on occasion they recoil to such a degree that they even claim that they are of the same mind as us, disagreeing only in words, lying against themselves on account of their awkwardness. For while we say that the existence of the Holy Spirit is not also from the hypostasis of the Son, they say that He is also from the hypostasis of the Son, making it impossible for us to be united in one concept. For, one is the only-begotten[13] and the existence of the Spirit is one. In any event, since the denial is always the contrary to its affirmation, the one proposition is always false if the other is true, and it is not possible to affirm and deny the very same thing about the same subject and be with the truth.[14]

But I think that no one among those with a sound mind[15] and not in agreement with them [sc. the Latins], will dispute that they not only speak things contrary to us but also think contrary to us. Nor will such a man dispute the fact that they dogmatize not only against us but also against the very word of truth itself, which has been preserved among us undiminished, and without increase, and entirely unaltered.[16] You all precisely know this without a need for logical demonstration (by 'you' I am referring to the fullness of the pious). Nevertheless, God willing, it will also be shown through this present treatise here, so that "every mouth" which disputes this "may be shut",[17] and those who are ambivalent may be established upon one confession.[18]

Ἀλλ᾽, ὦ Θεέ τοῦ παντός, ὁ μόνος δοτήρ καί φύλαξ τῆς ἀληθινῆς
θεολογίας καί τῶν κατ᾽ αὐτήν δογμάτων καί ρημάτων, ἡ μόνη
μοναρχικωτάτη τριάς, οὐ μόνον ὅτι μόνη τοῦ παντός ἄρχεις,
ἀλλ᾽ ὅτι καί μίαν ἐν σεαυτῇ μόνην ἔχεις ὑπεράρχιον ἀρχήν, τήν
μόνην ἀναίτιον μονάδα, ἐξ ἧς προάγεσθον καί εἰς ἥν ἀνάγεσθον
ἀχρόνως καί ἀναιτίως ὁ Υἱός τε καί τό Πνεῦμα, Πνεῦμα τό ἅγιον,
τό κύριον, τό ἐκ Θεοῦ Πατρός ἐκπορευτῶς τήν ὕπαρξιν ἔχον,
καί δι᾽ Υἱοῦ τοῖς ὀρθῶς πιστεύουσιν εἰς σέ καί διδόμενον καί
πεμπόμενον καί φαινόμενον· Υἱέ μονογενές, ἐκ Θεοῦ Πατρός
γεννητῶς τήν ὕπαρξιν ἔχων καί διά τοῦ ἁγίου Πνεύματος ταῖς
καρδίαις τῶν εἰς σέ πιστευόντων ἐμμορφούμενος καί ἐνοικῶν καί
ἀοράτως ὁρώμενος· Πάτερ ἀγέννητε μόνε καί ἀνεκπόρευτε, καί,
τό σύμπαν εἰπεῖν, ἀναίτιε, ὁ μόνος πατήρ τῶν ἀνεκφοιτήτων καί
ὁμοτίμων σοι φώτων, ἕν κράτος, μία δύναμις, ἡ δημιουργός τῶν
ποιητῶν καί ὑπό χεῖρά σοι φώτων, ἡ πάσης γνώσεως δότειρα, ἡ
πολυειδεῖς ἰδέας παραγαγοῦσα γνωστικῶν τε καί γνωστῶν καί
καταλλήλως τοῖς γινώσκουσι καί φυσικῶς ἐνθεῖσα τάς γνώσεις,
τοῖς μέν νοεροῖς ἁπλᾶς καί ἀπαθεῖς νοήσεις, τοῖς δέ αἰσθητικοῖς
πολυμερεῖς καί παθητάς αἰσθήσεις, τοῖς δέ μικτοῖς ἡμῖν ἀμφότερα·
ἡ καί τήν περί σοῦ κατά τό ἐγχωροῦν γνῶσιν μόνοις τοῖς λογικοῖς
σου κτίσμασιν ἀφάτῳ χρηστότητι χαριζομένη, δός καί ἡμῖν ἀρτίως
εὐαρέστως σοι θεολογῆσαι καί τοῖς ἀπ᾽ αἰῶνος ἔργῳ σοι καί
λόγῳ εὐαρεστήσασι συμφώνως· ὡς ἄν καί τούς μή θεαρέστως σε
θεολογοῦντας ἀπελέγξωμεν, καί τούς ἐν ἀληθείᾳ σε ζητοῦντας πρός
τήν ἀλήθειαν στηρίξωμεν, ἵνα σε γινώσκωμεν πάντες μίαν μόνην
πηγαίαν θεότητα, τόν μόνον Πατέρα τε καί προβολέα, καί σοῦ Υἱόν
ἕνα καί Υἱόν μόνον, ἀλλ᾽ οὐχί καί προβολέα, καί σόν ἕν Πνεῦμα
ἅγιον, καί πρόβλημα μόνον, ἀλλ᾽ οὐχί καί ποίημα· καί δοξάζοιμεν
ἕνα Θεόν, ἐν μιᾷ μέν καί ἁπλῇ, πλουσίᾳ δ᾽, ἵν᾽ οὕτως εἴπω, καί
ἀστενοχωρήτῳ θεότητι, καί ἀντιδοξαζοίμεθα παρά σοῦ ἐν πλουσίᾳ
θεώσει καί τρισσοφαεῖ φωτοχυσίᾳ, νῦν καί εἰς τούς ἀκαταλήπτους
αἰῶνας. Ἀμήν.

But, O God of all, Thou who alone art the Bestower and Preserver of genuine theology and of the dogmas and expressions related to it; Thou who art the Most Monarchial Trinity, [19] not only because Thou alone reignest over all, but also because Thou hast one single origin in Thine own self, the origin prior to all origination, the only uncaused Monad, from whom originate and back to whom refer, timelessly and causelessly, the Son and the Spirit; O Holy Spirit, Lord, Thou who hast being by procession from the Father, [20] and through the Son hast been given and sent [21] and manifested to those who rightly believe in Thee; [22] O Son, Only-Begotten, Thou who hast being by generation from the Father [23] and through the Holy Spirit art formed and indwelling [24] and seen invisibly in the hearts of those who believe in Thee; [25] O Father, Thou who alone art Unbegotten and Unproceeding and, to express the entirety, Uncaused, the only Father of Thine inseparable and equally-honored Lights, [26] one dominion, one power, the Creator of the created lights under Thine hand; Thou who art the Bestower of all knowledge, who broughtest forth diverse kinds of the congitive and the knowable, and hast emplaced knowledge naturally and fittingly in those who know, thus in the noetic beings placing simple and passionless perceptions, although in the sensual beings emplacing many divided and passionate sensations, and to us, who are of a mixed composition, emplacing both; [27] Thou who by Thine ineffable goodness grantest only to Thy rational creatures, according to their capacity, the knowledge concerning Thee: grant unto us, also, as it is fitting, as it is well pleasing to Thee, to theologize harmoniously with those who, from the ages, in word and deed, have pleased Thee well: so that we may refute those who do not theologize Thee as befitteth Thee as God; so that we may firmly strengthen them in the truth, who in truth seek Thee; so that we may all know Thee as the one and only Fount of Divinity, as the only Father and Originator, and Thy Son as One and Only Son but not also an Originator, and Thy One Holy Spirit as the only Procession but not made; and may we glorify One God, in one and simple yet bountiful – that I may say it thus – and unconstricted divinity, and may we be glorified in return by Thee in rich deification and threefold pouring-forth of light, now and unto the endless ages. Amen.

Κοινὴ μέν ἥδε ἡ εὐχή πᾶσι τοῖς μίαν σέβουσιν ἀρχήν. Ὑμεῖς δέ τί φατε οἱ τάς δύο λέγοντες ἐπί τῆς θεότητος ἀρχάς; Τί γάρ, εἰ μή φανερῶς τοῦτο λέγετε, ἀλλ᾽ ἐξ ὧν λέγετε τοῦτο συνάγεται; Τοιαῦτα τά βαθέα τοῦ Σατανᾶ, τά τοῦ πονηροῦ μυστήρια, ἅ τοῖς ὑπέχουσιν αὐτῷ τά ὦτα ψιθυρίζει οὐ χαλῶν καί ὑπεκκλύων τόν τόνον τῆς φωνῆς, ἀλλά τό βλαβερόν ὑποκρύπτων τοῦ νοήματος. Οὕτως καί τῇ Εὔᾳ ὡς ἔγωμαι, ἐφιθύρισεν.

Ἀλλ᾽ ἡμεῖς διδαχθέντες ὑπό τῆς θεοσοφίας τῶν Πατέρων αὐτοῦ τά νοήματα μή ἀγνοεῖν, ἀφανῆ τήν ἀρχήν ὡς ἐπίπαν τοῖς πολλοῖς τυγχάνοντα, οὐδέποτ᾽ ἄν ὑμᾶς κοινωνούς δεξαίμεθα μέχρις ἄν καί ἐκ τοῦ Υἱοῦ τό Πνεῦμα λέγητε.

Ἆρα γάρ οὕτω λέγοντες οὐ φανερῶς διατελεῖτε προστιθέντες πρῶτον μέν τῇ περί τοῦ ἁγίου καί προσκυνητοῦ Πνεύματος ἐκφαντορικῇ θεολογίᾳ τῆς αὐτοαληθείας Χριστοῦ, ὅς Θεός ὤν προαιώνιος δι᾽ ἡμᾶς καί θεολόγος ἐγεγόνει, ὅς αὐτόχρημα ὤν ἀλήθεια διά φιλανθρωπίαν κῆρυξ ἡμῖν ἀναπέφηνε τῆς ἀληθείας, ὅς διά τοῦτο εἰς τον κόσμον ἦλθεν, ἵνα μαρτυρήσῃ τῇ ἀληθείᾳ, οὗ καί πᾶς ὁ ὤν ἐκ τῆς ἀληθείας καί ταύτην ἐν ἀληθείᾳ ζητῶν, ἐπαΐει τῆς ἀληθινῆς φωνῆς;

Ἆρ᾽ οὖν οὐ πρώτῳ μέν τούτῳ ἀντιπίπτετε τῷ καί πρώτῳ πάντων οὕτω θεολογήσαντι («τό Πνεῦμα γάρ, φησί, τῆς ἀληθείας, ὅ παρά τοῦ Πατρός ἐκπορεύεται»), ἔπειτα τοῖς αὐτόπταις καί αὐτηκόοις γεγενημένοις μαθηταῖς καί ἀποστόλοις αὐτοῦ, μᾶλλον δέ πρό τούτων καί αὐτῷ τῷ ἁγίῳ Πνεύματι, ὅ καί ἦλθε κατά τήν δεδομένην ὑπό τοῦ Σωτῆρος αὐτοῖς ἐπαγγελίαν, ὅ καί ἐδίδαξεν αὐτούς τά πάντα, ὅ τοῦτο οὐκ ἐδίδαξεν ὡς οὐκ ἐκ μόνου τοῦ Πατρός ἐκπορεύεται τῶν φώτων, ἀλλά καί ἐκ τοῦ Υἱοῦ; Εἰ γάρ οὕτω τούτους τοῦτο ἐδίδαξε, καί ἡμᾶς ἄν οὗτοι ὁμοίως ἐδίδαξαν.

Ἐπεί καί διά τοῦτο διδαχθέντες τε καί φωτισθέντες ἀπεστάλησαν,

This prayer indeed is common to all those who revere a single origin. But you, why do you say there are two origins for the divinity? For, what does it matter if you do not plainly say this but if it is deduced from what you are saying? Such things are the depths of Satan,[28] the mysteries of the evil one, which he whispers to those who lend their ears to him. He whispers not in the sense of softening or lowering the tone of his voice, but rather by concealing the intended harm. For my part, I believe this is how he also whispered to Eve.

But since we have been taught by the divine wisdom of the Fathers that we should not be ignorant of his devices,[29] which initially happen to be practically invisible to the masses, we would never at any time receive you into communion as long as you say that the Spirit is also from the Son.

So, when you speak in this way, are you not evidently managing to add, first, to the revelatory theology revealed by the Truth Himself, Christ, about the holy and worshipful Spirit? He, being the pre-eternal God, had also become a Theologian for our sake.[30] For the sake of His love for mankind, He who was in truth the truth, was shown forth as a herald of the truth for us. He came into the world for this cause, that He might bear witness to the truth, and His truthful voice is heeded by everyone that is of the truth and seeks it in truth.[31]

Therefore, does this not mean that you are first of all resisting Him who was also the first of all to theologize thus: "the Spirit of truth which proceedeth from the Father"?[32] Next, are you not resisting those who were eye-witnesses, who had heard with their own ears, who had become his disciples and apostles? Or rather, even before them, are you not resisting the Holy Spirit Himself,[33] who came to them according to the promise which had been given by the Savior, who then also taught them all things[34], but who did not teach that He does not proceed from the Father of lights[35] alone but also from the Son? For if He taught them thus, they would have likewise taught us as well.

After they had been taught and enlightened, they were sent precisely

ἵνα διδάξωσιν ὡς ἐδιδάχθησαν, ἵνα φωτίσωσιν ὡς ἐφωτίσθησαν, ἵνα κηρύξωσιν ἐν παρρησίᾳ, ὃ εἰς τό οὖς ἀκούσειαν, τουτέστιν οὐκ ἐν ἐπηκόῳ πάντων, ἵν᾽ εἴπωσιν ἐν τῷ φωτί, δηλονότι φανερῶς τοῖς πᾶσιν, ἃ τούτοις εἴρηται ἐν τῇ σκοτίᾳ, ὡς ἔγωγ᾽ ἄν φαίην, δι᾽ ἀποκαλύψεως ἐν ὑπερφώτῳ γνόφῳ, ἔστω δέ καί παραβολικῶς, καί οἷος ὁ παρά τῷ Σολομῶντι σκοτεινός λόγος ὁ τῷ μετειληχότι τῆς σοφίας τρανούμενος. Εἰ δέ βούλει, τό κατά μόνας ἡ σκοτία δηλούτω καί ἀποκρύφως καί μήπω τοῖς πολλοῖς ἐγνωσμένως.

Ἀλλά πρός ὃ νῦν ἡμῖν ὁ λόγος, ὃ μή τούτοις εἴρηται τοῖς παρρησιασαμένοις τήν ἀλήθειαν, ὃ μή ἀνήγγειλε τό Πνεῦμα τό πᾶσαν ἀπαγγεῖλαν τήν ἀλήθειαν, ὃ μή ἐμαρτύρησεν ἤ ἐγνώρισεν ὁ πάντα ὅσα ἤκουσε παρά τοῦ Πατρός τοῖς ἀγαπητοῖς γνωρίσας, καί διά τοῦτο ἐλθών, ἵνα μαρτυρήσῃ τῇ ἀληθείᾳ, πῶς ὑμεῖς τοῦτο τολμᾶτε λέγειν οὕτως ἔκφυλον εἰσάγοντες προσθήκην ἐν τῷ τῆς πίστεως ὅρῳ, ὃν οἱ πρόκριτοι πατέρες κοινῇ συνειλεγμένοι πνευματοκινήτως, σύμβολον ἀψευδοῦς δόξης τῆς εἰς Πατέρα καί Υἱόν καί ἅγιον Πνεῦμα καί βάσανον εἰλικρινοῦς θεογνωσίας καί ὁμολογίαν ἀσφαλῆ πᾶσι τοῖς ὀρθοτομεῖν προῃρημένοις τόν λόγον τῆς ἀληθείας συνεγράψαντό τε καί παραδεδώκασιν;

1

Ἥν γάρ ὑπολογίζεσθε πρόφασιν, ὡς ἔστιν ὧν λεγόντων οὐκ ἴσον εἶναι τῷ Πατρί τόν Υἱόν, ὅτι μή καί αὐτός ἔχει τό ἐκπορεύειν, ὑμεῖς ἴσον δεικνύναι σπεύδοντες τήν προσθήκην εἰσηνέγκατε ταύτην, οὐδαμόθεν ἔχει τό εὔλογον. Εἰ γάρ τινες φαῖεν χρῆν εἶναι καί τό γεννᾶν ἔχειν τοῦτον, ὡς μή τούτου προσόντος τό ἴσον ἀφαιρουμένου, ἀνάγκη προστιθέναι καί τοῦτο πειθομένους τοῖς ἀσυνέτοις· καί ἁπλῶς μή μείζω λέγειν τῷ αἰτίῳ τοῦ Υἱοῦ τόν Πατέρα, ἵνα μή τό πρός αὐτόν ἴσον τοῦ Υἱοῦ ἀθετήσωμεν.

to this end, that they might teach as they had been taught; that they might enlighten as they had been enlightened; that they might boldly proclaim what they would have heard spoken in their ear, that is, not in the hearing of all;[36] that they might speak in the light, that is, openly to all, what had been said to them in darkness, as I would say, through revelation in a darkness transcending light, or even in parables and like the dark saying of Solomon, which is made clear to him that has partaken of wisdom.[37] Or, if you prefer, let the darkness indicate this, that it was spoken privately and in a hidden manner, and that it had not yet been made openly known to the many.

But to the point of our present treatise, this addition [the Filioque], which of course has not been uttered by those who boldly proclaimed the truth; which the Spirit did not announce, although He announced all truth;[38] to which the Savior did not bear witness or make known, although He had made known to His beloved as many things as He heard from the Father[39] and came for that very reason, to bear witness to the truth:[40] how was it that you, then, have the audacity to speak it, innovatively introducing an alien addition into the boundary of the Faith? The chosen Fathers[41], when they convened together, having been moved by the Spirit, composed this and handed it down to be a Symbol free from false belief in the Father and the Son and the Holy Spirit, to be a sincere touchstone of genuine knowledge of God and a sure Confession for all those who have chosen to rightly divide the word of truth.[42]

1

For, your justification—that, on account of those who claim that the Son would not be equal to the Father if He were not also able to cause procession, you have introduced this addition in an attempt to show the Son equal to the Father—is not reasonable at all. For then if some were to say that the Son must also possess the power to beget, since if this does not belong to Him He is deprived of equality, we would have to add this too, obeying the unwise, and in general to say that the Father is not greater than the Son with respect to cause, lest we despise the equality of the Son to the Father.

Ὅπερ ἄρα δοκεῖτε καί ὑποβάλλειν δολίως πρός ἀντίθεσιν τῶν εὐαγγελικῶν δογμάτων καί διδαγμάτων· ὁ γάρ καί τόν Υἱόν αἴτιον θεότητος λέγων αὐτόν ἀθετεῖ τόν Υἱόν ἐν τῷ εὐαγγελίῳ σαφῶς εἰπόντα «ὁ πατήρ μου μείζων μού ἐστιν», οὐχ ὡς ἀνθρώπου μόνον, ἀλλά καί ὡς Θεοῦ, τῷ τῆς θεότητος αἰτίῳ. Διό καί οὐχ ὁ Θεός εἶπεν, ἀλλ' ὁ Πατήρ· οὐ γάρ ὡς Θεός μείζων τοῦ Υἱοῦ, ἄπαγε τῆς ἀσεβείας, ἀλλ' ὡς αἴτιος θεότητος, καθάπερ καί οἱ θεοφόροι πατέρες ἡμῖν ἡρμήνευσαν. Τούτοις οὖν ὡς ἔοικε τοῖς θεοφόροις καί Χριστῷ τῷ Θεῷ τῶν θεοφόρων ἀντιλέγετε, τῷ Πατρί τόν Υἱόν οὐκ ἴσον κατά τό αἴτιον λέγουσιν.

Ἀλλ' ἡμεῖς καί τό ἴσον ἴσμεν τοῦ Υἱοῦ πρός τόν Πατέρα κατά τήν φύσιν καί τό μεῖζον τοῦ Πατρός ὁμολογοῦμεν κατά τό αἴτιον, ὅπερ ἄμφω, τό τε γεννᾶν καί ἐκπορεύειν, συμπεριβάλλει. Καί αὐτοῖς δέ τοῖς συγγραψαμένοις τήν ἀρχήν ὑπέρ τῆς πρός τόν Πατέρα τοῦ Υἱοῦ συμφυΐας, ταὐτό δ' εἰπεῖν ὁμοτιμίας, οὔσης τῆς ἀγωνίας, χωρίς τῆς παρ' ὑμῶν προσθήκης ἀποχρῶν ἐνομίσθη τό τῆς πίστεως σύμβολον.

Οὔκουν εὐλόγως οὐδέ εὐσεβῶς ταύτην εἰσάγετε τήν προσθήκην ἐν τῷ τῆς πίστεως ὅρῳ, ὅν οἱ πρόκριτοι πατέρες κοινῇ συνειλεγμένοι, πνευματικινήτως συνεγράψαντό τε καί παραδεδώκασιν. Ὧ καί προσθῆναι ἤ ἀφελεῖν ὅλως οὐκ ἐφεῖται μετά την τῷ χρόνῳ δευτερεύουσαν ἐκείνης τῶν ἁγίων σύνοδον, δι' ἧς καί ὁ τοῦτο τολμήσων ἀραῖς ὑποβάλλεται καί τῆς ἐκκλησίας ἐκβάλλεται, καί ταῦτα προσθήκην οὐκ εἰρημένην ὡς εἴρηται τῷ λόγῳ, οὐκ ἀποκεκαλυμμένην τῷ Πνεύματι, οὐχ εὑρημένην ἐν τοῖς τῶν ἁγίων ἀποστόλων ἀναγράπτοις λογίοις.

Οἷς συμφώνως καί οἱ ἐκθέμενοι τόν τῆς πίστεως τοῦτον θεῖον ὅρον ἐξέθεντο καί οἱ μετ' αὐτούς γεγονότες συνέθεντο, εἰ καί μή συνεξέθεντο. Οὐ γάρ ἔχετε λέγειν, ὡς οὐχί οὕτως οἱ μέν ἐξέθεντο, οἱ δέ τοῖς τήν ἀρχήν ἐκθεμένοις συνέθεντο, ὑπό τε τῶν ἀναγραφάντων τά καθέκαστα τῶν ἁγίων ἁπασῶν συνόδων ἐξελεγχόμενοι, καί αὐτῆς τῆς ἐξ ἐκείνων μέχρι καί νῦν, μᾶλλον δέ καί ἐσαεί συμφωνίας τῶν τεσσάρων πατριαρχικῶν θρόνων, καί αὐτῶν τῶν πολλῶν καί

So, then, you appear to propose this deceitfully in opposition to the evangelical dogmas and statutes, because whoever says that the Son is a cause of divinity despises the Son, who clearly said in the Gospel, "My Father is greater than Me."[43] He said the Father was greater than Him, not only as a human, but also as God with respect to the cause of divinity. He did not say "God" but the "Father." For, the Father is not greater than the Son because He is God – away with the irreverence! – but as the Cause of divinity, just as all the God-bearing Fathers interpreted to us. Therefore, as it seems, you are contradicting these God-bearers and Christ, the God of the God-bearers, who say that the Son is not equal to the Father with respect to the cause.

But we both acknowledge the equality of the Son with the Father according to nature and also confess the greatness of the Father according to cause, which includes both begetting and causing procession. Even for those who in the beginning composed a defense of the con-naturality of the Son with the Father, which is the same as saying equality of honor, this being the point of contention, the Symbol of Faith without your addition was considered sufficient.

So, then you neither reasonably nor reverently introduce this very addition into the Symbol of Faith, which the chosen Fathers, when they convened together, being moved by the Spirit, composed and handed down. Herein it is entirely forbidden to add or subtract after the chronologically second Council of the Saints, whereby whoever will dare to make an addition is submitted to denunciations and is expelled from the Church—especially an addition not utttered by the Word, not revealed by the Spirit, not found in the recorded pronouncements of the holy Apostles.[44]

The drafters articulated this divine Symbol of the Faith in agreement with the Apostles, and they that came after them agreed with them, although they did not compose it with them. You cannot say that the former did not articulate it in this way or that the latter did not agree with those who articulated it in the beginning, since you are refuted by those who recorded the minutes of all the Holy Councils, and by the very harmony of the four patriarchal thrones from the time of those Councils until today, or rather forevermore, and by

διαφόρων καί γενῶν καί γλωσσῶν ἀδιάφορον φερουσῶν τήν ἐξ
ἀρχῆς ἔκθεσιν καί ἀμεταποίητον.

Καί τοίνυν αἱ μέν ἐκφαντορικαί κοιναί φωναί τῶν θεοφόρων
θεολόγων, εὐαγγελιστῶν, ἀποστόλων, καί τῶν πρό αὐτῶν ἐξ αἰῶνος
προφητῶν οὕτως ὁμολογουμένως ἔχουσι περί τοῦ Πνεύματος
καί οὕτως ὁμολόγως τῷ Θεανθρώπῳ λόγῳ· πρός δέ καί αἱ κατά
διαφόρους αἰτίας καί καιρούς ὑπέρ εὐσεβείας συγκροτηθεῖσαι πᾶσαι
σύνοδοι, ταὐτό δε σχεδόν εἰπεῖν πᾶσα γλῶσσα θεοφόρος· ἐν οὐδεμιᾷ
γάρ τῶν συνόδων τούτων καί ἐκ τοῦ Υἱοῦ τεθεολόγηται τὸ Πνεῦμα
τό ἅγιον. Ἔδειξα δ᾽ ωφφδᾶν ἀρτίως τοῦτ᾽ αὐτό καί τους θεηγόρους
πάντας αὖθις ἕκαστον ἐν μέρει στέργοντας ἀπαραλλάκτως διά τῶν
ἰδίως ἑκάστῳ τούτων ἐξενηνεγμένων λόγων ἐφεξῆς.

Ἀλλ᾽ οὐκ ἐπί τοσοῦτον ἀνέξεται τὸ φίλερι τοῦ λατίνου μακρούς
ἡμῶν ἀποτεινόντων λόγους, ἀλλ᾽ ἀπαντήσει λέγον· πῶς οὖν καί
ὑμεῖς καί πόθεν εὑρόντες τήν προσθήκην ταύτην, παρά μόνου τοῦ
Πατρός ἐννοεῖτε τὸ Πνεῦμα τὸ ἅγιον ἐκπορεύεσθαι, διό καί ἡμᾶς
ἑτεροδόξους οἴεσθε, τοῦ Χριστοῦ τοῦτο μή εἰπόντος, ἀλλ᾽ οὐδέ
τῶν ἐκείνου μαθητῶν τινος;

Πρός ὅ νῦν ἡμεῖς εὐθύς ἀπαντήσομεν, οὕτω λέγοντες. Τὸ τῶν
εὐσεβούντων πλήρωμα χεῖλος γεγονότες ἕν ἐπ᾽ ἀγαθῷ, πύργον
εὐσεβείας ᾠκοδόμησαν, δυσσεβείας νοητοῦ κατακλυσμοῦ
παντάπασιν ἀνώτερον. Ἐπεδήμησε γάρ καί αὐτοῖς οἰκοδομεῖν
ἐπιχειροῦσιν ἡ τελεσιουργός τῶν ἀγαθῶν τριάς οὐ συγχέουσα,
ἀλλά συνδέουσα καί τάς δόξας καί τάς γλώσσας εἰς εὐσεβεστάτην
καί ὀρθόδοξον ὁμοφροσύνην. Αὐτοῦ τοίνυν ἡμεῖς ἐπ᾽ ἀσφαλοῦς
ὀχυρώματος ἱστάμενοι τούς ἀπεναντίας τῶν ὀρθῶν δογμάτων
φερομένους πρῶτον μέν ἐντεῦθεν εὐστοχώτατα καί γενναιότατα
βαλοῦμεν, ἅμα δέ καί λυσιτελῶς αὐτοῖς, εἰ βούλοιντο. Μετά τοῦτο
δέ τάς πολλαχόθεν, μᾶλλον δέ τῶν πανταχόθεν ἀναφαινομένων
ἀποδείξεων τῆς ἀληθείας, ἔστιν ἅς προκομίσομεν αὐτοῖς
πρός πόθον ταύτης καί αὐτούς ἐπαίροντες, ἵν᾽ εἴπω κατά τό
γεγραμμένον· «εἰ ἄραγε ψηλαφήσειαν αὐτήν καί εὕροιεν, καί γε οὐ
μακράν ὑπάρχουσαν αὐτῶν». Νῦν δέ μᾶλλον τούτους οὐχ ἡμεῖς,

the many and diverse races and tongues themselves, which retain the original exposition unchanged and unaltered.

Accordingly, the common revelatory voices of the God-bearing theologians, evangelists, apostles, and prophets that came before them from time immemorial are thus in confessed agreement concerning the Spirit and thus in agreement with the Theanthropic Word. In addition, the same is the case with all the councils that were convened for various causes and on different occasions for the sake of piety; in other words, with nearly every God-bearing tongue. For in not one of these councils had it been theologized that the Holy Spirit is also from the Son. And on this point, I could perfectly display hereafter that the divinely-inspired, one after another, all warmly embraced this very point in exactly the same way, each one in turn, through the treatises published by each one individually.

The Latin's love of debate, however, will not control itself for so long, should we extend long treatises. So he[45] will retort saying, "So where and how did you find your addition, supposing that the Holy Spirit proceeds only from the Father?[46] Why do you consequently think that we are heterodox when Christ did not say this, neither did any of His disciples?"

We shall now straightway respond to this objection, speaking thus: the full assembly of the pious, when they had become of one speech for the protection of the good, built a revered tower,[47] which was altogether higher than the noetic cataclysmic flood of irreverence.[48] And similarly the Trinity, the Perfecter of good things, met them, too, who were trying to build, not putting to confusion but binding together both the beliefs and languages into the most pious and orthodox oneness of mind.[49] We, accordingly, set ourselves upon this same citadel, against the enemies of right dogmas. From within the citadel, we shall launch the first volleys, those which, while they are the most accurate and most brave, are simultaneously for the enemies' advantage, if, on their part, they be willing. After this, we shall bring forth to them demonstrations of the truth which are apparent from many perspectives, or rather, from all perspectives, to create in them a longing for the truth and lift them up toward it. To express myself as it has been written, "If haply they might feel after the truth, and find it, though it be not far from them".[50] But

ἀλλ' αὐτό τό οἷον λογικόν τῆς εὐσεβείας περιτείχισμα καί βαλεῖ καί πατάξει καί τροπώσεται, εἰ δέ βούλει, καί ἰάσεται. Τοιοῦτος γὰρ ὁ τῶν θείων θεῖος ὅρος οὗτος· οὐ περιβάλλει μόνον τούς ἐμμένοντας καὶ καθίστησιν ἐν ἀσφαλείᾳ, ἀλλὰ καὶ προπολεμεῖ καὶ ἀνυποστάτως ἀντιτάττεται τοῖς ἐπανισταμένοις· τό δ' ὅπως, ἄκουε.

2

«Πιστεύω εἰς ἕνα Θεόν, πατέρα, παντοκράτορα», «καί εἰς ἕνα Κύριον Ἰησοῦν Χριστόν, τόν Υἱόν τοῦ Θεοῦ, τόν μονογενῆ, τόν ἐκ τοῦ Πατρός γεννηθέντα πρό πάντων τῶν αἰώνων». Ἆρ' οὖν οὐ συννοεῖται οὐδέ συνυπακούεται τό μόνου, οὐδ' ἐκ μόνου τοῦ Πατρός γεγέννηται, εἰ καί μή προστέθειται τό μόνου; Καί πάνυ μέν οὖν συνυπακούεται, καί οὐχ ἧττον ἢ προσκείμενον, εἰ ὅλως εὐσεβεῖν ἐθέλεις, εἴποις ἄν. Ἐντεῦθεν τοίνυν καί περί τοῦ Πνεύματος διδάσκου. Καί ἡνίκ' ἄν ἀκούοις ἐπί τοῦ αὐτοῦ συμβόλου, «τό Πνεῦμα τό ἅγιον τό ἐκ τοῦ Πατρός ἐκπορευόμενον», εὐθύς ἐξ ἀνάγκης συνυπακουόμενον νόμιζε τό «μόνου» καί μή προσθήκην ἄλλως νόμιζε ἡμῶν, ὑπέρ ἀληθείας διά τήν σήν ἀθέτησιν ἐν ταῖς πρός ὑμᾶς διαλέξεσι προστιθέντων ἀκροώμενος. Εἰ δέ μή, οὐδ' ἐπί τῆς ἐκ τοῦ Πατρός τοῦ Υἱοῦ γεννήσεως ἐάσεις συνυπακούεσθαι τό «μόνου»· καί οὕτω σου πολυπλασιάσεις τό δυσσέβημα.

3

Καί τοῦτο δέ μοι λάβε κατά νοῦν, ὡς ἐπί τοῦ τῆς πίστεως συμβόλου τόν Υἱόν ἐκ τοῦ Πατρός ἀκούοντες γεννηθέντα πρό πάντων τῶν αἰώνων καί τῷ ἐκ τοῦ Πατρός συννοούμενόν τε καί συνυπακουόμενον ἔχοντες τό «μόνου», καθάπερ ἄν καί αὐτός ἡμῖν συμφήσαις, ὅμως οὐδείς οὐδέποτε τό «μόνου» προσέθηκεν ἐκεῖ, ὥστε καί τήν σήν δόξαν ὅτι καί ἐκ τοῦ Υἱοῦ τό Πνεῦμα ἐκπορεύεται, εἰ καί ἀνωμολογημένον ἦν, καί ἡμῖν καί ἁπλῶς πάσῃ τῇ τοῦ Χριστοῦ Ἐκκλησίᾳ συνδοκοῦν, οὐδ' οὕτως ἐχρῆν ἐν τῷ τῆς πίστεως συμβόλῳ προστεθῆναι παρ' ὑμῶν.

now, not we, but instead this same Citadel, like a rational defense
of piety, will both shoot at them with the demonstrations of the
truth and strike them and turn them to flight and, if you will, also
heal them.[51] For, this divine Symbol of divine things is such that
it not only encloses those who abide in it and establishes them in
safety but also defends them and irresistibly meets in battle those
who have risen in rebellion. But as to how exactly it does this, listen

2

"I believe in One God, the Father, Almighty… and in One Lord
Jesus Christ, the Son of God, the Only-Begotten, begotten of the
Father before all ages." Is not the word "only" implicitly understood
and taken for granted, although it is not stated? Or has the Son
not been begotten only from the Father because the word "only" is
not added? If you wanted to be reverential in any sense you would
say, "This is implicitly understood very well, no less than if it were
added." From that vantage point, then, be also taught concerning
the Spirit. And so, should you hear from the same Symbol, "the
Holy Spirit which proceedeth from the Father," straightway, out of
sheer necessity, consider the word "only" to be understood, and do
not consider it to be our addition when you hear us adding it in
our conversations with you. We add it for the sake of the truth and
because of your rejection of it. Otherwise, neither will you concede
that the word "only" is implicitly understood in the case of the
generation of the Son from the Father; and thus you will multiply
your impieties.

3

Now do oblige me and take the following into consideration. Although
we hear in the Symbol of Faith that the Son has been begotten of
the Father before all the ages and we consider the word "only" to be
implicitly understood and taken for granted in the phrase "from the
Father", exactly as you yourself would agree with us, yet no one ever
added "only" to the Symbol. As a result, even if your belief that the
Spirit proceeds also from the Son were agreed upon and it seemed
good to us, as well as to the entire Church of Christ, even then you
should not have added it to the Symbol of Faith.

4

Ἦν οὖν ἄρα τῶν δικαιοτάτων μηδέ λόγου ἀξιοῦν ὑμᾶς, εἰ μή τοῦ προστιθέναι τῷ ἱερῷ συμβόλῳ παύσησθε· τῆς δέ παρ' ὑμῶν προσθήκης παρ' ὑμῶν ἐκβεβλημένης πρότερον, ἔπειτα ζητεῖν, εἰ καί ἐκ τοῦ Υἱοῦ ἤ οὐχί καί ἐκ τοῦ Υἱοῦ τό Πνεῦμα τό ἅγιον, καί τό ἀναφανέν τοῖς θεοφόροις συνδοκοῦν κυροῦν· ἀλλ' οὐδ' οὕτω προστιθέναι τῷ συμβόλῳ τῆς πίστεως, καθάπερ ἐπί τῶν δύο τοῦ ἑνός Χριστοῦ φύσεων καί θελημάτων καί ἐνεργειῶν, τῆς τε καθ' ὑπόστασιν ἑνώσεως καί τοῦ ἐπωνύμου τῆς παρθενομήτορος, οἱ πρό ἡμῶν πεπράχασι καλῶς τε καί φιλευσεβῶς, ὡς μετά τῆς εὐσεβείας καί τῆς κοινῆς εἰρήνης ἀντιποιούμενοι, καίτοι πολλάκις ἔπειτα κοινῇ συνειλεγμένοι, συνεκκλησιαζόντων ἤ συνευδοκούντων καί τῶν κατά καιρούς τῆς παλαιᾶς Ρώμης ἀρχιερατικῶς προϊσταμένων. Οὔκουν ἔχει τις ὑπολογίζεσθαι τήν τοῦ περιόντος πάπα περιωπήν· οὐ γάρ διά τοῦτον ἤ τούτους τούς μετ' ἐκείνους ἀποστερκτέον τούς τοσούτους καί τηλικούτους καί μακαρίῳ τέλει τήν ἡγιασμένην καί πολυειδῶς παρά Θεοῦ μεμαρτυρημένην κατακλείσαντας ζωήν.

5

Ἀλλά γάρ οὐ μόνον τό τῆς ὀρθοδόξου πίστεως σύμβολον,—δεῖ γάρ τῶν εὐγνωμόνως ἀκουσομένων ἕνεκα λέγειν·—μή μόνον οὖν τό τῆς πίστεως σύμβολον, ἀλλά καί πᾶσα σχεδόν γλῶσσα θεολόγος ἐκ Πατρός γεννηθέντα τόν Υἱόν κηρύττουσα καί παρά τοῦ αὐτοῦ Πατρός τό Πνεῦμα τό ἅγιον ἐκπορευόμενον, οὐ προστίθησι τό «μόνου»· ὡς κἄν μή προσκέηται, ἐξ ἀνάγκης συνυπακουόμενον, καί τοῦτ' εἴσῃ ἀνελίττων καί διεξιών αὐτάς τάς θεολόγους βίβλους. Σήν δ' ὅμως χάριν, καί ἡμεῖς ὀλίγ' ἄττα προενέγκωμεν καί διά βραχέων γεγραμμένα. Ὁ γοῦν μέγας Ἀθανάσιος, «τί ἐστι», φησί, «Θεός; Ἡ πάντων ἀρχή κατά τόν Ἀπόστολον, λέγοντα, "εἷς Θεός ὁ Πατήρ, ἐξ οὗ τά πάντα", καί γάρ ὁ λόγος ἐξ αὐτοῦ γεννητῶς καί τό Πνεῦμα ἐξ αὐτοῦ ἐκπορευτῶς». Ὁρᾷς ὁμοίως ἐπ' ἀμφοῖν τό ἐξ αὐτοῦ καί οὐδαμοῦ ρήματι προσκείμενον τό «μόνου»; Καί σύ τοίνυν ὁμοίως

4

Thus, it was most just not to deem you worthy even of conversation as long as you add to the sacred Symbol. Now, after you have cast out your addition, then one should inquire whether the Holy Spirit is also from the Son or not also from the Son and ratify what has been shown to be in agreement with the God-bearers – but not even then should one add to the Symbol of Faith, just as, with respect to the two natures and wills and energies of the one Christ, and the hypostatic union, and the title of the Virgin Mother,[52] those before us have acted well and reverently in striving for the common peace as well as for piety,[53] even though they afterwards convened together many times, and the presiding hierarchs of Old Rome at each time were also convening and gave consent. So, no one is obliged to take into consideration the prominent position of the present Pope. For we should not, for the sake of him or them that came after, reject so many and such great men who concluded their sanctified lives with a blessed end, to which lives God testified in many ways.

5

For, not only does the Symbol of the Orthodox Faith not add the "only" (it needs to be said, for the sake of those who will listen with good will)—therefore, not only does the Symbol of Faith not add the "only", but also nearly every theological tongue, when it proclaims the Son was begotten from the Father and the Holy Spirit proceeds from the same Father, does not add the "only". For, even if it is not added, it is necessarily implied, and if you open and go through the same theological books, you will also know this. For your sake, however, let us also succinctly put forth some small examples.
And so, of course, Athanasius the Great says, "What is God? The Source of all, according to the Apostle, who says, 'there is One God, the Father, of whom are all things.'[54] And, thus, the Word is from Him by way of begetting and the Spirit from Him by way of procession.'[55] Do you see that the "from Him" is used similarly for both and that nowhere is the "only" added to the phrase? And so, accordingly, you will either understand your addition similarly for

ἐπ᾽ ἀμφοῖν ἤ τήν σήν προσθήκην λήψῃ ἤ τό μόνου ἐξ ἀνάγκης συνυπακουόμενον νοήσεις.

Τί δέ ὁ μετ᾽ αὐτόν εὐθύς τῷ χρόνῳ καί οὐ μετ᾽ αὐτόν τῇ μεγαλειότητι παρά Θεῷ, τό φερωνύμως βασίλειον ἱεράτευμα, ἆρ᾽ οὐ συμφωνήσει τε καί συμφρονήσει; Ἀλλ᾽ ἄκουε καί μάνθανε· «κυρίως ὁ Υἱός ἐκ τοῦ Θεοῦ, ἐπειδή ὁ Υἱός ἐκ τοῦ Πατρός ἐξῆλθε καί τό Πνεῦμα ἐκ τοῦ Πατρός ἐκπορεύεται· ἀλλ᾽ ὁ μέν ἐκ τοῦ Πατρός γεννητῶς, τό δέ ἀρρήτως ἐκ τοῦ Θεοῦ». Ἰδού πολυπλασίως ὁμοίως ἐπ᾽ ἀμφοῖν τέθεικε τό ἐκ τοῦ Πατρός· ἔχεις οὖν ὅλως λέγειν ἔτι, ὡς οὐκ ἐκ μόνου τοῦ Πατρός τό Πνεῦμα τό ἅγιον, ὅτι μή πρόσκειται τό «μόνου»;

Βούλει δή καί τοῦ μεγάλου θεολόγου ἀκοῦσαι Γρηγορίου, ἐν βραχεῖ τό πᾶν συνάγοντος καί τήν σήν ὥσπερ τινί σμιλίῳ ἀποσμιλεύοντος προσθήκην καί ἀμφοτέροις τό ἐκ μόνου ἐφαρμόζοντος; καί τό θαυμασιώτερον, οὐχ ὅτι προστίθησιν, ἀλλ ὅτι μή προστίθησιν. «Ἡμῖν εἷς Θεός», φησίν, «ὅτι μία θεότης, καί πρός ἕν τά ἐξ αὐτοῦ τήν ἀναφοράν ἔχει, κἄν τρία πιστεύηται». Ἀκήκοας; Ἐξ αὐτοῦ εἶπεν ἄμφω. Ἆρ᾽ οὖν οὐ νοήσομεν τό «μόνου», ἀλλά νοήσομεν τό «οὐκ ἐκ μόνου», καί φρονήσομεν καί προσθήσομεν, ὅτι ἐκ τοῦ Πατρός καί ἐξ ἑτέρου τινός προέρχεται ἀμφότερα, ὅτι μή πρόσκειται τό «μόνου», καί τοῦ μόνου Θεοῦ τῆς ἀνωτάτω Τριάδος διά τοῦτο ἐκπεσούμεθα; Μή σύ γε τοῦτο πάθῃς, μᾶλλον δέ μή διαμείνῃς ἀνίατος παθών· γνωστόν γάρ ἤδη γέγονέ σοι τό ὀρθόν.

6

Καί μήν ἐκ τοῦ Πατρός φαμεν εἶναι τόν Υἱόν, ὡς ἐκ τῆς θείας οὐσίας γεννηθέντα, δηλονότι κατά τήν πατρικήν ὑπόστασιν· ἡ γάρ οὐσία μία τῶν τριῶν ἐστιν· ὥστε τό γεννᾶν τῇ πατρικῇ ὑποστάσει ἐφαρμόζεται καί οὐκ ἔστιν εἶναι τόν Υἱόν ἐκ τοῦ Πνεύματος. Ἐπεί οὖν καί τό Πνεῦμα τό ἅγιον ἐκ τοῦ Πατρός, ἐκ τῆς θείας οὐσίας καί

both, or you will necessarily consider that the "only" is implicitly understood for both.

But why will he, who is immediately after Athanasius in time and not inferior to him with respect to Majesty from God, who bears the name of the Royal priesthood, namely, St Basil the Great, not harmonize and not agree? Well, listen and learn, "strictly speaking the Son is from God, since the Son came forth from the Father and the Spirit proceeds from the Father. And while the one is from the Father by way of begetting, the other, in contrast, is from God in an ineffable way"[56]. Behold, in multiple instances he similarly asserted that both were from the Father. In short, then, are you able to say that the Holy Spirit is not only from the Father because the "only" is not in the text?

On this point, do you wish to hear also from the great theologian, Gregory? He briefly sums up the entire matter and removes your addition as with a scalpel, and applies the "only from" to both. And the most marvelous thing is not that he adds, but that he does not add. He says, "for us there is one God, because one is the Divinity, and to the One those that are from Him have their reference, although He is believed in as three."[37] Did you hear? He said both came "from Him." So will we not infer "only from [Him]"? Will we rather infer "not only from [Him]" and believe and add that both come forth from the Father and from something else, because the word "only" is not added, and thus fall away from the only God, from the Most High Trinity? May you not suffer this, or rather, may you not continue to suffer incurably, for what is right has already been made known to you.

6

Certainly, we affirm that the Son is from the Father since He was begotten from the divine essence, that is, by the paternal hypostasis (for the essence is one for the three). As a result, begetting is fittingly joined to the paternal hypostasis, and so the Son cannot be from the Spirit. Likewise, since the Holy Spirit is from the Father, He, too, is

αὐτό κατά τήν πατρικήν ὑπόστασιν ἐκπορευόμενόν ἐστιν· ἡ γάρ οὐσία πάντῃ τε καί πάντως μία τῶν τριῶν. Οὐκοῦν τό ἐκπορεύειν τῇ πατρικῇ ὑποστάσει ἐφαρμόζεται καί οὐκ ἔστιν εἶναι τό Πνεῦμα καί ἐκ τοῦ Υἱοῦ, οὐ γάρ ἐστι τά τῆς πατρικῆς ὑποστάσεως ἔχειν τόν Υἱόν.

Κατά γάρ τόν ἱερόν Δαμασκηνόν, «τήν διαφοράν τῶν θείων ὑποστάσεων ἐν μόναις τρισίν ἰδιότησιν ἐπιγινώσκομεν, τῇ ἀναιτίῳ καί πατρικῇ, τῇ αἰτιατῇ καί υἱϊκῇ, καί τῇ αἰτιατῇ καί ἐκπορευτῇ». Ὁρᾷς ὡς ἡ τοῦ Υἱοῦ ὑπόστασις οὐχί καί αἰτία, ἀλλ' αἰτιατή μόνον ἐστί; Μόνην γάρ, φησί, ταύτην ἔχει τήν ἰδιότητα, καθάπερ καί ἡ τοῦ Πνεύματος. Συνορᾷς δέ καί τοῦτο, ὡς ἡ πατρική, καθό πατρική ἰδιότης, ἄμφω τό γεννᾶν καί ἐκπορεύειν συμπεριβάλλει; Τοιγαροῦν, εἰ καί ἐκ τοῦ Υἱοῦ τό Πνεῦμα τό ἅγιον, εἴη ἄν καί ὁ Υἱός αἴτιός τε ἅμα καί Πατήρ ὡς αἴτιος.

7

Οὔκουν ἔνι τι τῶν τῆς πατρικῆς ὑποστάσεως ἔχειν τόν Υἱόν· εἰ δ' ἔχει, ἤ δύο ἔσονται τά αἴτια, ὡς ἐν δυσίν ὑποστάσεσι τοῦ ἐκπορεύειν ὄντος (οὕτω γάρ δύο καί τά αἰτιατά, ὡς τοῦ αἰτιατοῦ ἐν δυσίν ὑποστάσεσι θεωρουμένου), ἤ συνδραμοῦνται εἰς μίαν τήν ὑπόστασιν ὁ Πατήρ καί ὁ Υἱός. Ἐκ μόνου ἄρα τοῦ Πατρός ἐκπορεύεται τό Πνεῦμα τό ἅγιον, καί προσεχῶς καί ἀμέσως ἐκ Πατρός, ὡς καί ὁ Υἱός ἐκ τοῦ Πατρός γεννᾶται.

Διό καί Γρηγόριος ὁ Νύσσης θεῖος πρόεδρος, «τά τοῦ ἀνθρώπου», φησί, «πρόσωπα πάντα, οὐκ ἀπό τοῦ αὐτοῦ προσώπου κατά τό προσεχές ἔχει τό εἶναι, ὡς πολλά καί διάφορα εἶναι πρός τοῖς αἰτιατοῖς καί τά αἴτια. Ἐπί δέ τῆς ἁγίας Τριάδος οὐχ οὕτως· ἕν γάρ πρόσωπον καί τό αὐτό τοῦ Πατρός, ἐξ οὗπερ ὁ Υἱός γεννᾶται καί

proceeding from the divine essence, by the paternal hypostasis. For the essence is in every way and entirely one for the three. Therefore, causing procession is fittingly joined to the paternal hypostasis and so the Spirit cannot be also from the Son, since it is not possible for the Son to have the things of the paternal hypostasis.

For, according to the sacred Damascene, "we acknowledge the difference of the divine hypostases only in three personal properties: in the causeless and paternal, in the caused and filial, and in the caused and proceeding".[58] Do you see that the hypostasis of the Son is not also a cause but is only caused? For St. John says that He has only this property of being caused, just as it is with the hypostasis of the Holy Spirit. And do you also comprehend this, that the paternal property, inasmuch as it is paternal, encompasses both begetting and causing procession? So, because of this, if the Holy Spirit is also from the Son, the Son too would be both a cause and simultaneously a Father, by virtue of being a cause.

7

Therefore, the Son cannot possibly possess any of the things belonging to the paternal hypostasis. But, if He does possess, either there will be two causes, since causing procession is in two hypostases (for, in this way, there will also be two caused, since the caused will be contemplated as being in two hypostases), or the Father and the Son will coalesce into one hypostasis. Therefore, the Holy Spirit proceeds only from the Father, both directly and without mediation from the Father, as the Son also is begotten from the Father.

For this cause also, Gregory the divine primate of Nyssa[59] says, "all the persons of mankind do not have being from the same person with an immediate connection, as the causes, as well as the caused, are many and diverse. But in the case of the Holy Trinity, it is not like this, for there is one and same person, the Father, from whom precisely the Son is begotten and the Holy Spirit proceeds. It is

τό Πνεῦμα τό ἅγιον ἐκπορεύεται. Διό καί κυρίως τό ἕνα αἴτιον μετά τῶν αὐτοῦ αἰτιατῶν ἕνα Θεόν φαμεν τεθαρρηκότως».

Ἆρα νοῦν ἔλαβες πληγείς τῷ τῆς ἀληθείας λόγῳ καί μεταμανθάνεις τήν ἀλήθειαν καί πείθῃ Θεῷ καί τοῖς κατά Θεόν πατράσιν, ὡς ἐκ τοῦ Πατρός ἀκούων τό Πνεῦμα συνυπακούειν τό ἐκ μόνου καί μηκέτι ἐκ διαφόρων προσώπων τήν ὕπαρξιν αὐτῷ παρέχειν, ἀλλ᾽ ἐκ τοῦ ἑνός, τοῦ Πατρός, κατά τό προσεχές θεολογεῖν, οὐ τόν Υἱόν μόνον, ἀλλά καί τό Πνεῦμα τό ἅγιον ἕν πρόσωπον τό αἴτιον τῶν αὐτοῦ αἰτιατῶν εἶναι δοξάζων τόν Θεόν, ἀλλ᾽ οὐχ ἕν αἴτιον ὡς τῆς αὐτῆς οὐσίας τά δύο πρόσωπα λέγων τοῦ ἑνός, οὕτω γάρ πολλά γίνεται τά αἴτια, ὡς ἐφ᾽ ἡμῶν συμβαίνει, καί οὐκέτι Θεός εἷς, ὥσπερ οὐδ᾽ ἡμεῖς εἷς οἱ πάντες ἄνθρωπος, εἰ καί τῆς αὐτῆς ἐσμεν οὐσίας;

Ἆρ᾽ οὖν πείθῃ κατά ταῦτα Θεῷ καί τοῖς κατά Θεόν θεολογοῦσιν ἤ ζητεῖς ἔτι καί διά βροντῆς ἀκηκοέναι κατά τούς μετά τάς πολλάς Ἰησοῦ θεοσημίας σημεῖον ζητοῦντας ἐκ τοῦ οὐρανῶν ἰδεῖν; Ἄκουε δή καί τῆς βροντῆς, Ἰωάννου καί θεολογικωτάτου τῶν τοῦ Κυρίου μαθητῶν, ὅς φησιν· «εἴδομεν τήν δόξαν αὐτοῦ, δόξαν ὡς μονογενοῦς παρά πατρός». Τί οὖν, οὐκ ἐροῦμεν τόν μονογενῆ παρά μόνου τοῦ Πατρός, ἐπεί μή πρόσκειται τοῦ «μόνου»; Ἀλλά καί ὁ Κύριος αὐτός πρός Ἰουδαίους λέγων, «εἰ ὁ Θεός πατήρ ὑμῶν ἦν, ἠγαπᾶτε ἄν ἐμέ, ἐγώ γάρ ἐκ τοῦ Θεοῦ ἐξῆλθον καί ἥκω», καί πάλιν, «οὐχ ὅτι τις ἑώρακε τόν πατέρα, εἰ μή ὁ ὤν παρά τοῦ Θεοῦ, οὗτος ἑώρακε τόν πατέρα», πῶς οὐ προσέθηκε τό «μόνου» λέγων "ἐκ τοῦ Πατρός μόνου ἐξῆλθον", ἤ "ὁ ὤν παρά μόνου τοῦ Πατρός", οὐχ ὡς ἐξ ἀνάγκης συννοούμενον;

Τοσαυτάκις οὖν εἰρημένου περί τοῦ Υἱοῦ ὅτι παρά τοῦ Πατρός καί μηδαμοῦ τοῦ «μόνου» προσκειμένου, αὐτός τε πανταχοῦ συνυπακούεις τοῦτο καί τοῖς πανταχοῦ συνυπακούουσιν οὐ

principally for this reason that we boldly say that the one Cause, with those who are caused by Him, are one God."[60]

So, did you get some sense by suffering a blow from the word of truth? Are you properly learning the truth, and will you also, then, obey God and the godly Fathers, so that, when you hear that the Spirit is from the Father, you may agree about the "only from" and no longer grant to the Spirit existence from different persons, but theologize that not only the Son but also the Holy Spirit is from the one, the Father, without mediation, thinking that one person, God, is the cause of His Caused. Will you stop saying that the two persons are the one cause of the one person because they are of the same essence? For, in this way the causes become many, as happens with us, and God will no longer be one, just as we are not all one man, although we are of the same essence.

Therefore, will you obey God concerning these things and obey those who theologize in agreement with God? Or do you still seek to hear these things even through a roar of thunder, like those who, after the many divine signs of Jesus, were still seeking to see a sign from heaven? Listen here to the thunder, to John, the most theological of the disciples of the Lord, who says, "We beheld his glory, the glory as of the only begotten of the Father."[61] What is it, then? Will we not say that the Only-Begotten is only from the Father, as there is no addition of the word "only"? But the Lord Himself says to the Jews, "If God were your Father, ye would love me: for I proceeded forth and came from God".[62] And again, "Not that any man hath seen the Father, save He which is of God, he has seen the Father".[63] Why did He not add the word "only" saying, "I came only from the Father" or "which is only of the Father", if it was not necessarily understood?

Therefore, when it has been said, so many times, concerning the Son, that He is from the Father, and nowhere at all is the "only" added, you yourself also everywhere understand this and are not displeased with those who do everywhere take this for granted.

δυσχεραίνεις. Μᾶλλον μέν οὖν καί τοῖς μή συννοοῦσι τοῦτο ἐς τά μάλιστα δυσχερανεῖς καί ὡς δυσεβέσιν ἤ καί ἀσεβέσιν ἐγκαλέσεις. Περί δέ τοῦ ἁγίου Πνεύματος ἐκ τοῦ Πατρός ἀκούων, εἶτα τί παθών, οὐ συννοεῖς τό ἐξ ἀνάγκης συνυπακουόμενον, ἀλλά καί εἰς τήν ἐναντίαν ἐξετράπης δόξαν, ὅ ἄν ἐνεκάλεσας δικαίως τοῖς περί τοῦ Υἱοῦ κακῶς νοοῦσι, τοῦτ᾽ αὐτός ἀδίκως πεπονθώς ἐπί τοῦ Πνεύματος, ἐκ μηδεμιᾶς ὅλως τό δυσσεβές προξενούσης ἀφορμῆς;

8

Οὐ γάρ μόνον ὅτι λέγεται παρά τοῦ Πατρός τό Πνεῦμα, ὡς ὁ Θεός Λόγος πρό αἰώνων παρά τοῦ Πατρός, ἐξ ἀνάγκης παρά μόνου τοῦ Πατρός ἐκπορευόμενον νοεῖται, ἀλλ᾽ ἐπεί καί κατά τόν σοφόν μάρτυρα τῆς ἀληθείας Ἰουστῖνον, «ὡς ὁ Υἱός ἐστιν ἐκ τοῦ Πατρός, οὕτω καί τό Πνεῦμα τό ἅγιον ἐκ τοῦ Πατρός, πλήν τοῦ τρόπου τῆς ὑπάρξεως· ὁ μέν γάρ γεννητῶς ἐκ φωτός ἐξέλαμψε, τό δέ, φῶς μέν ἐκ φωτός καί αὐτό, οὐ μήν γεννητῶς, ἀλλ᾽ ἐκπορευτῶς προῆλθεν». Εἰ ὁ Υἱός ἀμέσως ἐκ Πατρός, καί τό Πνεῦμα ἐκ Πατρός ἀμέσως· καί εἰ ὁ Υἱός οὐχί καί ἐκ τοῦ Πνεύματος, καί τό Πνεῦμα οὐχί καί ἐκ τοῦ Υἱοῦ· καί εἰ ὁ Υἱός ἐκ μόνου τοῦ Πατρός, καί τό Πνεῦμα ἐκ μόνου τοῦ Πατρός. Ἐπεί γάρ τό Πνεῦμα τό ἅγιον ἐκπορευτόν ἐκ τοῦ Πατρός, ὡς ὁ Υἱός γεννητός ἐκ τοῦ Πατρός, τό δέ ὡς ὁ Υἱός γεννητός ἐκ τοῦ Πατρός ἐκπορευτόν, ἐκ μόνου τοῦ Πατρός ἐκπορευτόν, τό Πνεῦμα ἄρα τό ἅγιον ἐκ Θεοῦ Πατρός μόνου ἐκπορευτῶς προερχόμενος.

Ταῦτα ἄρα καί ὁμοίως λέγεταί τε καί ἔστιν, ὁμοῦ τε καί χωρίς ἑκάτερον, διά μέν τοῦ ὁμοίως εἶναι τήν ἀπόδειξιν ἡμῖν τῆς ἀληθείας αἰτιώδη παρεχόμενα, διά δέ τοῦ ὁμοίως λέγεσθαι τεκμηριώδη· οὐ γάρ ὅτι ἅμα ἐξ ἀϊδίου ὁ Υἱός τε καί τό Πνεῦμα, διά τοῦτο οὐκ ἐκ τοῦ Υἱοῦ τά τοῦ Πνεύματος γνωρίσομεν, ἀλλ᾽ ὅτι γνωριμώτερα ἡμῖν

Rather, you are utterly displeased with those who do not understand it in this way and you would accuse them as irreverent or even ungodly. But, concerning the Holy Spirit, when you hear that He proceeds from the Father, then what happens to you, that you do not understand that the "only" is also necessarily implied and you turn aside to the opposite belief? That, for which you would have justifiably accused those who wrongly thought this concerning the Son, has unjustifiably happened to yourself with reference to the Spirit, without any evidential support at all to warrant the impiety.

8

For, the Spirit is considered to proceed, by necessity, only from the Father, not only because He is said to be from the Father as God the Word is from the Father before the ages, but also since, according to the wise witness of the truth, Justin, "as the Son is from the Father, the Holy Spirit is similarly from the Father as well, apart from manner of existence. For, the One, indeed, shone forth from the Light by way of begetting, but the Other, while He too was certainly Light from the Light, came forth not by way of begetting, but by way of procession."[64] If the Son is immediately from the Father, the Spirit is also from the Father immediately. And if the Son is not from the Spirit, the Spirit is also not from the Son. And if the Son is only from the Father, the Spirit also is only from the Father. Since the Holy Spirit is proceeding from the Father as the Son is begotten from the Father, and since that which is proceeding as the Son is begotten is proceeding only from the Father, therefore, the Holy Spirit comes forth by way of procession only from God the Father.

So, the begetting of the Son and the procession of the Spirit are similar and are similarly described, both when taken together and separately. By existing similarly they furnish us on their own with the deductive proof of the truth, while by being described similarly they furnish us with the demonstrative proof of the truth. For, it is not because both the Son and the Spirit are simultaneously from eternity that we shall not acknowledge the things of the Spirit to

ἐστι τά τοῦ Υἱοῦ, ἐκ τῶν γνωριμωτέρων τούτων καί τό Πνεῦμα ἀποδείξομεν. Ἄλλως τε οὐδέ ἐκ τοῦ Υἱοῦ ἁπλῶς, ἀλλ᾽ ἐκ τοῦ εἶναι ὡς ὁ Υἱός τό Πνεῦμα ἐκ Πατρός, ἐκ μόνου τοῦ Πατρός ὑπάρχον ἀποδέδεικται.

9

Καί μήν κατά τόν θεῖον Παῦλον Πνεῦμα καί νοῦς λέγεται Χριστοῦ τό Πνεῦμα τό ἅγιον, καθάπερ ὁ Μέγας Βασίλειος ἐν τοῖς πρός Εὐνομιανοὺς περί τοῦ Πνεύματός φησιν γράφων· «τό ἐκ Θεοῦ τό Πνεῦμα εἶναι τρανῶς ἀνεκήρυξεν ὁ ἀπόστολος λέγων, ὅτι "τό Πνεῦμα ἐκ τοῦ Θεοῦ ἐλάβομεν"· καί τό δι᾽ Υἱοῦ πεφηνέναι σαφές πεποίηκεν, Υἱοῦ Πνεῦμα ὀνομάσας αὐτό καθάπερ Θεοῦ, καί νοῦν Χριστοῦ προσειπών, καθάπερ καὶ Θεοῦ Πνεῦμα, ὡς τό τοῦ ἀνθρώπου».

Καθάπερ οὖν τῶν ἀνθρώπων ἕκαστος τόν οἰκεῖον ἔχει νοῦν καί αὐτοῦ μέν ἐστιν ἑκάστου τούτων ὁ οἰκεῖος νοῦς, ἀλλ᾽ οὐκ ἐξ αὐτοῦ, ἀλλ᾽ ἐξ οὗπερ καί αὐτός, οὐκ ἐξ αὐτοῦ τοίνυν ἑκάστου ὁ οἰκεῖος νοῦς, εἰ μή ἄρα κατ᾽ ἐνέργειαν, οὕτω καί τό θεῖον Πνεῦμα φυσικῶς ἐνυπάρχον ὡς Θεῷ τῷ Χριστῷ, καί Πνεῦμα καί νοῦς ἐστιν αὐτοῦ. Καί κατά μέν τήν ἐνέργειαν αὐτοῦ ἐστι καί ἐξ αὐτοῦ ὡς ἐμφυσώμενον καί πεμπόμενον καί φανερούμενον, κατά δέ τήν ὕπαρξιν καί τήν ὑπόστασιν αὐτοῦ μέν ἔστιν, οὐκ ἐξ αὐτοῦ δέ, ἀλλ᾽ ἐκ τοῦ γεννήσαντος αὐτόν.

10

Ἵν᾽ οὖν σοι πανταχόθεν τάς κατά τῆς ἀληθείας ἐκκρούσωμεν λαβάς, ὁ Υἱός καί Λόγος τοῦ Θεοῦ, φύσει ὢν ἐκ τοῦ Θεοῦ, φύσει γεννᾶται, ἀλλ᾽ οὐ χάριτι γίνεται ἐκ τοῦ Πατρός. Ἐπεί δέ ὁ γεννῶν πηγαία θεότης καί πηγή θεότητος, πηγάζεται ὁ γεννώμενος. Ἐπεί δέ μόνος πηγή θεότητος καί πηγαία θεότης ὁ Πατήρ, ὡς Διονύσιος

be from the Son. Instead, because the things of the Son are better known to us, from these better-known matters we shall also prove the Spirit. Besides, it has been proven that the Spirit exists only from the Father not simply from the things of the Son but from the fact that the Spirit is from the Father as the Son is from the Father.

9

And certainly, according to the divine Paul, the Holy Spirit is called the Spirit and mind [nous] of Christ, just as Basil the Great says about the Spirit in his letters to the Eunomians when he writes, "the apostle distinctly proclaimed that the Spirit is from God when he says, 'we have received the Spirit from God';[65] and he made it clear that the Spirit was manifested through the Son since he named Him the Spirit of the Son just as he named Him the Spirit of God. He also named Him the mind [nous] of Christ,[66] just as he also named Him the Spirit of God, as is the case with the spirit of man."[67]

So, just as each man has his own intellect [nous] and each man's intellect is his own, yet his intellect is not from himself but from the source from which the man himself is, and so each man's own intellect is not from himself except in the sense of activity [energeia], so also, the divine Spirit naturally exists in Christ as in God and is thus His Spirit and intellect [nous]. And while according to activity the Spirit is His and from Him, since He is insufflated and sent and manifested, yet, according to His existence and hypostasis, He is indeed His, but not from Him, being instead from Him that begat the Son.

10

So, from every avenue of attack, let us repel the blows of your arguments against the truth. The Son and Word of God, being by nature from God, is begotten by nature, and does not come into being from the Father by grace. And seeing as the Begetter is the spring of divinity and the source of divinity, the Begotten springs forth. And seeing as the only source of

ὁ Ἀρεοπαγίτης καί Ἀθανάσιος ὁ μέγας συνῳδά φθέγγονται, ἐκ
μόνου ἄρα ὁ φύσει Υἱός ὑπάρχει τοῦ Πατρός· ὁ δέ θέσει οὐκ ἐκ
μόνου ἀλλά δι᾽ Υἱοῦ ἐκ τοῦ Πατρός, καίτοι οὐχ Υἱός μόνον, ἀλλά
καί Πνεῦμα χάριτί ἐστιν· «ὁ γάρ κολλώμενος τῷ Κυρίῳ ἕν Πνεῦμά
ἐστι», φησίν ὁ ἀπόστολος. Τό δέ Πνεῦμα τό ἅγιον οὐ χάριτι, ἀλλά
φύσει ἐστίν ἐκ τοῦ Θεου ὡς καί ὁ Υἱός καί Λόγος τοῦ Θεοῦ ἐκ τοῦ
Θεοῦ. Τό δέ φύσει ὄν Πνεῦμα ἐκ Θεοῦ φύσει ἐκπορεύεται ἐκ τοῦ
Θεοῦ· τό δέ φύσει ἐκπορευόμενον πηγάζεται ἐκ τοῦ Θεοῦ· τό δέ
πηγαζόμενον ἐκ τοῦ Θεοῦ ἐκ τῆς πηγαίας θεότητος πηγάζεται, ἥτις
ἐστί μόνος ὁ Πατήρ. Τό Πνεῦμα ἄρα τό ἅγιον φύσει Θεός, ἐκ Θεοῦ
Πατρός μόνου ἐκπορευτῶς πηγαζόμενον.

11

Εἰ δέ τις τοῦτ᾽ οὕτως ἔχειν οὐχ ὁμολογεῖ, καί περί τοῦ Υἱοῦ κακῶς
δοξάζων ἐξελεγχθήσεται. Τῇ γάρ τῆς ἀληθείας ἀποδείξει ταύτῃ
συμμαρτυρῶν καί ὁ θεολογικώτατος Γρηγόριος, «τί», φησίν, «οὐ
προσαγορεύεται τό Πνεῦμα ὧν ὁ Υἱός, πλήν γεννήσεως»; Καί
«πάντα ὅσα τοῦ Υἱοῦ, καί τοῦ Πνεύματος, πλήν τῆς υἱότητος».
Δαμασκηνός δε ὁ θεῖος, «διά τόν Πατέρα», φησί, «τουτέστι διά
τό εἶναι τόν Πατέρα, ἔχει ὁ Υἱός καί τό Πνεῦμα πάντα ἅ ἔχει,
τουτέστι διά τό τόν Πατέρα ἔχειν αὐτά, πλήν τῆς ἀγεννησίας καί
τῆς γεννήσεως καί τῆς ἐκπορεύσεως».

Ἑκάτερον ἄρα τούτων οὐκ ἔχει τό γεννᾶν καί ἐκπορεύειν· καί ὡς
τό Πνεῦμα κατ᾽ οὐδένα τρόπον ἔχει τήν γέννησιν, οὕτω ὁ Υἱός
κατ᾽ οὐδένα τρόπον ἔχει τήν ἐκπόρευσιν. Τοιγαροῦν ὁ αὐτός Υἱοῦ
καθάπερ ὅρος καί τοῦ Πνεύματος, πλήν τοῦ γεννητῶς τε καί
ἐκπορευτῶς, καθ᾽ ἅ καί μόνα διενηνόχασιν ἀλλήλων.

Καί τοῦτ᾽ ἄρα τηρητέον ἐφ᾽ ἅπασι τόν μή βλασφημεῖν ἀλλά
θεολογεῖν ἐθέλοντα. Ὡς γάρ εἷς καί μόνος γεννητός ὑπάρχει, ὁ Υἱός,

divinity and spring of divinity is the Father, as Dionysios the Areopagite[68] and Athanasius the Great harmoniously proclaim,[69] therefore the Son exists by nature only from the Father, whereas the one who is adopted is not "only from"[70] but is from the Father through the Son; although that person is not a son only, but is also a spirit by grace; for, the Apostle says, "he that is joined unto the Lord is one spirit".[71] Now the Holy Spirit is not by grace, but is by nature from God, just as also the Son and Word of God is from God. And so, the Spirit, being by nature from God, proceeds by nature from God. But what proceeds by nature springs forth from God. And what springs forth from God springs forth from the only source of divinity, which is the Father alone. Therefore, the Holy Spirit is God by nature, springing forth by means of procession from the Father alone.

11

Now if someone does confess that this is so, he will be refuted for thinking wrongly concerning the Son as well. For, when he bears witness to this very same proof of the truth, Gregory, who is incomparable in his theology, says, "what is not given as a name to the Spirit, of those which are also the Son's, apart from begottenness?"[72] Further, "all things, as many as are of the Son, are also the Spirit's, except Sonship".[73] Note that the divine Damascene says, "because of the Father, that is, on account of the Father's being, the Son and the Spirit have all things which They have. That is, because the Father has these same things they also have these things, apart from unbegottenness and begottenness and procession".[74]

Therefore, neither of them is able to beget and to cause procession, and as the Spirit does not possess begottenness by any mode, so the Son does not have procession by any mode. Consequently, the description is the same: just as it is for the Son, so it is for the Spirit, apart from being either begotten or proceeding, as according to this and this alone are they differentiated from each other.

And so, one who desires not to blaspheme but to theologize must maintain this for all the persons. For, as the Son is one and He alone

διόπερ καί μονογενής, οὕτως ἕν καί μόνον ἐκπορευτόν ὑπάρχει, Πνεῦμα ἅγιον· καί ὡς ὁ Υἱός γεννητός ἐκ μόνου τοῦ Πατρός, οὕτω καί τό Πνεῦμα τό ἅγιον ἐκπορευτόν ἐκ μόνου τοῦ Πατρός· καί ὡς ὁ Υἱός ἀμέσως ἐκ Πατρός γεννητός, οὕτω καί τό Πνεῦμα τό ἅγιον ἐκπορευτόν ἐκ τοῦ Πατρός ἀμέσως.

12

Ὁρᾷς ὅτι τό μέν παρ' ἡμῶν προσκείμενον ἔκφανσίς ἐστι τῆς ἀληθείας συνεκφωνουμένη διά τήν σήν πρός τήν ἀλήθειαν ἀθέτησιν; Καί γάρ παρόν τε καί ἀπόν τό αὐτό δίδωσι νοεῖν. Τό δέ σόν οὐ προσθήκη λέγοιτ' ἄν κυρίως, ἀλλά σαφής ἐναντιότης καί ἀνατροπή τοῦ εὐσεβοῦς φρονήματος· περιτρέπει γάρ τήν τῶν ἀκουόντων διάνοιαν εἰς τοὐναντίον καί ἀντί μιᾶς δύο δίδωσι δοξάζειν ἐπί τῆς μιᾶς θεότητος ἀρχάς καί τῇ πολυθέῳ πλάνῃ πάροδον παρέχει. Τίς γάρ τό ἕν ἐξ ἀμφοτέρων ἀκούων ἤ λέγων ἤ πιστεύων ἑτέρως ἄν φρονῆσαι;

Ἀλλ' οὐδέν ἄτοπον, φησίν, εἴ τις δύο μέν ἀρχάς λέγει, οὐκ ἀντιθέτους μέντοι, ἀλλά τήν ἑτέραν ἐκ τῆς ἑτέρας, ὡς καί Γρηγόριος ὁ θεολόγος περί τοῦ Υἱοῦ φησιν, «ἡ ἐκ τῆς ἀρχῆς ἀρχή»· οὕτω γάρ πάλιν μία ἔσται ἡ ἀρχή καί τό τῆς μοναρχίας δόγμα περισώζεται. Πρός ὅ λέγομεν ἡμεῖς, ὅτι καί Θεόν ἐκ Θεοῦ φαμεν, ἀλλ' οὐ δύο ποτέ θεούς.

13

Ἄλλως τε τό δημιουργικόν ταύτης σημαινούσης τῆς ἀρχῆς οὐ δύο μόνον ἄν εἴποι τις, εἰ καί μή καλῶς, ἀλλά καί πλείους. Τρισυπόστατος γάρ αὕτη ἡ ἀρχή· φύσει δέ οὖσα καί κοινή ἐστι· κοινήν δέ οὖσαν πῶς οὐκ ἄν ἔχοι καί τό Πνεῦμα ταύτην τήν ἀρχήν; Καί ὁ τῷ Ἰώβ δέ προσδιαλεγόμενος ὑπέρ τῆς τοῦ Θεοῦ δικαιοσύνης Ἐλιούς, «Πνεῦμα, λέγων, Κυρίου τό ποιῆσάν με» οὐ ποιητικήν ἀρχήν

is begotten (for which reason He is also called only-begotten), so the Holy Spirit exists as one and the only-proceeding. And as the Son is begotten only from the Father, so also the Holy Spirit is proceeding only from the Father. And as the Son is begotten directly from the Father, so also the Holy Spirit is proceeding from the Father directly.

12

Do you see, that the addition from us[75] is certainly an expression of the truth, which is uttered together with the text because of your disdain towards the truth? For, this addition, both when it is present and absent, gives us to understand the same thing. Yet yours would literally not be called an addition, but a clear opposition and overturning of a godly mindset. For, it diverts the mind of those who hear it to the opposite, and gives two origins to think of for the one divinity, and provides an inroad to the error of polytheism. For, who would think otherwise when he hears or says or believes that the One is from both?

"But there is nothing logically absurd," he retorts, "if someone does, in fact, say that there are two origins, for, they are not opposed, but the one is from the other, as Gregory the Theologian says concerning the Son: 'the origin from the origin.'[76] For, again in this way there will be one origin and the dogma of monarchy will be preserved".
 We respond to this, saying that we affirm God is from God, but not that there are ever two gods.

13

Put otherwise, since this same origin signifies the creative capacity, someone could say, although unsoundly, that there are not only two but more origins. For, this same origin is tri-hypostatic; and, being by nature, it is common; and, it being common, how could the Spirit not also have this same origin? Note also: when Elioud was dialoguing with Job about the righteousness of God saying, "the Spirit of the Lord hath made me",[77] did he not call the Spirit

τό Πνεῦμα λέγει; Καί ὁ θεῖος ᾠδικός Δαβίδ, «λόγῳ μέν Κυρίου τούς οὐρανούς στερεωθῆναι» ψάλλων, «Πνεύματι δέ τάς τῶν οὐρανῶν δυνάμεις» οὐχ ὥσπερ τῷ Υἱῷ, οὕτω καί τῷ Πνεύματι, τήν δημιουργικήν ἀρχήν προσμαρτυρεῖ; Εἰ τοίνυν διά τό γεγράφθαι «ἡ ἐκ τῆς ἀρχῆς ἀρχή» δύο εἰπεῖν ἀρχάς οὐδέν κωλύει κατά σέ, οὐκοῦν καί διά τό γεγράφθαι καί τό πνεῦμα ποιητήν, δύο ποιητάς εἰπεῖν οὐδέν κωλύει· ἤ διά τό «Λόγῳ Θεοῦ καί Πνεύματι τήν κτίσιν στερεοῦσθαι», ταὐτό δ᾽ εἰπεῖν συνίστασθαι, τρεῖς ἀρχάς εἰπεῖν οὐδέν ἄτοπόν ἐστιν.

Ἀλλ᾽ οὐδαμοῦ τῶν θεολόγων εἶπέ τις οὔτε δύο οὔτε τρεῖς. Ὥσπερ γάρ Θεόν ἑκάστην τῶν τριῶν προσκυνητῶν ἐκείνων ὑποστάσεών φαμεν καί Θεόν ἑκατέραν ἐκ Θεοῦ, ἀλλ᾽ οὐ παρά τοῦτο τρεῖς ἤ δύο ποτέ θεούς, οὕτω καί ἀρχήν ἐξ ἀρχῆς φαμεν, ἀλλ᾽ οὐ δύο ποτέ ἀρχάς· δευτέραν γάρ ἀρχήν οὐδέπω καί τήμερον ὑπό τῶν εὐσεβῶν ἀκηκόαμεν, ὥσπερ οὐδέ θεόν δεύτερον. Ἀλλ᾽ εἷς ἡμῖν Θεός καί μοναρχία τό προσκυνούμενον, οὐκ ἐκ δύο θεῶν, οὐδ᾽ ἐκ δύο ἀρχῶν συνιόντα εἰς ἕν· ἐπεί μηδέ κατά ταυτά μεριστόν ἡμῖν τό σεβόμενον. Καί μήν οὐδέ κατά τό αὐτό μερίζεταί τε καί συνάγεται· διαιρεῖται μέν γάρ ταῖς ὑποστατικαῖς ἰδιότησι, ταῖς δέ κατά τήν φύσιν ἑνοῦται. Εἰ γοῦν δύο ἀρχάς εἰπεῖν οὐδέν κωλύει, λοιπόν αὗταί εἰσι, καθ᾽ ἅς μερίζεται· ἑνωθῆναι τοίνυν αὖθις κατ᾽ αὐτάς ἀδύνατον· οὐκ ἄρ᾽ αἱ δύο μία.

Μᾶλλον δέ ἀναλαβόντες καί ἑτέραν ἀρχήν τῷ λόγῳ δόντες τά τῆς μοναρχικωτάτης ἀρχῆς εἰς δύναμιν διατρανώσωμεν, ὡς ἄν φερωνύμως ἔχοντά τε δείξωμεν τόν τῆς θεολογίας ἐπώνυμον καί

a creative origin? Further, when the composer of odes, the divine David, chanted, "By the Word of the Lord were the heavens established, and all the might of them by the Spirit,"[78] was he not attributing the creative origin as belonging to the Spirit just as it belongs to the Son? Therefore if, according to you, because it has been written "the origin from the origin," nothing prevents us from saying that there are two origins, then, because it has been written that the Spirit is also a creator, nothing prevents us from saying there are two creators. Or, because of the phrase "by the word of God and by His Spirit the creation is established" (that is to say, constituted), it is not inconsistent to premise that there are three origins.

Yet nowhere did any of the theologians say that the origins were either two or three. For, just as we affirm that each of those three worshipful hypostases is God and the two are God from God, but do not say that thereby there are ever two or three gods, thus we also affirm an origin from the origin, but never at any time do we affirm two origins. For, we have never heard from someone revered about a second origin even to this day, just as we have not heard of a second god. But for us there is one God, and what is worshipped is a monarchy,[79] not from two gods nor from two origins coming together into one, since what is revered by us is not divisible in those same respects [in terms of "God" and "origin"]. And certainly, God is not both parted and joined together in respect to the same thing. For He is divided in respect to the hypostatic properties; yet according to the natural properties He is united. So, if nothing prevents us from saying there are two origins, it remains, then, that these origins refer to that in which God is divided. So, again, it is not possible for these origins to be united. Therefore, the two are not one.

But rather, taking this up again and giving a new beginning to the discourse, let us clearly disclose, to the greatest extent, the truths of this absolutely singular-source origin. Thus, let us show that the namesake of theology worthily bears his name and in doing so refute those who dogmatize that there are two origins for the Holy

ἀπελέγξωμεν τούς τοῦ ἑνός ἁγίου Πνεύματος δύο δογματίζοντας ἀρχάς, ὅτι τε τοῦτο δογματίζουσι καί ὅτι οὐ καλῶς.

14

Ἡ δημιουργική ἀρχή μία ἐστίν, ὁ Πατήρ καί ὁ Υἱός καί τό Πνεῦμα τό ἅγιον. Ὅταν οὖν ἐκ τοῦ Θεοῦ τά ἐκ τοῦ μή ὄντος προηγμένα λέγωμεν, τήν τε ἀγαθότητα, δι᾽ ἥν τό εἶναι ἔσχον, καί τήν ἐγγεγενημένην χάριν, ὅθεν ἕκαστον τοῦ εὖ εἶναι καταλλήλως μετεσχήκασι, καί τήν ἐπιγεγενημένην ὕστερον, δι᾽ ἥν πρός τό εὖ εἶναι τά διαπεπτωκότα ἐπανῆλθον, ὅταν ταῦτά τε καί περί τούτων ποιώμεθα τούς λόγους, ἀρχήν καί πηγήν καί αἴτιον τόν Υἱόν ἐν ἁγίῳ Πνεύματί φαμεν, οὐχ ἑτέραν ἄπαγε, ἀλλά τήν αὐτήν ὡς τοῦ Πατρός δι᾽ αὐτοῦ ἐν ἁγίῳ Πνεύματι καί προάγοντος καί ἐπανάγοντος καί συνέχοντος καλῶς τά πάντα. Ὁ δέ Πατήρ πρός τῷ πηγή τῶν πάντων εἶναι διά τοῦ Υἱοῦ ἐν ἁγίῳ Πνεύματι, καί πηγή καί ἀρχή ἐστι θεότητος μόνος θεογόνος ὤν. Καί τοῦτ᾽ ἐσμέν εἰδότες κρεῖττον ἤ κατά ἀπόδειξιν, διά τῶν θεοπνεύστων λογίων τρανῶς ἐκπεφασμένον.

Ὅταν οὖν ἀκούσῃς ὅτι ὁ Υἱός, «ἡ ἐκ τῆς ἀρχῆς ἀρχή» καί «ὁ καλῶν αὐτόν ἀπό γενεῶν ἀρχήν» καί «μετά σοῦ ἡ ἀρχή ἐν ἡμέρᾳ τῆς δυνάμεώς σου», τῶν δημιουργημάτων νόει, καθάπερ καί Ἰωάννης ἀριδήλως ἐν τῇ Ἀποκαλύψει περί αὐτοῦ βοᾷ, «ἡ ἀρχή τῶν κτισμάτων τοῦ Θεοῦ», οὐχ ὡς καταρχή, ἄπαγε, Θεός γάρ, ἀλλ᾽ ὡς δημιουργός αὐτῶν· κοινωνός γάρ ἐστι τῆς ἐξ ἧς ταῦτα πατρικῆς ἀρχῆς, ἤ καί τῆς πάντων δεσποτείας ἐστίν ἐπώνυμον.

Τοῦ δέ Πνεύματος τόν Υἱόν ἀρχήν ἐπί τῆς σημασίας ταύτης πῶς ἄν φαίη τις, εἰ μή καί τό Πνεῦμα δοῦλον καί κτιστόν; Ἀλλ᾽ ἐπεί Θεός τό Πνεῦμα, οὐκ ἀρχή αὐτοῦ κατά τοῦτο ὁ Υἱός, εἰ μή ἄρα ὡς θεότητος

Spirit, showing both that they do dogmatize this and that they do not do so soundly.

14

The creative origin is one: the Father and the Son and the Holy Spirit. So, whenever we say that the things which have been brought forth into being from non-being are from God, whenever we mention the goodness, through which they acquired being, and the engendered grace, from which each one appropriately participated in well-being, and the grace that came to be later, by which those that had fallen returned to well-being, whenever we say these things and discourse concerning them, we are affirming that the Son is an origin and fount and cause in the Holy Spirit. Not that the Son is a different origin -- banish the thought! -- but the same origin, since the Father, through Him, in the Holy Spirit, both brings forth and leads back and sustains all things well. And the Father, besides being the fount of all things through the Son in the Holy Spirit, is also the Fount and origin of the divinity, being the only one capable of generating divinity. Further, we know this better than by logical demonstration, as it has been transparently expressed through the God-inspired oracles.

Therefore, whenever you hear that the Son is the "origin from the origin [ἀρχή]", and "who calleth him the origin [ἀρχή] from generations",[80] and "with Thee is dominion [ἀρχή] in the day of Thy power",[81] understand that these refer to Him as to the origin of created things, just as John so clearly shouts out about Him in Revelation as "the beginning [ἀρχή] of the creation of God",[82] not as the temporal beginning [καταρχή] — banish the thought! — but as their Creator. For He is a communicant of that from which these same things issue, the Paternal origin [ἀρχή], which is also a name of His dominion over all.[83]

Now, how could someone say that the Son is the origin of the Spirit in the same sense, unless the Spirit were also a servant and created? But since the Spirit is God, the Son is not His origin in this respect.

ἀρχή. Εἰ δέ τῆς τοῦ ἁγίου Πνεύματος θεότητος ὁ Υἱός ἐστιν ἀρχή, κοινωνεῖν δέ κατά ταύτην τήν ἀρχήν τῷ Πατρί ἀμήχανον, μόνος γάρ τεθεολόγηται πηγαία θεότης ὁ Πατήρ, ἑτέρας ἄρα διαφόρου τινός θεότητος ὁ Υἱός ἐστιν ἀρχή καί διέσπασε τό Πνεῦμα τῆς πηγαζούσης ἐκ τοῦ Πατρός θεότητος. Ἢ δύο διαφόρους θεότητας δώσωμεν τούτῳ τῷ ἑνί, οἱ καί τοῖς τρισί μίαν ἀνομολογοῦντες θεότητα;

Πῶς δέ καί αἱ δύο κατά Λατίνους τοῦ Πνεύματος ἀρχαί μία ἐστίν ἀρχή; Οὐ γάρ ἀξιώσουσιν ἡμᾶς πίστει δέχεσθαι τούτων τά προβλήματα, ἀλλά μηδέ σοφιστικῶς ἀποκρινέσθωσαν, ἄλλην ἀντ' ἄλλης ποιούμενοι τήν ἀπόκρισιν. Ἡμῶν γάρ ἐρωτώντων πῶς δύο κατ' αὐτούς τοῦ ἑνός Πνεύματος ἀρχαί, μίαν ἐκεῖνοι διισχυρίζονται τῶν δύο εἶναι τήν ἀρχήν. Ἡμεῖς δέ οὐ περί τῶν δύο προσώπων ἐρωτῶμεν, ἀλλά περί τοῦ ἑνός· περί τούτου γὰρ πρός αὐτούς ποιούμεθα τόν λόγον. Ὡς ἐπεί τῶν δύο μία ἡ ἀρχή καλῶς, πῶς τοῦ ἑνός δύο ἔσονται ἀρχαί καί πῶς αἱ δύο μία κατ' αὐτούς;

Φασίν οὖν, διότι ἡ μία ἐστίν ἐκ τῆς ἑτέρας. Τί οὖν Σήθ, ἐκ μιᾶς ἄρα γεγέννηται ἀρχῆς ὅτι ἡ Εὔα ἦν ἐκ τοῦ Ἀδάμ, καί οὐ δύο εἰσί τούτου τοῦ ἑνός ἀρχαί, ὅτι ἡ μία ἐστίν ἐκ τῆς ἑτέρας; Τί δέ ἡ Εὔα, οὐ δευτέρα ἀρχή τῶν ἐξ αὐτῆς, ὅτι καί αὐτή τήν ἀρχήν ἔσχεν ἐξ Ἀδάμ; Καίτοι ἀμφοῖν τό γόνιμον αὐτοῖς, ἀλλά διάφορον καί ἐν διαφόροις ὑποστάσεσι· διόπερ οὐδέ μία ἐστίν αὗται αἱ ἀρχαί, καθάπερ καὶ τὸν Νύσσης θεῖον πρόεδρον ἀνωτέρω προηνέγκαμεν εἰπόντα, καίτοι ἡ μία τούτων ἐστίν ἐκ τῆς ἑτέρας.

Εἰ γοῦν ἐνταῦθα οὗ εἰ καί μή ἕν, ὅμως ἐστί τό γόνιμον ἀμφοῖν, οὐκ ἔνι τοῦ ἑνός μίαν εἶναι τήν ἀρχήν, πῶς ἐπί τῆς ἀνωτάτω Τριάδος αἱ δύο κατ' αὐτούς τοῦ ἑνός ἁγίου Πνεύματος μία εἰσίν ἀρχαί, ἐν ᾗ μηδαμῶς ἐστι κατά τό θεογόνον κοινωνία; μόνος γάρ τεθεολόγηται θεότης θεογόνος ὁ Πατήρ.

Therefore, He can only be so as an origin of divinity. Now, if the Son is an origin of the divinity of the Holy Spirit, and if it is impossible for Him to share in this same origin with the Father (for, only the Father has been theologized as the divine Source), this would imply that the Son is the origin of some other, different divinity and by implication has sundered the Spirit from the divinity springing forth from the Father. Or will we, who confess one divinity in the three, concede two different divinities to this One?

Furthermore, how are the Spirit's two origins—according to the Latins—one? For they cannot demand that we accept their propositions by faith, but neither let them answer as sophists,[84] making one response instead of the other. For when we ask how—according to them—are there two origins of the one Spirit, they assert that the origin of the two is one. We, however, are not asking about the two persons but about the one, since it is for this matter that we are addressing to them the treatise. If the origin of the two is one (which is true), how will there be two origins of the one and how are these two one, according to them?

Therefore, they say, "because the one is from the other." What, then, of Seth? Has he, therefore, been begotten from one origin because Eve was from Adam? Are there not two origins for this one person [Seth] because the one is from the other? And what of Eve? Is she not a second origin for those born from her because she had her origin from Adam?[85] And yet, both of them had the generative power, but it was different and in different hypostases. Consequently, neither are these origins one (just as the divine primate of Nyssa stated, as we forementioned), although the one is from the other.

So if here, in this example, where both persons have the generative power, even though it is not one, the origin of the one [Seth] cannot be one, how is it possible in the most high Trinity, in whom there is no communication at all of the generation of divinity, for the two origins (according to them) of the one Holy Spirit to be one? For, only the Father has been theologised as the divinity-generating divinity.

Πάλιν ἡ Εὔα ἐκ μόνου οὖσα τοῦ Ἀδάμ, ἐκ μιᾶς ἐστιν ἀρχῆς· ὁ δέ Ἀδάμ ἐκ γῆς ἐστιν. Ἀλλ᾽ οὐ παρά τοῦτο ἡ Εὔα ἐκ τῆς γῆς καί τοῦ Ἀδάμ. Ὁ γάρ Ἀδάμ μόνος ἐκ τῆς γῆς. Ἢ τοίνυν καί αὐτοί ἐκ τοῦ Υἱοῦ μόνου λεγέτωσαν τό Πνεῦμα καί οὕτως αὐτό ἐκ μιᾶς ἀρχῆς λεγέτωσαν, ἑαυτοῖς μέν ἀκολούθως ἀλλ᾽ οὐκ εὐσεβῶς, οὐ γάρ ἐκ τῆς αὐτῆς ἀφ᾽ ἧς καί ὁ Υἱός, κἀντεῦθεν πάλιν δύο εἰσίν ἐπί τῆς θεότητος ἀρχαί καί οὐκέτ᾽ ἐστί μείζων ὁ Πατήρ τῷ αἰτίῳ τοῦ Υἱοῦ, ἐπίσης γάρ καί αὐτός αἴτιος θεότητος, ἤ ἐκ μόνου τοῦ Πατρός αὐτό λέγοντες μίαν καί τῷ Πνεύματι ὡς καί τῷ Υἱῷ εὐσεβῶς διδότωσαν ἀρχήν. Μέχρι γάρ ἄν ἐκ τοῦ Υἱοῦ ἤ ἐξ ἀμφοτέρων λέγωσιν, ἀλλ᾽ οὐκ ἐκ μόνου τοῦ Πατρός, οὐκ ἔστι μίαν εἶναι τῆς θεότητος τοῦ ἑνός Πνεύματος ἀρχήν.

Συνάπτων γάρ τις ἐπί τῶν τοιούτων, εἰ καί μίαν φαίη τήν ἀρχήν, ἀλλ ὁμωνύμως, ὥστε οὐ μία. Εἰ δέ διαιρῶν κατά μίαν ὁρᾷ τάς ὑποστάσεις, τῆς μιᾶς ἐξ ἀνάγκης δύο φανερῶς γίνονται ἀρχαί. Ἐμοί δ᾽ ἔπεισι θαυμάζειν καί τό ὑπερβάλλον τῆς ἀνοίας τῶν τάς δύο ταύτας, ἅς φασιν ἀρχάς, μίαν λεγόντων τε καί οἰομένων· εἰ μέν γάρ κοινωνεῖ τῷ Πατρί κατά τό θεογόνον ὁ Υἱός προβαλλόμενος τό Πνεῦμα, καί ἐν αὐτοῖς τό θεογόνον καὶ ἡ ἐκ τούτων αὕτη πρόοδος, τῆς φύσεως ἄρα τοῦτο καὶ οὐ δύο εἰσίν ἀρχαί, οὐδ᾽ αἱ δύο μία, ἀλλὰ ἁπλῶς μία, καί ἀπεξένωται τῆς θείας φύσεως αὐτό τό Πνεῦμα, μή καί αὐτό κατά θεογόνον κοινωνοῦν. Εἰ δέ μή κοινωνεῖ ὁ Υἱός κατά τοῦτο τῷ Πατρί, μηδέ ἕν αὐτοῖς τοῦτο τό προβάλλειν, καθ᾽ ὑπόστασιν τῷ Υἱῷ ἡ πρόοδος τοῦ Πνεύματος· διάφορος ἄρα αὕτη τῆς ἐκ τοῦ Πατρός τοῦ Πνεύματος προόδου· τά γάρ ὑποστατικά διάφορα.

15

Πῶς οὖν μία αἱ διάφοροι ἀρχαί, καί μήν τοῦ μεγάλου Διονυσίου ἐν

Again, since Eve is only from Adam, she is from one origin. Now consider that Adam is from the earth, but this does not mean that Eve is from the earth and from Adam, since only Adam is from the earth. In view of that, the Latins have two alternatives: either let them say that the Spirit is only from the Son and thus that He is from one origin (which, however, would not be the same origin as the one from which the Son is, and therefore again there will be two origins for the divinity and the Father will no longer be greater than the Son in cause, since He [the Son] will likewise be a cause of divinity), or let them instead say that He [the Holy Spirit] is only from the Father and thus reverently grant one origin to the Spirit, just as to the Son. For, as long as they say that He is from the Son or from both, but not only from the Father, there cannot possibly be one origin of the divinity of the one Spirit.

For when someone joins such things, although he might say that the origin is one, he speaks equivocally, so that it is not one. For, once he divides and looks at the hypostases one by one, necessarily the origins of the one hypostasis clearly become two. Now, they make me marvel at their exceeding folly who say and think that these two 'origins', as they say, are one. For if the Son actually communicates with the Father in the generation of divinity by emanating the Spirit, and the generation of divinity is one for them, and this progression from them is likewise one, then this property is natural and there are not two origins, nor are the two one, but simply one, and the Spirit Himself has been estranged from the divine nature, since He does not communicate in the generation of divinity. If, however, the Son does not communicate with the Father in the generation of divinity and the ability to emanate divinity is not one for them, the progression of the Spirit is hypostatic for the Son. This progression, then, is different from the progression of the Spirit from the Father; for the hypostatic properties are different.

15

How is it possible, then, that the different origins are one, and

δευτέρῳ κεφαλαίῳ τοῦ Περί θείων ὀνομάτων λόγου λέγοντος «ὅσα ἐστί τοῦ Πατρός καί τοῦ Υἱοῦ, ταῦτα καί τῷ θεαρχικῷ Πνεύματι κοινῶς καί ἡνωμένως ἀνατίθεσθαι», καί τοῦ μεγάλου Βασιλείου ἐν τοῖς πρός Εὐνομιανούς Ἀντιρρητικοῖς αὐτοῦ κεφαλαίοις γράφοντος, «πάντα τά κοινά Πατρί τε καί Υἱῷ κοινά εἶναι καί τῷ Πνεύματι»; Εἰ μέν κοινόν ἐστι Πατρί τε καί Υἱῷ τό ἐκπορεύειν, κοινόν ἔσται τοῦτο καί τῷ Πνεύματι, καί τετράς ἔσται ἡ Τριάς· καί τό Πνεῦμα γάρ ἐκπορεύσει Πνεῦμα ἔτερον. Εἰ δέ μή κοινόν ἔστι κατά Λατίνους τῷ Πατρί καί τῷ Υἱῷ τό ἐκπορεύειν, ὡς τοῦ μέν Πατρός ἐμμέσως κατ᾽ αὐτούς, τοῦ δέ Υἱοῦ ἀμέσως ἐκπορεύοντος τό Πνεῦμα, οὕτω γάρ καί ὑποστατικῶς ἔχειν τόν Υἱόν τό προβλητικόν φασιν, οὐκοῦν κατ᾽ αὐτούς καί τό δημιουργεῖν καί ἁγιάζειν καί ἁπλῶς ἅπαντα τά φυσικά οὐ κοινά Πατρός τε καί Υἱοῦ, ἐπειδή ὁ μέν Πατήρ διά τοῦ Υἱοῦ κτίζει τε καί ἁγιάζει, καί διά μέσου τοῦ Υἱοῦ δημιουργεῖ καί ἁγιάζει, ὁ δέ Υἱός οὐ δι᾽ Υἱοῦ. Τοιγαροῦν κατ᾽ αὐτούς ὑποστατικῶς ἔχει τό δημιουργεῖν καί ἁγιάζειν ὁ Υἱός· ἀμέσως γάρ καί οὐχ ὡς ὁ Πατήρ ἐμμέσως· καί οὕτω κατ᾽ αὐτούς τά φυσικά τῶν ὑποστατικῶν διενήνοχεν οὐδέν· οὐκοῦν καί ἡ φύσις τῆς ὑποστάσεως, ὡς μή τρισυπόστατον ἤ τριφυᾶ κατ᾽ αὐτούς εἶναι τόν Θεόν.

Εἰ δ᾽ ἄρα φαῖεν διά τοῦ Πνεύματος τόν Υἱόν δημιουργεῖν καί ἁγιάζειν, ἀλλά πρῶτον μέν οὐ σύνηθες τοῖς θεολόγοις διά τοῦ Πνεύματος τόν Υἱόν ἤ τόν Πατέρα δημιουργόν εἶναι λέγειν τῶν κτισμάτων, ἀλλ᾽ ἐν ἁγίῳ Πνεύματι. Ἔπειτα πρός τῷ μηδ᾽ οὕτω τό ἀνωτέρω δεδειγμένον ἄτοπον αὐτούς ἐκφεύγειν, οὐ γάρ δι᾽ Υἱοῦ πάλιν ὁ Υἱός ἀναφαίνεται δημιουργός καθάπερ ὁ Πατήρ, συμβήσεται τούτοις μηδέ κοινόν εἶναι λέγειν καί τῷ Πνεύματι τό δημιουργεῖν καί ἁγιάζειν, ὡς μή δι᾽ ἑτέρου, μηδέ ὡς ὁ Πατήρ ἤ καί ὁ Υἱός αὐτοῦ ταῦτα ἐνεργοῦντος. Κατ᾽ αὐτούς οὖν ὑποστατικῶς ἔχει

particularly when the great Dionysius, in the second chapter of his treatise Concerning the Divine Names, says, "all that belongeth to the Father and to the Son are also ascribed in common to the divine Spirit",[86] and how can it be so, when Basil the Great writes in his rebuttal chapters To the Eunomians, "all things common to the Father and to the Son are also common to the Spirit"?[87] If it were common both to the Father and to the Son to cause procession, then this causing of procession will also be common to the Spirit, and the Trinity will be a tetrad, since the Spirit also will make another Spirit proceed. But if causing procession is not common to the Father and the Son, as the Latins say, since the Spirit proceeds from the Father mediately—according to them—while from the Son immediately (for this is how they say that the Son has the emanating power hypostatically), then—according to them—both creating and sanctifying and quite simply all natural things will not be common to the Father and the Son, since the Father both fashions and sanctifies through the Son, and again through the mediation of the Son He creates and sanctifies, while the Son does not do so through a son. Consequently, according to them, the Son has the power of creating and sanctifying in His hypostasis, since He acts immediately and not mediately like the Father. And thus, according to them, the natural properties are no different from the hypostatic properties, and so neither is the nature different from the hypostasis, as if—according to them—God were not tri-hypostatic or of a threefold nature.

Now then, were they to say that the Son creates and sanctifies through the Spirit, we respond that, in the first place, it certainly is not customary with the theologians to say that the Son or the Father is the Creator of creatures through the Spirit, but rather in the Holy Spirit. Next, so that even by this argument they may not escape the absurdity shown above (for, again, the Son is not shown to be a Creator through a son as the Father is), they will have to say that not even creating and sanctifying are common to the Spirit, since He does not effect these things through another, nor does He do so like the Father or the Son. So, according to them, the Spirit has

τό Πνεῦμα τό δημιουργεῖν καί ἁγιάζειν, ὡς οὐκ ἐμμέσως καθάπερ ὁ Πατήρ κτίζον τε καί ἁγιάζον. Ἐντεῦθεν δή πάλιν κατ' αὐτούς, ταῦτά τε εἶναι καί ἀδιάφορα δείκνυται τοῖς ὑποστατικοῖς τά φυσικά. Εἰ δέ τοῦτο, καί ἡ φύσις ταῖς ὑποστάσεσι ταὐτόν τε καί ἀδιάφορον. Ἆρ' οὐ σαφῶς τῆς ἀνωτάτω Τριάδος ἐκπεπτώκασι καί τῆς ἑνότητος τῆς πίστεως καί τῆς κοινωνίας τοῦ ἁγίου Πνεύματος οἱ ταῦθ' οὕτω λέγοντές τε καί φρονοῦντες;

Ἀλλά γάρ ἐπανέλθωμεν ὅθεν ἐξέβημεν. Τίς γάρ τό Πνεῦμα τό ἅγιον τήν ὕπαρξιν ἔχειν ἐξ ἀμφοτέρων Υἱοῦ τε καί Πατρός ἀκούων ἤ λέγων ἤ πιστεύων καί παρά μέν τοῦ Υἱοῦ ἀμέσως, παρά δέ τοῦ Πατρός ἐμμέσως καί τά παρ' αὐτῶν θρυλλούμενά τε καί περιᾳδόμενα προσεχῆ τε καί ἐφεξῆς καί πόρρω, τίς ταῦτ' ἀκούων καί πιστεύων οὐ δύο δοξάσει τοῦ ἑνός Πνεύματος ἀρχάς; Πῶς δέ οὐκ ἄν εἴη ὁ Υἱός τῷ Πατρί συναίτιος, εἰ μή μάτην λέγεται καί ἐξ αὐτοῦ; Πῶς δέ οὐκ ἄν τό Πνεῦμα εἴη κτίσμα; Ἐπί γάρ τῶν κτισμάτων τῷ Πατρί συναίτιος.

16

Καί μήν ἐπί τῆς κτίσεως, ἐφ' ἧς φανερῶς αἴτιός ἐστι καί ὁ Υἱός καί τῷ Πατρί συναίτιος, ὡς ἐκ Πατρός δι' αὐτοῦ καί ἐξ αὐτοῦ τό εἶναι λαβούσης, ἀσεβές παντάπασιν εἰπεῖν ὅτι τήν κτίσιν ἐκ τοῦ Υἱοῦ οὐ λέγομεν καί ὅτι τό δημιουργικόν ἰδιότης ἐστί τῆς τοῦ Πατρός ὑποστάσεως. Τοιγαροῦν εἰ καί τό ἐκπορευτῶς ὑπάρχον Πνεῦμα ἅγιον ἐκ Πατρός δι' Υἱοῦ καί ἐξ Υἱοῦ τό εἶναι εἶχεν, οὐκ ἄν ἦν ὅλως εὐσεβοῦς εἰπεῖν, ὡς ἐκ τοῦ Υἱοῦ τό Πνεῦμα οὐ λέγομεν καί ὡς ἡ ἐκπορευτική ἰδιότης τῷ Πατρί μόνῳ πρόσεστιν.

Ἐπεί δέ οἱ ταῦτα λέγοντες Δαβίδ ἐστιν ὁ θεοπάτωρ καί Γρηγόριος ὁ Νυσσαέων φανότατος φωστήρ καί Δαμασκηνός ὁ θεοφόρος, κατά

the creating and sanctifying power hypostatically, since He does not create and sanctify mediately as the Father does. And herein, again, according to them, the natural properties are shown to be the same and no different from the hypostatic properties. But if this is so, the nature also is the same and no different from the hypostases. Have those that speak and think these things in this way not obviously fallen away from the Most High Trinity, from the unity of the Faith, and from the communion of the Holy Spirit?

But let us continue from where we digressed. When someone hears, or says, or believes that the Holy Spirit has existence from both the Father and the Son (from the Son immediately, but from the Father mediately) and believes the things that they keep repeating and disseminating, things both adjacent and subsequent and remote – who, when hearing and believing these things, will not be of the opinion that there are two origins for the one Spirit? How would the Son not be a joint cause with the Father, unless to nought the Spirit is said to be from Him? And how would the Spirit not be a creature? For, the Son is a joint cause with the Father with respect to created things.

16

And certainly, with respect to creation, for which the Son is also manifestly a cause and a joint cause with the Father since creation received being from the Father through Him and from Him, it is entirely impious to say that creation is not from the Son and that the creative property is of the hypostasis of the Father. Consequently, if the Holy Spirit, who exists by procession, had His being from the Father through the Son and from Son, it would be entirely impious to say that the Spirit is not from the Son and that the property of causing procession is attributed to the Father only.

But since David, the ancestral father of God, and Gregory of Nyssa the most bright, and the God-bearing Damascene are the ones saying these things,[88] then by utter necessity those who say that the

πᾶσαν ἀνάγκην οἱ συναίτιον τῷ Πατρί τόν Υἱόν λέγοντες ἐπί τοῦ παναγίου Πνεύματος καί ἐκ τοῦ Πατρός διά τοῦ Υἱοῦ καί ἐκ τοῦ Υἱοῦ τήν ὕπαρξιν αὐτῷ διδόντες, τοσοῦτον ἀπέχουσι τῆς εὐσεβείας, ὅσον ἀντέχονται ταύτης οἱ προαπηριθμημένοι τῶν ἁγίων καί οἱ τούτοις συνῳδά θεολογοῦντες.

17

Καί τοῦτο δέ συνορᾶν τῶν ἀναγκαιοτάτων, ὡς καθάπερ ἐκ τοῦ Πατρός δι᾽ Υἱοῦ καί ἐξ Υἱοῦ τήν γένεσιν ἔχοντες ἡμεῖς, Πατέρα καί ποιητήν ὁμοῦ τε καί χωρίς ἑκάτερον ἐπικαλούμεθα καί ἀνομολογοῦμεν, οὕτω καί τοῦ θείου Πνεύματος ὁμοῦ τε καί χωρίς ἑκάτερος Πατήρ ἄν ἐλέγετο καί προβολεύς, εἴπερ ἐκ Πατρός δι᾽ Υἱοῦ καί ἐξ Υἱοῦ τήν ὕπαρξιν τό Πνεῦμα εἶχεν. Ἀλλά τά τοιαῦτα πάντα πολυειδῶς συγχέοντα τάς θείας ὑποστάσεις παρίστησι σαφῶς, ὡς οὐχί καί ἐκ τοῦ Υἱοῦ τήν ὕπαρξιν ἔχει τό Πνεῦμα τό ἅγιον.

18

Καί μέν δή, «πάντα ὅσα ἔχει ὁ Πατήρ, τοῦ Υἱοῦ ἐστι», κατά τόν θεολόγον Γρηγόριον, «ἄνευ τῆς αἰτίας. Ποίας αἰτίας; Τῆς τῶν κτισμάτων; Ἄπαγε˙ τούτων γάρ ἀρχή καί αἴτιος καί ὁ Υἱός. Τοιγαροῦν ἄνευ τῆς αἰτίας καί ἀρχῆς τῆς ἐν Τριάδι νοουμένης θεότητος˙ πάντα οὖν ἔχει ὁ Υἱός τοῦ Πατρός, ἄνευ τοῦ ἀρχή καί αἴτιος εἶναι καί αὐτός τῆς θεότητος τοῦ Πνεύματος. Ἐκ μόνου ἄρα τοῦ Πατρός ἐκπορεύεται τό Πνεῦμα τό ἅγιον, καθάπερ ὁ Υἱός ἐκ μόνου τοῦ Πατρός γεννᾶται, καί προσεχῶς καί ἀμέσως τοῦ Πατρός ἔχεται καθ᾽ ὕπαρξιν, καθά καί ὁ Υἱός, εἰ καί διά τοῦ Υἱοῦ Πατρός εἶναι Πνεῦμα ἔσχεν, ὡς τοῦ ἐκπορεύοντος ὄντος καί Πατρός.

Son is jointly a cause with the Father for the All-Holy Spirit and who concede that His existence is from the Father through the Son and from the Son distance themselves as far from piety as the saints listed above and those who theologize in unison with these saints cling close to it.

17

Now here is another thing that must be necessarily understood, that, just as we have our genesis from the Father through the Son and from the Son, and as we invoke and confess each as a Father and Creator simultaneously and separately, in this way also, if the Spirit had existence from the Father through the Son and from the Son, each simultaneously and separately would be called Father and Generator of the divine Spirit. But all such things, in fusing together the divine hypostases in different ways, clearly prove that the Holy Spirit does not have existence from the Son.

18

Again, it is certain here, according to Gregory the Theologian, that "all things that the Father has are the Son's apart from the Cause."[89] What particular cause? The cause of creatures? Banish the thought! For, the origin and Cause of created things is also the Son. Consequently, it means "apart from the Cause and origin of the divinity considered in a Trinity". And so, the Son has everything of the Father's, without being Himself the origin and Cause of the divinity of the Spirit. The Holy Spirit, therefore, proceeds from the Father alone, exactly as the Son is begotten from the Father alone. And, according to His existence, He clings to the Father both directly and immediately, just like the Son, although it is through the Son that He acquired the power to be the Father's Spirit, since the One causing procession is also a Father.

19

Ἐπεί δέ καί δύο ἀνθρώπων ἡ μαρτυρία ἀληθής ἐστι κατά τόν τοῦ
Κυρίου λόγον, «καί διά δύο ἤ τριῶν μαρτύρων σταθήσεται πᾶν
ῥῆμα», καί ἡμεῖς τό νῦν εἶναι τῶν ἄλλων ἀφέμενοι διά τό μῆκος
τρεῖς παραστήσομέν σοι μάρτυρας, σαφῶς ἀπαγορεύοντάς σου
τήν προσθήκην. Καί δή παρίτω πρῶτος ὁ καί τῷ χρόνῳ πρότερος
Βασίλειος ὁ μέγας· ἐν γάρ τοῖς Κατ' Εὐνομίου κεφαλαίοις, «γεννᾷ»,
φησίν, «ὁ Θεός οὐχ ὡς ἄνθρωπος, γεννᾷ δέ ἀληθῶς· καί τό
γεγεννημένον ἐξ αὐτοῦ ἐκφαίνει λόγον οὐκ ἀνθρώπινον, ἐκφαίνει
δέ λόγον ἀληθῆ ἐξ αὐτοῦ· ἐκπέμπει Πνεῦμα διά στόματος, οὐχ οἷον
τό ἀνθρώπινον, ἐπεί μηδέ στόμα Θεοῦ σωματικῶς· ἐξ αὐτοῦ δέ τό
Πνεῦμα καί οὐχ ἑτέρωθεν». Ὁρᾷς ὅτι οὐχ ἑτέρωθεν, ἀλλ' ἐκ μόνου
τοῦ καί τόν Υἱόν γεννῶντος; Ὥστε οὐκ ἐκ τοῦ Υἱοῦ τό Πνεῦμα, ἐπεί
καί λόγος ὁ Υἱός, ἀλλ' οὐ στόμα τοῦ Πατρός ἐνταῦθα τῷ μεγάλῳ
τεθεολόγηται. Ὅς ἀλλαχοῦ δεικνύς καί τόν λόγον τοῦτον ἐκ τοῦ
αὐτοῦ προϊόντα στόματος, «εἰ γάρ τό Πνεῦμα μή πιστεύεις», φησίν,
«ἐκ στόματος Θεοῦ προεληλυθέναι, οὐδ' ἄν τόν λόγον πιστεύσεις».
Ὁρᾷς σαφῶς ὅτι Λόγος ὁ Υἱός, ἀλλ' οὐ στόμα τοῦ Πατρός· ἐξ οὗ
στόματος κατά τόν μέγαν Βασίλειον πρόεισι καθ' ὕπαρξιν ὡς τό
Πνεῦμα τό ἅγιον;

Τόν αὐτόν δέ τρόπον καί ὁ ἀδελφός αὐτῷ καί ἀδελφά φρονῶν
Γρηγόριος ἐν τῷ Περί θεογνωσίας λόγῳ, «Πνεῦμα δέ», φησί, «τό
τῆς πατρικῆς ἐκπορευόμενον ὑποστάσεως. Τούτου γάρ ἕνεκα
καί Πνεῦμα στόματος ἀλλ' οὐχί καί τόν λόγον στόματος ὁ Δαβίδ
εἴρηκεν, ἵνα τήν ἐκπορευτικήν ἰδιότητα τῷ Πατρί μόνῳ προσοῦσαν
πιστώσηται».

Μετ' αὐτόν τόν ἀψευδῆ τῆς ἀληθείας μάρτυρα, ὁ ζῶν φωστήρ
γεγονώς Ἀλεξανδρείας Κύριλλος, συμμαρτυρήσων παρελθέτω·

19

Now since the witness of two men is true, according to the word of the Lord, "and by two or three witnesses every word will be established",[90] although we presently desire to bring more witnesses, on account of the length we shall present to you but three witnesses, who clearly forbid your addition. And on this point, let us present Basil the Great first, since he was also prior chronologically. For, he says in his chapters "Against Eunomius", "God begets, not like a man, but He truly begets; and He shines forth what has been begotten from Him, a word, not a human word but a true word from Him. He sends forth the Spirit through His mouth, not like that which is human, since neither does the mouth of God send forth bodily; and the Spirit is from Him, and not from another [source]".[91] Do you see, then, that the Spirit is not from another source, but is only from the One who begets the Son? As a result, the Spirit is not from the Son, since in this passage the Son has been theologized by Basil the Great as being the Word but not the mouth of the Father. St. Basil indicates in another passage that this Word proceeds from the same mouth, when he says, "for, if you will not believe that the Spirit has come forth from the mouth of God, neither will you believe that the Word [has come forth from the mouth of God]." Do you see clearly that the Son is the Word but not the mouth of the Father, from which mouth, according to Basil the Great, He comes forth, according to His existence, as does the Holy Spirit?

Now in the same manner Gregory, who is his brother and thinks the same with him as a brother, says in his treatise Concerning Divine Knowledge, "the Spirit proceeds from the paternal hypostasis. For this sake, David also said 'the spirit of His mouth' but not 'the word of His mouth', in order to confirm that the property of causing procession is an attribute of the Father alone".[92]

After this witness of the truth, free from falsehood, Cyril, who became a living luminary of Alexandria, will bear witness, as well.

φησί γάρ ἐν τῷ Περί τῆς ἁγίας Τριάδος· «αἱ προσκυνηταί τρεῖς ὑποστάσεις γινώσκονται καί πιστεύονται ἐν Πατρί ἀνάρχῳ καί ἐν Υἱῷ μονογενεῖ καί ἐν Πνεύματι ἁγίῳ τῷ ἐκπορευομένῳ ἐκ τοῦ Πατρός, οὐ γεννητῶς καθάπερ ὁ Υἱός, ἀλλ᾿ ἐκπορευομένῳ καθάπερ εἴρηται ἐκ μόνου τοῦ Πατρός ὡς ἀπό στόματος, πεφηνότι δέ διά τοῦ Υἱοῦ καί λαλήσαντι ἐν τοῖς ἁγίοις πᾶσι προφήταις τε καί ἀποστόλοις». Καί ἀλλαχοῦ πάλιν· «οὐχ ὥσπερ ὁ Υἱός ἀπὸ τοῦ Πατρός γεννητῶς οὕτω καί τό Πνεῦμα τό ἅγιον ἀπό τοῦ Υἱοῦ ἐκπορευτῶς, ἄπαγε τῆς βλασφημίας καί πολυθεῖας· εἷς γάρ παρ᾿ ἡμῖν ἀμφοῖν τοῖν προσώποιν αἴτιος καί σύνδεσμος, ὁ Πατήρ».

Ἆρ᾿ ἔστι τρανότερον ἔλεγχον τῆς σῆς δυσσεβείας παρελθεῖν; Ἀνθρώπῳ μέν οὐκ ἄν ἔδοξεν. Ἀλλά καί τοῦθ᾿ ἡμῖν τό Πνεῦμα δέδωκε τόν ἐκ Δαμασκοῦ σοφίσαν Ἰωάννην· «τό Πνεῦμα γάρ», φησίν οὗτος, «τοῦ Υἱοῦ μέν λέγομεν, ἐκ δέ τοῦ Υἱοῦ οὐ λέγομεν· δι᾿ Υἱοῦ δέ πεφανερῶσθαι καί μεταδιδόσθαι ἡμῖν ὁμολογοῦμεν».

Ἀφείς δέ σοι τούς ἄλλους συνείρειν ἐφεξῆς ὅτι πλείστους ὄντας καί σχεδόν ὅσοι τῶν πατέρων οὐδέν ἧττον ἤ ζῶντες ἐν τοῖς καθ᾿ ἑαυτούς συγγράμμασι λαλοῦσιν, ἐκ τῶν λόγων σου κρινῶ σε· πάντως δέ καί ὁ Θεός. Σοῦ γάρ αὐτοῦ λέγοντος ἐκ τοῦ Πατρός καί τοῦ Υἱοῦ ἐκπορεύεσθαι τό Πνεῦμα καί τό «μόνων» οὐ προστιθεμένου, ἆρ᾿ οὐδ᾿ ἐκ τούτων μόνων τό Πνεῦμα ἐννοεῖς, οὐδέ συνυπακούεις τό μόνων, κἄν μή συνεκφωνῇς; Ἀλλά ζητήσομεν κατά τήν σήν, ἵν᾿ οὕτως εἴπω, φιλοπολυεκπόρευτον διάνοιαν, καί ἐξ ἄλλου του ἐκπορεύεσθαι τό Πνεῦμα διά τήν σήν περί τοῦ μόνου ἄγνοιαν;

20

Οὐ μήν, ἀλλ᾿ ἵνα πάλιν ἐκ τῶν αὐτῶν σοι συσκευάσω τῆς ὡς

Let him be brought forth. For he says in Concerning the Holy
Trinity, "the three worshipful hypostases are recognized and are
believed in the beginningless Father, and in the Only-Begotten
Son, and in the Holy Spirit, who proceeds from the Father, not by
begetting, as with the Son, but by proceeding, as it has been said,
from the only Father as from a mouth, but who has been manifested
through the Son and has spoken in all the saints and prophets and
apostles".[93] And, again, in another place, "the Holy Spirit is not from
the Son by procession as the Son is from the Father by begetting.
Away with the blasphemy and polytheism! For, among us there is
one cause and connection for both persons, namely, the Father."[94]

Is it, then, even possible to bring forth a more convincing refutation
of your irreverence? Certainly no man would have thought so.
But the Holy Spirit has given to us even this very thing, John from
Damascus, having made him wise. For, he says, "while we say 'the
Spirit of the Son', yet we do not say 'the Spirit from the Son', but
we confess that He has been manifested and is communicated to
us through the Son."[95]

Nonetheless, I shall forgo compiling in succession the others
because they are very many, nearly as many of the Fathers as are
alive in their writings, and from your words I shall judge you. God
will certainly judge you, too. For when you yourself say that the
Spirit proceeds from the Father and the Son, and you do not add
the "only", do you perhaps consider that the Spirit is not only from
these? Do you perhaps not imply the "only", whether pronounced
together with "from the Father and the Son" or not? Or will we
enquire, according to your reasoning which is so fond of many
processions, so to speak,[96] whether the Spirit proceeds from some
other one too, on account of your ignorance concerning the word
"only"?

20

Nevertheless let me from the same sources once more prepare the

ἀληθῶς πληγῆς τό ἴαμα καί τῶν δυσσεβῶν ἐκσπάσω καί δογμάτων
καί ρημάτων, εἰπέ μοι, ὦ βέλτιστε, εἴ τις ἔροιτό σε περί τοῦ Υἱοῦ,
ὡς ἐπειδήπερ γέγραπται ὅτι, «εἴδομεν τήν δόξαν αὐτοῦ, δόξαν ὡς
μονογενοῦς παρά Πατρός», καί ὅτι «πιστεύω εἰς ἕνα Υἱόν τόν ἐκ
τοῦ Πατρός πρό αἰώνων γεννηθέντα», καί τ' ἄλλ' ὅσα σοι ἀνωτέρω
ἀπηρίθμηται, οἷς οὐ πρόσκειται τό «μόνου», ἐκ τοῦ Πατρός καί ἐκ
τοῦ ἁγίου Πνεύματος προσθείς φαίης ἄν γεγεννῆσθαι τόν Υἱόν,
τοῦτ' αὐτό προφασιζόμενος ὅτι μή πρόσκειται τό «μόνου»; Ἄπαγε
δήπου, φαίης ἄν. Καί αὐτῆς ἐκπέσοι τῆς ἄνωθεν ἀναγεννήσεως ὁ
τοῦτο προστιθείς καί μή ἐκ μόνου δοξάζων γεγεννῆσθαι τοῦ Πατρός
τόν Λόγον. Οὐδαμοῦ γάρ γεννήτωρ εἴρηται τό Πνεῦμα σύν ἡμῖν
καλῶς ἐρεῖς, οὐδέ κοινόν ἔχει τι Πατρί, ὅ μή ἔστι κοινόν καί τῷ Υἱῷ·
οὐδ' ἐκ τῆς δυάδος προάγεται τό ἕν, οὐδ' εἰς τήν δυάδα ἀναφέρεται·
οὐδ' ἡ μονάς εἰς μονάδα κινηθεῖσα καί εἰς ἑτέραν αὖθις μονάδα ἡ
δυάς, «ἀλλ' ἡ μονάς θεοπρεπῶς εἰς δυάδα κινηθεῖσα, μέχρι τριάδος
ἔστη». Καί «εἷς ἡμῖν Θεός· οὐ μόνον ὅτι μία θεότης, ἀλλ' ὅτι καί
εἰς ἕν ἀμφότερα τά ἐξ αὐτοῦ τήν ἀναφοράν ἔχει. Καί μία πηγαία
θεότης, ὁ Πατήρ καί μόνος αἴτιος καί μόνος πηγή θεότητος».
Οὐκοῦν καί ταῦτ' ἐστίν αὐτοῦ τά ἰδιάζοντα τῶν γνωρισμάτων·
μόνος γάρ· οὐδεμίαν ἄρα τήν κοινωνίαν ἕξει πρός ταῦτα τό Πνεῦμα
τό ἅγιον, ἐπεί καί «τά τῆς ὑπερουσίου θεογονίας οὐκ ἀντιστρέφει
πρός ἄλληλα», Διονύσιος αὖθις ἄν εἶπεν ὁ οὐρανόφρων.

Ἀλλ' εὖγέ σοι τῆς ἐν τούτοις πρός τε τούς θεοσόφους τῶν πατέρων
καί ἡμᾶς τούς ἐξ ἐκείνων σοφισθέντας ἀπαραλλάκτου συμφωνίας.
Ἑάλως δ' ὅμως, τό τοῦ λόγου, τοῖς σαυτοῦ πτεροῖς καί λυσιτελῶς
ὄντως ἐπατάχθης τῷ τοῦ ὀρθοῦ προπολεμοῦντι λόγῳ· τό γάρ εἰς

medicine for your real wound and draw you out of these irreverent dogmas and words. Tell me, O good man: if someone should ask you concerning the Son—inasmuch as it has been written that "we beheld His glory, the glory as of the only-begotten of the Father,"[97] and that "I believe in one Son, begotten of the Father before the ages," and the rest, as many as have been enumerated for you earlier in the treatise, in which the "only" is not placed in the text—would you make an addition and say that the Son has been begotten from the Father "and from the Holy Spirit", making the very same excuse, that the "only" is not present in the text? Surely, you would say, "Away with the idea! Whoever adds this and does not think that the Word has been begotten only from the Father shall fall away even from the very regeneration from above." You will correctly say with us that nowhere is the Spirit called "begetter", nor does He share anything with the Father which is not also shared in common with the Son. Neither does the one proceed from the dyad, nor does it refer back to the dyad; nor did the monad move into a monad and [this] dyad again [move] into another monad, "but the monad moved in a God-befitting manner into a dyad, until it stood as a triad".[98] And, "our God is one, not only because the divinity is one, but also because the two which are from Him have their reference to the One. Further, there is one fountainhead of divinity, the Father, who is also the only Cause and only Fount of divinity."[99] So then, these same things are His individuating characteristics; for He is "only". Consequently, the Holy Spirit will have no communion with respect to these things, especially seeing that Dionysius, the celestially minded, again in this case would have said,"The attributes of the super-essential divine generation are not interchangeable".[100]

But congratulations for your perfect harmony in these matters both with the Godly-wise fathers and with us who have been made wise by them! Yet you were caught, as the saying goes, by your own feathers[101] and you were indeed profitably struck by the [foregoing] argument which fought to defend what is right. As far as the argument is concerned, you were not only stricken but also

αὐτόν ἧκον, οὐ μόνον ἐπατάχθης, ἀλλά καί ἰάθης κατά τό εἰρημένον ὡς ὑπό Θεοῦ, «πατάξω καί ἰάσομαι».

Ἅ γάρ ἄν εἶπες μεθ᾽ ἡμῶν τε καί τῆς ἀληθείας πρός τούς ἐκ Πατρός τε καί ἐκ τοῦ Πνεύματος λέγοντας γεγεννῆσθαι τόν Υἱόν, ἄλλας τε προφάσεις προφασιζομένους ἐν ἁμαρτίαις, μᾶλλον δέ δυσσεβείαις, καί ὅτι μή προστέθειται τῷ γεγεννῆσθαι ἐκ Πατρός τό "μόνου", ταῦτα καί αὐτός ἀρτίως ἀφ᾽ ἡμῶν τε καί τῆς ἀληθείας ἄκουε, ἐκ τοῦ Πατρός καί τοῦ Υἱοῦ λέγων ἐκπορεύεσθαι τό Πνεῦμα τό ἅγιον· ἑτέρωθέν τε τοῦτο πειρώμενος πιστοῦσθαι καί τοῦ μή προσκεῖσθαι τῷ ἐκ Πατρός ἐκπορεύεσθαι τό "μόνου"· καί αὐτῆς γάρ ἐκπεσεῖται τῆς διά τοῦ ἁγίου Πνεύματος υἱοθεσίας ὁ καί ἐξ Υἱοῦ τό Πνεῦμα λέγων.

21

Ποῦ γάρ τῶν θεοπνεύστων λογίων προβολέα τόν Υἱόν εὕροι τις ἄν ὠνομασμένον, καίτοι Γρηγορίῳ τῷ μεγάλῳ θεολόγῳ τῶν τοῦ Υἱοῦ προσηγοριῶν πασῶν καί πολλάκις ἀπηριθμημένων καί οὐκ ἀπηριθμημένων μόνον ἀλλά καί τεθεωρημένων; Ὅς καί τό "μονογενής" ἐξηγούμενος, «οὐχ ὅτι», φησί, «μόνος ἐκ μόνου καί μόνον, ἀλλά καί μονοτρόπως»· ὅ ἀλλαχοῦ μόνως εἶπε καί ἰδιοτρόπως, τοῦτ᾽ αὖθις ἐξηγούμενος. Τό δέ "μόνος" ὡς εἷς· τό δ᾽ "ἐκ μόνου" ὡς ἐν παρθενίᾳ γεννήσαντος, ταὐτό δ᾽ εἰπεῖν ὡς οὐκ ἀπό συζυγίας. Τό δέ "μόνον" τί ἄν ἄλλο εἴη ἤ ὅτι μόνος Υἱός, ἀλλ᾽ οὐχί καί Πατήρ οὐδέ προβολεύς; Εἰ δέ καί ὁ Πατήρ, Πατήρ μόνον λέγεται, εἰκότως — καί γάρ ἐκ Πατρός τό Πνεῦμα — καί Πατρός λέγεται Πνεῦμα καί ὁ Πατήρ καί τοῦ Πνεύματος λέγοιτ᾽ ἄν ὡς αἴτιος· Πατέρα γάρ τῶν φώτων τοῦτον εἶπεν ὁ μέγας Ἰάκωβος ὁ ἀδελφόθεος, τουτέστιν Υἱοῦ καί Πνεύματος, ὡς καί Ἀθανάσιος ὁ

healed, as it has been written as by God, "I shall strike and I shall also heal."[102]

For, the things which you would have said together with us and with the truth to those who say that the Son has been begotten both from the Father and from the Spirit and make excuses in sins,[103] or rather in impieties, and say as an excuse, among other things, that the "only" is not added to the phrase "begotten of the Father", you yourself should now hear the exact same things both from us and from the truth, when you say that the Holy Spirit proceeds from the Father and the Son and logically attempt to certify this on the basis of other things and that the "only" is not present in the procession from the Father. For one who says that the Spirit is also from the Son will fall away even from the very adoption through the Holy Spirit Himself.

21

For where in the God-inspired utterances can someone possibly find the Son named "generator", although the great theologian Gregory many times enumerated all the appellations of the Son, and not only enumerated but also inspected them? He, in interpreting the meaning of the word "only-begotten", says, "It does not only mean 'only the only one, only from Him', but also 'in a unique manner' [μονοτρόπως],"[104] once more interpreting what he had elsewhere also called "uniquely and in a distinctive manner [ἰδιοτρόπως]."[105] He used the phrase "the only one" in the sense of "one", while by the phrase "only from" he meant one that begat in virginity, which is the same as to say, not from coupling. And so, what else could the first "only" be but that He is only a Son, not also a Father, neither a generator? Now, if the Father is called a Father only, since the Spirit is from the Father it is reasonable for the Spirit to be called the Spirit of the Father, and the Father would also be called the Father of the Spirit, since He is the Cause. For, the great James, the Brother of God, called Him Father of Lights,[106] that is, of the Son and the Spirit, as Athanasius the Great says when he exegetes.[107] But

μέγας ἐξηγούμενος λέγει. Εἰ δέ τοῦθ' οὕτως ἔχει, ὥσπερ οὖν ἔχει, λέγοιτ' ἄν καί ὁ Υἱός Πατήρ φωτός, τουτέστι τοῦ ἁγίου Πνεύματος, εἰ καί ἐξ αὐτοῦ κατά σέ τό Πνεῦμα.

Εἰ γοῦν ταῦτ' ἦν ὀνομάσαι, οἷον Πατέρα φωτός ἤ προβολέα τοῦ ἁγίου Πνεύματος, πῶς ἄν οὐχί τῶν ἄλλων αὐτοῦ σχεδόν πάντων ὀνομάτων ὁ μέγας ἐν θεολογίᾳ Γρηγόριος προΰθηκε, καίτοι τό πρός τόν Πατέρα ἀγωνιζόμενος δεικνύναι; Διό φησιν· «εἰ μέγα τῷ Πατρί τῷ μηδαμόθεν ὡρμῆσθαι, οὐκ ἔλαττον τῷ Υἱῷ τό ἐκ τοιούτου Πατρός. Καί πρόσεστιν τῷ Υἱῷ τό τῆς γεννήσεως πρᾶγμα τοσοῦτον». Εἰ γοῦν προσῆν τό προβολέα εἶναι, πῶς οὐκ ἄν εἶπε πρᾶγμα τοσοῦτον, δι' ὅ καί μᾶλλον ἄν δεικνύειν ἔδοξεν ἴσον τῷ Πατρί; Ἀλλ' οὐκ εἶπεν· οὐκοῦν οὐδέ πρόσεστιν.

22

Ὁ γάρ μέγας οὗτος θεολόγος οὐδ' ἁπλῶς οὕτω τό ἐκπορευόμενον ἴδιον τίθησι τοῦ Πνεύματος, ἀλλά τό ἐκ τοῦ Πατρός ἐκπορευόμενον, προορῶν δήπου καί προανατρέπων σου τήν δυσσεβῆ προσθήκην. Ἀνωτέρω γάρ μικρόν εἰπών, τόν μέν Πατέρα γεννήτορα καί προβολέα, τόν δέ Υἱόν προβολέα μέν οὐ, γέννημα δέ μόνον, προϊών, ἡμεῖς δέ, φησίν, «ἐπί τῶν ἡμετέρων ὅρων ἱστάμενοι, τό ἀγέννητον εἰσάγομεν καί τό γεννητόν καί τό ἐκ τοῦ Πατρός ἐκπορευόμενον». Οὐκ εἶπε τό ἐκπορευόμενον ἁπλῶς ἴδιον τοῦ Πνεύματος ὑπάρχειν, ἵνα μή τις ἐκ τοῦ Υἱοῦ ἤ καί ἐκ τοῦ Υἱοῦ ἐκπορεύεσθαι νομίσῃ τό Πνεῦμα τό ἅγιον· τό μέν γάρ γεννητόν συνεισάγει τῇ διανοίᾳ τόν Πατέρα, τό δέ ἐκπορευτόν οὐχ οὕτω. Διά τοῦτο τό ἐκ Πατρός ἐκπορευόμενον ἴδιον τέθηκε τοῦ Πνεύματος· «τοῦτο γάρ», φησί καί Βασίλειος ὁ μέγας, «γνωριστικόν τῆς κατά τήν ὑπόστασιν ἰδιότητος σημεῖον ἔχει τό Πνεῦμα τό ἅγιον, τό μετά τόν Υἱόν καί σύν αὐτῷ γνωρίζεσθαι καί ἐκ τοῦ Πατρός ὑφεστάναι». Ἀλλ' ὁρᾷς, ὅπως παρ' ἡμῶν δικαίως ἀπελήλασθε τῆς κοινωνίας, οὐκ ἐπί τῶν ἡμετέρων ὅρων καί τῆς εὐσεβείας ἱστάμενοι;

if this holds true, which it does, then the Son would also be called Father of Light, that is, of the Holy Spirit—if, according to you, the Spirit is from Him.

Well, then, if these were the names that we are to give, like "Father of Light" or "Originator of the Holy Spirit", why did Gregory, who was greatly versed in theology, not place these names before almost all his other designations, though he painstakingly toiled to show the Son's equality to the Father? And so, he says, "If the Father's greatness lies in not being moved into being from anywhere, it is not lesser for the Son to be from such a Father. Such a great thing as being begotten belongs to the Son".[108] If origination, then, belonged to Him, why did he not mention something so important, through which he would prove even more strongly that He is equal with the Father? But he did not say it; so it is not attributed to Him.

22

For, this great theologian does not make the thesis that the characteristic of the Spirit is simply "procession", but rather makes the thesis, "procession from the Father", surely foreseeing your irreverent addition and overturning it aforehand. And so having said a little above that the Father, on one hand, is Begetter and Originator, while the Son, on the other hand, is not the Originator but only one begotten, he then goes on to say, "but standing firm in our definitions, we introduce the Unbegotten, and the Begotten, and Him who proceeds from the Father."[109] He did not say that merely procession is the idiom[110] of the Spirit, lest someone think that the Holy Spirit proceeds from the Son or also from the Son. For, while begottenness conveys the thought of a Father, yet procession is not so. On account of this, he set forth procession "from the Father" as an idiom of the Spirit. For, Basil the Great says, "the Holy Spirit has this sign, indicative of His property as far as hypostasis is concerned, namely to become known[111] after the Son and with Him, and to subsist from the Father." So, do you not see that you all were justifiably banned from communion with us, not standing fast upon our definitions and upon piety?

Ἢ γάρ καί τόν Υἱόν Πατέρα προσερεῖς, ὡς καί ἀνωτέρω δέδεικται, ἵν’ ἐκπορευόμενον εἴη σοι καί ἐξ αὐτοῦ τό Πνεῦμα, ἢ τό ἐκ τοῦ Πατρός ἐκπορεύεσθαι οὐκ ἄν ἴδιον εἴη σοι τοῦ Πνεύματος, οὐδέ τό ἐκπορεύειν ἴδιον εἶναι νομίσεις τοῦ Πατρός, καί ἀπ’ ἐναντίας θεολογήσεις τοῦ τό θεολογεῖν ἐπωνυμίαν κτησαμένου καί πρός τήν ἐναντίον ὄντως μοῖραν στήσῃ καί παρ’ ἡμῶν ἐκκήρυκτος γενήσῃ· τάς γάρ αὐτοῦ φωνάς ἐκφαντορίας οὔσας ἴσμεν τοῦ ἁγίου Πνεύματος. Ἀλλά γάρ, ὥσπερ τῆς νοτίδος ἐξ ὑγρῶν σωμάτων ἐκπορευομένης καί τοῦτ’ ἴδιον ἐχούσης καί τῶν ὑγρῶν σωμάτων ἴδιόν ἐστι τό νοτίδα ἐκπορεύειν, τόν αὐτόν τρόπον καί τοῦ Πνεύματος ἴδιον ἔχοντος τό ἐκ τοῦ Πατρός ἐκπορεύεσθαι καί τοῦ Πατρός ἐξ ἀνάγκης ἴδιόν ἐστι τό τό Πνεῦμα ἐκπορεύειν.

Μόνου ἄρα τοῦ Πατρός ἡ τοῦ Πνεύματος ἐκπόρευσις· καί ἀεί ἐκ μόνου τοῦ Πατρός ἐκπορεύεται τό Πνεῦμα καθ’ ὑπαρκτικήν ἀλλ’ οὐκ ἐκφαντικήν προέλευσιν. Καί ἐν οἷς γάρ τῷ ἐκπορευτῷ μή συνεκφωνεῖται τό ἐκ τοῦ Πατρός, συνυπακουόμενόν ἐστιν ἀεί τοῖς συνετῶς ἀκούουσιν, ὥσπερ καί ἐπί τοῦ Υἱοῦ τῷ γεννητῷ συνυπακούεται. Γεννητός γάρ καί ἡμῶν ἁπάντων ἕκαστος· γεννητός δέ ἐκ τοῦ Πατρός, ταὐτόν δ’ εἰπεῖν ἐκ Θεοῦ Πατρός, μόνος ὁ Υἱός, ὥστε τό συνημμένον τοῦτ’ ἔστιν ἴδιον αὐτοῦ καί ἀεί συννοεῖται, κἄν μή συνεκφωνεῖται. Τόν αὐτόν οὖν τρόπον ἐκπορευτόν ἄν εἴποις καί τό πνεῦμα τό ἡμέτερον. Οὐκοῦν οὐ τό ἁπλῶς ἐκπορευτόν ἴδιον τοῦ ἁγίου Πνεύματος, ἀλλά τό ἐκ τοῦ Πατρός ἐκπορευτόν· ἐκεῖνος γάρ ἀεί Πατήρ. Τῶν ἀδυνάτων ἄρ’ ἐστίν ἐκ τοῦ Υἱοῦ ἐκπορευτόν ὑπάρχειν, εἰ μή καί ὁ Υἱός εἴη σοι Πατήρ. Οὐ μόνον δέ τό ἐκ τοῦ Πατρός τῷ ἐκπορευτῷ συνυπακούεται, ἀλλά καί τό ἐκ μόνου τοῦ Πατρός, καθάπερ καί τῷ γεννητῷ· ὡς γάρ οἱ ἔνθεοι θεολόγοι διδάσκουσιν ἡμᾶς, ὅ καί ἀνωτέρω ἔφημεν, χωρίς τοῦ γεννητῶς τε καί ἐκπορευτῶς, ὡς ὁ Υἱός ἐκ τοῦ Πατρός, οὕτω καί τό Πνεῦμα· τοιγαροῦν παντάπασιν ἀδύνατον εἶναι καί ἐκ τοῦ Υἱοῦ.

For either you would characterize the Son also as a Father, as has been shown above, so that in your eyes the Spirit may proceed from Him also, or, in your eyes, to proceed from the Father would not be an idiom of the Spirit,[112] nor would you think that causing procession is the idiom of the Father [alone]. But, in that case, you will be theologizing against him that acquired the title of theologian, and in all reality you will be standing with the opposing party and be renounced by us. For, we know that his utterances are revelations of the Holy Spirit. But to return to the topic, just as, when humidity proceeds from bodies of water and has this idiom, it is an idiom also of the bodies of water to cause the humidity to proceed, in this same manner, since the Spirit has an idiom of proceeding from the Father, so too it necessarily belongs to the Father to cause the Spirit to proceed.

Therefore, the procession of the Spirit is only from the Father, and the Spirit always proceeds only from the Father according to His existential, although not in His revelatory, coming forth. For, in those passages in which the phrase "from the Father" is not expressed along with the "proceeds", [the phrase "from the Father"] is always understood by those who hear with understanding, just as it is understood with the Son in respect to His begottenness. For, every one of us is begotten; but only the Son is begotten from the Father, that is to say, from God the Father. Thus, this appendage "from the Father" is His idiom and is ever understood, even if it be not expressed. In the very same way then, you would say that our own spirit proceeds. Therefore, the idiom of the Holy Spirit is not simply "proceeding" but "proceeding from the Father"; for that one is always Father. So, it is impossible for Him to exist as proceeding from the Son, unless the Son also might be in your eyes a Father. Not only is the fact that it is from the Father implicitly understood with the "proceeding", but also that it is from the Father alone, precisely as it is understood with the "begotten". For as the inspired theologians teach us, which we also affirmed above, apart from the manner being by begetting or procession, as the Son is from the Father so also is the Spirit. And so accordingly, in every way entirely, it is impossible for Him to be also from the Son.

23

Πρός δέ, εἰ καί ἐκ τοῦ Υἱοῦ τό Πνεῦμα καί δι' αὐτοῦ τήν ὕπαρξιν ἔχει κατά σέ, αὐτός ἐστιν ἕνωσις Πατρός καί Πνεύματος. Πῶς οὖν ὁ αὐτός μέγας ἐν θεολογίᾳ Γρηγόριός φησιν, «ἄναρχον καί ἀρχή καί τό μετά τῆς ἀρχῆς εἷς Θεός», «φύσις δε τοῖς τρισί μία· ἕνωσις δέ ὁ Πατήρ, ἐξ οὗ καί πρός ὅν ἀνάγεται τά ἑξῆς, οὐχ ὡς συναλείφεσθαι, ἀλλ' ὡς ἔχεσθαι»; Ἀκούων γάρ τις διά τοῦ Υἱοῦ τό Πνεῦμα τῷ Πατρί συναπτόμενον, νοεῖν ἄν ἔχοι τοῦτο λεγόμενον, διά τήν κατά τήν ὁμολογίαν ἐκφώνησιν, μέσου κειμένου τοῦ Υἱοῦ. Καί ὅτι Πατρός Πνεῦμα οὐκ ἄν ἄλλως λέγοιτο, εἰ μή διά τόν Υἱόν. Ἕνωσις δέ ὁ Πατήρ πῶς ἄν εἴη, εἰ μή προσεχῶς ἔχει πρός ἑκάτερον ἀμέσως προβαλλόμενος ἑκάτερον; Ἀλλά καί τό οὐχ ὡς συναλείφεσθαι δέ, ἀλλ' ὡς ἔχεσθαι, τήν προσεχῆ καί ἄμεσον ἑκατέρου σχέσιν πρός αὐτόν δηλοῖ.

24

Τί δέ, ὅτι «τό ἄναρχον καί ἡ ἀρχή καί τό μετά τῆς ἀρχῆς εἷς Θεός»; Εἰ γάρ ἐξ Υἱοῦ τό Πνεῦμα ᾔδει, τό ἐκ τῆς ἀρχῆς ἄν εἶπεν, οὐ τό μετά τῆς ἀρχῆς.

25

Οὐκοῦν ὅταν ἀκούσῃς διά τοῦ Υἱοῦ τό Πνεῦμα ἐκπορεύεσθαι, ὡς συμπαρομαρτοῦν τῷ λόγῳ νόησον. Οὕτω γάρ καί τήν "διά" οὐκ εἰς τήν "ἐκ" κακῶς, ἀλλ' εἰς τήν "μετά", τῷ τῆς θεολογίας ἐπωνύμῳ συνάδων μεταλήψῃ. «Πνεῦμα γάρ», φησί, «μεμαθήκαμεν», Δαμασκηνός ὁ θεῖος, «τό συμπαρομαρτοῦν τῷ λόγῳ καί φανεροῦν

23

Moreover, if the Spirit is also from the Son and through Him has His existence according to you, the Son is the union of the Father and Spirit. Then, how does the same Gregory, great in theology, say, "the unoriginate and the origin and what is with the origin are one God" and "Now the nature is one in three; and the Father is the union, from whom and to whom are led back those who follow, not so as to fuse together, but so that they may possess [their being] themselves"?[113] For, when someone hears that the Spirit is conjoined to the Father through the Son, he may understand that this is said on account of the [doxological] pronouncement[114] that concerns the confession, with the Son placed in the middle; and that He would not be called "Spirit of the Father" for a different reason, except on account of the Son. But how would the Father be the union, unless He relates to each directly, emanating each immediately? But the phrase "not so as to fuse together, but so that they may possess [their being] themselves" shows the direct and immediate relation of each to Him.

24

But why does he say, "the unoriginate and the origin and what is with the origin are one God?" For, if he knew that the Spirit is "from the Son", he would have said "what is from the origin," not "what is with the origin."

25

Therefore, whenever you hear that the Spirit proceeds through [διὰ] the Son, understand Him to be accompanying the Word, because, in doing so, you would not take the word "through" wrongly, in the sense of "from," but in the sense of "with," thus harmonizing with the namesake of theology.[115] For, the divine Damascene says, "We have learned the Spirit which accompanies the Word and manifests

αὐτοῦ τήν ἐνέργειαν». Συμπαρομαρτεῖν δέ ἐστι τό συνακολουθεῖν, ὡς ὁ αὐτός ἐκεῖ φησιν ὥστε οὐχί καί ἐκ τοῦ Υἱοῦ, ἀλλά σύν τῷ Υἱῷ τό Πνεῦμα ἐκ Πατρός, συνακολουθούσης ἀδιαστάτως τε καί ἀχρόνως τῇ γεννήσει τῆς ἐκπορεύσεως. Μεμαθήκαμεν δέ εἶπεν, ὡς τῶν πρό αὐτοῦ θεοφόρων οὕτω διδασκόντων, παρ' ὧν μυηθείς οὕτω νοεῖν τό Πνεῦμα δι' Υἱοῦ, τό ἐκ τοῦ Υἱοῦ τοῦτο λέγειν παντάπασιν ἀπηγόρευσεν.

Εἰ δ' ὁ μέγας Βασίλειος οὐδέν εἶναί φησιν ἀπᾷδον εἰς τήν "ἐκ" τήν "διά" μεταλαμβάνειν, ἀλλ' ἐπί τῶν κτισμάτων, διό καί τόν ἀπόστολον προήγαγεν εἰπόντα, «ἐξ αὐτοῦ καί δι' αὐτοῦ καί εἰς αὐτόν τά πάντα», παρ' αὐτοῦ γάρ δεδημιούργηνται καί δι' αὐτοῦ συνέχονται καί πρός αὐτόν ἐπιστρέφονται τά ὄντα πάντα, ὁ δέ ἱερός Δαμασκηνός κἄν τῷ ἑβδόμῳ τῶν Θεολογικῶν αὐτοῦ κεφαλαίων προθείς πάλιν ὅ καί ἀνωτέρω ἔφημεν, μετά τινα συνᾴδων τῷ Κατηχητικῷ λόγῳ τοῦ Νύσσης ἐνθέου Γρηγορίου, «τό ἅγιον Πνεῦμα δύναμιν εἶναί φησιν οὐσιώδη, αὐτήν ἐφ' ἑαυτῆς ἐν ἰδιαζούσῃ ὑποστάσει θεωρουμένην καί αὐτοῦ, δηλονότι τοῦ Λόγου, οὖσαν ἐκφαντικήν, οὐ χωρισθῆναι τοῦ Θεοῦ ἐν ᾧ ἐστι καί τοῦ Λόγου ᾧ συμπαρομαρτεῖ δυναμένην», ἆρ' οὐ σαφές κἀντεῦθεν, ὡς οὐχί καί ἐκ τοῦ Υἱοῦ τό Πνεῦμα τό ἅγιον;

26

Οὐ μήν, ἀλλ' ἐπεί παρά τῶν θεολόγων ποτέ μέν ὁ Πατήρ μέσος εἶναι λέγεται Υἱοῦ καί Πνεύματος, ποτέ δέ ὁ Υἱός μέσος τοῦ Πατρός τε καί Πνεύματος, ποτέ δέ τό Πνεῦμα μέσον Πατρός τε καί Υἱοῦ, οὐκ ἄν εἴη τό Πνεῦμα τρίτον ἀπό τοῦ Πατρός, οὐδ' ἄν ἐκ τοῦ Πατρός διά τοῦ Υἱοῦ τό εἶναι ἔχοι. Τοῖς γάρ ἐφεξῆς τρισί σημείοις, οὐκ ἄν εἴη ποτέ τι τῶν ἑκατέρωθεν κειμένων ἄκρων μέσον· ἀλλ'

His energy".[116] Now "to accompany" means "to follow along with"
as he himself says there in that passage. As a result, the Spirit is not
"and from the Son" but from the Father together with the Son, since
the procession accompanies the begetting timelessly and without
any intervening distance. Now, he said "we have learned" because
the God-bearers, who were before him, taught thus, and since by
them he was initiated to think in this way, that the Spirit is "through
the Son", he completely forbade us from saying "the Spirit is from
the Son."

Now if Basil the Great says that there is nothing inharmonious
in transforming "through" into "from", yet he said this for created
beings. This is why he then brought forth the Apostle, who said,
"all things are from Him and through Him and to Him",[117]
For, all beings have been created by Him and through Him are
sustained and are returned to Him. And the sacred Damascene
in his seventh theological chapter, having first placed once more
the passage which we cited earlier above, after some other things,
says the following in harmony with the Catechetical Treatise of
the inspired, divine Gregory of Nyssa: "The Holy Spirit is an
essential power, contemplated itself by its own self in a particular
hypostasis, revelatory of Him, that is, of the Word, and not able to
be separated from God, in whom He is, nor from the Word, whom
He accompanies."[118] So, is it not clear, from this passage here too,
that the Holy Spirit is not also from the Son?

26

Nevertheless, since by the theologians sometimes the Father is said
to be in the middle of the Son and the Spirit, and sometimes the
Son is said to be in the middle of both the Father and the Spirit,
and sometimes the Spirit is said to be in the middle of both the
Father and the Son, the Spirit would not be the third from the
Father neither would He have His being from the Father through
the Son. For with three consecutive points, never could one of the
endpoints that lie on either side be the midpoint. Instead, when

ἔοικεν ἡ ἐπί τῆς θεολογίας μεσότης νοουμένη τοῖς ἐπί τῶν γωνιῶν τοῦ ἰσοπλεύρου τριγώνου σημείοις ἄκροις· ἐκεῖ γάρ ἕκαστον μέσον ἑκατέρων εὑρίσκεται. Ἄν δέ καί τόν μεσότητα πρῶτον ἔχοντα ἐν ἀριθμοῖς ἐπισωρεύσας ὡς ἐν ἐπιπέδῳ θῇς, οὕτω τόν τε πρῶτον ἐνεργείᾳ τρίγωνον ἀποτελέσεις ἀριθμόν, καί ἥν ἄν λάβοις τῶν ἐν αὐτῷ μονάδων μέση δυοῖν ὑπολοίποιν ἔσται. Εἴ τις οὖν ἀρχήν καί αἴτιον τῶν δύο κέντρων ὑποθοῖτο τό ἕν, προσεχῶς καί ἀμέσως ἐξ ἀνάγκης ἐκεῖνο πρός ἑκάτερον ἔχει κἄν ταῖς μονάσι δήπου τόν αὐτόν τρόπον.

27

Τί δέ, οἱ λέγοντες ὡς ἕν ἕκαστον αὐτῶν ἔχει πρός τό ἕτερον οὐχ ἧττον ἤ πρός ἑαυτό, ἆρ᾽ οὐκ ἀριδήλως ἀμέσως ἔχειν παριστῶσι πρός ἄλληλα;

28

Τί δ᾽ ὁ ἐμμέτροις Ἔπεσι θεολογικῶς τε ἅμα καί πατρικῶς ἐγκελευόμενος, ὡς εἴπερ ἀκούσαις περί Υἱοῦ καί Πνεύματος, «ὥς ρα Θεοῖο τά δεύτερα Πατρός ἔχουσιν, οὕτω νοεῖν κέλομαί σε λόγους σοφίης βαθυκόλπου»· ὡς εἰς ῥίζαν ἄναρχον ἀνέρχεται, οὐ θεότητα τέμνει. Εἰ γάρ μή ἀμέσως ἦν ἐκ τοῦ Πατρός τό Πνεῦμα, οὐκ ἄν δεύτερον καί τοῦτ᾽ ἀπό τοῦ Πατρός ἐτίθει, καθά καί τόν Υἱόν.

29

Καί μήν ἐκπόρευσις, ἐφ᾽ οὗπερ ἄν λέγοιτο, πρόοδός τις καί κίνησίς ἐστι, κατάλληλος τῷ τε ἐκπορεύοντι καί τῷ ἐκπορευομένῳ. Ἡ δέ τοῦ Πνεύματος πρόοδος διττή διά τῆς θεοπνεύστου κηρύττεται Γραφῆς· προχεῖται γάρ ἐκ τοῦ Πατρός διά τοῦ Υἱοῦ, εἰ δέ βούλει καί

considered, theological middleness is like the three endpoints on the corners of an equilateral triangle. For in that case each point is found to be in the middle of the other two. And if you were to pile up the first number to be in the middle and place it as if on the second dimension, in this way you will actually make the first a triangular number,[119] and whichever one you take of the units that are in it, that unit will be in the middle of the other two. Therefore, should one postulate that the one tip is the origin and cause of the two, then necessarily that tip will surely, in the same way, have a direct and immediate relationship to each of the other two in the units as well.

27

What then? Do those who say, that each one of them relates to the other not less than to its own self, not then clearly prove that they relate directly to one another?

28

What then of the Theologian, who bids you with poetic utterances, both theologically and paternally, that, should you happen to hear concerning the Son and Spirit, "'that they have the second position after the Father,' this is how I urge you to understand the words of deep-bosomed wisdom";[120] [namely,] that he is ascending to an unoriginate root: he is not dividing the divinity. For if the Spirit were not directly from the Father, he would not have likewise placed Him second from the Father, as he also placed the Son.

29

And certainly procession, wherever indeed it be mentioned, is some type of progression and motion, befitting both the one causing procession and the one proceeding. The progression of the Spirit, however, is proclaimed through the God-inspired Scripture to be twofold. For, He is poured forth from the Father through the

ἐκ τοῦ Υἱοῦ, ἐπί πάντας τούς ἀξίους, οἷς καί ἐπαναπαύεται καί ἐνοικεῖ. Αὕτη οὖν ἡ κίνησίς τε καί πρόοδος, εἰ δέ βούλει καί ἐκπόρευσις – οὐδέ γάρ περί τῶν ὀνομάτων ζυγομαχοῦντες ἀσχημονήσομεν, ἐπεί καί ὁ Δαβίδ λέγει, «ὁ Θεός ἐν τῷ ἐκπορεύεσθαί σε ἐν μέσῳ τοῦ λαοῦ σου, ἐν τῷ διαβαίνειν σε ἐν τῇ ἐρήμῳ, γῆ ἐσείσθη», ἐκπόρευσιν ἐνταῦθα λέγων τήν τοῦ Πνεύματος ἔκχυσιν ἐπί πᾶσαν σάρκα τήν εἰς Χριστόν πιστεύσασαν, ἥτις ἔρημος ἦν πρότερον τῆς χάριτος, ὥσπερ καί σεισμόν τῆς γῆς τήν ἐξ εἰδωλολατρίας πρός Θεόν μετάθεσιν – αὕτη οὖν ἡ ἐκ τοῦ Πατρός καί τοῦ Υἱοῦ πρόοδος τοῦ Πνεύματος οὐκ ἄν εἴη πάντως καί διά τῶν ἀξίων· καί ταῦτα πρός τούς αὐτούς πάλιν, ἐν οἷς οἰκεῖ τε καί ἀναπαύεται χάριτι τό Πνεῦμα τό ἅγιον. Ἀνάπαυσις γάρ ἐστιν ἐν τούτοις, ἀλλ᾽ οὐκ ἐξ αὐτῶν κίνησις τοῦ Πνεύματος, ἀλλά μᾶλλον τῆς ἐπ᾽ αὐτούς κινήσεως παῦλα· κἄν τινες μεταδιδόναι δύναμιν ἐκτήσαντο, ἀλλ᾽ ἑτέρῳ πάντως τρόπῳ.

Ἡ μέντοι ἐκ Πατρός δι᾽ Υἱοῦ, ἥν ἔφημεν, πρόοδος τοῦ Πνεύματος καλεῖται καί εὐδοκία Πατρός τε καί Υἱοῦ, ὡς διά φιλανθρωπίαν πάντως τελεσθεῖσα, καί ἀποστολή καί δόσις καί συγκατάβασις, καί χρονικῶς ἀεί προάγεται καί πρός τινας καί δι᾽ αἰτίας, ἵνα ἁγιάσῃ καί διδάξῃ καί ὑπομνήσῃ καί τούς ἀπειθεῖς ἐλέγξῃ· μία μέν οὖν αὕτη κίνησις καί πρόοδος τοῦ Πνεύματος.

Ἔστι δέ καί ἡ ἀναιτίως τε καί ἀπολελυμένως πάντῃ καί ὑπέρ εὐδοκίαν καί φιλανθρωπίαν, ὡς μή κατά θέλησιν ἀλλά κατά φύσιν μόνην ἐκ τοῦ Πατρός οὖσα προαιώνιος καί ὑπερφυεστάτη τοῦ Πνεύματος ἐκπόρευσις καί κίνησις καί πρόοδος. Ζητῆσαι δή χρεών ἡμᾶς καί κατά ταύτην τήν ἄφραστόν τε καί ἀπερινόητον κίνησιν τό Πνεῦμα προερχόμενον ἐκ τοῦ Πατρός, ἆρ᾽ ἔχει κατά τάς γραφάς καί «ἐν ᾧ ἀναπαύεται» θεοπρεπῶς; Ζητοῦντες οὖν

Son, or, if you prefer, from the Son as well, upon all those who are worthy, upon whom He rests and indwells. Therefore, this very movement and progression, or, if you prefer, this procession—for, we do not wish to shamelessly join in a debate about names, since David also says, "O God, when Thou wentest forth before Thy people, when Thou didst traverse the wilderness, the earth was shaken"[121] (the "going forth" here describes the outpouring of the Holy Spirit on all flesh believing in Christ, which previously was a wilderness bereft of grace, just as also the shaking of the earth was the transition from idolatry to God)[122]—this progression, then, of the Holy Spirit from the Father and the Son would certainly not also be through the worthy men, although these are the same ones in whom the Holy Spirit both dwells and rests by grace. For there is a rest of the Holy Spirit in them, but not a movement of the Holy Spirit from them, rather a cessation of the movement [that occurs] on them; and although some acquired the power of transmission, yet they did so in a completely different way.

Now the progression from the Father through the Son, which we mentioned, is also called the good pleasure of the Father and the Son, as it was assuredly wrought on account of the love of God for mankind. It is also called a sending, and a giving, and a condescension, and it always comes forth temporally and to certain persons and for certain causes, that it might sanctify, and teach, and bring to remembrance, and reprove the disobedient. So then, this is one movement and progression of the Spirit.

But there is also a pre-eternal and supernatural procession and movement and progression of the Spirit, which is causeless and in everything separate and transcendentally beyond both good pleasure and love for man, since it is from the Father, not according to will[123] but only according to nature. Therefore, we are obligated to examine: here, too, [as before,] in this inexpressible and incomprehensible movement, does the Spirit, coming forth from the Father, have the one "in whom He rests", according to the Scriptures, in a God-befitting manner? So, when we enquire, we

εὑρίσκομεν εὐδοκιμήσαντα τόν Πατέρα τοῦ μονογενοῦς Θεοῦ διδάξαι καί ἀποκαλύψαι τοῦτο πρῶτον Ἰωάννῃ τῷ τοῦ Κυρίου προδρόμῳ τε καί βαπτιστῇ, ὅς φησι· «κἀγώ οὐκ ᾔδειν αὐτόν, ἀλλ' ὁ πέμψας με βαπτίζειν ἐν ὕδατι, ἐκεῖνός μοι εἶπεν· ἐφ' ὅν ἄν ἴδοις τό Πνεῦμα καταβαῖνον καί μένον ἐπ' αὐτόν, οὗτός ἐστιν ὁ βαπτίζων ἐν Πνεύματι ἁγίῳ». Διό «καί ἐμαρτύρησεν ὁ Ἰωάννης λέγων ὅτι τεθέαμαι τό Πνεῦμα καταβαῖνον ὡσεί περιστεράν ἐξ οὐρανοῦ καί ἔμεινεν ἐπ' αὐτόν».

Ἀλλ' ἵνα μή τις, νομίσας διά τήν ἐνανθρώπησιν τοῦ Κυρίου ταῦτα λεχθῆναί τε καί τελεσθῆναι παρά τοῦ Πατρός, οὐχ ἱκανόν εἶναι δεῖγμα τοῦτ' εἴπῃ πρός εὕρεσιν τοῦ ζητουμένου ἀκουέτω Δαμασκηνοῦ τοῦ θείου γράφοντος ἐν ὀγδόῳ τῶν Δογματικῶν, «πιστεύομεν καί εἰς ἕν Πνεῦμα ἅγιον, τό ἐκ Πατρός ἐκπορευόμενον καί ἐν Υἱῷ ἀναπαυόμενον», καί ἐν τῷ περί θείου τόπου, «Θεός τό Πνεῦμα τό ἅγιόν ἐστι, δύναμις ἁγιαστική ἐνυπόστατος ἐκ τοῦ Πατρός ἀδιαστάτως ἐκπορευομένη καί ἐν Υἱῷ ἀναπαυομένη». Διό καί ταμίας τοῦ θείου Πνεύματος ὁ Χριστός ἐκ Θεοῦ γνήσιος Υἱός ἐστί τε καί λέγεται. Ὅ καί ὁ θεῖος Κύριλλος ἐν Θησαυροῖς δεικνύς, «ἀνάγκη πᾶσα», φησί, «τῆς θείας φύσεως εἶναι λέγειν τό Πνεῦμα τό ἅγιον, ἧς καί ἔστιν ἀπαρχή κατά τόν ἀπόστολον· εἰ δέ τοῦτο, οὐκ ἔστι κτίσμα, Θεός δέ μᾶλλον ὡς ἐκ Θεοῦ καί ἐν Θεῷ». Καί πάλιν, «Θεός ἄρα τό Πνεῦμά ἐστι τό ἐν Υἱῷ παρά Πατρός φυσικῶς ὑπάρχον καί ὅλην αὐτοῦ τήν ἐνέργειαν ἔχον». Ἀλλά καί ὁ τοῦ Διαλόγου θεῖος Γρηγόριος ἐν τῷ τελευταίῳ αὐτοῦ λόγῳ φησίν, ὅτι «τό Πνεῦμα τό ἅγιον ἐκ τοῦ Πατρός ἐκπορεύεται καί ἐν τῷ Υἱῷ μένει». «Οὕτω γάρ ἄν θεώμενοι σεφθείημεν πηγήν ζωῆς εἰς ἑαυτήν χεομένην καί ἐφ' ἑαυτῆς ἑστῶσαν ὁρῶντες», κατά τόν μέγαν θεοφάντορα Διονύσιον.

Καί τοίνυν τό Πνεῦμα τό ἅγιον κατά τήν προαιώνιον ἐκείνην καί ἀπερινόητον ἐκπόρευσίν τε καί πρόοδον ἐκ τοῦ Πατρός ἐκπορευόμενον καί ἐν Υἱῷ ἀναπαυόμενον, πῶς ἄν διά τοῦ Υἱοῦ ἐν ᾧ ἀναπαύεται ταύτην ἔχει τήν πρόοδον; Οὐκοῦν εἰ καί ἐκ τοῦ

find that the Father of the only-begotten God was well pleased to teach and reveal this first to John, the Forerunner and Baptist of the Lord, who says, "And I knew him not: but he that sent me to baptize with water, the same said unto me, Upon whom thou shalt see the Spirit descending, and remaining on him, the same is he which baptizeth with the Holy Spirit."[124] And so "John bare record, saying, I saw the Spirit descending from heaven like a dove, and it abode upon him."[125]

But, if someone should say that this is not a sufficient proof for the discovery of what is sought, thinking that these things were said and accomplished by the Father because of the incarnation of the Lord, let him hear the divine Damascene when he writes in the eighth chapter of his dogmatics, "We believe also in one Holy Spirit, who proceeds from the Father and rests in the Son;"[126] and, in the passage concerning the divine place, "the Holy Spirit is God, an enhypostatic[127] power capable of sanctifying, who proceeds from the Father without distance and rests in the Son."[128] Wherefore also Christ, a genuine Son born from God, both is and is described as the treasurer of the divine Spirit, which is also what the divine Cyril had shown in his Treasuries, saying, "We must absolutely say the Holy Spirit is of the divine nature, of which He also is the firstfruits, according to the Apostle. But, if this is so, He is not a creature. Instead, He is God, as being from God and in God".[129] And again, "so the Spirit is God, who exists naturally and possesses all His activity in the Son from the Father".[130] But also the divine Gregory the Dialogist, in his final treatise, says that "the Holy Spirit proceeds from the Father and abides in the Son".[131] For, according to Dionysius, the great revealer of God, "in this way, having been deified, we would find ourselves revering a fountain of life, beholding it flowing into itself and standing over itself."[132]

And so, as the Holy Spirit proceeds from the Father and rests in the Son according to that aforementioned pre-eternal and incomprehensible procession and progression, how could He possess this progression from the Son on whom He rests? Therefore, if it

Υἱοῦ πάλιν προέρχεσθαι θεολογεῖται, οὐ κατ᾽ ἐκείνην πάντως, ἀλλά καθ᾽ ἑτέραν πρόοδον, ἥτις ἐστίν ἡ πρός ἡμᾶς φανέρωσις καί πρός τούς ἀξίους μετάδοσις. Ὁ γάρ Χριστός ἐστι κατά τόν θεολόγον Γρηγόριον ὁ τοῦ Πνεύματος ταμίας, ὡς Θεός τε καί Θεοῦ Υἱός. Ὁ δέ ταμίας οὐκ ἐξ ἑαυτοῦ πάντως τά διδόμενα προβάλλεται, καίτοι φυσικῶς ἔχει ἐν αὐτῷ τό Πνεῦμα τό ἅγιον ὁ ἐκ Θεοῦ Θεός καί φυσικῶς ἐξ αὐτοῦ προϊόν εἰς τούς ἀξίους, ἀλλ᾽ οὐχί τήν ὕπαρξιν ἔχον ἐξ αὐτοῦ. Ταῦτ᾽ ἄρα καί αὐτός ὁ Κύριος, «ὅταν ἔλθῃ», φησίν, «ὁ παράκλητος, ὅν ἐγώ πέμψω ὑμῖν παρά τοῦ Πατρός», ὡς παρά τοῦ Πατρός ἐκπορευόμενον καί ἐν αὐτῷ ἀναπαυόμενον καί οὕτω πεμπόμενον πρός τούς οἰκείους.

30

Εἰ δ᾽ ὡς τήν ὕπαρξιν ἔχον ἐκ τοῦ Υἱοῦ, ὡς δι᾽ Υἱοῦ παρ᾽ αὐτοῦ τό Πνεῦμα πέμπεται, ἀρχήν οὐκοῦν ἔχει καί τοῦτο τόν Υἱόν καί τῶν γεγονότων ἐστίν ἕν. Καί μαρτυρείτω πάλιν ἡ θεολόγος φωνή· «τηροῖτο γάρ», φησίν, «ὡς ὁ ἐμός λόγος, εἷς μέν Θεός, εἰς ἕν αἴτιον καί Υἱοῦ καί Πνεύματος ἀναφερομένων, καί κατά τό ἕν καί ταὐτόν τῆς θεότητος, ἵν᾽ οὕτως εἴπω, κίνημά τε καί βούλημα καί τήν τῆς οὐσίας ταυτότητα. Αἱ δέ τρεῖς ὑποστάσεις μηδεμιᾶς ἐπινοουμένης συναλοιφῆς ἤ ἀναλύσεως ἤ συγχύσεως, Πατρός μέν ὡς ἀνάρχου καί ἀρχῆς ἐπινοουμένου καί λεγομένου, ἀρχῆς δέ ὡς αἰτίου καί ὡς πηγῆς καί ὡς ἀϊδίου φωτός, Υἱοῦ δέ ἀνάρχου μέν οὐδαμῶς, ἀρχῆς δέ τῶν ὅλων». Εἰ οὖν καί τοῦ Πνεύματος εἴη ἀρχή ὁ Υἱός, ἕν τῶν ὅλων ἔσται κατά σέ τό Πνεῦμα· τούτων γάρ ἀρχή καί ὁ Υἱός.

Ἵν᾽ οὖν αὖθις εἴπω τό τοῦ θεολόγου, «δεῖξον ὅτι γέγονε τό Πνεῦμα καί τότε τῷ Υἱῷ δός», ὥστε δι᾽ αὐτοῦ ἤ καί ἐξ αὐτοῦ τήν ὕπαρξιν κεκτῆσθαι, — ἐπεί καί ὁ θεῖος Κύριλλος πρός τούς λέγοντας ὡς,

is theologized that He proceeds from the Son, again, this definitely does not refer to that progression but to another one, which is the manifestation unto us and the transmission to those who are worthy. For, Christ is, according to Gregory the Theologian, the Treasurer of the Spirit, as being both God and Son of God. The Treasurer, however, absolutely does not emanate from Himself what is being given, although God from God naturally has in Himself the Holy Spirit, which also naturally proceeds from Him to the worthy but does not possess existence from Him. Therefore, the Lord Himself says the same: "When the Comforter is come, whom I will send unto you from the Father,"[133] as proceeding from the Father and resting in Him and being in this way sent to those of His household.

30

But if the Spirit is sent by the Son as having his existence from the Son as through the Son, then He, too, has the Son as His origin and is one of the things that have come into being.[134] Let the voice of the Theologian, once again, testify to this. For, he says, "Let this be observed as my word: There is one God, with both the Son and the Spirit referring back to one cause, and also with respect to the divinity's one and identical movement and will and the identity of the essence. But, there are three hypostases, with no coalescence or division or confusion being conceived, with the Father conceptualized and spoken of as unoriginate and origin (as an origin, since He is a cause and a source and everlasting light), while the Son is not unoriginate at all, but is the origin of all things".[135] So, if the Son were also the origin of the Spirit, the Spirit would be one of all things, according to you; since of these things the Son is also an origin.

So, let me once again repeat the phrase of the Theologian: "Demonstrate that the Spirit came into being and then attribute it to the Son",[136] that is, that through Him or also from Him He [the Holy Spirit] has acquired existence. This is especially so, since, to

εἰ καί ἐκ τοῦ Θεοῦ τό Πνεῦμα, ἀλλ' οὐ κυρίως οὐδ' ἐξῃρημένως, ἵν' ἐντεῦθεν ὁμοούσιον νοῆται τό ἐξ οὗ, γέγραπται γάρ ὅτι καί τά πάντα ἐκ Θεοῦ «μένει», φησί, «τῷ ἁγίῳ Πνεύματι κυρίως τό ἐξ οὗ, διά τό ἐκ Θεοῦ Πατρός πρός τό εἶναι τά οὐκ ὄντα δραμεῖν, δι' Υἱοῦ δέ» — δεῖξον οὖν, ἵνα πάλιν εἴπω, τό θεῖον Πνεῦμα ἐκ μή ὄντων, καί τότε καί ἐκ τοῦ Υἱοῦ τήν ὑπόσταστιν αὐτῷ παράσχου, ταὐτό δ' εἰπεῖν παρ' ἀμφοτέρων. Ἐξ ἀμφοτέρων οὖν ὑπάρχον τό Πνεῦμα οὐκ ἔστι μή ἕν τῶν πάντων εἶναι ἤ τό τάχα μετριώτερον δοκοῦν, μή καί ἀμφοτέρους τό ἕν αἰτίους ἔχειν καί ἀρχήν ἑκάτερον. Ὡς γάρ ἐξ ἀμφοτέρων τῆς κτίσεως ἁπάσης προηγμένης ἑκάτερός ἐστιν ἀρχή τῶν ὅλων, οὕτως ἐξ ἀμφοτέρων τοῦ Πνεύματος ἐκπορευομένου, κατά τούς λατινικῶς φρονοῦντας, ἑκάτερος ἔσται τοῦ πνεύματος ἀρχή, καί δύο κἀντεῦθεν ἔσονται ἀρχαί τῆς μιᾶς θεότητος.

Εἰ γάρ συντελεῖ τι κἀνταῦθα, ὥσπερ κἀκεῖ δήπου συνδημιουργεῖ, αἴτιος ὁμολογουμένως καί αὐτός τοῦ Πνεύματος· εἰ δέ μή συντελεῖ τι, μάτην εἴληπται καί ὡς ἐκ γεωμετρικοῦ πορίσματος μάταιοι ὄντως ἀνεφάνησαν οἱ λατίνοι θεολόγοι· οὐ γάρ ταῦτ' ἔχουσι λέγειν. Ὡς, καθάπερ ἐπί τῶν δημιουργημάτων ἑκατέρου ὑπάρχοντος ἀρχῆς, μία οὐδέν ἧττόν ἐστιν ἀρχή, οὕτω δή κἀνταῦθα μία ἔσται, κἄν ἐξ ἀμφοτέρων λέγηται. Ἐκεῖ μέν γάρ, καθάπερ ἔφημεν, φυσική ἐστιν, ἀλλ' οὐχ ὑποστατική, διά τοῦτο ἡ δημιουργική δύναμις μία καί ἀμφοῖν· ἐνταῦθα δέ οὐχί τό γόνιμον ἀμφοῖν.

Ἠκούσαμεν γάρ μικρόν ἀνωτέρω τοῦ τῆς θεολογίας ἐπωνύμου, τόν μέν Πατέρα πηγήν καί ἀρχήν εἰπόντος ἀϊδίου φωτός, τόν δέ Υἱόν ἄναρχον μέν οὐδαμῶς ἀρχήν δέ τῶν ὅλων. Διό καί «μόνη πηγή τῆς ὑπερουσίου θεότητος ὁ Πατήρ», ὁ μέγας εἶπε Διονύσιος ὁ Ἀρεοπαγίτης· καί αὖθις· «ἔστι πηγαία θεότης ὁ Πατήρ, ὁ δέ

those who were claiming that, although the Spirit was from God, yet He was not from Him literally or in an exceptional way (such that the source-from-which might be thought to be consubstantial, insofar as it has been written that all things are also from God), to these the divine Cyril says, "The source-from-which abides in the Holy Spirit literally, because what did not exist came toward existence from God the Father but through the Son."[137] Demonstrate then, to repeat the Theologian's words, prove that the divine Spirit is from things which are non-existent [ex nihilo], and then grant Him a hypostasis that is also from the Son, that is to say, from both. Therefore, if the Spirit exists from both, He cannot but be one of all things, or, what seems perhaps more moderate, the one cannot but have both as causes and each as an origin. For as with all creation that came forth from both, each is the origin of all, so also, according to those who think like the Latins, when the Spirit proceeds from both, each will be an origin of the Spirit, and on this basis there will be two origins of the one divinity.

For if the Son contributes something in this case, too, just as in that case also He doubtlessly co-creates, He, too, is admittedly a cause of the Spirit. If, however, He does not contribute anything, He has been assumed in vain, and so as with a geometric proof the Latin theologians are genuinely proven vain; for they cannot say that "just as with created things, although each divine person exists as an origin, nonetheless the origin is one, so here, too, it is one, even if it is spoken of as from both." Of course [this cannot stand, since] just as we have said, in the former case, the creative power is actually natural, not hypostatic, and because of this the creative power is one and in both. In the latter case, however, the generative capacity is not in both.

For, a little earlier up we heard from Gregory, the namesake of theology, who said that the Father is a source and an origin of "everlasting light, while the Son is not unoriginate at all, but is the origin of all things". Wherefore the great Dionysius the Areopagite said, "The Father alone is source of the super-essential Godhead",

Υἱός καί τό Πνεῦμα τῆς θεογόνου θεότητος, εἰ οὕτω χρή φάναι, βλαστοί θεόφυτοι καί οἷον ἄνθη καί ὑπερούσια φῶτα»· καί πάλιν· «διακεκριμένα δέ ἐστι τό Πατρός ὑπερούσιον ὄνομα καί χρῆμα καί Υἱοῦ καί Πνεύματος, οὐδεμιᾶς ἐν τούτοις ἀντιστροφῆς ἤ ὅλως κοινότητος ἐπεισαγομένης». Κἀν τῷ Περί μυστικῆς θεολογίας τρίτῳ, «ἐκ τοῦ ἀΰλου», φησί, «καί ἀμεροῦς ἀγαθοῦ τά ἐγκάρδια τῆς ἀγαθότητος ἐξέφυ φῶτα, καί τῆς ἐν αὐτῷ καί ἐν ἑαυτοῖς καί ἐν ἀλλήλοις συναϊδίου τῇ ἀναβλαστήσει μονῆς ἀπομεμένηκε ἀνεκφοίτητα»· καί αὖθις· «τά τῆς ὑπερουσίου θεογονίας οὐκ ἀντιστρέφει πρός ἄλληλα».

31

Εἰ τοίνυν εἴποις προβολέα τόν Υἱόν ὁ Πατήρ οὐδέποτ' ἄν εἴη προβολεύς· κοινωνήσει γάρ κατά τό θεογόνον τῷ Υἱῷ· ἀλλά τοῦτ' ἀπείρηται. Εἰ δέ τόν Πατέρα φαίης, ὥσπερ οὖν ἐστιν, ὁ Υἱός οὐκ ἄν εἴη προβολεύς, οὐκ ἄρα ἐξ αὐτοῦ τό Πνεῦμα· μόνος γάρ θεότης θεογόνος ὁ μόνος γεννήτωρ καί προβολεύς· κατά ταῦτα γάρ καί θεογόνος. Ταύτην δή τήν κοινωνίαν καί ὁ μέγας Βασίλειος ἀπαγορεύων πρός τόν ἑαυτοῦ γράφων ἀδελφόν, «τό Πνεῦμα», φησί, «τό ἅγιον τοῦ Υἱοῦ μέν ἤρτηται, ᾧ ἀδιαστάτως συγκαταλαμβάνεται· τῆς δέ τοῦ Πατρός αἰτίας ἐξημμένον ἔχει τό εἶναι, ὅθεν καί ἐκπορεύεται, τοῦτο γνωριστικόν τῆς κατά τήν ὑπόστασιν ἰδιότητος σημεῖον ἔχον, τό μετά τόν Υἱόν καί σύν αὐτῷ γνωρίζεσθαι καί ἐκ τοῦ Πατρός ὑφεστάναι. Ὁ δέ Υἱός τό ἐκ τοῦ Πατρός ἐκπορευόμενον Πνεῦμα δι' ἑαυτοῦ καί μεθ' ἑαυτοῦ γνωρίζων, μόνος μονογενῶς ἐκ τοῦ ἀγεννήτου φωτός ἐκλάμψας, οὐδεμίαν κατά τό ἰδιάζον τῶν γνωρισμάτων τήν κοινωνίαν ἔχει πρός τόν Πατέρα ἤ τό Πνεῦμα τό ἅγιον».

and again, "The Father is originating Godhead, while the Son
and the Spirit are (so to speak) divine off-shoots and, as it were,
blossoms and super-essential shinings of the divinity-generating
divinity"; and again, "The differentiated names are the super-
essential names and connotations of 'Father,' 'Son,' and 'Spirit.' In
these cases the titles cannot be interchanged, nor are they held in
common."[138] Likewise, in his third chapter on Mystical Theology, he
says, "from the immaterial and indivisible Good the interior rays if
Its goodness have their being, remaining immovably in that state
of rest which within their origin and within themselves and each
other is co-eternal with the act by which they spring from It;"[139] and
again, "The attributes of the super-essential divine generation are
not interchangeable."[14]

31

Accordingly, if you were to say that the Son is generator, then
the Father would never be generator.[141] For [otherwise] the Father
would communicate with the Son with respect to the generation
of divinity—but this has been forbidden. Conversely, in the event
that you are affirming the Father to be generator, then (as is the
case) the Son would not be generator, and therefore the Spirit is
not from Him, since of course the only begetter and generator is
the only generator of divinity. For, it is in those respects that He is
generator of divinity. On this point, Basil the Great also forbids this
very same communion and says, writing to his own brother, "While
the Holy Spirit is attached to the Son, with whom He is understood
together inseparably, yet He has existence dependent on the cause
of the Father, from whom He also proceeds, having this as a sign
that distinguishes His own hypostatic property, namely to be known
after the Son and together with Him and to have His subsistence
from the Father. Yet while the Son makes known the Spirit, which
proceeds from the Father, through Himself and with Himself, being
the only one that shone forth as only-begotten from the unbegotten
Light, He has no communion with the Father or the Holy Spirit
regarding the individual characteristics."[142]

Ὁρᾷς ὅπως ἔχει πρός τε τόν Πατέρα καί τόν Υἱόν τό Πνεῦμα τό ἅγιον καί τίνα Υἱοῦ καί Πνεύματος τά γνωρίσματα; «Γνωρίζει τοίνυν ἡμῖν», φησί, «καί φανεροῖ τό Πνεῦμα τό ἅγιον, δι' ἑαυτοῦ τε καί μεθ' ἑαυτοῦ ὁ τοῦ Θεοῦ μονογενής Υἱός, ἀλλ' οὐχί καί ἐκπορεύει, ἵνα μή κοινωνίαν ἔχῃ κατά τό ἰδιάζον τῷ Πατρί. Τῆς γάρ τοῦ Πατρός, φησίν, αἰτίας ἐζημμένον ἔχει τό εἶναι τό Πνεῦμα τό ἅγιον, ἥτις ἰδιότης μόνου τοῦ Πατρός ἐστι· «Πάντα γάρ», φησίν ὁ θεολόγος, «ὅσα ἔχει ὁ Πατήρ, τοῦ Υἱοῦ ἐστιν, ἄνευ τῆς αἰτίας». Τίς οὖν ἐκ τοῦ παντός αἰῶνος τῶν ἐνθέων θεολόγων τά ἴδια ἑκάστου τῶν τριῶν τῆς μιᾶς θεότητος προσώπων τοῖς δυσίν ἤκουσται προσνείμας, ἀλλά μή ἀσύγχυτα φυλάξας; Ὅτι δέ τοῦ Πατρός ἴδιον τό ἐκπορεύειν δῆλον· Τῆς γάρ αὐτοῦ, φησίν, αἰτίας ἐζῆπται τό Πνεῦμα, ὅθεν καί ἐκπορεύεται, παρ' οὗ καί ὑφέστηκεν· εἰ καί μετά τόν Υἱόν καί σύν αὐτῷ γνωρίζεται.

32

Ἐπεί δέ τά κοινά ἐπί τῆς ἀνωτάτω καί προσκυνητῆς Τριάδος ἐπίσης ἔνεστιν, οἷς ἐστι κοινά, τό δέ ἐκ τοῦ Πατρός εἶναι κατά τούς Λατίνους οὐκ ἐπίσης πρόσεστι τῷ Υἱῷ καί τῷ ἁγίῳ Πνεύματι, — ὁ μέν γάρ προσεχῶς ἐξ αὐτοῦ γεγέννηται καί ἐκ μόνου τοῦ Πατρός, τό δέ ἐμμέσως καί οὐ προσεχῶς ἐκπορεύεται καί οὐκ ἐκ μόνου τοῦ Πατρός ὥς γε αὐτοί φρονοῦσιν — εἰ οὖν κατ' αὐτούς οὐκ ἐπίσης πρόσεστιν, οὐδέ κοινόν Υἱῷ καί Πνεύματι τό εἶναι ἐκ Πατρός· εἰ δέ μή κοινόν τοῦτ' ἔστιν αὐτοῖς, οὐδ' ἐκ τοῦ Πατρός ὅλως οὐδέτερον αὐτῶν. Θάτερον γάρ ὁποιονοῦν ἐκ τοῦ Πατρός ὑπάρχον, θάτερον ἐκβάλλεται μή κοινωνοῦν, καί δι' ἀλλήλων ἀμφότερα. Οὕτως οὐδέν ἄν διαφύγοις τῶν ἀτόπων ὁ λατινικῶς φρονῶν, ὥσπερ οὐδ' οἱ ἐκ τοῦ Πνεύματος εἰπόντες τόν Υἱόν, ἀλλ' οἷς ἄν ἐπιχειρήσῃς

Do you see how the Holy Spirit relates both to the Father and to the Son, and what, in particular, are the identifying characteristics of the Son and of the Spirit? Accordingly, he says that the only-begotten Son makes known to us and manifests the Holy Spirit through Himself and with Himself, but He does not also cause procession, lest He have communion in what individuates the Father; since he says that the Holy Spirit "has existence dependent on the cause of the Father," which is a characteristic of the Father alone. "For, all things whatsoever that the Father has are the Son's, except the cause," says the Theologian.[143] So, who of the inspired theologians of any age was heard to have granted the properties of each of the three persons of the one divinity to the two of them, except a theologian that did not guard them unconfused? As for the causing of procession being the property of the Father, that is obvious. For, he says, the Spirit depends upon Him as His cause, from whom He also proceeds, from whom He also has His subsistence—although He is made known after the Son and together with Him.

32

Now, since the things which are common regarding the most high and worshipful Trinity exist equally in those in whom they are common, and seeing that being from the Father, according to the Latins, is not an attribute of the Son and of the Holy Spirit equally (for the one has been begotten directly from the Father and from the Father alone, while the other proceeds mediately and not directly, and not from the Father alone, at least as they think)—if, according to them, being from the Father is not an attribute of both equally, then neither is it common to the Son and Spirit. But if this is not common to them, then neither of them is from the Father at all. For, when either one of the two exists from the Father, the other one is expelled and does not share; and both are expelled through each other. In this way, you who think like the Latins will not avoid any of the logical absurdities, just as neither can they escape who say that the Son is from the Spirit. But with whichever arguments you attempt to escape, these very same arguments will they use, and

διαφεύγειν, τοῖς αὐτοῖς ἐπιχειρήμασι κἀκεῖνοι χρήσονται καί σοι δι’ ἑαυτῶν ἄφυκτον ἀποδείξουσι τόν τῶν ἀτόπων ἑσμόν.

Εἰ γάρ ὅτι μετά τόν Υἱόν λέγεται τό Πνεῦμα ὑπαριθμούμενον ἐρεῖς, ὅ σοι δοκεῖ τῶν ἐπιχειρημάτων ἀσφαλέστερον, ὡς ἔγωγ’ ἄν φαίην οὐχ ἧττον τῶν ἄλλων σφαλερόν, κἀκεῖνοί σοι τόν Υἱόν δείξουσιν, ἔστιν οὐ λεγόμενον μετά τό Πνεῦμα, προαριθμουμένου δηλαδή τοῦ ἁγίου Πνεύματος. Ἀμφοτέροις δέ ἡμεῖς μετά τῆς ἀληθείας ἀντεροῦμεν λέγοντες, οὐκ ἐν τῇ τάξει τῶν ὀνομάτων, ὦ οὗτοι, κεῖνται τά πράγματα.

Εἰ γάρ τοῦτο, τί κωλύει κατά τόν αὐτόν λόγον τῆς συναριθμήσεώς τε καί προαριθμήσεως ἐπαλαττομένης παρά τῇ θείᾳ Γραφῇ, ποτέ μέν γεννᾶν τε καί προβάλλειν, ποτέ δέ τά αὐτά γεννᾶσθαί τε καί προβάλλεσθαι; Οὐδέ γάρ προκαταρκτικόν, οὐδέ πρῶτον αἴτιον ἐπί τοῦ Πνεύματος, ὡς ὑμεῖς, τόν Πατέρα λέγομεν, δεύτερον δέ τόν Υἱόν, εἰ καί διά τό δημιουργικόν αἴτιον ταῦτα καλεῖται ὁ Πατήρ. Κἀκεῖθεν οὕτω κεκλημένος, ἔσθ’ ὅτε παρά τῶν θεολόγων οὕτως ὀνομάζεται καί περί τῶν ἀκτίστων τόν λόγον ποιουμένων, ὥσπερ καί Πατήρ διά τόν Υἱόν καλεῖται. Ἀλλ’ ἔσθ’ ὅτε καί περί τῶν κάτω ποιούμενοι τούς λόγους, οὕτω τοῦτον ὀνομάζομεν· οὐδέ γάρ πρῶτον μέν Θεόν τόν Πατέρα σέβομεν, δεύτερον δέ τόν Υἱόν, τρίτον δέ τό Πνεῦμα τό ἅγιον, ἵν’ ἀεί τό δεύτερον μετά τό πρῶτον λέγωμεν καί μετ’ αὐτό τό τρίτον, ὑπό τάξιν ἐξ ἀνάγκης ἄγοντες τά ὑπεράνω τάξεως, ὥσπερ καί τῶν ἄλλων πάντων.

33

Ὁ γάρ χρυσοῦς τήν γλῶτταν Ἰωάννης ἐξηγούμενος τό παρά τοῦ Ἀβραάμ πρός τόν οἰκεῖον οἰκέτην εἰρημένον, «θές τήν χεῖρά σου ὑπό τόν μηρόν μου», κατά τήν ὁμιλίαν προϊών φησι· «κηρυττέσθω Πνεῦμα ἅγιον· ὑψούσθω ὁ μονογενής· δοξαζέσθω ὁ Πατήρ. Μηδείς ἀνατετράφθαι τήν ἀξίαν νομιζέτω, εἰ Πνεύματος πρῶτον

they will prove to you by their own example that there is no escape from the stream of absurd conclusions.

For if you will say that, when the Spirit is numbered in order, He is named after the Son (which appears to you to be the safest argument but which is no less perilous than the others, at least as I myself would say), these [who say that the Son is from the Spirit] will also show to you that the Son is sometimes spoken of after the Spirit, that is, when the Holy Spirit is numbered prior. But we, along with the truth, will counter both by saying, "O such people! The actual realities do not lie in the order of their names".

For if this were so, according to this same argument, since the co-numbering and fore-numbering alternate in the divine Scripture, what would prevent the same things from begetting and causing procession on one occasion, but on another occasion from being begotten and from proceeding? For we do not call the Father an initial or a first cause regarding the Spirit while calling the Son a second cause, as you do; these names are applied to the Father on account of the creative cause.[144] And having been called by this name from that [context of creation], He is sometimes so called by the theologians when they are speaking of uncreated things as well, just as He is called Father on account of the Son. There are times, however, when we also name Him thus while making treatises about things below. For we do not revere the Father as a first God, the Son as a second one, and the Holy Spirit as a third, so as to always name the second after the first and after Him the third, [thus] bringing under order by necessity what transcends order and all other things as well.

33

For John, golden in tongue, while explaining what was said by Abraham to his own domestic servant, "Put thy hand under my thigh",[145] advancing in the course of his homily, says, "Let the Holy Spirit be proclaimed, let the Only-Begotten be exalted, let the Father be glorified. Let no one think that the worthiness has

μνημονεύομεν, εἶτα Υἱοῦ, εἶτα Πατρός· ἢ Υἱοῦ πρῶτον, εἶτα Πατρός. Οὐ γάρ ἔχει τάξιν ὁ Θεός, οὐχ ὡς ἄτακτος, ἀλλ᾿ ὡς ὑπέρ τάξιν ὤν. Οὐδέ γάρ σχῆμα ἔχει ὁ Θεός, οὐχ ὡς ἀσχήμων, ἀλλ᾿ ὡς ἀσχημάτιστος».

Ὑπέρ τάξιν οὖν, ἀλλ᾿ οὐχ ὑπό τάξιν ὁ Θεός. Εἰ δ᾿ ἔστι καί τάξις ἐπί τοῦ Θεοῦ διά τό τρισυπόστατον τῆς θεότητος, ἀλλ᾿ οὐκ ἔστιν ἡμῖν ἐγνωσμένη διά τό ὑπέρ πᾶν εἶδος τάξεως εἶναι. Τήν μέν γάρ κατά τήν ἐκφώνησιν τάξιν ἴσμεν, διδαχθέντες παρά τῆς θεοπνεύστου Γραφῆς, παρ᾿ ἧς καί ἐπαλλαττομένην ταύτην εὐσεβῶς διδασκόμεθα. Τήν δ᾿ ἐκ τῆς φυσικῆς ἀκολουθίας προσοῦσαν, καί μάλιστα τοῖς δυσί προσώποις, τῷ τε Υἱῷ καί τῷ ἁγίῳ Πνεύματι, οὐδαμῶς ἴσμεν. Διό Γρηγορίων ὁ θεολογικώτατος ἐν τῷ δευτέρῳ τῶν Εἰρηνικῶν φησιν, «οὕτω φρονοῦμεν καί οὕτως ἔχομεν, ὡς ὅπως μέν ἔχει ταῦτα σχέσεώς τε καί τάξεως, αὐτῇ μόνῃ τῇ Τριάδι συγχωρεῖν εἰδέναι καί οἷς ἄν ἡ Τριάς ἀποκαλύψῃ κεκαθαρμένοις, ἢ νῦν ἢ ὕστερον».

Ἀλλ᾿, ὁ μέγας, φασί, Βασίλειος, ὡς κεκαθαρμένος ἐξ ἀποκαλύψεως, τοῦτο μαθών εἶπεν ἐν τοῖς Κατ᾿ Εὐνομίου. Συγχωρεῖν δέ καί Γρηγόριον τόν θεολόγον εἰδέναι ταύτην, οἷς ἄν ἡ Τριάς ἀποκαλύψῃ κεκαθαρμένοις. Ἀλλ᾿ εἰ τοῦτο, πῶς τοῦ Εὐνομίου μαθεῖν εἰπόντος ἐκ τῶν ἁγίων τρίτον τῇ τάξει καί τῷ ἀξιώματι τό Πνεῦμα τό ἅγιον, δυσχεράνας οὔμενουν ἠρέμα τούτῳ καί λίαν ἐπαχθῶς ἐνεγκών ὁ θεῖος Βασίλειος, «παρά τῶν ἁγίων», φησίν, «εἶπε μεμαθηκέναι· τίνες δέ οἱ ἅγιοι καί ἐν ποίοις αὐτῶν λόγοις τήν διδασκαλίαν πεποίηνται εἰπεῖν οὐκ ἔχει; Δῆλον ὡς οὐκ ὄντων τῶν εἰπόντων ἁγίων.

Εἶτα, ἐπειδήπερ ἐκεῖνος ἐκ τοῦ τρίτον εἶναι τῇ τάξει καί τῷ ἀξιώματι τό Πνεῦμα τό ἅγιον τρίτον εἶναι καί τῇ φύσει συνήγαγε, καίτοι

been overthrown if we commemorate the Spirit first, then the Son, then the Father, or the Son first, then the Father. For God does not have order, not because He is disorderly but because He transcends order. Neither does God have a form, not because He is formless, but because He is incapable of being represented".[146]

Therefore, God transcends order and is not subject to order. But even if there is an order for God, because of the tri-hypostatic characteristic of the divinity, it is not known to us on account of it being transcendent to every form of order. For, we certainly know the order used during the exclamation, because we have been taught it by the God-inspired Scripture, from which we are also reverently taught that it alternates. But the order that is attributed to them from the course of [the divine] nature, and especially to the two persons, to the Son and to the Holy Spirit, that we do not know at all. Wherefore, the most theological of Gregories says in the second chapter of his Orations of Peace, "We are of this mind and thus do we hold, that the way in which these things exist in respect to relation and order be conceded as known only to the Trinity Itself or to those purified ones to whom the Trinity will reveal it, either now or afterward".[147]

"But," they say, "Basil the Great, as one that had been purified by revelation, said in his chapters Against Eunomius that he did learn this. Gregory the Theologian, too, makes allowance for this to be known to those purified ones to whom the Trinity might reveal it". But if this is so, when Eunomius said that he learned from the saints that the Holy Spirit is third in order and in dignity, why was the divine Basil on the contrary quietly displeased at him and bore it very grievously and said, "He said he learned it 'from the saints,' but who the saints are or in which of their particular treatises they have laid down this teaching he cannot say".[148] It is clear that there are no saints who said this.

Then, seeing that, on the basis that [according to Eunomius] the Holy Spirit was third in order and in dignity, Eunomius concluded

μηδέ παρά τοῦτο συναγόμενον, ἐνδούς ὁ μέγας καί καθ᾽ ὑπόθεσιν
παραδεξάμενος, «εἰ καί τρίτον εἶναι», φησί, «τῇ τάξει καί τῷ ἀξιώματι
τό Πνεῦμα τό ἅγιον ὁ τῆς εὐσεβείας ἴσως παραδίδωσι λόγος, ἵνα
καί ὅλως συγχωρήσωμεν, ἀλλ᾽ οὐκ ἀνάγκη παρά τοῦτο τρίτον
εἶναι αὐτό καί τῇ φύσει». Ὡς οὖν καθ᾽ ὑπόθεσιν παραδεξάμενος,
ἀλλ᾽ οὐ τοῦτο δογματίζων αὐτός, ἀμφισβητικῶς ἔχοντα τόν λόγον
προήγαγεν.

Ὁ δέ φησιν ἐν τῷ πρώτῳ τῶν Πρός αὐτόν Εὐνόμιον, ὡς «ἔστι
τάξεως εἶδος οὐ κατά τήν ἡμετέραν θέσιν, ἀλλ᾽ ἐκ τῆς κατά φύσιν
αὐτοῖς ἐνυπαρχούσης ἀκολουθίας», οὐ περί τοῦ Υἱοῦ καί τοῦ
Πνεύματος ἀλλά περί τοῦ Πατρός καί τοῦ Υἱοῦ ποιούμενος τήν
διάλεξίν φησιν, ἐν οἷς ἐγνωσμένον τε καί ἀνωμολογημένον ἅπασιν
αἰτιατόν μέν εἶναι τόν Υἱόν, τόν δέ Πατέρα αἴτιον καί τοῦ αἰτιατοῦ
προεπινοούμενον ἐξ ἀνάγκης, εἰ καί μή κατά χρόνον, ὡς αὐτός ἐκεῖ
φησι. Ταῦτ᾽ ἄρα καί χωρίς ἐνδοιασμῶν τε καί ἀμφισβητήσεων, τόν
μέν Πατέρα προτετάχθαι τοῦ Υἱοῦ φησι, τόν δέ Υἱόν δευτερεύειν
τοῦ Πατρός, γράφων· «ἡμεῖς δέ, κατά μέν τήν τῶν αἰτίων πρός τά
ἐξ αὐτῶν σχέσιν, προτετάχθαι τοῦ Υἱοῦ τόν Πατέρα φαμέν, κατά
δέ τήν τῆς φύσεως διαφοράν οὐκέτι, οὐδέ κατά τήν τῶν χρόνου
ὑπεροχήν». Ἐν δέ τῷ τρίτῳ πάλιν, «τάξει μέν», φησί, «δεύτερος τοῦ
Πατρός, ὅτι ἀπ᾽ ἐκείνου, καί ἀξιώματι, φύσει δέ οὐκέτι δεύτερος».

Οὕτως οἶδεν ὁμολογουμένως ἐκ τοῦ Πατρός εἶναι τόν Υἱόν, ἀλλ᾽
οὐχί καί τό Πνεῦμα ἐξ Υἱοῦ. Εἰ γάρ τοῦτ᾽ ἐγίνωσκεν, οὐκ ἄν ὅλως
ἠμφισβήτει, οὐδ᾽ ἄν ἀπηγόρευε τρίτον εἶναι τῇ τάξει ἀπό τοῦ
Πατρός τό Πνεῦμα τό ἅγιον· ἀλλ᾽ οὐδέ κατά τοῦ Εὐνομίου καί τοῦτ᾽
εἰπόντος λίαν ἐδυσχέραινε. Πρός δέ τούτοις καί τό δευτερεύειν τοῦ
Υἱοῦ τό Πνεῦμα σύν ἀμφιβολίᾳ πολλῇ καί καθ᾽ ὑπόθεσιν, ἀλλ᾽ οὐχ
ὡς αὐτός δοξάζων παραδεξάμενος, δείκνυται μηδ᾽ αὐτός εἰδέναι,
ὅπως ἔχουσι πρός ἄλληλα ὁ Υἱός τε καί τό Πνεῦμα σχέσεώς τε καί
τάξεως.

that He was also third in nature (although this does not follow from that), the great one conceded and, having accepted it hypothetically, he said, "Even if perhaps the pious tradition hands down that the Holy Spirit is third in order and in dignity (let us even completely concede the point), yet this does not necessitate that He is also third in nature".[149] So he presented this saying argumentatively, accepting this as though hypothetically but not dogmatizing it himself.

But what he says in the first of the letters Against Eunomius, that "there is a form of order, not according to our positioning, but from the course of nature existing in them",[150] this he says discoursing not on the Son and the Spirit, but on the Father and the Son, in whom it is known and confessed by all that the Son is caused while the Father is the cause and is thus necessarily conceptualized before the caused, although not temporally, as he himself says there. Therefore, he asserts without any apprehension or doubt that the Father has indeed been ranked before the Son, while the Son is placed second from the Father. He writes, "While we say that the Father is categorized before the Son with respect to the relationship of the causes with those caused from them, we do not say this with respect to the difference of nature or to a temporally based superiority".[151] And again, in his third letter he says, "He is second in order from the Father (since He is from Him) and second in dignity, but He is not second in nature."[152]

So, he confessedly knows that the Son is from the Father, but not also that the Spirit is from the Son. For, if [Saint Basil] held [that the Spirit is from the Son], then there would be no argument at all, nor would he forbid the Holy Spirit from being third in order from the Father, nor would he have been greatly displeased with Eunomius when the latter said this. Furthermore, since it was with much uncertainty and hypothetically that he accepted that the Spirit is second from the Son (not as if he himself was thinking this way), so he shows that neither does he himself know the manner in which the Son and the Spirit have relationship and order between themselves.

Ὅτι μέν γάρ ἅμα ἐξ ἀϊδίου ὁ Υἱός τε καί τό Πνεῦμα τό ἅγιον, ἐν
ἀλλήλοις τε ὄντα καί ἀλλήλων ἐχόμενα καί δι᾽ ἀλλήλων ἀφύρτως
τε καί ἀμιγῶς χωροῦντα, καί ὅτι τούτων ἕκαστον τάξεώς τε καί
σχέσεως εἶδος, καί ὡς ὁ Υἱός τε καί τό Πνεῦμα τό ἅγιον ἐκ τοῦ
Πατρός ἅμα, εἰ καί οὐχ ὡσαύτως, καί ὅτι ὁμότιμα ἐξ ὁμοτίμου,
καί ὅτι τό ἐκπορεύειν ἰδιότης ὄν τῆς πατρικῆς ὑποστάσεως οὐκ
ἔστιν εἶναι τοῦ Υἱοῦ, καί ὡς ὁ λέγων καί τόν Υἱόν τό ἐκπορεύειν
ἔχειν σύγχυσιν ποιεῖ τῶν θείων ὑποστάσεων, δυσσεβῶς ἀθετῶν
τήν ἀνωμολογημένην τάξιν ἐπί τοῦ Θεοῦ — «δεῖ γάρ», φησί καί
Γρηγόριος ὁ τῆς θεολογίας ἐπώνυμος, «τάς ἰδιότητας μένειν Πατρί
καί Υἱῷ, ἵνα μή σύγχυσις ᾖ παρά θεότητι τῇ καί τά ἄλλα εἰς τάξιν
ἀγούσῃ» — ταύτην μέν οὖν τήν ἀνωμολογημένην τάξιν ἐπί τοῦ
Θεοῦ καί ἡμεῖς ἴσμεν· τήν δέ δεύτερον μέν ἐκ τοῦ Υἱοῦ, τρίτον δέ
ἀπό Πατρός τιθεῖσαν τό Πνεῦμα τό ἅγιον οὔθ᾽ ἡμεῖς ἴσμεν οὔτε οἱ
διδάσκαλοι καί προασπισταί τῆς Ἐκκλησίας.

Λατῖνοι δέ, ὤ τῆς ἀνοίας ὁμοῦ καί ἀπονοίας, τήν μέν εὐσεβῆ καί
ἀνωμολογημένην ἐκείνην ἐπί τοῦ Θεοῦ τάξιν ἀθετοῦσιν, ἅ δέ
Βασίλειος ὁ μέγας καί Γρηγόριος ὁ θεολόγος ὑπέρ τήν οἰκείαν
γνῶσιν ὁμολογοῦσιν εἶναι ὡς ἀπόρρητα ὄντα καί ὑπέρ ἡμᾶς, αὐτοί
καταλαβεῖν αὐχοῦσι καί περί τήν ἄφραστόν τε καί ἀπερινόητον
ἐκπόρευσιν τοῦ Πνεύματος καινοφωνοῦσι, βλασφημοῦσι δέ εἰπεῖν
οἰκειότερον, ἔμμεσόν τε καί ἄμεσον αὐτήν λέγοντες καί προσεχῆ
καί πόρρω, δι᾽ ὧν κινδυνεύουσι καί εἰς κτίσμα κατασπᾶν τό Πνεῦμα
τό ἅγιον. Διό οὐκ ἀναγκαίως οὐδ᾽ ἀεί μετά τόν Υἱόν παρά τῆς
θεοπνεύστου τίθεται Γραφῆς τό Πνεῦμα τό ἅγιον.

Τοῦτο γάρ Λατίνοις συμβαίνει, τοῖς ἐκ τῶν δύο, πρώτου αἰτίου
καί δευτέρου, λέγουσι τό ἕν καί μή κατά πάντα στέργουσι τήν
θεόπνευστον Γραφήν, ἀλλά κατ᾽ ἐξουσίαν ἄττα βούλονται

As for the admitted order in God—namely, that the Son and the Holy Spirit are simultaneously from eternity, being in each other, possessing each other, and pervading through each other unconfused and unmixed; that each of them constitutes a form both of order and of relationship; that both the Son and the Holy Spirit are from the Father at the same time, although not identically so; that the equally honorable are from the equally honorable; that, since causing procession is the idiom of the paternal hypostasis, it cannot be the Son's; that one who says that the Son also can cause procession creates a confusion of the divine hypostases, irreverently disregarding the admitted order in God—we too acknowledge this admitted order in God. Gregory, too, the namesake of theology, says, "The properties must remain in the Father and the Son, lest there be confusion with respect to the divinity that leads the others also into order."[153] Thus, we too acknowledge, on one hand, this admitted order in God; on the other hand, neither do we nor do the teachers and defenders of the Church acknowledge the order that places the Holy Spirit as second from the Son and third from the Father.

Now the Latins—O the simultaneous senselessness and madness!—they actually despise the reverend and confessed order in God. And those things which Basil the Great and Gregory the Theologian confess to be beyond their own knowledge, as being ineffable and transcending us, these things the Latins boast that they understand. Yet they innovate regarding the inexpressible and incomprehensible procession of the Holy Spirit, or, to speak more bluntly, they blaspheme, when they say that the procession is both indirect and direct, both proximate and far, by which they risk degrading the Holy Spirit into a creature. Therefore, the Holy Spirit is not by necessity nor is He always placed after the Son by the divinely inspired Scripture.

For, this happens to the Latins, who say that the one is from the two, from a first and a second cause, and who do not embrace the God-inspired Scripture in everything, but with their own authority they

προστιθεῖσί τε καί ἀφαιροῦσιν· ἡμῖν δέ τοῖς ἐκ τοῦ ἑνός εὐσεβοφρόνως σέβουσι καί εἰς ἕν ἀναφέρουσι τά δύο, ἥκιστα.

34

Ἵνα δέ σοι καί λόγον δῶμεν, μᾶλλον δέ καταξιώσωμεν διδάξαι· τίνος ἕνεκεν ὡς ἐπί πλεῖστον ὁ μέν Υἱός μετά τόν Πατέρα, τό δέ Πνεῦμα μετά τόν Υἱόν ἡμῖν ὑμνεῖται, καί μυεῖσθαι παραδέδοται; Ὁ Θεός καί Πατήρ, ἡ πάντων ἀρχή, Υἱοῦ Πατήρ ἐστι μονογενοῦς, ὅς καί πρίν ἤ προστεθῆναι τῷ Πατρί συννοεῖται πάραυτα. Πῶς οὖν ἀφέντες τόν καί πρίν ἤ λεχθῆναι προσεχέστατα τῷ Πατρί νοούμενον, εὐθύς ἄν τό Πνεῦμα μετά τόν Πατέρα θείημεν; Διά τοῦτο μετά τόν τοῦ Πατρός Υἱόν λέγεται τό Πνεῦμα· μή δυναμένων γάρ ἡμῶν ἄμφω προφέρειν διά γλώττης ἅμα, ὥσπερ ἄρα καί ἐκ τοῦ Πατρός προῆλθον, εἰ πρό τοῦ Υἱοῦ τό Πνεῦμα τῷ Πατρί συννημένον θείημεν, δόξαι ἄν Υἱός τό Πνεῦμα· τό γάρ "Πατήρ" ὄνομα εὐθύς συνεισάγεται τῇ διανοίᾳ τόν Υἱόν· προϊόντες δ' αὖθις καί μετά τό Πνεῦμα προσεχῶς εὐθύς τιθέντες τόν Υἱόν, Πατέρα τό Πνεῦμα ποιήσομεν νοεῖσθαι. Ὁ γάρ Υἱός, Πατρός Υἱός καί συνεισάγει τῇ διανοίᾳ τόν Πατέρα καί μάλιστα τόν πρό αὐτοῦ λεγόμενον· ὁ δέ Υἱός προσεχῶς τῷ Πατρί τιθέμενος καί τό μονογενές ἑαυτῷ φυλάττει καί τό ἐκπορευτῶς ἐκ Πατρός εἶναι τό Πνεῦμα οὐ κωλύει. Ὅ καί ὁ Νυσσαέων Γρηγόριός φησιν, οὗτινος οἱ λατινικῶς φρονοῦντες τό ὕψος τῆς διανοίας μή χωρήσαντες, πόρρω μέν τοῦ Πατρός, ὤ τῆς ἀσεβείας, δοξάζουσι τό Πνεῦμα, προσεχές δέ τοῦ Υἱοῦ. Ἀλλ' οὐχ ὅτι ὁ Πατήρ τε καί Υἱός ἄλληλα εἰσάγουσι τῇ διανοίᾳ κατά τοῦτο ὄντα προσεχῆ, διά τοῦτο πόρρω τό Πνεῦμα τοῦ Πατρός καί οὐκ ἀμέσως ἐξ αὐτοῦ. Ἀλλά περί μέν τούτων, ὕστερον.

Νῦν δ' ἵνα καί δευτέραν αἰτίαν ἀποδῶμεν, ἥτις καί αὕτη, ἵνα διά πάντων συνετίσωμέν σε, διά τήν προειρημένην γέγονε· πρῶτον

add and subtract what they wish. But this does not happen to us at all, who with a reverential mindset revere the two as being from one and refer the two to the one.

34

But let us even give you opportunity to speak, or rather let us deem you worthy to teach: for what reason is it that for the most part we hymn the Son after the Father and the Spirit after the Son, and in this order it has been handed down in tradition for us to be initiated? The God and Father, the origin of all things, is Father of the Only-Begotten Son, who is straightway understood together with the Father even before He is mentioned. How then could we abandon Him who is understood as near as possible to the Father even before He is named and position the Spirit directly after the Father? Because of this, the Spirit is mentioned after the Son of the Father, because we are not able to pronounce both of them at the same time with our tongue, just as they came forth from the Father. If we position the Spirit joined to the Father before the Son, the Spirit would seem to be a Son, since the name "Father" straightway conveys to our reasoning the Son. Advancing once more and having placed the Son directly after the Spirit, we would be making the Spirit to be considered a Father. For the Son is the Son of a Father and He brings the Father to mind, especially the one mentioned before Him. So, when the Son is placed directly with the Father, He preserves His own only-begottenness without hindering the Spirit from being from the Father by procession. This is also what Gregory of the Nyssans says, whose height of thought the Latin-minded could not comprehend. So, they think that the Spirit is far from the Father—O the irreverence!—yet proximate to the Son. But the fact that the Father and the Son bring each other to mind, being in this respect proximate to one another, is not a reason why [one should think that] the Spirit is far from the Father and not directly next to Him. But these matters are for later.

But now, so as to give you understanding by all means, let us propose a second cause, which also came to be on account of the

ἡμῶν τό γένος Θεόν ἔγνω τόν Πατέρα καί Πατέρα τόν Θεόν, τῆς αὐτοῦ θεότητος φανερωθείσης τε καί πιστευθείσης ἀμυδρῶς, ὥς γε συνήνεγκεν ἡμῖν. Εἰ γάρ ἐπίσης ὤν Πατήρ καί προβολεύς, τόθ᾿ ἡμῖν οὐ Πατήρ ἀλλά προβολεύς ἤ ἐκπορεύων ἐκηρύττετο, πῶς ἄν παραδεξάμεθα, μή δυνάμενοί πω χωρῆσαι διά τό νηπιῶδες ἔτι, τήν ἐπίγνωσιν τοῦ ἐμφύτου πλούτου τῆς θεότητος; Τό δέ "πατήρ" ὄνομα καί πρός ἡμῶν ἐστι καί οἷον κοινόν ἔχομεν αὐτό ταῖς ἐξ αὐτοῦ ὁμοουσίοις μέν αὐτῷ ἡμῖν δέ δεσποτικαῖς ἐκείναις ὑποστάσεσιν. Εἰ κἀκεῖνοι μέν φύσει καί ὑπέρ ἡμᾶς ἔχουσιν αὐτό, ἡμῶν δ᾿ ὑπό φιλανθρωπίας καλεῖσθαι κατηξίωσε – διό καί Ἰουδαῖοι ἔλεγον, «ἡμεῖς Πατέρα ἔχομεν τόν Θεόν» – σοφῶς οὖν ἄγαν καί οἷον ὑποκλέπτων τήν διάνοιαν ἡμῶν, μᾶλλον δέ ἡμᾶς ἀπό τῆς τοῦ πονηροῦ δουλείας καί ψευδοδοξίας καί ψευδολατρίας ἐπί τήν οἰκείαν δεσποτείαν πρός θεογνωσίαν ὑφαιρούμενος καί τήν τοῦ μονογενοῦς ὑπεμφαίνων συνεισέφερε θεότητα, Πατήρ κηρυττόμενος αὐτός. Μετ᾿ αὐτόν ὁ Υἱός πεφανέρωται τῷ κόσμῳ, διά σαρκός ἡμῖν ὀφθείς καί συναναστραφείς· ὅς σύν ἑαυτῷ καί τό Πνεῦμα ὑπεδείκνυ, λόγοις τε καί ἔργοις διά πάντων πιστούμενος, συνημμένον φύσει καί ὁμότιμον ἑαυτῷ καί τῷ Πατρί. Μετά τόν Υἱόν τό Πνεῦμα τό ἅγιον ἐπεδήμησε τῷ κόσμῳ, παρά μέν τοῦ Υἱοῦ πεμπόμενον, ὡς οὐκ ἀντίθεον οὐδέ ἀντίχριστον, καί πεμπόμενον οὐχ ἁπλῶς καί ἀπολύτως, ἀλλά χρονικῶς καί πρός τινας καί δι᾿ αἰτίαν· παρά δέ τοῦ Πατρός ἐκπορευόμενον οὐ δι᾿ αἰτίαν ὅλως, οὐδέ χρονικῶς ἤ πρός τινας, ἀλλ᾿ ἁπλῶς καί ἀπολύτως πάντη, ὡς ὁμόθεον καί ὁμοούσιον καί τῆς αὐτῆς οὐχ ἧττον ἐξημμένον τῷ Υἱῷ αἰτίας καί ἀρχῆς, παρ᾿ ἑαυτοῦ δέ ἐρχόμενον ὡς κύριον καί αὐτεξούσιον.

Ἐπεγένετο δέ καί τρίτη τις αἰτία τοῖς θεολόγοις, δι᾿ ἥν μετά τόν Υἱόν καί ἐκ τῶν τοῦ Υἱοῦ παριστᾶσιν ὡς ἐπί πλεῖστον τό συναφές καί τέλειον καί ὁμοούσιον Πατρί τῆς θεότητος τοῦ Πνεύματος· ὅτι μετά τό κατευνασθῆναι καί μετασκευασθῆναι τήν πλειόνων κατά τοῦ Υἱοῦ μανίαν, πολυειδῶς ἀποδειχθείσης καί ἀναφανείσης

preceding one. At the first, our race came to know the Father as God and God as a Father. His divinity had been manifested and believed indistinctly, as was, of course, to our profit. For if, being equally a Father and an Originator, He was instead preached not as Father but as Originator or as one causing procession, how could we have received it, since at that point, on account of still being childlike, we were not able to contain the knowledge of the innate richness of the divinity? The name "Father", however, is closer to us, and we share it, as it were, with those hypostases that are from Him and are consubstantial with Him though magisterial for us. While they possess it by nature and transcendently in comparison to us, yet He has deemed us worthy to call Him by this name on account of His love for mankind; and so the Jews also were saying, "We have God as Father."[154] Therefore, He very wisely beguiled our understanding, or better, by being proclaimed as Father, He indicated and introduced the divinity of the Only-Begotten so that He may draw us away from bondage to the wicked one and away from false belief and false worship, drawing us to His own dominion, to the knowledge of God. After Him, the Son has been manifested to the world: He was seen bodily and conversed with us.[155] Together with Himself, He was also indirectly indicating the Spirit, assuring everywhere in His words and deeds that the Spirit is joined by nature and equally honorable with Himself and the Father. After the Son the Holy Spirit sojourned in the world, being sent, on the one hand, from the Son, not as instead of God or instead of Christ, and was being sent not simply or unconditionally, but temporally and to certain people and for a cause. On the other hand, He proceeds from the Father not for any cause at all, nor temporally, nor to certain men, but simply and entirely unconditionally, as the same God, of the same substance, and united to the very same cause and origin as the Son, while coming of Himself as Lord and self-determining.

Finally, the theologians had a third particular reason for presenting (for the most part) the connection and perfection and consubstantiality of the Spirit's divinity with the Father as being after the Son and from the things of the Son. Namely, after the mania of the many against the Son was quenched and transformed, as

καί στηριχθείσης ἀσφαλέστατα τῆς τούτου πρός τόν Πατέρα
συμφυΐας καί ὁμοτιμίας ὁ κατά τοῦ θείου Πνεύματος ἐμφανέστερον
ἀνερριπίσθη πόλεμος. Ταῦτ' ἄρα καί τοῖς θεολόγοις ὁ λόγος ἅπας,
οὐ περί τοῦ τρόπου τῆς ὑπάρξεως, ἀλλά περί τήν πρός τόν Υἱόν
ὁμοουσιότητος τοῦ Πνεύματος, εἰ καί Λατῖνοι βιάζονται τάς ρήσεις,
μεθέλκοντες αὐτῶν τήν διάνοιαν εἰς τήν οἰκείαν κακόνοιαν.

35

Ἀλλά γάρ οὕτως ἡμῖν ὁ ἐν τρισίν ὑποστάσεσιν εἷς Θεός
ἐκπεφασμένος, οὕτω καί δοξάζεται· καί οὕτω μιᾶς εἰκόνος οὔσης
καί μορφῆς ἐπί τῆς μόνης ἀνειδέου καί προσκυνητῆς Τριάδος – «ἡ
γάρ Τριάς συνάπτεται μέν ἀδιαστάτως, σύνεστι δέ ἀϊδίως, εἰκόνα
δέ προφαίνει μίαν καί τήν αὐτήν», Ἀθανάσιος ὁ μέγας λέγει – μιᾶς
οὖν οὕτως εἰκόνος οὔσης ἐπί τῆς σεπτῆς Τριάδος, τόν μέν Υἱόν
τοῦ Πατρός μορφήν τε καί εἰκόνα λέγομεν, τό δέ Πνεῦμα τοῦ Υἱοῦ.
Οὕτω γάρ ἡμῖν ὡς εὐδόκησεν ἑαυτήν ἐγνώρισε καί οὕτως ἔχειν
πρός τόν Υἱόν τό Πνεῦμα λέγομεν, ὡς αὐτός πρός τόν Πατέρα·
ὁμοίως γάρ ἀμφότερα ἔχουσι πρός τόν Πατέρα, πλήν τοῦ τρόπου
τῆς ὑπάρξεως, ὡς ἀνωτέρω διά πλειόνων ἀποδέδεικται. Προσεχῶς
δέ τῷ Πατρί ὁ Υἱός ἔγνωσται ἡμῖν καί διά τοῦ προσεχῶς τούτου
ἐγνωσμένου τό Πνεῦμα τό ἅγιον ἐφανερώθη, κηρυχθέν τε καί
πεμφθέν ἐν τῷ ὀνόματι αὐτοῦ, ὡς καί οὗτος πρῴην ἦλθεν ἐν τῷ
τοῦ Πατρός ὀνόματι. Καί πάντα λέγομεν ἔχειν τόν Υἱόν τά τοῦ
Πατρός ἄνευ τῆς αἰτίας, πάντα δέ τά τοῦ Υἱοῦ τό Πνεῦμα ἄνευ
τῆς υἱότητος. Πάντα γάρ τοῦ Πατρός ὁμοίως ἔχει ὁ Υἱός τε καί τό
Πνεῦμα ἄνευ τῆς αἰτίας, συμπεριβαλλούσης ἄμφω τάς ὑπαρκτικάς
καθ' ὑπόστασιν διαφοράς. Διό καί πρό τοῦ Υἱοῦ ἔστιν οὗ τίθεμεν τό
Πνεῦμα, εἰ καί ὡς ἐπ' ἔλαττον, ὡς δέ ἐπί πλεῖστον μετά τόν Υἱόν
καί μετά τόν Πατέρα τοῦτον, ἵνα τῶν τριῶν ὑπέρ ἡμῶν μεγίστων
ἔργων καὶ θεοπρεπῶν καί προμηθεστάτων οἰκονομιῶν, συνεχῆ
καί ἀδιάλειπτον τήν μνήμην φέροντες, συντομωτάτην διά πάντων
ἀποδιδῶμεν τήν εὐχαριστίαν.

His con-naturality and equality of honor to the Father had been proven and plainly declared and most firmly established in many ways, then the war against the Divine Spirit was rekindled more openly. That is why the whole argument for the theologians is not about the mode of existence but about the consubstantiality of the Spirit with the Son, although the Latins do violence to the words, dragging the theologians' intellect down to their own poorly connected train of thought.

35

Nevertheless, since the one God in three hypostases has been expressed to us thus, thus He is also glorified. And in this way, since there is one image and form of the only formless, worshipful Trinity—"For the Trinity, on the one hand, is joined without interval and, on the other hand, is eternally together and shines forth one and the same image," as Athanasius the Great says[156]—since, then, in this way there is one image of the revered Trinity, we call the Son the form and image of the Father while calling the Spirit an image of the Son. For, this is how it pleased Him to make Himself known to us. And we say that the Spirit is in relation to the Son in the way in which the Son is in relation to the Father. For both are similarly related to the Father apart from the mode of existence, as has been demonstrated above in many ways. Now, the Son has become known to us as immediately proximate to the Father, and through Him who is known as proximate the Holy Spirit has been manifested, proclaimed, and sent in His name, just as the Son came earlier in the name of the Father. And we say that the Son has all things which are the Father's apart from the cause, while the Spirit has all things of the Son apart from sonship. For the Son and the Spirit in a similar way have all that is the Father's, except for the cause, which embraces both of the existential hypostatic differences. Consequently, we sometimes also place the Spirit before the Son, although more rarely, while for the most part we place Him after the Son and after the Father, so that we may bear in mind a continual and ceaseless remembrance of the three greatest works and most providential and God-befitting economies wrought for our sakes, and render the briefest possible thanksgiving for all things.

36

Εὐνόμιος δέ καί μετ' αὐτόν οἱ λατινικῶς φρονοῦντες μή συνετῶς
ἀκηκοότες τῆς πρός τόν Θεόν τοιαύτης εὐχαριστίας τῶν Πατέρων
καί τῆς ἐν ταῖς πρός τούς ἑτεροδόξους ἀντιρρήσεσιν οἰκονομίας
μή δυνηθέντες συνιδεῖν, συνήγαγον κακῶς ἐντεῦθεν τρίτον ἀπό
Πατρός εἶναι τό Πνεῦμα τό ἅγιον, μηδέ τοῦτο συνιδόντες, ὡς
εἴγε τοῦτο ἦν καί διά τοῦτο «ἡ φυσική τάξις τοῦ τε Υἱοῦ πρός τόν
Πατέρα καί τοῦ θείου Πνεύματος πρός τόν Υἱόν ἐδείκνυτο, οὐκ ἄν,
ἐπαλλαττομένης ἐν τῇ θείᾳ Γραφῇ τῆς συνεκφωνήσεως τῶν τριῶν
προσκυνητῶν προσώπων, ἔστιν οὗ μετά τό Πνεῦμα ὁ Υἱός ἐτίθετο,
προαριθμουμένου δηλαδή τοῦ ἁγίου Πνεύματος, καθάπερ καί ὁ
πολύς ἐν θεολογίᾳ φησί Γρηγόριος, ὅτι «τά αὐτά καί προαριθμεῖται
καί ὑπαριθμεῖται παρά τῇ Γραφῇ διά τήν ἰσοτιμίαν τῆς φύσεως»·
ἐν δέ τῇ παρουσίᾳ τῶν ἀπ' Αἰγύπτου ἐπισκόπων καί ἡμᾶς οὕτω
παραινεῖ θεολογεῖν, «μετά Παύλου», λέγων, «θεολόγησον, τοῦ
πρός τρίτον οὐρανόν ἀναχθέντος, ποτέ μέν συναριθμοῦντος τάς
τρεῖς ὑποστάσεις, καί τοῦτο ἐνηλλαγμένως, οὐ τετηρημένως ταῖς
τάξεσι, προαριθμοῦντος, ἐναριθμοῦντος, ὑπαριθμοῦντος τό αὐτό».

Ἀλλ' οὐδέ τό "δι' οὗ" μόνῳ τῷ Υἱῷ παρά τῆς θείας ἀπονενέμηται
Γραφῆς· ὁ γάρ θεῖος Κύριλλος ἐν Θησαυροῖς φησι, «Χριστοῦ τό
Πνεῦμα, ὡς τοῦ Θεοῦ Λόγου διά Πνεύματος ἡμῖν ἐνοικιζομένου».
Τούτων οὖν Εὐνόμιός τε καί τό τῶν Λατίνων γένος, μηδένα
ποιησάμενοι λόγον, τρίτον εἶναι τῇ τάξει καί τῷ ἀξιώματι τό
Πνεῦμα τό ἅγιον ἐδογμάτισαν, οὐ τῇ κατά τήν ὁμολογίαν
τάξει ἀλλά τῇ φυσικῇ, κακῶς. Ὅ γε μήν Εὐνόμιος ἐντεῦθεν
τρίτον ἀπό τοῦ Πατρός εἶναι καί τῇ φύσει, ὡς ἀμφοτέρων
κατ' αὐτήν διαφέρον, προσεδογμάτισεν, οἱ δέ Λατῖνοι καί ἐκ
τοῦ Υἱοῦ ἐκπορεύεσθαι τό Πνεῦμα τό ἅγιον κατασκευάζουσιν.

36

But Eunomius and, after him, those who think like the Latins, have not heard with understanding this thanksgiving of the Fathers to God, nor were they able to understand the economia used in the rebuttals toward the heterodox. Therefore, they wrongly deduced from this [thanksgiving] that the Holy Spirit is third from the Father. But neither did they understand this, that if in fact this were true and if by it the natural order of the Son to the Father and of the divine Spirit to the Son were being displayed, then, when the doxological proclamation of the three worshipful persons is alternated in the divine scripture, there would be no instances of the Son being placed after the Spirit, that is, with the Holy Spirit numbered before Him. Likewise, Gregory, great in theology, says that "These same ones are both numbered before and numbered after in the Scripture due to the natural equality of honor",[157] and in the presence of the bishops from Egypt he also exhorts us to theologize in this way saying, "Theologize together with Paul, who was taken up into the third heaven and would sometimes count together the three hypostases and do this in alternation, without holding the orders strictly, numbering the same one as first, middle, and last."[158]

But neither is the phrase "through whom" assigned only to the Son by the Holy Scripture. For, the divine Cyril in his Treasuries says, "The Spirit is of Christ, because God the Word is indwelling in us through the Spirit".[159] Therefore, having taken no account of these things, both Eunomius and the race of the Latins dogmatized that the Holy Spirit is third in order and dignity, not in the order [pronounced] during the confession, but in the natural order, which is wrong. From there Eunomius, at any rate, certainly dogmatized in addition that He is third from the Father in nature as well, as differing from both according to His nature, while the Latins construct their argument that the Holy Spirit proceeds also from the Son.

37

Ἡμεῖς δέ σύν τοῖς ἱεροῖς πατράσιν ὡς ἐπί τό πλεῖστον τό Πνεῦμα μετά τόν Υἱόν τιθέαμεν καί μετά τόν Πατέρα τοῦτον, ἵνα τῶν τριῶν ὑπέρ ἡμῶν μεγίστων ἔργων καί θεοπρεπῶν καί προμηθεστάτων οἰκονομιῶν συντομωτάτην ἀποδιδῶμεν διά πάντων τήν δοξολογίαν καί τήν εὐχαριστίαν καί τήν ἀνάμνησιν· οὐχ ὅτι δεύτερα καί τρίτα τῇ τιμῇ καί τῇ ἀξίᾳ – καί γάρ ὁμότιμα – οὐδέ τήν δυάδα ποιοῦντες τοῦ ἑνός ἀρχήν, οὐδ' εἰς τήν δυάδα ἀναφέροντες τό ἕν, ἀλλ' εἰς ἡμῖν Θεός, εἰς ἕν αἴτιον καί Υἱοῦ καί Πνεύματος ἀναφερομένων, ἐξ οὗ μόνου ἔχει καί τήν ὕπαρξιν ἑκάτερον αὐτῶν· καί ὅτι μία ἀρχή, ὁ Πατήρ, ὡς καί ὁ θαυματουργός Γρηγόριος λέγει, κατά τοῦτο τοίνυν εἷς Θεός· καί ὅτι μία φύσις τοῖς τρισίν, αὐτά γάρ τά δύο καί τά τρία καί τό ἐξ αὐτοῦ καί τό ἀναφέρεσθαι εἰς αὐτόν οὐ τήν φύσιν διαιρεῖ, ἀλλά περί αὐτήν διαιρεῖται, οὐδέ γοῦν ἐξ αὐτῆς ἐστι κυρίως, εἰ καί μή χωρίς αὐτῆς, οὐδ' εἰς αὐτήν ἀναφέρεται, εἰ καί μή ἄνευ ταύτης· τό γάρ ἕν, πῶς ἄν αὐτό ἑαυτό γεννήσαι τε καί προβάλοιτο καί εἰς ἑαυτό ἀναφέροιτο; Οὐδ' ἀρχή τοίνυν καί τά ἐξ αὐτῆς, οὐδέ αἴτιον καί αἰτιατόν αὐτό ἑαυτοῦ τό ἕν. Εἰ τοίνυν ταῦθ' ἅπαντα, κατά ταῦτα κυρίως καθ' ἅ καί μερίζεται, ταῦτα δ' ἐστίν αἱ τρεῖς ὑποστάσεις, εἴτ' οὖν τά τρία πρόσωπα τῆς μιᾶς τῇ φύσει θεότητος, ὅταν οἱ Λατῖνοι λέγωσιν ἐξ ἀμφοτέρων τό ἕν, τῶν προσώπων δηλαδή φασι· κατά τοῦτο γάρ καί ἀμφότερα, τό γάρ ἕν οὐκ ἄν ῥηθείη ποτέ ἀμφότερα.

Ἐπεί τοίνυν κατά ταῦτα λέγουσιν ἐκ τῶν δύο τό ἕν, καθ' ἅ καί ἡ ἀρχή καί τό αἴτιον καί νοεῖται καί λέγεται, ἐκ δύο ἀρχῶν λέγουσι τό ἕν καί δύο ἀρχάς καί δύο αἴτια καί πολυθεΐαν εἰσάγουσιν. Οὐ γάρ μόνον ὅτι μία φύσις εἷς Θεός, ἀλλ' ὅτι καί ἕν πρόσωπον τήν ἀναφοράν ἔχει τά ἐξ αὐτοῦ, καί εἰς ἕν αἴτιον καί μίαν ἀρχήν τά

37

But we, along with the sacred Fathers, for the most part position the Spirit after the Son and the Son after the Father, so that we may always render the briefest possible doxology and thanksgiving and remembrance for the three greatest works and most providential economies wrought on our behalf as befits God. We do not do so because they are second or third in honor or in worth (for there is equality of honor), nor do we thus make the dyad an origin of the one, nor are we refering the one back to a dyad. But for us there is one God, with the Son and the Spirit referring back to one cause, from which cause alone each of them has existence; and also because there is one origin, namely, the Father, as also Gregory the Wonderworker says, and it is therefore in this respect that there is one God; and also because there is one nature in the three; for, by themselves [the terms] "the two" and "the three" and the "from Him" and the "referring back to Him" do not divide the nature but are divided in connection with it, and so, of course, neither do they strictly derive from the nature, although they cannot be apart from it, nor do they refer to it, although they cannot be without it. For, how would it be possible for the one both to beget and to emanate His own self and to refer back to Himself? So, the one is not an origin and that which are from it, nor is it a cause and itself its own caused. Accordingly, since all of these references, in their chief sense, correspond to that in which they are also divided, and that is the three hypostases or three persons of the Divinity one in nature, therefore, whenever the Latins say that the one is from both, they are speaking of the persons, since it is with reference to this that they are called 'both'; for the one would never be called "both".[160]

Therefore, since they say "the one is from the two" in the same sense in which the origin and the cause are understood and spoken of, they mean that the one is from two origins and thus they introduce two origins and two causes and polytheism. For, there is one God not only because there is one nature, but also because those that are

ἐξ ἀρχῆς ἀναφέρεται· οὐ τά δύο μόνον ἄμφω, ἀλλά καί ἑκάτερον
αὐτῶν χωρίς. Καὶ διά τοῦτο μία τῆς θεότητος ἀρχή καί εἷς Θεός
ἐστι καί κατά ταύτην τήν ἀναφοράν· ὅτι καί ἑκάτερον ἀναφέρεται
εἰς ἕν ἀμέσως. Εἰ γάρ μή ἀμέσως καί τό Πνεῦμα ἐκ Πατρός, τό
ἐμμέσως τοῦτο δύο ἐξ ἀνάγκης τά αἴτια ποιεῖ τοῦ Πνεύματος, τό τε
μέσον καί τό ἄκρον, καί οὐκ ἔνι διά τήν οὕτως ἔχουσαν ἀναφοράν
ἕνα Θεόν τά τρία εἶναι· μᾶλλον δέ οὐδέ Θεόν εἶναι τό διά μέσης
θεότητος ἐκ τοῦ Πατρός· ἐπί γάρ τά κτίσματα ἦλθεν ὁ Πατήρ διά
μέσης θεότητος κατά τούς θεολόγους.

38

Οὐ γάρ ὡς Πατήρ ταῦτ' ἔκτισεν, ἀλλ' ὡς Θεός. Ὁ δέ Υἱός εἷς
Θεός μετά Πατρός· διά τοῦτο ἐκ Πατρός δι' Υἱοῦ ὡς ἐξ ἑνός Θεοῦ
κτίσματα καί μία ἡ ἀρχή τῶν κτισμάτων, ὁ Θεός. Γεννᾷ δέ ὁ Θεός
καί ἐκπορεύει ὡς Πατήρ τῶν αὐτῷ συναϊδίων φώτων. Εἰ γοῦν ἐκ
Πατρός δι' Υἱοῦ ὡς ἐξ ἑνός ἐστι τό Πνεῦμα τό ἅγιον, οὐχ ὡς ἐξ
ἑνός ἔσται Θεοῦ, τοῦ Πατρός καί τοῦ Υἱοῦ, ἀλλ' ὡς ἐξ ἑνός ὄντος
Πατρός, τοῦ Πατρός καί τοῦ Υἱοῦ. Καί ταύτης τῆς συγχύσεως τίς
ἄν ἀτοπωτέρα γένοιτο; Διό καί ταύτην οἱ Λατῖνοι φεύγοντες, ὡς ἐξ
ἑνός φασι Θεοῦ· ὅ χώραν οὐδαμόθεν ἔχει, καθάπερ ἀναπέφηνε· καί
ταῦθ' ὅτι καί τό Πνεῦμα εἷς Θεός ἐστι μετά Πατρός τε καί Υἱοῦ.
Τοιγαροῦν, ἐπειδήπερ πάντη τε καί πάντως εἷς ὑπάρχει ὁ Πατήρ,
οὐκ ἄμφω ὁ Υἱός τε καί τό Πνεῦμα, ἀλλά καί χωρίς ἑκάτερον μίαν
ἀρχήν καί ἕν αἴτιον ἔχει μόνον, τόν Πατέρα. Καί οὕτω μία τῆς
θεότητος ἀρχή, κἄν οἱ λατινικῶς φρονοῦντες ἐγκαλούμενοι, πῶς
δύο λέγουσιν ἐπί τῆς θεότητος ἀρχάς, ἀπολογεῖσθαι οἴωνται μίαν
ἀρχήν ἰσχυριζόμενοι δοξάζειν τοῦ Υἱοῦ τε καί τοῦ Πνεύματος·
σοφίζεσθαι γάρ ἡμᾶς βουλόμενοι τοῦτο διαβεβαιοῦνται, ὡς καί
τήν ἀρχήν ἔφθημεν εἰπόντες. Αὐτό γάρ τοῦτό ἐστι τό παρ' ἡμῶν
ἐγκαλούμενον αὐτοῖς· πῶς Υἱοῦ μέν καί τοῦ Πνεύματος μίαν τήν

from Him have one person as [their point of] reference, and because those from the origin refer back to one cause and one origin, not only both of the two, but also each one of them separately. And therefore one is the origin of divinity and there is one God even with respect to this reference, because each refers back to one directly. For, if the Spirit was not directly from the Father, this mediation would necessarily create two causes for the Spirit, both a middle and an end, and with such a reference it would be impossible for the three to be one God. Or rather, what is from the Father through a mediating divinity cannot be God at all: the Father came by a mediating divinity only in the case of created things, according to the theologians.

38

For He did not create these things as Father but as God. Now the Son is one God with the Father. Therefore, created things are from the Father through the Son as from one God, and the origin of created things is one, that is, God. God begets and causes procession as Father of the lights coeternal with Him. If, therefore, the Holy Spirit is from the Father through the Son as from one [as the Latins say], He will not be as from one God, from the Father and the Son, but as from one Father, namely, the Father and the Son. And what could be more absurd than this confusion? And so, fleeing this the Latins say, "as from one God," which is totally impossible, as has become apparent, especially seeing that the Spirit is also one God, with the Father and the Son.

Consequently, forasmuch as the Father is entirely and in every respect one, then, the Son and the Spirit, not only both but also each one separately, have only one origin and cause, the Father. And this is how there is one origin of the divinity, even if the Latin-minded, when challenged with "How do you say that there are two origins of the divinity?", think they are defending themselves by claiming that they believe the origin of both the Son and the Spirit to be one. For they insist on this, wishing to deceive us, as we said before at the outset. But this is precisely the accusation which we lay

ἀρχήν φασι, τοῦ δέ ἑνός Πνεύματος δύο λέγουσιν ἀρχάς; Ἐκεῖνοι δέ περί τοῦ ἑνός ἐρωτώμενοι, σοφιστικῶς περί τῶν δύο τήν ἀπόκρισιν ποιοῦνται· σφῶν αὐτῶν μᾶλλον ἤ τῶν πυνθανομένων κατασοφιζόμενοι.

39

Πατήρ μέν οὖν καί ἀρχή καί αἴτιον ἐπί Θεοῦ πάντῃ τε καί πάντως ἕν· προβολεύς γάρ παρ᾽ οὐδενός τῶν ἀποστόλων ἤ τῶν εὐαγγελιστῶν ἐκλήθη, ἀλλά καί ἀντί τούτου ἡ τοῦ Πατρός ἀπέχρησεν αὐτοῖς φωνή. Ἀρχήν δέ λέγω οὐ τήν καταρχήν, οὐδέ τήν δημιουργικήν, οὐδ᾽ ᾗ τό τῆς δεσποτείας ἐστίν ἐπώνυμον.

40

Καί τοίνυν ὁ Θεός καί Πατήρ, καθό Πατήρ, ἀρχή καί αἴτιός ἐστι· καί καθό ἀρχή, Πατήρ τῶν φώτων, δηλαδή Υἱοῦ καί Πνεύματος· καί καθό αἴτιος, αἴτιος, ἀρχή τε καί Πατήρ. Εἰ οὖν καί ὁ Υἱός αἴτιός ἐστι τοῦ Πνεύματος, ἐξ ἀνάγκη ἔσται καί ἀρχή καί Πατήρ ὡς αἴτιος· ὡς γάρ τοῦ ἀνθρώπου, καθό ἀνθρώπου ἐπιστήμης δεκτικοῦ ὑπάρχοντος, τόν ἐπιστήμης δεκτικόν οὐκ ἔνι μή καί ἄνθρωπον ὑπάρχειν, οὕτω καί ἐπί Θεοῦ· ἐπεί ὁ Πατήρ, καθό Πατήρ, ἀρχή καί αἴτιός ἐστι, τόν αἴτιον ὑπάρχοντα οὐκ ἔνι μή καί ἀρχήν εἶναι καί Πατέρα, καίτοι τοῦ θεολόγου Γρηγορίου γράφοντος, «οὕτως εἶναι Υἱόν κυρίως τόν Υἱόν, ὅτι μή ἔστιν οὗτος καί Πατήρ».
Ὁρᾷς ἀθετουμένην σαφῶς τήν μοναρχίαν καί τό καθ᾽ ὑπόστασιν ἑνιαῖον τοῦ Πατρός ὑπό τῶν λεγόντων καί ἐκ τοῦ Υἱοῦ τό Πνεῦμα καί μή ἀναγόντων ἑκάτερον τῶν προσώπων εἰς μίαν μόνην, τήν τῆς θεότητος πηγήν; Μία γάρ φύσις καί οἱ πάντες ἄνθρωποι, ἀλλ᾽ οὐχ εἷς οἱ πάντες ἄνθρωπος. Καίτοι δι᾽ ἀλλήλων, μᾶλλον δέ διά τῶν πρό ἡμῶν, ἀναχθείημεν ἄν εἰς ἕνα τόν προπάτορα, ἀλλ᾽ εὐθύς πολλά τά αἴτια, καί οὐκ ἐξ ἑνός ἡμεῖς διά τοῦτο καί οὐχ εἷς. Ἆρ᾽ οὐ φανερῶς καινοτομεῖς ὁ λατινικῶς φρονῶν;

against them: how exactly do they on the one hand affirm that the origin of the Son and the Spirit is one, but on the other hand say that there are two origins for the one Spirit? When, however, they are asked about the one, they sophistically make a response about the two, fooling their own selves rather than the inquirers.

39

So then, Father and origin and cause are altogether and entirely one with respect to God. For He has never been called an originator by any of the Apostles or Evangelists; instead of this, the name of Father was enough for them. And when I speak of origin, I refer not to the [temporal] beginning, nor to the creative origin, nor to what is a name of the dominion.[161]

40

And consequently, the God and Father, insofar as He is a Father, is an origin and a cause; insofar as He is an origin, He is the Father of Lights, meaning, of the Son and the Spirit, and insofar as He is a cause, He is a cause and an origin and a Father. So, if the Son is a cause of the Spirit, as cause He will necessarily also be both a father and an origin. For as with man, since [only] man has the capacity of understanding, he that has the capacity of understanding cannot but be a man, so it is also with God. Since the Father, inasmuch as He is a Father, is an origin and cause, he that is a cause cannot but be also an origin and a Father. And so, Gregory the Theologian writes, "In this way is the Son, properly speaking, a Son, because He is not also a Father".[162]

Do you see that the monarchy has been clearly disregarded, as also the hypostatic singularity of the Father, by those who say that the Spirit is also from the Son and who do not lead each of the persons up to one and only fount, the fount of divinity? For, all men are also one nature, but they are not all one man. Even though we could be led through each other, or rather through those before us, up to the one forefather, yet in the immediate [past] the causes are many, and we are not from one; therefore we are not one. So you who think like the Latins, are you not clearly innovating?

41

Καί εἰ μή πρό ὑμῶν ἐλλιπές ἦν τό καθ᾽ ἡμᾶς εὐαγγέλιον, ὅ «ἐκηρύχθη ἐν ἔθνεσιν, ἐπιστεύθη ἐν κόσμῳ», καί «ἡ τοῦ Θεοῦ σωτήριος χάρις» καί ἡ κατ᾽ αὐτήν θεογνωσία, ἡ πᾶσιν ἐκφανεῖσα καί διδάξασα πάντας, εἰ μή «κεκένωται ἡ πίστις», εἰ μή διέφθαρται τά τῆς ὁμολογίας, αἷς καί ἐνήθλησαν καί ἐνήσκησαν «τό τῶν μαρτύρων ἡμῖν περικείμενον νέφος», ὁ τῶν ὁσίων παμπληθής κατάλογος, ὁ τῶν διδασκάλων θεοδίδακτος θίασος, πάντες οἱ ἔργῳ καί λόγῳ καί τοῖς καθ᾽ ἑαυτούς παθήμασι μαρτυρήσαντες τῇ ἀληθείᾳ, ὑπέρ ἧς καί μεχρι θανάτου καλῶς ποιοῦντες ἐνέστησαν, καί οὐχ ὑπέρ αὐτῆς μόνον ἤ καί ἑαυτῶν, ἀλλά καί ὑπέρ τοῦ ἡμετέρου στηριγμοῦ – εἰ μή ταῦθ᾽ ἅπαντα καί ἡ τῶν ἀπό Χριστοῦ καλουμένων πίστις ἐλλιπής, διακενῆς ὄντως σύ προσθήκας ἐξευρίσκεις καί κατά τῆς σεαυτοῦ καινοτομεῖς ψυχῆς.

Εἰ μέν γάρ ἐγίνωσκον καί ἐξ Υἱοῦ τό Πνεῦμα, τίνος ἕνεκεν οὐ παρρησίᾳ διατέλεσαν κηρύττοντες καί διά τῶν ἱερῶν συνόδων πολλῶν καί πολλάκις γενομένων βεβαιώσαντες; Ἀλλ᾽ οὐκ ἐγνωσμένον ἦν αὐτοῖς; Οὐκοῦν οὐδ᾽ ἦν οὕτω τἀληθές· πάντα γάρ ἐγνώρισεν αὐτοῖς ὁ δι᾽ ἡμᾶς ἐγνωσμένος καθ᾽ ἡμᾶς. Καί πάντα κατά τήν ἐπαγγελίαν ἐδίδαξεν αὐτούς τό Πνεῦμα καί διά τοῦτ᾽ ἐδίδαξεν, ἵν᾽ ἡμᾶς οὗτοι διδάξωσιν, ὡς ἐδιδάχθησαν, ὡς καί ἀνωτέρω εἴρηται. Εἰ γάρ τοῦτο λέγειν τολμήσεις, ὡς οὐκ ἔγνωσαν οἱ πρό ἡμῶν θεολόγοι τἀληθές, ὡς καί τοῦτο μηδέν ἧττον βλάσφημον ἀποπεμψόμεθα.

Τίς γάρ εἰ ὁ τοῦτο γρύζαι τολμῶν; Ποία δ᾽ ἰσάριθμος σύνοδος, μᾶλλον δέ πόσαι καί ποῦ μαρτυρηθεῖσαι παρά τοῦ Πνεύματος, ὅ καί ζῶσιν ἐκείνοις καί γεγονόσιν ἐξ ἀνθρώπων συνεμαρτύρησε, καί ἀεί συμμαρτυρεῖ τε καί συμμαρτυρήσει διά τῶν ἐπί τοῖς σοροῖς τούτων τελουμένων τε καί τελεσθησομένων θαυμάτων; Ἀλλ᾽

41

Unless prior to you our gospel was deficient, which was "preached unto the gentiles, believed on in the world";[163] unless likewise deficient was "the grace of God that bringeth salvation"[164] and the knowledge of God that comes by it, which has been revealed to all and has taught all; unless the "faith is made void";[165] unless the [articles] of the confession are corrupted, for which "the cloud of witnesses surrounding us"[166] struggled and ascetically strove, as also did the replete registry of the sanctified, the God-taught brotherhood of teachers, all who bore witness to the truth in deed and in word and in their own sufferings, for the sake of which they stood steadfast doing well even unto death, and not for the sake of truth alone or for themselves but also for our own strengthening—unless all these things and the faith of those called after Christ are deficient, truly you are vainly inventing additions and you innovate against your own soul.

For had they actually known that the Spirit is also from the Son, why did they not boldly continue to preach it and confirm it through the many sacred councils which many times occurred? But it was not known to them, was it? Then neither was it true. For He that was known among us for our sake, He made known all things to them. The Spirit also taught them all things, according to the promise,[167] and it was for this reason that He taught them, that they might teach us as they had been taught, as was also mentioned above.[168] For if you dare to say this, that the theologians before us did not know the truth, we shall dismiss this too as nothing less than blasphemy.

For who are you that dare mutter this? What sort of council [testifies to your claims], equal in number [with previous councils], or better, how many are there and where, to which the Spirit has borne witness, who has attested together with those saints, both when they were alive and when they had gone out from among men, and who always attests, and will attest, by wonders that are wrought, and will be wrought, upon their tombs? Yet the Latin

ἔχω κἀγώ, φησί, πολλοὺς τῶν πατέρων συμμαρτυροῦντάς μοι τῇ προσθήκῃ. Τί οὖν, ἕτερα μέν οὗτοι κοινῇ συνειλεγμένοι παρεδίδουν ἐκκλησίᾳ, ἕτερα δέ καθ᾿ ἑαυτοὺς ἐδογμάτιζον; Οὔμενουν. Ἀλλ᾿ ἤ παραχαράττεις αὐτός ἤ παραλογίζῃ καί παρεξηγῇ, μή μετά τοῦ Πνεύματος ἑρμηνεύων τά εἰρημένα διά τοῦ Πνεύματος.

42

Οὐ μήν, ἀλλ᾿ εἰ καί τοῦτο θείημεν, ὅπερ οὐκ ἔστιν, οὐ προσδεκτέα μᾶλλον τά κοινῇ παραδεδομένα τῶν ἰδίως εἰρημένων ἑκάστῳ; Ἐκεῖνα μέν γάρ πρός τῷ πάντων εἶναι καί ἀνεπιχείρητα τοῖς κακουργοῦσι καί τῷ παραχαράττειν δολοῦσι τόν τῆς ἀληθείας λόγον, πᾶσιν ἐγνωσμένα σοφοῖς τε καί ἰδιώταις καί διά στόματος ἀεί φερόμενα. Τά δέ μή ἐπί τοσοῦτο καθωμιλημένα ὕποπτά ἐστι καί μάλιστα προαγόμενα παρά Λατίνων, οἵ καί τῷ φανερωτάτῳ τῆς πίστεως συμβόλῳ διά προσθήκης ὑπεβούλευσαν. Οἱ γάρ τῷ ἐν τοῖς τῶν ὡς ἀληθῶς χριστιανῶν ἁπάντων στόμασι κειμένῳ καί τῆς ἡμέρας ἑκάστης πολλάκις ἀνακηρυττομένῳ προσθήκην ἐπινοήσαντές τε καί τολμήσαντες, τί οὐκ ἄν ἔδρασαν ἐν τοῖς ἀγνοουμένοις παρά τῶν πλειόνων; Τά γοῦν μή κοινά μηδέ καθωμιλημένα ὕποπτά ἐστι, μή πονηρός ἄνθρωπος ἐνέσπειρεν αὐτοῖς ζιζάνια. Ταῦτα ἄρα, κἄν μέν ὁμολογῶσι τῇ κοινῇ ὁμολογίᾳ, προσδεκτέα· ἄν δέ μή, οὐχί.

Ὅμως ἐν δευτέρῳ λόγῳ τά δοκοῦντα συμμαρτυρεῖν σου τῇ καινοτομίᾳ ὀψόμεθα καί ἀπελέγξομεν, Θεοῦ διδόντος, οὐκ ἐκεῖνα, ἄπαγε, ἀλλά σέ τά καλῶς λελεγμένα ἐκλαμβάνοντα κακῶς, καί μή τοῖς σαφέσι τά ἀσαφῆ καί τοῖς παρρησίᾳ εἰρημένοις τά ἐν τῷ κρυπτῷ συμβιβάζοντα πρός δύναμιν.

says, "I also have many of the Fathers who attest to my addition."
What, then? Were these same fathers delivering one thing to the
Church when they convened publicly and dogmatizing something
different by themselves? Absolutely not. Rather, either you yourself
are falsifying them or you are misled by fallacious reasoning and
so misunderstand them, not interpreting with the Spirit things that
have been said through the Spirit.

42

Nevertheless, even if we were to assume this (which is not possible),
must not the things that have been handed down publicly be
accepted rather than what has been spoken by each privately? For,
because those writings belong to all, they cannot be attacked by the
malicious workers and by the efforts of deceitful people to recoin
the Word of truth, since they are known to all, both the educated[169]
and to the private laymen, and are ever borne in their speech. But
writings not so familiar are suspicious, and especially as they are
produced by the Latins, who through their addition have plotted
even against the conspicuous Symbol of Faith. For having invented
and audaciously ventured an addition into a text that is in the
mouths of all true Christians and which is proclaimed many times
every day, what else would they not have done in the texts unknown
to the masses? Therefore, writings which are not common nor
familiar are held in suspicion, for fear lest an evil man have sown
tares among them. These very writings, if in fact they agree with
the common confession, must be received, but if they do not, they
cannot be received.

In a second discourse, however, we shall look at what things appear
to corroborate your innovation and, God willing, refute them; not
refuting them—banish the thought!—but refuting you who take
wrongly the things that have been spoken well and who do not
reconcile, as much as possible, the unclear statements with the clear
ones and what has been said in secret with what has been said with
bold certitude.

Νῦν δ' ἀνακεφαλαιωσώμεθα τόν νῦν λόγον, κᾶθ' οὕτω τά λείποντα προσθῶμεν.

1.) Πρῶτον μέν οὖν ἐξελήλεκται κενή τυγχάνουσα παντάπασιν ἡ τῆς προσθήκης τούτων πρόφασις.

2.) Ἔπειτα δέδεικται συνυπακουόμενον τό "μόνου", ὅταν λέγηται παρά τοῦ Πατρός ἐκπορευόμενον τό Πνεῦμα τό ἅγιον· ἐπεί κἄν τῷ αὐτῷ συμβόλῳ παρά τοῦ Πατρός ἀκούοντες γεννηθέντα τόν Υἱόν, ἐκτός ἀντιλογίας πάσης δεχόμεθα συνυπακουόμενον τό "μόνου".

3.) Τούτῳ συνείρομεν ἑξῆς· ὡς εἰ καί ἀνεπιλήπτως εἶχε τό λέγειν καί ἐκ τοῦ Υἱοῦ τό Πνεῦμα, τῷ συμβόλῳ προστεθεῖσθαι παρά Λατίνων οὐκ ἐχρῆν. Ἐπεί κἄν εὖ ἔχον εἰς τό ἑξῆς ἀναφανῇ, προσθετέον οὐκ ἄν εἴη· καί τοῖς πρό ἡμῶν γάρ, καίτοι συνεληλυθόσι καί συνεζητακόσι πᾶσι καί αὐτοῖς τοῖς τῆς παλαιᾶς Ῥώμης προεστῶσιν, οὐδέν τῶν ἀναφανέντων εὐσεβῶς ἔχειν προσετέθη.

4.) Κἀντεῦθεν ἀνεφάνη τῶν δικαίων ὄν πρῶτον ἀπαιτεῖν αὐτούς τήν προσθήκην ἐξελεῖν καί μή διά τήν περιωπήν τοῦ περιόντος πάπα τούς μεμαρτυρημένῳ παρά Θεοῦ τέλει κατακλείσαντας τόν βίον ἀποστέργειν, εἶτα συζητεῖν μετ' αὐτῶν ἀνέχεσθαι περί αὐτῆς.

5.) Μετά τοῦτο πρός τούς εὐγνωμόνως τῶν λόγων ἀκρωμένους λέγομεν, ὡς καί ἀμφότερα ἐκ τοῦ Πατρός ἀκούοντες, ἔχομεν συνυπακούειν τό "ἐκ μόνου", κἄν μή συνεκφωνῆται.

6.) Ἀλλά καί ἐκ τοῦ Πατρός ἐκπορευτῶς τό Πνεῦμα λέγοντες τό ἐκπορεύειν τῇ πατρικῇ ὑποστάσει ἐφαρμόζομεν· ἡ γάρ οὐσία πάντῃ τε καί πάντως μία τῶν τριῶν, οὐκ ἔνι δέ τά τῆς πατρικῆς ὑποστάσεως ἔχειν τόν Υἱόν· ὥστε οὐχί καί ἐκ τοῦ Υἱοῦ τό Πνεῦμα.

But now, let us summarize the present treatise, and then let us thus add what is left.

1.) Therefore, at the first, it was proven that their excuse for the addition is entirely vain.

2.) Then, it has been shown that the "only" is implied whenever it is said that the Holy Spirit proceeds from the Father, since, when we hear in the same Symbol that the Son has been begotten from the Father, we accept without any argument that the "only" is implied.

3.) To this we add in order that, even if it were possible to say without censure that the Spirit is from the Son, it still should not have been added to the Symbol by the Latins, since, even if in the future it should be shown to be good, it should not be added; furthermore, because nothing that was shown to be pious was added by our forebears, although they had all gathered, even the superiors of Old Rome themselves, and examined the matter at hand together.

4.) Hence, it was demonstrated that it is just, first, to demand from them to remove this addition and not to reject those who concluded their life with a blessed end (testified by God) in deference to the prominent position of the present Pope; and then to discuss with them whether this should be tolerated.

5.) After this, we say to those listeners that are receptive of the arguments: when hearing that both are from the Father, we must understand "only from" as implied, even if it is not expressed in the text.

6.) But also when we say that the Spirit is from the Father by way of procession, we attribute causing procession to the paternal hypostasis. For the essence is in every way and entirely one for the three. It is not, then, possible for the Son to have that which is of the paternal hypostasis. Therefore, the Spirit is not also from the Son.

7.) Μετά τοῦτο ἐζηλέχθησαν οἱ λατινικῶς φρονοῦντες μηκέτι ἐξ
ἑνός δύνασθαι τά δύο πρόσωπα τῆς θεότητος φρονεῖν, ὡς ἐν δυσί
προσώποις τό αἴτιον τιθέμενοι καί ταῦτα διαφόρως, ἀλλ᾽ οὐδέ Θεόν
ἕνα λέγειν διά τήν τοιαύτην πρός τό ἕν ἀναφοράν· οὐδέ γάρ εἷς
ἄνθρωπος πάππος, πατήρ τε καί υἱός, κατά τόν σοφόν τῆς Νύσσης
πρόεδρον, ἐπειδήπερ εἰς δύο πρόσωπα τό αἴτιον ἀναφέρεται. Καί
πρός τούτῳ παρεστήσαμεν, ὡς, καθάπερ δύο τά αἰτιατά, ἐπειδήπερ
τό αἰτιατόν ἐν δυσίν φασιν αὐτοί προσώποις.

8.) Πρός δέ τούτοις, ἐπεί κατά τούς θεοσόφους θεολόγους, ὡς ὁ
Υἱός ἐκ τοῦ Πατρός ἐστιν, οὕτω καί τό Πνεῦμα, πλήν τοῦ γεννητῶς
τε καί ἐκπορευτῶς, εἰ ὁ Υἱός ἀμέσως καί οὐχί καί ἐκ τοῦ Πνεύματος,
ἀλλ᾽ ἐκ μόνου τοῦ Πατρός, καί τό Πνεῦμα ἐκ τοῦ Πατρός ἀμέσως,
ἀλλ᾽ οὐχί καί ἐκ τοῦ Υἱοῦ.

9.) Προσαπεδείξαμεν ὡς, ἐπεί καί νοῦς λέγεται Χριστοῦ τό Πνεῦμα,
καθάπερ καί ἡμῶν ἑκάστου ὁ οἰκεῖος, κατά μέν τήν ἐνέργειαν αὐτοῦ
ἐστι καί ἐξ αὐτοῦ, κατά δέ τήν ὑπόστασιν αὐτοῦ μέν ἐστι φυσικῶς,
ἀλλ᾽ οὐκ ἐξ αὐτοῦ, ἀλλ᾽ ἐκ μόνου τοῦ Πατρός.

10.) Πρός τούτῳ τοῦ μή χάριτι, φύσει δέ εἶναι ἐκ Πατρός τό Πνεῦμα,
ἐκ μόνου τοῦ Πατρός ἔχειν τήν ὕπαρξιν ἐδείχθη.

11.) Καί ἀπό τοῦ πάντα ἔχειν ἑκάτερον τά τοῦ Πατρός, ἄνευ τῆς
ἀγεννησίας καί τῆς γεννήσεως καὶ τῆς ἐκπορεύσεως κατά τούς
θεολόγους.

12.) Κἀντεῦθεν ἀναπεφήνασιν οἱ μέν Λατῖνοι προστιθέντες καί
κατά διάνοιαν ἐν τῷ τῆς πίστεως συμβόλῳ· ἡμεῖς δέ ἀναπεφήναμεν
μηδέ κατά τόν ἔξω λόγον τῇ κατά τό θεῖον σύμβολον εὐσεβεῖ
διανοίᾳ προστιθέντες.

7.) After this, it was proven that the Latin-minded are no longer able to maintain that the two persons of the divinity are from one, since they place the cause in two persons, and differently at that. But neither are they able to say that God is one, on account of such a reference back to the one. For neither is a grandfather, a father, and a son one man, according to the wise primate of Nyssa, forasmuch as the cause refers to two persons. Besides this we proved that, just as two are the caused, [so the causes will also be two, according to them,] inasmuch as they themselves say that what is caused is in two persons.

8.) Furthermore, according to the divinely wise theologians, as the Son is from the Father, so also is the Spirit, except for being by begetting or procession. Thus, if the Son is directly and not also from the Spirit but from the Father alone, the Spirit will also be directly from the Father and not also from the Son.

9.) We have also demonstrated that, since the Spirit is called the mind of Christ, just as is the case with the individual intellect of each one of us, according to energy the Holy Spirit is His and from Him, while according to hypostasis He is His naturally, yet not from Him but only from the Father.

10.) Moreover, it has been shown that the Spirit has existence only from the Father by the fact that He is from the Father not by grace but by nature;

11.) And from the fact that each of them possesses all things of the Father, apart from unbegottenness, begottenness, and procession, according to the theologians.

12.) Hence it was shown plainly that the Latins added to the Symbol of Faith on the basis of their reasoning, while we did not add to the reverential reasoning of the divine Symbol on the basis of external argumentation.

13.) Κατηγορήσαμεν τῶν Λατίνων ὡς ἐκεῖνα δογματιζόντων, ἐξ ὧν δύο ἀναφέρονται τοῦ ἑνός Πνεύματος ἀρχαί. Οἱ δέ μηδέν κωλύειν πρός τό μίαν εἶναι ταύτας ἔφησαν, ἐπειδήπερ ἡ μία ἐστίν ἐκ τῆς ἑτέρας· καί ἀπεδείχθησαν καί κατά τοῦτο βλασφημοῦντες.

14.) Εἶτ᾽ αὖθις ἡμεῖς ἀναλαβόντες τόν περί τῆς ἀρχῆς λόγον, ἐδείξαμεν κατ᾽ οὐδένα τρόπον δύο εἶναι τοῦ ἑνός Πνεύματος ἀρχάς.

15.) Παρεστήσαμεν ἐκ τοῦ τά κοινά Πατρί τε καί Υἱῷ, καί τῷ Πνεύματι κοινά εἶναι μαρτυρεῖσθαι, ὅτι οὐχί καί τοῦ Υἱοῦ τό ἐκπορεύειν· ἦν γάρ ἄν τοῦτο καί τοῦ Πνεύματος· ἐν ᾧ προσεξηλέγξαμεν αὐτούς, ἀδιάφορα τοῖς φυσικοῖς τά ὑποστατικά ποιοῦντας. Εἰ δέ τοῦτο, καί ταῖς προσκυνηταῖς ὑποστάσεσι τήν θείαν φύσιν.

16.) Ἐκ τοῦ ἀσεβές εἶναι τήν δημιουργικῶς διά τοῦ Υἱοῦ τό εἶναι σχοῦσαν κτίσιν ἐκ τοῦ Υἱοῦ μή λέγειν, ἀλλά τήν δημιουργικήν ἰδιότητα μόνῳ διδόναι τῷ Πατρί, κατ᾽ ἀνάγκην ἀκολούθως συνηγάγομεν, ὡς, εἰ καί ἐκπορευτῶς τό Πνεῦμα δι᾽ Υἱοῦ τό εἶναι εἶχε, δυσσεβοῦς ἦν ἄν λέγειν, ὅτι Πνεῦμα ἐκ τοῦ Υἱοῦ οὐ λέγομεν καί ὡς ἡ ἐκπορευτική ἰδιότης μόνον τοῦ Πατρός ἐστιν. Ἐπεί δ᾽ οἱ ταῦθ᾽ οὕτω λέγοντες οὐκ εὐσεβεῖς μόνον, ἀλλά καί θεοφόροι, δυσσεβεῖς οὐκοῦν οἱ λέγοντες καί ἐξ Υἱοῦ τό Πνεῦμα.

17.) Καί ὡς, εἰ δι᾽ Υἱοῦ τό Πνεῦμα, ὁμοῦ τε καί χωρίς ἑκάτερος Πατήρ ἄν λέγοιτο καί προβολεύς, ὡς καί ἐπί τῆς κτίσεως, ποιητής τε καί Πατήρ.

18.) Ἐκ τοῦ πάντα ἔχειν θεολογεῖσθαι τόν Υἱόν τά τοῦ Πατρός ἄνευ τῆς αἰτίας, ἥτις οὐκ ἄν ἡ τῶν κτισμάτων εἴη, τοιγαροῦν ἡ τοῦ Υἱοῦ καί τοῦ Πνεύματός ἐστιν, ἀπεδείξαμεν αὖθις οὐχί καί ἐκ τοῦ Υἱοῦ τό Πνεῦμα ἐκπορεύεσθαι.

13.) We accused the Latins of dogmatizing things from which flows [the idea of] two origins of the one Holy Spirit. They, however, said that there is nothing to prevent these from being one, forasmuch as the one [the Son] is from the other [the Father]. They have been proven to be blaspheming in this regard, as well.

14.) Afterward, resuming our discussion concerning the origin, we have shown that there cannot in any way exist two origins of the Holy Spirit.

15.) Based on the fact that what things are common to the Father and to the Son are also testified to be common to the Spirit, we presented that to cause procession is not also the Son's; for if this were so, it would also be the Spirit's. Herein, we censured them for rendering the hypostatic properties of no difference from the natural properties. But if this be so, then they are also making even the divine nature of no difference from the worshipful hypostases.

16.) From the fact that it is irreverent to say that creation, which acquired being creatively through the Son, is not from the Son, but rather to attribute the creative property to the Father alone, we necessarily concluded that it follows that, if the Spirit had existence also from the Son by means of procession, it would have been impious to say that the Spirit is not from the Son and that the processional property is only the Father's. Since, however, those who say these things thus are not only pious but also God-bearers, then impious are those who say that the Spirit is also from the Son.

17.) Also we showed that, if the Spirit were through the Son, then, both together and separately, each would be called Father and Originator, as in creation each of them is called Creator and Father.

18) From it being theologized that the Son has all things of the Father except the cause (which would not be the cause of created things and so it would be the cause of the Son and Spirit), we have demonstrated again that the Spirit does not proceed also from the Son.

19.) Καί μάρτυρας παρηγάγομεν ἀπαγορεύοντας τήν λατινικήν προσθήκην.

20.) Ἐδείξαμεν αὖθις ἐκ τοῦ μή τόν Υἱόν καί ἐκ τοῦ Πνεύματος ὑπάρχειν, ὅτι καί τό Πνεῦμα οὐχί καί ἐκ τοῦ Υἱοῦ τό εἶναι ἔχει.

21.) Εἶτα, ἐκ τῶν ἀπηριθμημένων καί τεθεωρημένων τοῖς ἁγίοις ὀνομάτων τοῦ Υἱοῦ, παρεστήσαμεν ὡς οὐχί καί ἐκ τοῦ Υἱοῦ τό Πνεῦμα τό ἅγιόν ἐστι.

22.) Πάλιν ἐκ τοῦ μή ἐκπορευτόν ἁπλῶς, ἀλλά τό ἐκ τοῦ Πατρός ἐκπορευτόν ἴδιον εἶναι τοῦ θείου Πνεύματος, τούς θεολόγους μαρτυρεῖν παρεστήσαμεν ἐκ μόνου τοῦ Πατρός τό Πνεῦμα τό ἅγιον.

23.) Καί ἀπό τοῦ ἕνωσιν Υἱοῦ καί Πνεύματος εἶναι τόν Πατέρα· ἡ γάρ τῶν ἄλλων ἑκατέρου μεσότης ἐν τοῖς ὀνόμασι κεῖται.

24.) Καί ἀπό τοῦ μή ἐκ τῆς ἀρχῆς τό Πνεῦμα λέγεσθαι, ἀλλά μετά τῆς ἀρχῆς, ἀρχῆς εἶναι θεολογουμένου τοῦ Υἱοῦ.

25.) Καί ὡς ὁ δι' Υἱοῦ καθ' ὕπαρξιν τό Πνεῦμα λέγων καί εἰς τήν 'ἐκ' τήν 'διά' μεταλαμβάνων ἁμαρτάνει. Ὡς γάρ συμπαρομαρτοῦν τῷ λόγῳ δι' αὐτοῦ τό Πνεῦμα λέγεται καί οὐκ ἐξ ἐκείνου, ἀλλά σύν ἐκείνῳ, γεννηθέντι ἐκ τοῦ Πατρός, καί τό Πνεῦμα ἐκπορεύεται.

26.) Αὖθις ἐκ τοῦ θεολογεῖσθαι τῶν τριῶν προσώπων ἕκαστον, τῶν καθ' ὑπόστασιν ἑτέρων δύο μέσον.

27.) Καί πρός ἄλληλα ἔχειν ὡς ἕκαστον πρός ἑαυτό.

28.) Καί τῷ δεύτερον ἀπό τοῦ Πατρός καί τό Πνεῦμα λέγεσθαι, καθά καί ὁ Υἱός, ἀμέσως ἑκάτερον ὑπάρχον ἐκ Πατρός ἐδείχθη μή ἐοικυίας τῆς θεολογικῆς μεσότητος τοῖς κειμένοις ἐφεξῆς τρισί σημείοις, ἀλλά τοῖς ἐπί τῶν τοῦ τριγώνου γωνιῶν.

19.) We also presented witnesses who forbid the Latin addition.

20.) We have shown, again, that the Spirit does not have being from the Son on the basis that the Son also does not have existence from the Spirit.

21.) Then, from the names of the Son that have been enumerated and inspected by the saints, we presented that the Holy Spirit is not also from the Son.

22.) Again, from the fact that the property of the divine Spirit is not simply to proceed, but to proceed from the Father, we presented that the theologians witness that the Holy Spirit is only from the Father;

23.) And from the fact that the Father is the union of the Son and the Spirit; for the medial position of each of the others is found in the names;

24.) And from the fact that the Spirit is said to be not from the origin but with the origin, when the Son is theologized as being the origin;

25.) And that he sins who says that the Spirit has existence through the Son and interprets "through" as meaning "from". For, the Spirit is said to be through Him and not from Him, since He accompanies the Word; but the Spirit proceeds together with Him, who was begotten from the Father.

26.) Again, from the fact that each of the three persons is theologized as a middle point of the other two hypostatically.

27.) And that they are related to one other as each is related to Himself.

28.) And by the Spirit being called second from the Father, just as the Son, it has been shown that each exists directly from the Father, since theological middleness is not likened to three points lying in a row but to the three points of the corners of a triangle.

29.) Μετά τοῦτο διττῆς φανερῶς δειχθείσης τῆς τοῦ Πνεύματος προόδου, προσεδείχθη καί τῶν προόδων ἑκατέραν κατάλληλον τήν παῦλαν ἔχειν. Κἀντεῦθεν πάλιν, ὡς οὐχί καί ἐκ τοῦ Υἱοῦ τό εἶναι ἔχει τό Πνεῦμα τό ἅγιον.

30.) Πάλιν ἐκ τοῦ λέγειν καί τόν Υἱόν ἀρχήν τοῦ θείου Πνεύματος ἀναπεφήνασιν οἱ λατινικῶς φρονοῦντες τοῖς κτιστοῖς συντάττοντες τό θεῖον Πνεῦμα.

31.) Αὖθις ἐκ τοῦ μή ἔχειν κοινωνίαν κατά τό θεογόνον τόν Πατέρα καί τόν Υἱόν παρίσταται μή εἶναι καί ἐκ τοῦ Υἱοῦ τό Πνεῦμα.

32.) Πρός δέ τούτοις, ἐκ τοῦ τά κοινά τῆς ἀνωτάτω Τριάδος ἐπίσης εἶναι τῶν θείων ὑποστάσεων ἑκάστῃ, ἀνεφάνησαν οἱ λατινικῶς φρονοῦντες μήτε τόν Υἱόν μήτε τό Πνεῦμα λέγοντες ἐκ τοῦ Πατρός, μηδ᾽ ὑποστατικάς ἔχειν τόν Θεόν διαφοράς.

33.) Εἶτα περί τῆς ἐν Θεῷ τάξεως ποιησάμενοι τόν λόγον προσαπεδείξαμεν μή γνωστόν εἶναι τοῖς ἁγίοις, ὅπως ἔχει πρός ἄλληλα σχέσεώς τε καί τάξεως ὁ Υἱός τε καί τό Πνεῦμα τό ἅγιον· καί συμφωνεῖν κἄν τούτῳ παρεστήσαμεν τούς μεγάλους, Βασίλειον καί Γρηγόριον καί Ἰωάννην τόν χρυσοῦν θεολόγον, πρός δέ καί τήν εὐσεβῆ καί ἀνωμολογημένην ἐπί τοῦ Θεοῦ τάξιν παρεστήσαμέν τε καί διευκρινήσαμεν. Κἀντεῦθεν ἀπηλέγχθησαν οἱ λατινικῶς φρονοῦντες τήν μέν εὐσεβῆ τάξιν ἀγνοοῦντες, ἅ δέ οἱ θεολόγοι μή εἰδέναι ὁμολογοῦσιν ὡς ὑπέρ ἡμᾶς, αὐτοί ταῦτα γινώσκειν ἀκριβῶς αὐχοῦντες καί οὕτω καινοφωνοῦντές τε καί βλασφημοῦντες περί τήν ἐκπόρευσιν τοῦ παναγίου Πνεύματος.

34.) Ἡμεῖς δέ καί λόγον ἐκδεδώκαμεν πολυειδῶς δεικνύοντες τίνος ἕνεκεν ὡς ἐπί πλεῖστον ὁ μέν Υἱός μετά τόν Πατέρα, τό δέ Πνεῦμα μετά τόν Υἱόν ἡμῖν ὑμνεῖται καί τοῖς μυουμένοις παραδίδοται.

35.) Καί ὡς ἑπόμενοι καλῶς οἱ θεολόγοι τῷ λόγῳ τῆς μυήσεως, ἐπί

29.) After this, when it was clearly shown that the procession of the Spirit is twofold, it was also shown that each of the processions has a corresponding resting point. This shows again that the Holy Spirit does not have being also from the Son.

30.) Again, by saying that the Son also is an origin of the divine Spirit, the Latin-minded have been plainly shown to place the divine Spirit in the same rank as creatures.

31.) Again, from the fact that the Father and the Son cannot share in the generation of divinity, it is presented that the Holy Spirit does not have being from the Son.

32.) In addition to this, from the fact that the things which are common for the Most High Trinity likewise belong to each of the divine hypostases, it was shown that the Latin-minded say that neither the Son nor the Spirit is from the Father and that God does not have hypostatic differences.

33.) Next, after we had made an argument concerning the order in God, we have demonstrated that it is not known to the saints how the Son and the Holy Spirit have order and relationship in relation to each other. We further presented that the great theologians agree in this, Basil and Gregory and John the golden theologian. Besides this, we also presented and further clarified the pious and traditionally confessed order of God. And in this, the Latin-minded have been refuted, shown to be ignorant of this pious order, boasting that they exactly know those things which the theologians admit they do not know as they transcend us, and thus they innovate and blaspheme regarding the procession of the All-Holy Spirit.

34.) We have put forward an explanation showing in many ways for what reason, for the most part, we hymn the Son after the Father and the Spirit after the Son and why we traditionally hand this down to those that are being initiated.

35.) And that the theologians who followed the initiating word

πάντων τῶν κοινῶς ἐνθεωρουμένων τοῖς τρισίν, οὕτω φασίν ἔχειν πρός τόν Υἱόν τό Πνεῦμα, ὡς πρός τόν Πατέρα ὁ Υἱός.

36.) Καί ὅτι τοῦτο μή συνετῶς ἀκούσαντες Εὐνόμιός τε πρότερον καί οἱ λατινικῶς πεφρονηκότες ὕστερον, τρίτον ἀπό τοῦ Πατρός ἐδογμάτισαν τόν Πνεῦμα τό ἅγιον· κἀντεῦθεν ὁ μέν Εὐνόμιος τρίτον καί τῇ φύσει, Λατῖνοι δέ καί ἐκ τοῦ Υἱοῦ τό εἶναι ἔχειν προσεδογμάτισαν.

37.) Ἔτι δείκνυμεν, ὡς οὐκ ἄμφω μόνον ὁ Υἱός τε καί τό Πνεῦμα, ἀλλά καί ἑκάτερον αὐτῶν χωρίς, ἀμέσως ἀναφέρεται πρός τόν Πατέρα· καί ὡς, εἰ μή τοῦθ᾽ οὕτως ἔχει, οὐδέ Θεός εἷς ἔσται.

38.) Πρός δέ τούτοις ἐκ τοῦ τόν Θεόν καί Πατέρα ὡς Θεόν ἀλλ᾽ οὐχ ὡς Πατέρα κτίζειν, γεννᾶν δέ καί ἐκπορεύειν ὡς Πατέρα, δείκνυμεν, ὡς εἰ κατά Λατίνους ἐκ τοῦ Πατρός καί ἐκ τοῦ Υἱοῦ, ὡς ἐξ ἑνός τό Πνεῦμα, οὐχ ὡς ἐξ ἑνός [Θεοῦ, ἀλλ᾽ ὡς ἐξ ἑνός] ἔσται Πατρός, τοῦ Πατρός καί τοῦ Υἱοῦ. Καί οὕτω τό λατινικόν φρόνημα τελέως ἐξελέγχεται, καί ὡς ἐξ ἀμφοτέρων αὐτῶν δυσσεβῶς καθ᾽ ὕπαρξιν τό Πνεῦμα λέγον καί ὡς ἐξ ἑνός Θεοῦ τῶν ἀμφοτέρων.

39.) Ἔτι μετά τοῦτο περί ἀρχῆς φαμεν, καί ὡς οἱ λατινικῶς φρονοῦντες σοφιστικῶς ἀποκρίνονται πρός τούς ἐρωτῶντας αὐτούς, εἰ δύο λέγουσιν ἀρχάς τῆς θεότητος τοῦ Πνεύματος.

40.) Ἐντεῦθεν πάλιν ἐκ τοῦ Πατέρα φώτων θεολογεῖσθαι παρά τοῦ ἀποστόλου τόν Πατέρα, καί τόν Υἱόν κἀντεῦθεν Πατέρα λέγοντες οἱ λατινικῶς φρονοῦντες ἀποδείκνυται· καί ἀθετοῦντες σαφῶς τήν μοναρχίαν καί τό καθ᾽ ὑπόστασιν ἑνιαῖον τοῦ Πατρός.

41.) Ἀναφαίνομεν τό αἰδέσιμον ἔχειν καί ἀπό τῆς ἀρχαιότητος τό καθ᾽ ἡμᾶς δόγμα, καί ὡς ἀνελλιπές μηδαμῶς προσθήκης δεῖσθαι.

42.) Ἔπειτα καί τοῦτ᾽ εἰπόντες, ὅτι τά κοινῶς εἰρημένα παρά

well say that, inasmuch as all things are perceived as common in the three, the Spirit is related toward the Son as the Son is related toward the Father.

36.) And we showed that Eunomius first, and later the Latin-minded, not having listened wisely to this, dogmatized the Holy Spirit as third from the Father. It was on this basis that Eunomius dogmatized that He is third also by nature, while the Latins dogmatized that He has existence also from the Son.

37.) We further show that the Son and the Spirit refer directly to the Father not only together but also each of them separately; and that, unless this is so, God will not be one.

38.) Furthermore, from the fact that God the Father creates as God, not as Father, while he begets and causes procession as Father, we show that, if according to the Latins the Spirit is from the Father and from the Son as from one, it will not be as from one God but as from one Father, from the Father and the Son.[170] And so the Latin mindset is absolutely checked, as it impiously states that the Spirit is existentially both from the two of them and as from one God, the two of them.

39.) Further, we speak concerning the origin, and that those minded like the Latins answer like sophists to those enquiring whether they hold that there are two origins of the divinity of the Spirit.

40.) Thenceforth, once again, given that the Father is theologized as Father of the Lights according to the Apostle,[171] it has been demonstrated that the Latin-minded [stance] implies that the Son is a Father and they are clearly despising the monarchy and the hypostatic singleness of the Father.

41.) We show that even from ancient times our dogma is venerable, and, since it lacked nothing, there is no need for an addition at all.

42.) Then, we also said this, that what has publicly been spoken

τῶν πατέρων στερκτέα μᾶλλον τῶν ἰδίως τισί τούτων εἰρημένων ἑκάστῳ, καί ὅτι τά μή καθωμιλημένα ὕποπτά ἐστι, καί μάλιστα παρά Λατίνων προαγόμενα τῶν καί τοῖς φανεροῖς παρεγχειρούντων, ὑπεσχέθημεν, σύν Θεῷ δ᾽ ὁ λόγος ἐν δευτέρῳ λόγῳ τά διαφωνεῖν δοκοῦντα συμφωνοῦντα παραστήσειν.

Ταῦτα μέν οὖν ἀνωτέρω διά πλειόνων ἀποδέδεικται· καί ὡς ἡμεῖς καί ἡ καθ᾽ ἡμᾶς ὁμολογία πανταχόθεν ἔχει τό ἀσφαλές καί στέφανος ἡμῖν ἐστι καυχήσεως καί ἀκαταίσχυντος ἐλπίς. Εἰ γάρ μή οὕτω καί ἡμεῖς κατά ταύτην ἐλλιπεῖς, πολλῷ μᾶλλον οἱ ἐκ παλαιοῦ καί μυηθέντες ἄνωθεν καί τό καθ᾽ ἡμᾶς γένος θεοκινήτως μυήσαντες ἀπόστολοι, προφῆται, σεπταί σύνοδοι πατέρων πολλαί τε καί πολυάριθμοι. Εἰ δέ καί γινώσκοντες ἑτέρως, ὡς νῦν ἰσχυρίζονται τό τῶν Λατίνων γένος, οὐ πεφανερώκασιν ἡμῖν, καί ταῦτα τοῦ Κυρίου πρός αὐτούς εἰπόντος, «ἅ ἠκούσατε ἐν τῇ σκοτίᾳ, κηρύξατε ἐν τῷ φωτί», πῶς οὐκ ἄν τῶν ὑπευθύνων εἶεν; Ἀλλ᾽ ὁ Θεός αὐτούς δι᾽ ἔργων κἀνταῦθα μεγίστων ἐδικαίωσεν.

Οὐ γάρ ἐφρόνουν κατά τούς Λατίνους, ἄπαγε, ὡς καί τοῦτο δέδεικται, ἀλλά καί ἐγνώκασι καί παραδεδώκασιν ἡμῖν μίαν καί μόνην ἀρχήν τῆς θεότητος, ἕνα Πατέρα ἀγέννητον, ἕνα Υἱόν ἐξ αὐτοῦ γεννητῶς προερχόμενον, ἕν Πνεῦμα ἅγιον συναΐδιον, ἐκ τοῦ Πατρός καί αὐτό ἐκπορευόμενον πρό αἰώνων καί εἰς αἰώνας· καί ἔτι καί συνδοξαζόμενον τῷ Πατρί καί τῷ Υἱῷ νῦν καί ἀεί καί εἰς τούς αἰῶνας τῶν αἰώνων. Ἀμήν.

by the Fathers must be affectionately embraced, rather than those things said privately by certain of them, and that the unfamiliar texts are suspect, especially when they are produced by the Latins, who interfere even with texts in plain sight. We have promised, with God's help, in a second treatise to prove that what appears to be discordant is actually harmonious.

And so, these points have been thoroughly and logically demonstrated above in the treatise, and also that we and our confession are safe in every way and it is our crown of boasting and a hope which cannot be put to shame. For if this were not so and we are deficient with respect to this confession, then the men of old would have been much more deficient, who were initiated from above and who, being moved by God, initiated our race: the apostles, the prophets, the many and numerous revered councils of the Fathers. But if they knew differently (as the race of the Latins is now contending), and since they have not clearly revealed this to us, even though the Lord said to them, "That which you heard in the darkness, proclaim it in the light,"[172] how would they not be liable? But herein God vindicated them through the greatest works.

For they were not thinking like the Latins—far from it—as this has already been shown. On the contrary, they have both known and delivered to us that there is one, and only one, source of divinity, one unbegotten Father, one Son, who comes forth from Him by being begotten, one co-eternal Holy Spirit, Himself also proceeding from the Father before the ages and unto the ages and, furthermore, glorified with the Father and the Son now and ever and unto the ages of ages. Amen.

NOTES

[1] Cf. Gen.3:1. Δεινός in the sense of clever, as the context elaborates.

[2] The parallelism is to the Trinity, the fount of goodness, in contrast. The Trinity has a single head, the Father.

[3] Gen. 3:15. Cf. Rom. 16:20.

[4] Cf. Ps. 72:8.

[5]Arianism: A heresy named for its notorious proponent, Arius (250-336),who asserted that Christ was not equal to the Father in divinity. Arius's confrontation with Saints Alexander and Athanasius led to the calling of the First Ecumenical Council at Nicaea in 325 AD, where he was condemned and the original Nicene Creed was proclaimed. Christ was proclaimed consubstantial (*homoousios*) with the Father, which remains the foundation of Orthodox Christology.

[6]Eunomianism: A subsequent and more extreme form of Arianism. Aëtius, its founder, was influenced by Arius in Alexandria and Antioch. Influential from the middle of the fourth century until 380 AD, Aëtius applied Aristotelian syllogisms to defend his doctrines, and claimed Christ was *anomoios*, *unlike* the Father, in order to contradict the orthodox definition of *homoousios*. Eunomius carried on his teachings through dialectic and a strict doctrine of divine simplicity that proclaimed man's ability to comprehend the divine essence. "God knows no more of His own substance than we do."

[7]Macedonianism (also known as Pneumatomachianism): Named for its founder, Macedonius, who denied the divinity of the Holy Spirit, whom he claimed to be a creation of the Son, and a servant of the Father and the Son. They also held to a semi-Arian belief of Christ being of "similar substance" (*homoiousios*) but not of the "same essence" (*homoousios*) of that of God the Father. It was condemned by the Second Ecumenical Council at Constantinople in 381.

[8]The familiar biblical metaphor is that the church was a fruitful plant and that the evil one sought to ravage ("λυμήνασθαι") the vineyard of the Lord,. This word is used here, and again in the second treatise. The evil one did lay waste to the Latin church. So Saint Gregory is comparing the two churches: the Latin has been ravaged in Treatise 2, here the Church of God survived. Cf. Is. 5:1-2: " Now will I sing to my well-beloved a song of my beloved touching his vineyard. My well beloved hath a vineyard in a very fruitful hill: [2] And he fenced it, and gathered out the stones thereof, and planted it with the choicest vine, and built a tower in the midst of it, and also made a winepress therein: and he looked that it should bring forth grapes." The next verse is an amplification of the thought, with the causal particle, explaining how it was not laid waste. "For, his fangs also were in turn shattered by those who had been pierced by him, meaning, by those who have truly made Christ their own Head." Cf. Psalm 80:8-11, "[8]Thou hast brought a vine out of Egypt: thou hast cast out the heathen, and planted it. [9]Thou preparedst room before it, and didst cause it to take deep root, and it filled the land.[10] The hills were covered with the shadow of it, and the boughs thereof were like the goodly cedars.[11] She sent out her boughs unto the sea, and her branches unto the river."

[9]Cf. the 6th priestly prayer of Orthros ("crush under their feet the invisible and warring enemies") and Rom. 16:20.

[10] Cf. Gen. 3:14.

[11] The Greek word here translated as "looking out", "ἐπιτηρητής", comes from the same root as the verb translated as "bruise" in Gen. 3:15: "he shall bruise thy

head, and thou shalt bruise [τηρήσεις] his heel".

[12] According to Aristotle, common principles (κοιναὶ ἀρχαί) are the foundational laws of logic, including the law of non-contradiction. namely, the laws of identity, non-contradiction, and the excluded middle. Cf. Aristotle, *Metaphysics* IV (Γ), 1003-6.

[13] Cf. St. Gregory the Theologian, "Nor is the Spirit Son because He is of God, for the Only-begotten is one" ("οὔτε τὸ πνεῦμα υἱὸς ὅτι ἐκ τοῦ θεοῦ, εἷς γὰρ ὁ μονογενής", Fifth Theological Oration §9; NPNF2 7.320).

[14] This is a paraphrase of the logical law of non-contradiction. Cf. Aristotle, *Metaphysics*: "τὸ γὰρ αὐτὸ ἅμα ὑπάρχειν τε καὶ μὴ ὑπάρχειν ἀδύνατον τῷ αὐτῷ καὶ κατὰ τὸ αὐτό...αὕτη δὴ πασῶν ἐστὶ βεβαιοτάτη τῶν ἀρχῶν": "It is impossible that the same thing belong and not belong to the same thing at the same time and in the same respect...this is the most certain of all principles" (1005b19-20, 22).

[15]*Phronema* is notoriously difficult to convey in English. The mind stops like brakes at truth and is fixed on it. Hence a mindset. Theologically, the Church is said to "have the phronema of Christ". The Church as the continuation of the Incarnation is indwelt with the same animating and life-giving Spirit, and thus the very way of thinking, or mindset, of Christ, which is preserved among Orthodox Christians. Experiencing the phronema of Christ presupposes two things. First, the hesychastic and mysterial life are the immediate means of connecting to the phronema of the Church. Secondly, it is actualized more deeply by our ascetic participation in the Cross, in other words, by repentance.

[16]Compare his later statement, concerning the Creed: "you are refuted by those who recorded the minutes of all the Holy Councils, and by the very harmony of the four patriarchal thrones...which retain the original exposition unchanged and unaltered."

[17] Rom. 3:19.

[18] Or an alternative reading: "what is ambivalent may be made more firmly supported by relating it to the one confession".

[19] "Monarchial" literally means "of one arche [ἀρχή]", which can mean both "rule, reign" and "origin, beginning".

[20] Cf. John 15:26, "But when the Comforter is come, whom I will send unto you from the Father, even the Spirit of Truth which proceedeth from the Father, He shall testify of Me."

[21] Cf. Gal.4:6, "And because ye are sons, God hath sent forth the Spirit of His Son into your hearts, crying, 'Abba, Father'".

[22] Cf. John 14:18-23, "I will not leave you comfortless; I will come to you. Yet a little while and the world seeth Me no more, but ye see Me. Because I live, ye shall live also. At that day ye shall know that I am in My Father, and you in Me, and I

in you. He that hath My commandments and keepeth them, he it is that loveth Me; and he that loveth Me shall be loved by My Father, and I will love him and will manifest Myself to him." Judas (not Iscariot) said unto Him, "Lord, how is it that Thou wilt manifest Thyself unto us, and not unto the world?" Jesus answered and said unto him, "If a man love Me, he will keep My words; and My Father will love him, and We will come unto him and make Our abode with him."

[23] Cf. John 1:18, "No man hath seen God at any time; *the only begotten Son*, who is in the bosom of the Father, He hath declared Him." "Only" also in the sense, as St. Gregory says elsewhere, from the Father. As the Son is only from the Father, so the Spirit is only from the Father.

[24] Cf. Gal. 4:19, " My little children, over whom I travail in birth again until Christ be formed in you."

[25] Cf. Eph. 3:16-19, "that He would grant you, according to the riches of His glory, to be strengthened with might by His Spirit in the inner man; that Christ may dwell in your hearts by faith; that ye, being rooted and grounded in love, may be able to comprehend with all saints what is the breadth and length and depth and height,and to know the love of Christ, which surpasseth knowledge, that ye might be filled with all the fullness of God."

[26] Cf. James 1:17, "Every good gift and every perfect gift is from above, and cometh down from the Father of lights, with whom is no variableness, neither shadow of turning."

[27] Saint Paul teaches that man is body, soul and spirit (1Thes. 5:23). Thus as a microcosm, he possesses sensual knowledge, like the beasts (2 Pet. 2:12), knowledge of himself, of his psyche (cf. 1 Cor. 2:14), and most importantly he possesses a knowledge of God, (John 17:3) which is possessed by beings who are *noeros*, intellectual, capable of spiritual cognition.

[28] Cf. Rev. 2:24.

[29] Cf. 2 Cor. 2:11, "lest Satan should get an advantage of us: for we are not ignorant of his devices."

[30] Cf. St. Gregory the Theologian, *Theological Oration 5*.

[31] Cf. John 18:37, "to this end was I born, and for this cause came I into the world, that I should bear witness unto the truth. Every one that is of the truth heareth my voice." Also, cf. John 10:27.

[32] John. 15:26.

[33] Cf. Acts 7:51.

[34] Cf. John 16:13.

[35] James 1:17.

[36] Cf. Mark 4:10-11, "And when he was alone, they that were about him with the twelve asked of him the parable.[11] And he said unto them, Unto you it is given

to know the mystery of the kingdom of God: but unto them that are without, all these things are done in parables."

[37] Cf. Prov. 1:6: "To understand a proverb ['parable' LXX], and the interpretation; the words of the wise, and their dark sayings."

[38] Cf. John.16:13, "Howbeit when he, the spirit of truth, is come, he will guide you into all truth: for he shall not speak of himself; but whatsoever he shall hear, that shall he speak: and he will show you things to come."

[39] Cf. John 15:15, "Henceforth I call you not servants; for the servant knoweth not what his Lord doeth: but I have called you friends; For all things that I have heard of my father I have made known unto you."

[40] Cf. John 18:37-8, "Pilate therefore said unto him, art thou a King then? Jesus answered, thou sayest that I am a King period to this end was I born, and for this cause came I into the world, that I should bear witness unto the truth. Everyone that is of the truth here with my voice."

[41] The role of the Fathers is not to be merely chosen in a representative sense, but they are chosen in the sense of being chosen to be instruments, being spiritually moved, to compose the Definition. Secondly, they are chosen in the sense of being holy. The Fathers, as elect or chosen vessels, were spiritually moved, in a way similar to the description given by St. Peter concerning the biblical authors. "Holy men of God spake as they were moved the Holy Ghost" (2 Pet.1:21). The spiritual dimension is brought out in the Synaxarion of the Sunday of the Holy Fathers, which reads, "Upon the conclusion of the Council, Saint Constantine summoned all of those holy men: they all came, and after praying for sometime, confirmed that it was the Queen of cities and dedicated it to the Mother of the Word, by order of the Emperor. And thus, each of the Saints returned home."

[42] Cf. 2 Ti. 2:15.

[43] John 14:28.

[44] The text which supports this is generally held to be Canon 7 of the 4th Ecumenical Council, as follows: "Canon VII. When these things had been read, the holy Council decreed that it is unlawful for any man to bring forward, or to write, or to compose a different (ἑτέραν) Faith as a rival to that established by the holy Fathers assembled with the Holy Ghost in Nicæa. But those who shall dare to compose a different faith, or to introduce or offer it to persons desiring to turn to the acknowledgment of the truth, whether from Heathenism or from Judaism, or from any heresy whatsoever, shall be deposed, if they be bishops or clergymen; bishops from the episcopate and clergymen from the clergy; and if they be laymen, they shall be anathematized. And in like manner, if any, whether bishops, clergymen, or laymen, should be discovered to hold or teach the doctrines contained in the Exposition introduced by the Presbyter Charisius concerning the Incarnation of the Only-Begotten Son of God, or the abominable and profane doctrines of Nestorius, which are subjoined, they shall be subjected to the sentence of this holy and ecumenical Council. So that, if it be a bishop,

he shall be removed from his bishopric and degraded; if it be a clergyman, he shall likewise be stricken from the clergy; and if it be a layman, he shall be anathematized, as has been afore said" (Schaff, Phillip, ed. Seven Ecumenical Councils. Vol. 14. Peabody, MA: CBD, 2001, 437).

[45] The subject is the love for debate, which is personified. For the sake of the reader, it is changed to "he", the Latin.

[46] Cf. Ott, 62: "*Since the 9th century*, the Greek Orthodox Church has taught that the Holy Ghost proceeds from the Father alone. A Council at Constantinople in the year 879, under the Patriarch Photius, rejected the 'filioque' of the Latins as heretical. In contrast to this, the Second General Council of Lyons (1274) declared... (The Holy Ghost eternally proceeds from the Father and Son as from one principle and only one spiration.)"

[47] The Saint characterizes the Symbol of Faith as "a revered tower" (or lit. "a tower of piety"), the godly converse of the tower of Babel (cf. Gen. 11).

[48] Cf. Josephus, *Antiquities of the Jews* 2.4: "[Nimrod] said, 'He would be revenged on God, if He should have a mind to drown the world again: for that he would build a Tower too high for the waters to be able to reach."

[49] Cf. Doxastikon of the Vesperal Verses for the feast of Pentecost, "Of old the tongues were confounded because of the audacity in the building of the tower, but now the tongues are made wise because of the glory of Divine knowledge. There God condemned the impious because of their offence, and here Christ hath enlightened the fishermen by the Spirit. At that time confusion of tongues was wrought for punishment, but now the concord of tongues hath been inaugurated for the salvation of our souls."

[50] Cf. Acts 17:27.

[51] Cf. Isa. 19:22.

[52] Namely, 'Theotokos.'

[53] I.e. even though the two natures and wills and energies of Christ were many times proclaimed in council, in obedience to the Second Ecumenical Council the Fathers never made any addition to the Symbol of Faith lest they cause unnecessary discord.

[54] 1 Cor. 8:6.

[55] St. Athanasius the Great, *Testimonies from Scripture*, 48 (PG 28:72,49).

[56] St. Basil the Great, *Against the Sabellians and Arius et the Anomoeans,* 7 (PG 31:616,39).

[57] St. Gregory the Theologian, *On the Holy Spirit Oratio 31,* 14.

[58] St. John of Damascus, *Exact Exposition of the Orthodox Faith* 3, 5 (49).

[59] The Greek term is *proedros*, literally president, which, if translated as such, carries modern connotations. St. Gregory was elected bishop of Nyssa in 372,

from which he was deposed in 376, but subsequently regained it in 378. Present at the Council of Antioch in April 379, he attempted reconciliation of heretical groups. Notably as a primate, he participated in the Second Ecumenical Council of Constantinople, in 381.

[60] St. Gregory of Nyssa, 'That When We Speak of Three Persons in the Godhead We Do Not Speak of Three Gods: To the Greeks, From the Common Notions' (PG 45:180).

[61] John 1:14.

[62] John 8:42.

[63] John 6:46.

[64] St. Justin the Philosopher and Martyr, *Exposition of the Right Faith*, 9.

[65] 1 Cor. 2:12.

[66] See 1 Cor. 2:16.

[67] St. Basil the Great, *Against Eunomius 5* (PG 29:733,13).

[68] St. Dionysios the Areopagite, On the Divine Names, 2,5. The exact text is "Μόνη δὲ πηγὴ τῆς ὑπερουσίου θεότητος ὁ πατὴρ οὐκ ὄντος υἱοῦ τοῦ πατρὸς οὐδὲ πατρὸς τοῦ υἱοῦ, φυλαττόντων δὲ τὰ οἰκεῖα τῶν ὕμνων εὐαγῶς ἑκάστῃ τῶν θεαρχικῶν ὑποστάσεων": "The Father alone is the source of the super-essential Godhead, and the Father is not a Son, nor is the Son a Father; for the divine persons all preserve, each without alloy, His own particular attributes of praise."

[69] St. Athanasios the Great, *On Dionysius* 18 et seq., *Homily I Against the Arians*, 19.

[70] "The one who is adopted is not 'only from' but is from the Father through the Son": In order to show that the *filioque* relegates the Spirit to a position of adoption, Saint Gregory brings in the theology of adoption. We are sons from the Father through the Son. Our adoption (θέσις) is by grace, not by nature. If the Spirit is from the Father through the Son as the *filioque* teaches, this would make Him to be a creature. Saint Gregory will argue this later.

[71] 1 Cor. 6:17.

[72] St. Gregory the Theologian, *On Pentecost, Oration 41* (PG 36:441,41).

[73] Ibid., *On Those Who Came From Egypt, Oration 34* (PG 36:252,4).

[74] St. John of Damascus, *Exact Exposition of the Orthodox Faith*, 1, 8.

[75] That the Holy Spirit is "only" from the Father. See section 2.

[76] St. Gregory the Theologian, *On Theophany, Oration 38* (PG 36:325,20).

[77] Job 33:4.

[78] Ps. 32:8.

[79] Monarchy (Gr. μοναρχία), from μόνος (alone) and ἀρχή (see footnotes 19 and 83): there is but a single origin in the Trinity.

[80] Isa. 41:4. This phrase has been translated anew to best capture the meaning most relevant to the present context.

[81] Ps. 109:3.

[82] Rev. 3:14.

[83] In this passage, the words "origin", "beginning", and (in its first instance) "dominion" are all rendering the one Greek word "ἀρχή", which has all of these related but not identical meanings. On the contrary, the word "καταρχή" only has the meaning of a temporal beginning, while the second occurrence of "dominion" translates the word "δεσποτεία", another narrower synonym of "ἀρχή".

[84] Cf. the preamble, where sophistry is a characteristic of the serpent.

[85] Aquinas, ibid.,"Reply to Objection 1. In every action two things are to be considered, the "suppositum" acting, and the power whereby it acts; as, for instance, fire heats through heat. So if we consider in the Father and the Son the power whereby they spirate the Holy Ghost, there is no mean, for this is one and the same power. But if we consider the persons themselves spirating, then, as the Holy Ghost proceeds both from the Father and from the Son, the Holy Ghost proceeds from the Father immediately, as from Him, and mediately, as from the Son; and thus He is said to proceed from the Father through the Son. So also did Abel proceed immediately from Adam, inasmuch as Adam was his father; and mediately, as Eve was his mother, who proceeded from Adam; although, indeed, this example of a material procession is inept to signify the immaterial procession of the divine persons."

[86] St. Dionysius the Areopagite, *On the Divine Names* 2, 1.

[87] St. Basil the Great, *Against Eunomius* 5 (PG 29:712,3).

[88] Psalm 32:6; St. Gregory of Nyssa, 'That When We Speak of Three Persons in the Godhead We Do Not Speak of Three Gods: To the Greeks, From the Common Notions' (PG 45: 180); St. John of Damscus, *Exact Exposition of the Orthodox Faith* 1,7.

[89] St. Gregory the Theologian, *On Those Who Came From Egypt, Oration 34*, 10 (PG 36:252,1).

[90] Mt. 18:16.

[91] SSt. Basil the Great, *Against Eunomius* 5 (PG 29:736,23).

[92] This is a reference to a work by St. Gregory of Nyssa, or, at least here attributed to St. Gregory of Nyssa by St. Gregory Palamas, Περὶ Θεογνωσίας, which has been lost. The Psalmic reference is Ps. 32:6.

[93] St. Cyril of Alexandria, *On the Holy and Consubstantial Trinity, Oration 2* (PG 75:724A).

[94] St. Cyril of Alexandria, *Confession of Faith*, Johannes Vegelinus, De sacrosancta

Trinitate 1604, p. 121.

[95] St. John of Damascus, *Exact Exposition of the Orthodox Faith*, 1, 8.

[96] So as to describe the Latin reasoning, St Gregory coined the word "φιλοπολυεκπόρευτον" ("fond of much procession"), which is why he excuses himself with "so to speak".

[97] John 1:14.

[98] St. Gregory the Theologian, *On the Son, Oration 29*, 2.

[99] St. Dionysius the Areopagite, O*n the Divine Names, 2*, 5.

[100] Ibid.

[101] Cf. Aeschylus, Fragment 139; said of the eagle, shot by an arrow adorned with eagle's feathers.

[102] Dt. 32:39.

[103] Cf. Ps 140:4.

[104] St. Gregory the Theologian, *On the Son, Oration 30*, 20.

[105] St. Gregory the Theologian, *On the Holy Spirit, Oration 31* (or 25, 16).

[106] James 1:17.

[107] Commentary on Psalm 32, 15.

[108] St. Gregory the Theologian, *On the Son, Oration 29*, 11 (PG 36:87C).

[109] Ibid.

[110] An idiom, in theological usage, is equivalent to a natural property or personal attribute.

[111] Or "recognized".

[112] Ott, 63. "That the Holy Ghost proceeds from the Father and from the Son as from One Single Principle and through One Single Spiration, is clear from John 16, 15: "All that the Father has, is mine." If the Son, by virtue of His eternal generation from the Father, possesses everything that the Father posesses except the Fatherhood and the ungeneratedness which are not communicable, then He must also possess the power of spiration (vis spirativa) and with it the being a Principle in relation to the Holy Ghost."

[113] St. Gregory the Theologian, *The Last Farewell, Oration 42*, 15 (PG 36:476,12).

[114] "Doxological pronouncement": a translation of *ekphonesis;* for instance, "Glory to the Father, and to the Son, and to the Holy Spirit".

[115] I.e. Saint Gregory the Theologian.

[116] St. John of Damascus, *Exact Exposition of the Orthodox Faith*, 1, 7.

[117] Rom. 11:36. Cf. St. Basil, *On the Holy Spirit 5*.

[118] St. John of Damascus, *Exact Exposition of the Orthodox Faith*, 1, 7 (PG 94:806C).

[119] In geometry, triangular numbers represent numbers arranged in the form of an equilateral triangle. See Figure 1. In the Latins' view, the Trinity is like three consecutive points: the Father begets the Son and together they make the Holy Spirit to proceed. This is a straight line, which is one-dimensional. To make it into a two-dimensional shape, i.e. into a plane (ἐπίπεδον), width must be added to length by pushing the midpoint upwards, thus "piling [it] up" over the other two (Fig. 2.2). The result is the second triangular number (Fig. 1 and 2.3). The units that St. Gregory mentions are the three dots that make up the triangle.

[120] St. Gregory the Theologian, *Theological Songs, On the Holy Spirit* v. 54-57 (PG 37:412 A).

[121] Psalm 67:8 et seq. The Greek for "going forth" (ἐκπορεύεσθαι) is the same word as the one translated "proceeding" when with reference to the Holy Spirit.

[122] St. Gregory the Theologian, *Oration 31*, 25.

[123] The statement from Aquinas is worthy of repetition: "I answer that, the procession of love in God ought not to be called generation. In evidence whereof we must consider that the intellect and the will differ in this respect, that the intellect is made actual by the object understood residing according to its own likeness in the intellect; whereas the will is made actual, not by any similitude of the object willed within it, but by its having a certain inclination to the thing willed. Thus the procession of the intellect is by way of similitude, and is called generation, because every generator begets its own like; whereas the procession of the will is not by way of similitude, but rather by way of impulse and movement towards an object. So what proceeds in God by way of love, does not proceed as begotten, or as son, but proceeds rather as spirit; which name expresses a certain vital movement and impulse, accordingly as anyone is described as moved or impelled by love to perform an action" (Summa Question 27; article 4; objection 3).

[124] John 1:33.

[125] John 1:32.

[126] St. John of Damascus, *Exact Exposition of the Orthodox Faith* 1, 8 (PG 94:808C).

[127] "Enhypostatic" is defined by Maximus the Confessor in his *Different Definitions*: "enhypostatic is what is common, according to the essence; that is, the form, which is in reality substantiated in individuals under it, and which is not conceived simply notionally." Put simply, hypostatic is what is in reality existent; enhypostatic is existent in a hypostasis, not merely the ahypostatic (i.e. not realized) form, or eidos. He is simply stating that this is natural, pertaining to the bestowal of substance.

[128] St. John of Damascus, *Exact Exposition of the Orthodox Faith* 1, 13 (PG 94:852B).

[129] St. Cyril of Alexandria, *Treasuries* (PG 75: 601C).

[130] St. Cyril of Alexandria, *Treasuries* (PG 75: 580C).

[131] St. Gregory the Dialogist, *Dialogue* 2 (PL 66:203 B).

[132] St. Dionysius the Areopagite, *Epistle 9* (PG 3:1104A).

[133] John 15:26.

[134] Cf. John 1:3.

[135] St. Gregory the Theologian, *Oration 20,* 7 (PG 35:1073,4).

[136] St. Gregory the Theologian, *On the Holy Spirit, Oration 31,*12 (PG 36:153C).

[137] St. Cyril, *Treasuries*, 33 (PG 75:569A).

[138] St. Dionysius the Areopagite, *On the Divine Names* 2.5, 2.7, 2.3 respectively (PG 3:645A).

[139] St. Dionysius the Areopagite, *On Mystical Theology* 3 (PG 3:1033).

[140] St. Dionysius the Areopagite, *On the Divine Names* 2, 5 (PG 3:644D).

[141] "Generator" is here used as a monolexical translation of "προβολεύς", which precisely means "one that causes emanation."

[142] St. Basil the Great, *Epistle* 38, 4 (PG 32:329D).

[143] St. Gregory the Theologian, *On the Son, Oration 30* (PG 36:116,11C). Cf. John 17:10.

[144] Cf. "In the creation [of the bodiless powers] understand the Father to be the originating cause of what came to be, the Son to be the creative [cause], the Spirit to be the perfecting [cause]. Thus, [understand] the ministering spirits to exist by the will of the Father, to be led to being by the action [ἐνεργείᾳ] of the Son, and to be perfected by the presence of the Spirit". Basil the Great, *De spiritu sancta*, 38, (PG 32:136B).

[145] Gen. 24:2

[146] St. John Chrysostom, *On the Saying of Abraham* 2 (PG 56: 555).

[147] St. Gregory the Theologian, *On Peace, Oration 23,* 11 (PG 35:1161,45).

[148] St. Basil the Great, *Against Eunomius 5* (PG 29:557,21).

[149] Ibid. 3, 1.

[150] St. Basil the Great, *Against Eunomius 1*, 20 (PG 29:262,1).

[151] Ibid.

[152] St. Basil the Great, *Against Eunomiums 3*, 1 (PG 29:656,11).

[153] St. Gregory the Theologian, *Oration 31* (PG 36:163B).

[154] Cf. John 8:41.

[155] Baruch 3:37.

[156] St. Athanasius the Great, *To the Sebellianizers* (doubtful) 11.

[157] St. Gregory the Theologian, *On the Holy Spirit, Oration 31*, 20 (PG 36:156B).

[158] St. Gregory the Theologian, *Oration 34*, 15 (PG 36:253C).

[159] St. Cyril of Alexandria, *Treasuries* (PG 75: 569C).

[160] Cf. the second paragraph of section 13 above.

[161] See footnote 99 above.

[162] St. Gregory the Theologian, *Oration 29*, 5 (PG 36:80B).

[163] 1 Tim. 3:16.

[164] Tit. 2:11.

[165] Rom. 4:14.

[166] Heb. 12:1.

[167] Cf. John 14:26.

[168] See the tenth paragraph of the Preamble, or second paragraph before the beginning of section 1 above.

[169] Lit. 'wise.'

[170] The Greek text in brackets is missing from Christou's edition of 1981 and was supplied hereinto from the edition of 1627.

[171] James 1:17.

[172] Mt. 10:27.

SECOND APODICTIC TREATISE
ON THE PROCESSION
OF THE HOLY SPIRIT

ΛΟΓΟΣ
ΔΕΥΤΕΡΟΣ

1

Ὧν μὲν οὖν ἔδει καὶ αὐτῷ τῷ τῶν εὐσεβούντων καταλόγῳ πρὸς διασάφησίν τε καὶ βεβαίωσιν τοῦ ὀρθοῦ φρονήματος καὶ δι᾽ ὧν ἐν βραχεῖ τὸ δυσσεβὲς ἅπαν τῶν ἐνισταμένων ἀναφαίνεται Λατίνων, πρότερον εἰς δύναμιν διεξελθόντες, ἃ δὲ αὐτοὶ προτείνουσι καθ᾽ ἡμῶν τε καί τῆς εὐσεβείας, καὶ δι᾽ ὧν ἰσχυρίζονται μηδὲν καινοτομεῖν, ἀλλὰ τοῖς αὐτοῦ Χριστοῦ θείοις λόγοις συνῳδὰ φρονεῖν καὶ λέγειν καὶ τοῖς κατὰ Χριστὸν θεολογήσασι κατ᾽ οὐδὲν ἀπάδοντα, ταῦτα δὲ μήπω πάνθ᾽ ἑξῆς εἰς τοὐμφανὲς παραγαγόντες μηδὲ ἀπελέγξαντες, νῦν ἴδωμεν καθ᾽ ἕκαστον ἅττα λέγουσι καὶ τίσι λογισμοῖς ἢ καὶ γραφικοῖς ῥήμασί τε καὶ νοήμασι χρησάμενοι, μᾶλλον δὲ παραχρησάμενοι, τῆς θεολέκτου τε καὶ πατροπαραδότου διαπεπτώκασιν ὁμολογίας. Καὶ τὸ δεινότατον ἁπάντων, οὐδ᾽ ἐπαναλῦσαι καὶ ἀσφαλῶς ἐπιλαβέσθαι οὗ διαπεπτώκασιν ἐθέλουσιν, ἀλλὰ τοῖς πρὸς ἐπανόρθωσιν διδοῦσι χεῖρα, ἀληθείας λόγου δύναμιν πρὸς ἀλήθειαν ἀναγωγόν, οἷά τινες ὡς ἀληθῶς ἀνάγωγοι, δυσχεραίνουσί τε ἐς τὰ μάλιστα καὶ ἀντιλέγουσι.

TREATISE TWO

1

Earlier, to the best of our ability, we went through the things that were necessary even to the register of the pious themselves, both for clarification and for confirmation of the correct mindset,[1] and by which in short course the entire impiety of the objecting Latins comes to light, but as for the things which the Latins themselves propose both against us and against piety and by which they claim that they do not innovate at all but think and speak in harmony with the divine words of Christ Himself and not out of harmony at all with those who have theologized according to Christ, we have not yet brought all these things into the light nor refuted them in order. Let us now individually look at what things they assert and what rationales or even scriptural expressions and concepts they used, or rather abused, and so have fallen from the God-chosen confession which was handed down from the Fathers. And the most fearful thing of all is that they do not desire to return and safely hold on to that from which they have fallen. Instead, like truly ill-bred men,[2] they are displeased to the highest degree and gainsay those giving their hand, the power of the word of truth leading up to the truth, unto correction.[3]

2

Τὸ μὲν οὖν ὀρθοῦ διαπεσεῖν κοινὸν ἐγένετο ταῖς ἐκκλησίαις ἁπάσαις, ἄλλοτε ἄλλῃ διὰ τοῦ μακροῦ χρόνου λυμηναμένου τοῦ χείρονος. Τὸ δὲ διαπεσοῦσαν μηκέτ᾽ ἐπανελθεῖν μόνης τῆς τῶν Λατίων ἐγένετο, καίτοι μεγίστης τε καὶ κορυφαίας οὔσης καὶ τῶν πατριαρχικῶν θρόνων ἐξόχου περιωπῆς· καὶ ταὐτὸν ταύτῃ συμβέβηκε, μεγίστῃ τῶν ἐκκλησιῶν οὔσῃ, τῷ μεγίστῳ τῶν ζῴων ἐλέφαντι. Ὃν φασι μηδ᾽ ὕπνου καιρὸν ἐπ᾽ ἐδάφους ἀνακλίνεσθαι πρὸς ἄνεσιν, τοῖς δὲ πλαγίοις ἄρθροις μικρὸν ἐποκλάζοντα διαναπαύεσθαι· ἂν δὲ πού τι παθὼν καταπέσῃ, μηκέτ᾽ ἀνίστασθαι δύνασθαι. Ἀλλὰ τοῖς μὲν ἐλέφασι τὸ βάρος τοῦ σώματος αἴτιον καὶ ἡ πολυσαρκία δύσχρηστός τε οὖσα καὶ κάτω πιέζουσα, καθάπερ τις ἐπικειμένη μόλυβδος πολυτάλαντος, τοῖς δὲ Λατίνοις ὁ τῦφος οἶμαι τὸ μόνον, μικροῦ δέω λέγειν, πάθος ἀνίατον, ὃ καὶ τῷ μόνῳ πονηρῷ κρίμα κατὰ τὸν ἀπόστολον ἰδιαίτατον· δι᾽ ὃ κἀκεῖνος εἰς αἰῶνας ἀνίατος.

Ἂν δὲ τὸ τῶν Λατίνων τοῦτο φῦλον τοῦτον ἀπόθωνται – δύνανται γάρ, καὶ γὰρ ἄνθρωποι – τάχ᾽ ἂν ἡμεῖς οἱ τοῦ ὀρθοῦ πάντες συναχθέντες εἰς ἓν καὶ οἷόν τισι προνομαίαις, ὃ καὶ τοῖς καταπεσοῦσιν ἐλέφασι παρά τῶν μὴ κειμένων ἡ φύσις ἐξεῦρε βοήθημα, τοῖς θεοπνεύστοις λογίοις χρησάμενοι διαναστήσομέν τε καὶ στήσομεν ὀρθίους, ἀπαρεγκλίτως ἐχομένους τοῦ κανόνος τῆς εὐσεβείας. Ἐθελοντὰς δὲ κειμένους ὀνήσει τὸ παράπαν οὐδέν, κἂν παρ᾽ αὐτῶν τῶν οὐρανίων νόων σκευάζηταί τε καὶ προσάγηται τὸ τῆς ψευδοδοξίας ἴαμα· τούτων γὰρ λόγος προφητικοῖς ῥήμασιν ἐκπεφασμένος, ὡς «ἰατρεύσαμεν τὴν Βαβυλῶνα καὶ οὐκ ἰάθη».

2

So, to fall away from what is right was something common to all the churches, as evil laid waste sometimes to the one, sometimes to another, through the length of time. But that a fallen one no longer return, this only occurred with the church of the Latins, even though she is both the largest and chief and possessing the most eminent summit of the patriarchal thrones. The same thing befell her, who is the greatest of the churches, that befell the elephant, which is the greatest of the animals. They say that it does not lay itself down on the ground for rest even during sleep, but it rests awhile by crouching for a little time on its sides; and if it were to suffer something and fall down, it is no longer able to get itself up again. But for the elephants, the cause is actually the weight of the body and the sheer enormity of their flesh, which is cumbersome and weighs them down, just like an overlying piece of lead weighing many talents. In contrast, with the Latins I gather that it is only pride — I would almost say, an incurable passion — which, according to the Apostle, is also most particularly the crime belonging to the only evil one, which is the reason why that one is forever incurable.

But should this tribe of the Latins push him back (they are able, since indeed they are human), immediately all we of the right mindset, gathered together into one, using as it were some sort of trunks, which nature has also provided as a help from the elephants that are not lying down for those that have fallen, thus having used the God-inspired oracles, we would raise them up and set them standing on their feet and unswervingly maintaining the rule of piety. Yet those who willingly lay themselves down will not profit at all, even if the remedy for pseudodoxy were to be prepared and administered by the celestial intellects themselves. For theirs is the saying that has been expressed by the prophetic words, "We have healed Babylon, but she was not is healed."[4]

3

Μικροῦ τοίνυν μάτην τούτοις δίδωσιν ὁ χεῖρα διδούς, τοῦτο μόνον εὖ ἄγαν ἑαυτῷ νείμας καὶ ἀποδοὺς τῷ Θεῷ τὴν τῆς οἰκείας καλοκαγαθίας ἐπίδειξιν, ἐκείνους δὲ μόνον ἐθελοκακοῦντας ἀποδείξας καὶ ἴσως στήσας τοῦ μὴ πρόσω τῶν ἀτοπημάτων χωρεῖν. Καὶ νῦν γάρ, εἰ μὴ σαφῶς ἑτεροφωνεῖν ἐθέλουσι, τί κρεῖττον ἂν σχοῖεν φάρμακον πρὸς ἐπανόρθωσιν, ἢ ὅτι περ ἐκ μόνου τοῦ Πατρός, ἀλλ᾽ οὐχὶ καὶ ἐκ τοῦ Υἱοῦ τὴν ὑπόστασιν ἔχει τὸ Πνεῦμα τὸ ἅγιον; Ὁ προαποδέδεικται διὰ πολλῶν καὶ διὰ τῆς ὑποφωνήσεως τοῦ "μόνου", ἀριδηλοτέρας γεγονυίας τῆς ὀρθοδόξου διανοίας περὶ τῆς τοῦ ἁγίου Πνεύματος ἀσφαλοῦς θεολογίας καὶ τῆς κατ᾽ αὐτοὺς προσθήκης ὑπεναντίας φανερῶς ἐληλεγμένης τοῦ ὀρθοτομοῦντος κηρύγματος τῆς ἀληθείας.

Ἀλλὰ καὶ χωρὶς τούτων οὐδέ τινά ποθεν ἀνάγκην ἐπαγομένην ὁρῶμεν μετακινεῖν τὰς πνευματικινήτους περὶ θεοσεβείας ψήφους τῶν ἀπ᾽ αἰῶνος ἱερῶν συνόδων καί μετασκευάζειν τὸ πατροπαράδοτον τῆς εὐσεβείας σύμβολον, ὡς προστιθέναι καὶ ἰσχυρίζεσθαι τὴν ὕπαρξιν ἔχειν καὶ ἐκ τοῦ Υἱοῦ τὸ Πνεῦμα τὸ ἅγιον. Τί γάρ, εἰ τῆς θεοπνεύστου Γραφῆς ἔστιν ἃ δοκοῦσι διαφωνεῖν πρὸς τὰ κοινῇ τοῖς θεολόγοις ἐκπεφασμένα, κἀντεῦθεν ἀνωμολογημένα πᾶσιν ἡμῖν, οὐκ ἐκεῖνα μᾶλλον συμβιβάσομεν τῇ πανταχόθεν ἐχούσῃ τὸ ἀναμβισβήτητον ἀληθείᾳ πρὸς δύναμιν, ἀλλ᾽ ἡμεῖς ἐκπεσούμεθα δι᾽ ἐκεῖνα τῆς ἀληθείας; Οὐδ᾽ εἴ τι καὶ τὴν ἡμετέραν ὑπερβαίνει διάνοιαν ὁμολογήσομεν καὶ ἄλλοις δή τισι τῆς κατ᾽ αὐτὰ συνέσεως παραχωρήσομεν, ὅστις ἂν ἀξιωθείη – κἂν τῶν ἐσχάτων ᾖ - τῶν βαθέων καὶ ἀποκεκρυμμένων μυστηρίων τοῦ Πνεύματος, ἡμᾶς δ᾽ αὐτοὺς ἀναξίους κρίναντες τούτων, ὑπὸ τὴν κραταιὰν χεῖρα τοῦ Θεοῦ ταπεινώσομεν, ἀλλ᾽ ὦ τοῦ πάθους, καὶ Θεὸν αὐτὸν ἀγνοήσομεν διὰ τὸ μηδὲν ἐθέλειν ὁμολογεῖν ἀγνοεῖν, ὥσπερ οἱ καὶ τὴν τοῦ Υἱοῦ θεότητα ἀγνοήσαντες διὰ τὰ δυσλήπτως περὶ αὐτοῦ γεγραμμένα; Οὔμενουν. Οὐδὲ γὰρ ἐκείνοις αἱ γραφικαὶ μαρτυρίαι,

3

Accordingly, whoever gives his hand to them gives it almost in vain, having very well handed out to himself only this and rendered to God the proof of his own goodness. But as for them, he has proven that they are only deliberately doing wrong and has perhaps checked them so as not to proceed to further fallacies. And now, unless they wish to obviously speak discrepantly, what better medicine could they have for their restoration than that the Holy Spirit has His hypostasis only from the Father and not also from the Son? This has previously been proven by many other proofs as well as by the hinting of the "only", while the orthodox understanding concerning the unerring theology of the Holy Spirit has become more distinct and their addition has been clearly refuted as contrary to the rightly dividing proclamation of the Truth.

But even apart from these things, we do not see anywhere any necessity compelling us to alter the spirit-incited decisions of the sacred synods of old concerning the reverence toward God or to change the Symbol of piety handed down by Tradition from the Fathers, so as to add and assert that the Holy Spirit has His existence also from the Son. Why? If in the God-inspired Scripture there are things that appear to disagree with what has been expressed in common by the theologians and hence acknowledged by all of us, will we not rather harmonize, to the best of our ability, those things with the truth, since it possesses indisputability from every angle? Shall we instead fall away from the truth because of them? Furthermore, if something exceeds our reasoning, will we not admit it and leave it to some others to understand these matters (whoever might be deemed worthy — even if he be one of the last — of the deep and hidden mysteries of the Spirit), and having judged ourselves unworthy of them, will we not humble ourselves under the mighty hand of God? But oh what a misfortune! Will we even become ignorant of God Himself because of being unwilling to admit ourselves ignorant of anything at all, just like those that

μὴ καλῶς ἐκληφθεῖσαι, δυνηθεῖεν ἂν συνάρασθαι παραιτουμένοις οὐ κατὰ καιρὸν ἢ τῆς ἀσεβείας αὐτοὺς καὶ τῆς δι᾽ αὐτὴν αἰωνιζούσης καταδίκης ἐξελέσθαι· ἀλλὰ κρίσιν τίσουσιν αἰώνιον, ὅτι τὰς σαφεῖς ἀθετήσαντες φωνὰς καὶ τὰς ἀσαφεῖς φυσιώσει γνώσεως ἀνερευνήσαντες, μᾶλλον δὲ μὴ ἐρευνήσαντες μηδὲ τοῖς ὡς ἀληθῶς ἐρευνήσασι πεισθέντες, ἐξ αὐτῆς ἐνδίκως τῆς πεφυσιωμένης γνώσεως τὴν ὄντως ἀφροσύνην ἐκαρπώσαντο.

4

Καίτοι πλεῖσταί εἰσιν αὗται αἱ φωναί, αἳ τοῖς μὴ διορατικωτάτοις τὸ πρὸς τὸν Πατέρα συνάναρχόν τε καὶ ὁμότιμον ἀφαιροῦνται τοῦ Υἱοῦ καὶ αὐτὸ δὲ τὸ δεσποτικὸν ἀξίωμα καὶ τὴν βασιλείαν τὴν ἄληκτον· «ὑποταγήσεται γάρ», φησί, «καὶ ὁ Υἱός», καὶ «χρὴ αὐτὸν βασιλεύειν ἄχρι τινός», καὶ «μείζων ὁ Πατήρ», καὶ «ἡ σοφία ἔκτισται», καὶ «ἀγνοεῖ τι τῶν ἐκτισμένων ὑπ᾽ αὐτοῦ», καὶ «ἀφ᾽ ἑαυτοῦ οὐδὲν δύναται ποιεῖν», καὶ «καταβέβηκεν οὐχ ἵνα τὸ οἰκεῖον θέλημα ποιῇ», καὶ «ἦν διανυκτερεύων ἐν τῇ προσευχῇ τοῦ Θεοῦ», καὶ «ἔμαθε», καὶ «προέκοψε», καὶ «ὑψώθη», καὶ «ἐδοξάσθη», καὶ «τετελείωται», καὶ ὅσα τῆς τοῦ ἡμετέρου φυράματος ταπεινότητος, καὶ ὅσα τῆς εὐγνωμοσύνης, ἵν᾽ οὕτως εἴπω, τοῦ γεννήματος πρὸς τὸν γεννήτορα, καὶ ὅσα τοῦ μὴ ἀντίθεος εἶναι δείγματα, καὶ ὅσα πρὸς ἡμᾶς δι᾽ ἔργων ἀρετῆς ὑποδείγματα.

Τί οὖν, διὰ ταῦτα τὸ ἑτέρωθεν προσμαρτυρούμενον τῷ Υἱῷ θεῖον οἷον ἀδιεξίτητον ὕψος ἀθετητέον, ὅτι «ἐν ἀρχῇ ἦν», «καὶ πρὸς τὸν Θεὸν ἦν, καὶ Θεὸς ἦν», καὶ «πρὸ πάντων βουνῶν γεννᾶται», καὶ «πρὸ τοῦ ἡλίου διαμένει τὸ ὄνομα αὐτοῦ», καὶ «οὗτος ὁ Θεὸς καὶ οὐ λογισθήσεται ἕτερος πρὸς αὐτόν», αὐτὸς γάρ ἐστιν ὁ «μετὰ ταῦτα

became ignorant of the divinity of the Son on account of what had been obscurely written regarding Him? Certainly not. For these scriptural witnesses, which have not been taken as they should, would neither be able to assist them in their untimely excuses nor to snatch them from their impiety and from the resulting eternal condemnation. Instead, they shall pay eternal damnation, because they despised the clear voices and searched out the unclear ones, being puffed up with knowledge, or rather they did not search nor were they obedient to those who truly did search, and so from this same puffed-up knowledge they have justly reaped genuine foolishness.

4

And yet there are multitudes of such expressions which, for all but the most discerning, take away both the shared dignity and the cobegininglessness of the Son in relation to the Father and even His dominical dignity and unending kingdom. For he says, "The Son also shall be subject"[5] and "He must reign till some point"[6] and "the Father is greater"[7] and "wisdom hath been builded"[8] and "He is ignorant of something of what has been made by Him"[9] and "He can do nothing of Himself"[10] and "He came down not to do His own will"[11] and "He continued all night in prayer to God"[12] and "He learned"[13] and "increased"[14] and "was lifted up"[15] and "was glorified"[16] and "has been perfected,"[17] and as many things as be proofs of the lowliness of our own substance, and of the gratitude, that I may so say, of the Begotten toward the Begetter, and of not being against God, and as many as be for us models of virtue through works.

What then? Should the so indescribable divine height which is testified to the Son from elsewhere be set at naught because of the foregoing statements, since "He was in the beginning, and He was with God, and He was God"[18] and "He is brought forth before all the hills"[19] and "before the sun doth His name continue"[20] and "This is our God and there shall no other be accounted of in comparison

τοῖς ἀνθρώποις συναναστραφείς», ὅτι τε αὐτὸς καὶ ὁ Πατήρ ἕν εἰσι, καὶ αὐτὸς ἐν τῷ Πατρὶ καὶ ὁ Πατὴρ ἐν αὐτῷ, καί «ὁ ἑωρακὼς αὐτὸν ἑώρακε τὸν Πατέρα», καὶ «μετ᾽ αὐτοῦ ἡ ἀρχὴ ἐν ἡμέρᾳ τῆς δυνάμεως αὐτοῦ», «καὶ κατακυριεύσει μετὰ τὸ ἀντανανιρεθῆναι τὴν σελήνην», καὶ «πᾶν αὐτῷ γόνυ κάμψει ἐπουρανίων καὶ ἐπιγείων καὶ καταχθονίων», καὶ «ἡ βασιλεία αὐτοῦ, βασιλεία αἰώνιος», καὶ «βασιλεῖ ἑτέρῳ οὐχ ὑπολειφθήσεται».

Ταῦτα τοίνυν καὶ τ᾽ ἄλλ᾽ ὅσα τούτοις παραπλήσια, τὰ τοσοῦτο θαυμαστά, τὰ ἐπὶ τοσοῦτον ὑψηλά, τὰ οὕτως ἀνυπέρβλητα, διὰ τὰ ταπεινοῦντα τῶν ῥημάτων συγκαθελκύσομεν αὐτοῖς; Ἀλλ᾽ οὐ ζητήσομέν τε καὶ στέρξομεν τὸ ἐγκεκρυμμένον τοῖς δοκοῦσι χαμερπέσιν ὑψηλὸν καὶ τοῦ εὐσεβοῦς νοήματος γενόμενοι διαλύσομεν τὸ προσιστάμενον; Ἀλλὰ τῷ φαινομένῳ προσπταίσομέν τε καὶ πεσούμεθα καὶ ἐναπομενοῦμεν τῷ γράμματι; Οὔμενουν· ἀποκτένει γὰρ τὸ γράμμα κατασπῶν ἀφ᾽ ὕψους τοὺς μὴ ἄνω πρὸς τὸ Πνεῦμα βλέποντας.

5

Ταῦτ᾽ ἄρα καὶ ἡμεῖς, ὅσοι καθαρῶς τοῦ Πνεύματος, ὅσοι καθάπερ αὐτὸ ἑαυτὸ διεσάφησε θεολογοῦμεν, ὅσοι μηδὲν ἀνάξιον αὐτοῦ καὶ φρονοῦμεν καὶ κηρύττομεν, μηδ᾽ ἐξ ὧν λέγομεν ἐκβαῖνον· ἡμεῖς τοίνυν, κἄν τι μὴ ὁμόφωνον δοκῇ τῇ περὶ τοῦ ἁγίου μόνου καὶ προσκυνητοῦ Πνεύματος θεολογίᾳ καὶ αὐτὸ τοῦ ἁγίου Πνεύματος διδόντος, νοήσομεν πνευματικῶς καὶ διευκρινήσομεν καὶ διαρρίψομεν τοὺς λίθους τοῦ προσκόμματος καὶ πᾶσι τρόποις ἀποδείξομεν τοῖς προτέροις τῶν Πατέρων ὁμολογοῦντας τοὺς ὑστέρους, κοινῇ τε καὶ ἰδίᾳ ἑαυτοῖς, καὶ ἡμᾶς αὐτοὺς αὐτοῖς καὶ κοινῇ πάντας τῷ κοινῷ τῇ φύσει δεσπότῃ καὶ κατὰ χάριν ἡμετέρῳ Πατρί.

of Him."[21] For He it is who "after these things conversed with men,"[22] since He and the Father are one,[23] and He is in the Father and the Father in Him,[24] and he that hath seen Him hath seen the Father,[25] and "with Him is dominion in the day of His power,"[26] "and He shall have dominion after the moon be taken away,"[27] and "every knee shall bow to Him, of things in heaven, and things in earth, and things under the earth,"[28] and "His kingdom is an eternal kingdom"[29] and "shall not be left to another king."[30]

Therefore shall we, on account of the humbling statements, drag down together with them these so marvellous, these so lofty, these so unsurpassable proclamations and whatever else resembles them? Will we not rather both seek out and ardently embrace the loftiness that has been hidden in the seemingly lowly expressions, and, once we have become of the pious understanding, will we not dissolve what gives offence? Will we instead both stumble upon appearances and fall and remain in the letter? Certainly not; for the letter indeed killeth,[31] dragging down from the heights those who do not look upwards to the Spirit.

5

Therefore we too, as many as theologize concerning the Spirit purely, as many as do so just as He personally clarified Himself, as many as neither think nor proclaim anything unworthy of Him, nor anything resulting from what we do say; we therefore, even if something should appear not to be in agreement with the theology concerning the only Holy and worshipful Spirit, although it too was given by the Holy Spirit, we shall understand these things spiritually and distinguish and scatter the stones of stumbling and demonstrate in every way that the later Fathers actually agreed in confession with those that were prior, both publicly together and privately by themselves, and that we ourselves agree with them, and that all of us in common agree with our common Master by nature and Father by grace.

Ἐπεὶ δὲ ὅσα σχεδὸν ἀγνοοῦσι τῶν Γραφῶν ὑπ' ἀπορίας ἢ κακοβουλίας πρὸς τὴν οἰκείαν κακοδοξίαν οἱ Λατῖνοι περιτρέπουσι στρεβλοῦντες, πλείονα δέ εἰσιν αὐτοῖς τὰ ἀγνοούμενα τῶν δοκούντων αὐτοῖς ἀναντιρρήτων καὶ δι' ὧν ὡς προφανῶν τὸν περὶ αὐτοὺς ἐξαπατῶσιν ὄχλον, τούτων ἡμεῖς ἀρτίως μνησθέντας καὶ ταῦτα κακῶς παρ' αὐτῶν ἐξειλημένα Θεοῦ συναιρομένου ἀπελέγξαντες, καὶ οἷόν τινας θεμελίους ὑποσπάσαντες, σαθρὸν αὐτῶν ἀποδείξομεν τὸ ὅλον τῆς δυσεβείας οἰκοδόμημα.

6

Φέρε δὴ προθῶμεν πρότερον τὸ καὶ πρότερον αὐτοῖς δοκοῦν παντάπασιν ἄμαχον, ὡς ὑπὸ τοῦ λόγου τῆς ἀληθείας εἰρημένον· «ἐνεφύσησεν αὐτοῖς καὶ εἶπε, λάβετε Πνεῦμα ἅγιον». Ὁρᾷς, φησί, πῶς σαφῶς καὶ ἐκ τοῦ Υἱοῦ τὸ Πνεῦμα τὸ ἅγιον; Ἆρ' οὖν ὅτι ἐμφυσήσας εἶπε «λάβετε Πνεῦμα ἅγιον», τὸ ἅγιον Πνεῦμα τὸ ἐμφύσημα ἦν, ὡς ταὐτὸν εἶναι τῷ διὰ σαρκὸς ἐμφυσήματι τὸ ἐκπόρευμα ἢ τῷ δεδόσθαι δι' ἐμφυσήματος τεκμηριοῦνται καὶ τῆς τοῦ Χριστοῦ θεότητος ἐμφύσημα εἶναι τὸ Πνεῦμα τὸ ἅγιον, κἀντεῦθεν παρὰ τοῦ Υἱοῦ ἐκπορεύεσθαι συμπεραίνουσιν; Ἀλλ' ὁπότερον τούτων λέγουσιν, ἐπιστομιζέσθωσαν αὐτόθεν πρῶτον διὰ βραχέων· οὐ γὰρ ἐμφυσήσας εἶπεν ὁ Κύριος, "λάβετε τὸ Πνεῦμα", ἀλλὰ χωρὶς τοῦ ἄρθρου, "λάβετε Πνεῦμα ἅγιον", δηλαδὴ βραχύ τι τοῦ Πνεύματος. Σαφὲς οὖν ὡς μερικὴν τοῦ Πνεύματος ἐνέργειαν διὰ τοῦ ἐμφυσήματος ἔδωκεν, οὐκ αὐτοῦ τὴν φύσιν ἢ τὴν ὑπόστασιν· ἀμερὴς γὰρ παντάπασιν ἡ τοῦ θείου Πνεύματος φύσις τε καὶ ὑπόστασις. Διὰ τί δὲ ἐμφυσήσας ἔδωκεν, ὅπερ ἔδωκεν; Ἵνα δείξῃ μίαν οὖσαν ἑαυτοῦ καὶ τοῦ θείου Πνεύματος τὴν ἐνέργειαν· κἀντεῦθεν ἀλλήλων, ἑαυτοῦ κἀκείνου, παραστήσῃ τὸ συναφὲς καὶ συμφυὲς καὶ ὁμότιμον, καθάπερ καὶ ὁ Χρυσόστομός φησι θεολόγος

Because the Latins distort and divert nearly all the passages of Scripture that they fail to understand toward their own cacodoxy, either out of perplexity or out of ill will, (and the things they do not understand are more than those which they deem indisputable, which they use as if obvious to deceive the multitude around them), we shall mention these things presently and, once we have proven, with the help of God, that they have been improperly understood by the Latins, once we have drawn them out from underneath like some foundations, we shall demonstrate that the entirety of their irreverent edifice is rotten.

6

Come now, let us set first propose for discussion what previously in their eyes seemed to be altogether incontrovertible, since it had been said by the word of truth: "He breathed upon them and said, 'Receive ye Holy Spirit.'"[32] Do you see, they say, how clearly the Holy Spirit is also from the Son? So, because he breathed upon them and said, "Receive ye Holy Spirit," was the Holy Spirit the breathing-upon,[33] so that the procession is identified with what He bodily breathed upon them? Or do they infer, from the fact that it was bestowed by breathing upon them, that the Holy Spirit is also a breathing-upon of the divinity of Christ and therefore conclude that He proceeds from the Son? But whichever one of them they are saying, let their mouths be bridled by the very same passage through brief arguments first. For, the Lord did not breathe upon them and say, "Receive ye the Spirit," but He said it without the article, "receive ye Holy Spirit," namely, some portion of the Spirit. So then, it is clear that He bestowed but a particular energy of the Spirit by breathing upon them, not His nature or hypostasis. For, both the nature and hypostasis of the divine Spirit is altogether indivisible. But why did He bestow whatever He bestowed by breathing upon them? He did this so as to prove that His own energy and the divine Spirit's energy are one, and so that from this He might show the conjunction and connaturality and equal honour of each, of Himself and of the Spirit, precisely as Chrysostom the

γράφων, «τινὲς μέν φασιν ὅτι οὐ τὸ Πνεῦμα ἔδωκεν, ἀλλ᾽ ἐπιτηδείους αὐτοὺς πρὸς ὑποδοχὴν δι᾽ ἐμφυσήματος κατεσκεύασεν. Οὐκ ἂν δέ τις ἁμάρτοι καὶ τότε εἰληφέναι αὐτοὺς λέγων ἐξουσίαν τινὰ πνευματικὴν καὶ χάριν, ὥστε ἀφιέναι ἁμαρτήματα. Διὸ ἐπήγαγεν, 'ὧν ἂν ἀφῆτε ἀφέωνται,᾽ δεικνὺς ποῖον εἶδος ἐνεργείας δίδωσι· καὶ γὰρ ἄφατος ἡ τοῦ Πνεύματος χάρις καὶ πολυειδὴς ἡ δωρεά. Τοῦτο δὲ γίνεται, ἵνα μάθῃς ὅτι μία ἡ δωρεὰ καὶ ἡ ἐξουσία Πατρὸς καὶ Υἱοῦ καὶ ἁγίου Πνεύματος».

7

Ὡς ἂν δὲ καὶ διεξοδικώτερον πρὸς αὐτοὺς ἀπαντήσωμεν, εἰ τὸ ἐμφύσημα τοῦ Κυρίου τὸ Πνεῦμα τὸ ἅγιον ἦν, καὶ ἡ ἀναπνοὴ λοιπὸν ᾗ ἐχρῆτο, δι᾽ ἧς καὶ τὸ ἐμφύσημα γέγονε, τὸ Πνεῦμα τὸ ἅγιον ἦν. Οὐκοῦν οὐ καθ᾽ ἡμᾶς ἐγένετο ἄνθρωπος, ἀλλ᾽ ἢ φαντασίᾳ, κατὰ τὴν φαντασίαν τῶν Ἀκεφάλων, ἢ καὶ πρὶν ἀνθρώποις συναναστραφῆναι τὴν σαρκώδη φύσιν ἐξ ἀρχῆς εἶχεν οὕτω πως συνισταμένην, κατὰ τὴν Ἀπολιναρίου ἄνοιαν· καὶ μὴ αὐτὸς ὁ Κύριος καὶ τοῦτ᾽ εἶπε πάντως· «τὰ ῥήματα, ἃ ἐγὼ λαλῶ, Πνεῦμά εἰσι καὶ ζωή εἰσι». Εἰ δὲ Πνεῦμα εἰσι, καὶ Πνεῦμα ἅγιόν εἰσι· πῶς γὰρ οὔ; Οὐκοῦν, κατὰ τὴν Ἰταλῶν περὶ τοῦ ἐμφυσήματος ἑρμηνείαν, καὶ τὸ Πνεῦμα Λόγος καὶ Θεοῦ Λόγος. Οὗ τί ἂν ἀκουσθείη καινότερον; Μᾶλλον δὲ λόγοι, καὶ Θεοῦ λόγοι· τὰ γὰρ ῥήματα, πλῆθος.

Ἐπιστῆσαι δὲ κἀνταῦθα δέον, ὡς οὐδὲ νῦν εἶπεν, ὅτι «τὰ ῥήματα ἃ ἐγὼ λαλῶ τὸ Πνεῦμά εἰσιν», ἀλλά χωρὶς τοῦ ἄρθρου, δηλῶν μὴ τοῦ Πνεύματος τὴν ὑπόστασιν εἶναι ταῦτα, τῆς δὲ τοῦ θείου Πνεύματος ἐνεργείας εἶναι πεπληρωμένα καὶ τὴν ζωοποιὸν τοῦ Πνεύματος δι᾽ αὐτῶν χορηγεῖσθαι ἐνέργειαν. Καὶ ἡνίκα τοίνυν ἐμφυσήσας εἶπε, "λάβετε Πνεῦμα ἅγιον", τοῦτ᾽ ἀντίκρυς ἔφη, ὅτι τὸ ἐμφύσημα τοῦτο τῆς τοῦ λύειν καὶ δεσμεῖν ἐξουσίας τοῦ θείου Πνεύματος πεπληρωμένον ἐστί.

theologian says when he writes, "Some actually say that He did not bestow the Spirit, but rendered them fit to receive Him, by the breathing-upon. Yet one would not be wrong in asserting that even then they received some spiritual power and grace, so as to remit sins. Wherefore He added, "Whose soever sins ye remit, they are remitted unto them,"[34] showing what particular kind of energy He was bestowing. For, the grace of the Spirit is ineffable and the gift is multiform. But this comes to pass, that you may learn that the gift and the power of the Father and of the Son and of the Holy Spirit is one."[35]

7

But let us give them as it were a more expanded answer. If the Lord's breathing-upon was the Holy Spirit, then the breath He was using, through which His breathing-upon happened, was the Holy Spirit as well. This means that He did not become a man as we are, but was either an illusion, like the illusion of the *Acephali*, or, even before He conversed with men, He had the fleshly nature constituted from the beginning in some such way, according to the senselessness of Apolinarius. And yet, the Lord Himself also said, at any rate, "The words that I speak, they are Spirit, and they are life."[36] But if they are Spirit, they are also Holy Spirit; for how could they not be? So, according to the interpretation of the Italians concerning the breathing-upon, the Spirit is also the Word, even God's Word. What greater novelty than this could be heard? Or better yet, the Spirit would be words, even God's words, for "the words" are many.

Here also we ought to pay attention to the fact that neither in this case did He say, "the words that I speak are 'the' Spirit," but without the article, indicating that these very things are not the hypostasis of the Spirit but are completely full of the energy of the divine Spirit and that the life-giving energy of the Spirit is supplied through them. And so when He breathed upon them and said, "receive holy Spirit," this is what He forthrightly meant, namely, that this breathing-upon is completely full of the authority of the divine Spirit to bind and loose.

8

Πρὸς ὃ δὲ νῦν ὁ Λόγος καὶ παρ' ἡμῶν τὰ τοῦ Κυρίου ῥήματα ἐξαγγέλλεται· «ἐν γὰρ τοῖς χείλεσί μου», φησίν, «ἐξήγγειλα πάντα τὰ κρίματα τοῦ στόματός σου». Ἆρ' οὖν καὶ ἐξ ἡμῶν ἐκπορεύεται τὸ Πνεῦμα τὸ ἅγιον; Ἀλλὰ καὶ ἐξερευνῶνται καὶ μελετῶνται καὶ τηροῦνται καὶ πράττονται καὶ κατανοοῦνται, εἰς ὅσα κατάγει τὸ Πνεῦμα ὁ τὰ τοῦ Πνεύματος ἑρμηνεύων οὐ διὰ τοῦ Πνεύματος, ὅση δὲ καὶ ἡ διαφορὰ τῶν τοῦ Κυρίου λόγων· ἐντολαί, νόμοι, μαρτύρια, δικαιώματα, κρίματα. «Καὶ ἐγένετο ῥῆμα Κυρίου ἐπὶ Ἰωάννην τὸν Ζαχαρίου», κατὰ τὸν θεῖον εὐαγγελιστὴν Λουκᾶν, καὶ «καθὼς ἐλάλησε Κύριος διὰ τῶν ἁγίων αὐτοῦ προφητῶν ποιῆσαι ἔλεος», ὁ Ζαχαρίας φησί, καὶ «ἐπὶ Ἰωνᾶν τὸν τοῦ Ἀμαθῆ Λόγος Κυρίου ἐγένετο», καὶ «ὁ Λόγος ὁ γενόμενος πρὸς Ἡσαΐαν» καὶ ἄλλοτ' ἐπὶ ἄλλον, καὶ «εἶπε Κύριος πρὸς Μωϋσῆν» καὶ τὸν δεῖνα ἢ τὸν δεῖνα καὶ ἐφ' ὅσους ἀρτίως οὐδὲ ἀριθμῆσαι ῥᾴδιον.

Τί οὖν, ταῦτα πάντα τὸ Πνεῦμα τὸ ἅγιον ἦν καὶ οὐκ ἐλάλησεν αὐτὸ διὰ τῶν προφητῶν κατὰ τὸ γεγραμμένον, ἀλλ' αὐτὸ ἐλαλήθη δι' αὐτῶν ἢ ἐλαλήθη πρὸς αὐτούς; Ἄπαγε τῆς βλασφημίας. Εἰ δὲ μὴ ταῦτα τὰ ἐκ τοῦ ἀσωμάτου Θεοῦ ἀσωμάτως λεγόμενα τὸ Πνεῦμα τὸ ἅγιον ἦν, πολλῷ μᾶλλον οὐδὲ τὰ τοῦ Χριστοῦ ῥήματα σωματικῶς προφερόμενα. Εἰ δὲ μὴ ταῦτα, οὐδὲ ἡ ἀναπνοὴ ἐν ᾗ τυποῦται αὐτὰ καὶ προάγεται. Εἰ δὲ μὴ αὕτη, οὐδὲ τὸ ἐμφύσημα τὸ γεγονὸς δι' αὐτῆς. Πρὸς δὲ τούτῳ, οὐδὲ τὸ παρ' αὐτοῦ αἰνιττόμενον. Εἰ γοῦν καὶ παντάπασιν ἀδύνατον, ὅμως ἔστω μὴ τῆς σαρκός εἶναι, ἀλλὰ τῆς θεότητος τοῦ Υἱοῦ τὸ ἐμφύσημα· μᾶλλον δέ, ἵν' αὐτὸ θῶμεν τὸ παρὰ τῶν Λατίνων λεγόμενον, ἔστω παρὰ τοῦ αἰσθητοῦ τὸ νοητὸν ἐκεῖνο παρὰ τοῦ Σωτῆρος σημαίνεσθαι. Ἀλλ' ἐνεφύσησεν οὗτος καὶ τὴν ἀρχὴν εἰς πρόσωπον τοῦ πρώτου πλάσματος. Τί δὲ ἐνεφύσησε;

8

Now as relates to our current discourse, the words of the Lord are also declared by us, since he says, "With my lips have I declared all the judgments of Thy mouth."[37] Does this mean that the Holy Spirit also proceeds from us? But all those things, to which he drags down the Spirit who does not interpret the things of the Spirit by the Spirit, are[38] both searched and meditated and observed and practiced and understood; and the same holds for the amount of difference between the words of the Lord: commandments, laws, testimonies, statutes, judgments. "The word of the Lord came unto John the son of Zacharias," according to the divine evangelist Luke,[39] and "as the Lord spake by His holy prophets to perform mercy,"[40] says Zacharias, and "Now the Word of the Lord came to Jonah, the son of Amittai,"[41] and "The Word that came to Isaiah"[42] and other times to others, and "The Lord said unto Moses" and unto so-and-so or so-and-so and to so many that it is not easy even to enumerate them perfectly.

What then? Were all these things the Holy Spirit? Did He not speak through the prophets as it has been written, but was Himself actually spoken through them or to them? Away with this blasphemy! Now if these words which were spoken bodilessly from the bodiless God cannot be the Holy Spirit, then much more neither were the words of Christ, pronounced with His body, the Spirit. And if these are not the Spirit, then neither is the breathing whereby He forms them and pronounces them. And if this is not the Spirit, then neither is His breathing-upon which happened through it. And beside this, neither is the Holy Spirit what was spoken by Him as a riddle. So although it is completely impossible, nevertheless let it be assumed that the breathing-upon is not of the Son's flesh but of His divinity; or rather, so that we may present the very thing said by the Latins, let it be assumed that the Savior was signifying the noetic by the sensible. In the beginning, however, the same One also breathed into the face of the first formed. And what did He breath into him?

Πνοὴν ζωῆς. Τί ἐστι πνοὴν ζωῆς; Ψυχὴν ζῶσαν. Διδασκέτω σε Παῦλος· «ἐγένετο ὁ πρῶτος ἄνθρωπος εἰς ψυχὴν ζῶσαν». Τί δὲ ἐστι ζῶσαν; Ἀείζωον, ἀθάνατον, ταὐτὸν δ' εἰπεῖν λογικὴν - ἡ γὰρ ἀθάνατος λογικὴ – καὶ οὐ τοῦτο μόνον, ἀλλὰ καὶ κεχαριτωμένην θείως. Τοιαύτη γὰρ ὄντως ζῶσα ψυχή. Τοῦτο δὲ τῷ κατ' εἰκόνα ταὐτόν, εἰ δὲ βούλει καὶ καθ' ὁμοίωσιν. Ὢ τῆς ζημίας, ἐκ τίνος εἰς τί μετεβάλομεν.

9

Ἑώρων οἱ τῶν ἀγγέλων ὀφθαλμοὶ τότε τὴν αἰσθήσει καὶ σαρκὶ συνημμένην τοῦ ἀνθρώπου ψυχὴν καὶ Θεὸν ἄλλον ἑώρων, μὴ γεγενημένον μόνον ἐπὶ γῆς δι' ἀγαθότητα θείαν, νοῦν τε καὶ σάρκα τὸν αὐτόν, ἀλλὰ δι' ὑπερβολὴν ταύτης καὶ κατὰ Θεοῦ χάριν μεμορφωμένον, ὡς εἶναι τὸν αὐτὸν σάρκα καὶ νοῦν καὶ Πνεῦμα καὶ τὸ κατ' εἰκόνα καὶ ὁμοίωσιν θείαν τὴν ψυχὴν ἔχειν ἐντελῶς ὡς ἑνιαίαν οὖσαν ἐν νῷ καὶ λόγῳ καὶ πνεύματι. Ἀλλ' εἶδε καὶ ὁ βάσκανος ὀφθαλμός, οὐκ ἤνεγκεν ὁ ἀρχέκακος ὄφις· τοσοῦτον ἐκαρτέρησεν, οἶμαι, ὅσον δραστικώτερον τὸν ἰὸν ὑπὸ τὴν γλῶσσαν κεράσαι καὶ οἷον συσκευάσαι καὶ μῖξαι δόλῳ, γλυκερῷ λόγῳ, τὸ δι' ἀκοῆς δηλητήριον· ἐπῆλθεν, ἔθελξεν, ἔτρωσεν — ὢ καὶ τῆς ἐμῆς εὐκολίας καὶ τῆς ἐκείνου κακίας — εἰσέχεε τῇ ψυχῇ τὸν ἰόν, ἐθανάτωσε τὸ ζῶν ἐκεῖθεν, τὸ σῶμα λέγω, τὴν δ' ἀφ' ἑαυτῆς ζῶσαν ψυχὴν ἠμαύρωσεν· ἀφῃρήμεθα τὸ θεῖον κάλλος, ἐστερήμεθα τῆς θείας μορφῆς, τὸ φῶς ἀπεβάλομεν, τὴν πρὸς αὐτὸ τὸ ἀνωτάτω φῶς ὁμοιότητα διεφθείραμεν· περιβαλόμεθα τὸν ζόφον ὡς ἱμάτιον, φεῦ, καὶ ὡς διπλοΐδα τὸ σκότος ἐνεδεδύμεθα. Ἀλλ' ἠλέησε δωρεάν, ἵνα μὴ μηκύνω λέγων, οὗ φύσις ἡ ἀγαθότης καὶ ὁ δι' αὐτὴν ἔλεος· καὶ δι' ἐμὲ τὸν πεσόντα κατῆλθε καὶ γέγονε, καθά φησιν ὁ ἀπόστολος, «εἰς Πνεῦμα ζωοποιοῦν», ὡς ἂν ζωοποιήσας ἀνακαινίσῃ τὴν ἀμαυρωθεῖσαν εἰκόνα.

A breath of life.[43] What is a breath of life? A living soul.[44] Let Paul instruct you: "the first man was made a living soul."[45] And what is "living"? Ever living, immortal, which is the same as to say rational (since what is rational is immortal), and not only this, but also divinely graced. For such is truly a living soul. And this is the same as being according to the image and, if you will, according to the likeness as well. O the injurious loss! From what into what we have been changed!

9

The eyes of the angels were beholding at that time the soul of man joined with sense and flesh, and they were beholding another God, which had not only come into existence upon the earth on account of divine goodness, being the same in both intellect and flesh, but had also been formed according to the grace of God on account of the exceeding greatness of this same goodness, so that the same man might be flesh and intellect and spirit and so that his soul might completely possess being according to the divine image and likeness, since it is unitary in intellect and reason and spirit. But the envious eye also beheld him. The principal source of vice, the serpent, did not bear it. He was patient, I think, just as much as was enough for to mix a more potent poison under the tongue and as if to prepare and mingle with deceit, with a sweet word, the aural poison. He came; he captivated; he wounded — O my docility and his malignity! He injected the virus into the soul, he killed what was living off of it (I am referring to the body), while he blackened the soul which had life in itself. We have lost the divine beauty; we have been deprived of the divine form; we cast away the light; we corrupted the likeness to the highest light itself. We put on darkness as a garment,[46] alas! and as with a double cloak we endued ourselves with darkness. But—to be succinct—He freely had mercy, He whose nature is goodness and the consequent mercy; and for me who had fallen He descended and He has become, just as the Apostle says, "a quickening Spirit,"[47] so that, having quickened, He may renew the tarnished image.

Τοῦτο τοίνυν ἤδη τελῶν καὶ δεικνὺς ὡς οὗτος ἐκεῖνος ὁ καὶ τὴν ἀρχὴν δημιουργήσας δι᾽ ἐμφυσήματος τοῖς μαθηταῖς ἐμφυσᾷ καὶ δι᾽ οἰκείου λόγου φανεροῖ τὸ δώρημα· οὐκ αὖθις λέγων ψυχὴν ἐντίθημι, ἀλλὰ Πνεῦμα, καὶ Πνεῦμα θεῖον αὖθις τῇ μεταδόσει τῶν χαρισμάτων τὴν ψυχὴν ἀπεργάζομαι. Εἰπέ, Παῦλε, πῶς, τὸν λόγον διαδεξάμενος· στόμα γὰρ ὄντα σε γινώσκω Χριστοῦ. Αὐτήν, φησί, συνάπτων, ὡς ἐκεῖνος ἂν εἶπε, τῷ ἐμῷ πνεύματι καὶ οἷον πνέειν μετ᾽ ἐμοῦ τοὺς ἐμοὺς καὶ κατὰ χάριν ἔχειν διὰ τῆς πρὸς ἐμὲ συναφείας τὴν τῷ θείῳ Πνεύματι φυσικῶς προσοῦσαν τοῦ λύειν καὶ δεσμεῖν ἐξουσίαν. «Ἡμεῖς γάρ», φησί, «νοῦν Χριστοῦ ἔχομεν», καὶ «ὁ κολλώμενος τῷ Κυρίῳ ἓν Πνεῦμά ἐστιν».

10

Ἀλλ᾽ ὁρᾷς πῶς τὸ ἐμφύσημα τοῦτο αἰνίττεται μὲν παρὸν τὸ Πνεῦμα καὶ τελεσιουργοῦν τὴν ἐπὶ τὸ κρεῖττον τῆς ἀνθρωπίνης ψυχῆς ἀνακαίνισιν, ἣν ἐκ Πατρὸς διὰ τοῦ Υἱοῦ ἐν ἁγίῳ Πνεύματι τελεῖσθαι πιστεύομεν, δίδωσι δὲ πνεῦμα καὶ Πνεῦμα ἅγιον, ἀλλὰ κατὰ τὴν δωρεὰν καὶ τὴν δύναμιν καὶ τὴν χάριν καὶ τὴν ἐνέργειαν, ἥτις τὸ τὰς ἁμαρτίας τῶν ἀνθρώπων δεσμεῖν καὶ λύειν ἐστίν, οὐκ αὐτὴν τὴν ὑπόστασιν τοῦ παναγίου Πνεύματος; Παρ᾽ οὐδενὸς γὰρ αὕτη λαμβάνεσθαι δύναται. Τὰ δὲ χαρίσματα τοῦ Πνεύματος, αἱ φυσικαὶ δυνάμεις καὶ ἐνέργειαι, μηδαμῶς αὐτοῦ χωριζόμεναι, λαμβάνονται μὲν παρὰ τῶν ἀξίων ἐνεργεῖσθαι παρὰ τοῦ Πνεύματος, οἳ διὰ τὸ ἡνῶσθαι τούτῳ καὶ τῇ τούτου ἐνεργείᾳ χρισθῆναι (μόνος γὰρ ὁ μόνος Χριστὸς ὅλῳ ἐχρίσθη τῷ χρίοντι, κατὰ τὸν εἰπόντα, Χριστὸς διὰ τὴν θεότητα, οὐκ ἐνεργείᾳ κατὰ τοὺς ἄλλους χριστοὺς ἁγιάζουσαν, παρουσίᾳ δὲ ὅλου τοῦ χρίοντος)· τῷ γοῦν ἡνῶσθαι διὰ τῆς ἐκεῖθεν θείας ἐνεργείας καὶ χρηματίσαι τοῦ Πνεύματος ὄργανα, καὶ δι᾽ ἑαυτῶν αὐτὸ φανεροῦν λαβεῖν λέγονται καὶ πρὸς αὐτοὺς δίδοσθαι διὰ τοῦ Υἱοῦ, εἰ δὲ βούλει καὶ παρὰ τοῦ Υἱοῦ, τὸ Πνεῦμα τὸ ἅγιον.

Accordingly, accomplishing this now and showing that He was the same one who also created in the beginning through His breathing-upon, He breathes upon His disciples and through His own word manifests the gift. He does not say, "I am once again emplacing a soul" but "a Spirit, and I am once again making the soul a divine Spirit, by the communication of gifts." Tell, O Paul, how is this done? For you have received the word; and I know that you are the mouth of Christ. He says, as [Christ] would have said, "By joining the soul with my spirit, and it is as if my disciples breathe with me and have by grace, through the connection to me, the authority to loose and to bind, which is by nature present in the divine Spirit." For he says, "We have the mind of Christ,"[48] and, "He that is joined unto the Lord is one Spirit."[49]

10

But do you see how, on the one hand, this breathing-upon hints that the Spirit is present and is perfectly accomplishing the renewal of the human soul to that which is better, which renewal we believe to be accomplished from the Father through the Son in the Holy Spirit, while on the other hand it bestows a spirit, even a Holy Spirit, but in relation to the gift and the power and the grace and the energy (which is to bind and to loose the sins of men), not the very hypostasis of the All-Holy Spirit? For this is not able to be received by anyone. However, the gifts of the Spirit, the natural powers and activities, while being in no way separated from Him, are received by those who are worthy to be energized by the Spirit, who, on account of being united with Him and anointed by His energy (for the only Christ[50] alone has been anointed by the entirety of the Anointer, according to him who said[51] that He is Christ on account of His divinity, which sanctifies not by energy like the other christs but by the presence of the entire Anointer) — so at any rate in having been united through the divine energy from Him and having been called instruments of the Spirit, they are said to manifest through themselves that they received the Holy Spirit and that He is given to them through the Son or, if you will, from the Son as well. The

Καὶ τοῦτ' ἔδειξεν ὁ Κύριος ἐμφυσήσας καὶ εἰπὼν τοῖς μαθηταῖς, «λάβετε Πνεῦμα ἅγιον», ὡς καὶ Δαμασκηνὸς ὁ θεῖος ἡμᾶς ἐδίδαξεν· εἰπὼν γάρ, «ὅτι ἐκ τοῦ Υἱοῦ τὸ Πνεῦμα οὐ λέγομεν, Πνεῦμα δὲ Υἱοῦ ὀνομάζομεν καὶ δι' Υἱοῦ πεφανερῶσθαι καὶ μεταδίδοσθαι ἡμῖν ὁμολογοῦμεν», εὐθὺς ἐπήνεγκεν· «ἐνεφύσησε γὰρ καὶ εἶπε τοῖς μαθηταῖς, λάβετε Πνεῦμα ἅγιον». Ἆρ' οὐ κατάδηλον, ὡς ὁ δαμασκηνὸς Πατὴρ ἀπὸ τοῦ ἐμφυσήματος τούτου μὴ εἶναι καὶ ἐκ τοῦ Υἱοῦ ἀλλὰ φανεροῦσθαι μόνον καὶ μεταδίδοσθαι δι' αὐτοῦ τὸ Πνεῦμα τὸ ἅγιον ἐνόησε καί ἀπέδειξε;

11

Λατῖνοι δὲ φρενοβλαβῶς ἀντιθετικῶς ἐκείνῳ νοοῦσι καὶ δογματίζουσιν· οὐ γὰρ συνορῶσιν ὡς τὰ χαρίσματα ταῦτα καὶ αἱ ἐνέργειαι, καθ' ἃς διὰ τοῦ Υἱοῦ χορηγεῖται τὸ Πνεῦμα τὸ ἅγιον, οὐ παρὰ τοῦ Υἱοῦ μόνον, ἀλλὰ καὶ παρ' αὐτοῦ δίδονται τοῦ ἀνωτάτω Πατρός. «Πᾶν γάρ», φησί, «δώρημα τέλειον ἄνωθέν ἐστι παρὰ τοῦ Πατρός τῶν φώτων». Τί δὲ τῆς ἐξουσίας τοῦ ὑφιέναι καὶ κρατεῖν τὰ ἁμαρτήματα τελεώτερον; Καὶ οὐ παρὰ τοῦ Πατρός καὶ τοῦ Υἱοῦ μόνον, ἀλλὰ καὶ δι' αὐτοῦ καὶ παρ' αὐτοῦ τοῦ ἁγίου Πνεύματος· «ἐκχεῶ γὰρ ἀπὸ τοῦ Πνεύματός μου ἐπὶ πᾶσαν σάρκα» διὰ τοῦ Ἰωὴλ εἶπεν ὁ Θεός· ἧς ἐκχύσεώς ἐστι πάντως καὶ τὸ τοῖς μαθηταῖς παρὰ Χριστοῦ δεδομένον Πνεῦμα δι' ἐμφυσήματος· καὶ «τῷ μέν», φησί, «διὰ τοῦ Πνεύματος δίδοται λόγος σοφίας, τῷ δὲ λόγος γνώσεως», καί πάνθ' ὅσα ἐφεξῆς τῷ ἐκλεκτῷ σκεύει τῶν χαρισμάτων ἀπηρίθμηται Παύλῳ, τῷ καὶ τῶν ἀποκαλύψεων τὴν ὑπερβολὴν διὰ τοῦ Πνεύματος ἠμοιρηκότι· διὸ καὶ λέγοντι, «ἡμῖν δὲ ἀπεκάλυψεν ὁ Θεὸς διὰ τοῦ Πνεύματος αὐτοῦ», οὐ μόνον τὰ μὴ ἐγνωσμένα τοῖς περιβοήτοις κατ' ἀρετὴν καὶ εὐσέβειαν πατράσιν, ἀλλὰ καὶ αὐτὴν τὴν τῶν ἀγγέλων ὑπερβαίνοντα γνῶσιν· «καὶ ταῦτα γινώσκομεν», φησὶν ὁ τῶν ἀποστόλων θεολογικώτατος Ἰωάννης, «ἐκ τοῦ Πνεύματος οὗ ἐλάβομεν παρ' αὐτοῦ». Καὶ ἁπλῶς πᾶσα ἐπὶ τὴν κτίσιν ἡ τῶν ἀγαθῶν χορηγία ἐξ αὐτοῦ πηγάζει· καὶ «οὐκ ἔστιν ὅλως δωρεά», φησὶν ὁ μέγας Βασίλειος, «ἄνευ τοῦ ἁγίου Πνεύματος εἰς τὴν κτίσιν ἀφικνουμένη»· ὃς καὶ πάντα ἀπαριθμησάμενος, τάς

Lord showed this when He breathed upon His disciples and said
to them: "Receive ye Holy Spirit," as the divine from Damascus
taught us. For after he stated, "We do not say that the Spirit is from
the Son; but we do name Him Spirit of the Son and confess that
He has been manifested and transmitted to us through the Son," he
immediately added, "For He breathed upon His disciples and said
to them, 'Receive ye Holy Spirit.'"[52] So is it not completely clear
that from this breathing-upon the Damascene Father understood
and proved that the Holy Spirit is not also from the Son but is only
manifested and transmitted through Him?

11

The Latins, however, insanely consider and dogmatize in a way
contrary to that man. For they do not comprehend that these gifts
and energies, by which the Holy Spirit is supplied through the Son,
are bestowed not only by the Son but also by the Most High Father
Himself. For he says: "Every perfect gift is from above, coming
down from the Father of lights."[53] But what is more perfect than the
authority to bind and loose sins? And they are not only from the
Father and the Son, but are also through and from the Holy Spirit
Himself; for God said through the prophet Joel: "I will pour out of
My Spirit upon all flesh."[54] The Spirit bestowed by Christ to His
disciples by the breathing-upon is by all means part of this effusion
as well. And he says, "To one is bestowed by the Spirit the word of
wisdom, to another the word of knowledge"[55] and all the things that
have been enumerated in order by that elect vessel of charisms Paul,
to whom also was fittingly apportioned the greatness of revelations
by the Spirit. Wherefore he also says, "God hath revealed them unto
us by His Spirit,"[56] not only the things that were unknown to those
Fathers renowned for virtue and piety but even things that transcend
the very knowledge of the angels. John, the most theological of the
Apostles, says, "We know these things by the Spirit, which we have
received from Him."[57] And simply all the supply of good things
upon the creation springs from Him. And Basil the Great says,
"There is absolutely no gift which comes to the creation without the

τε δωρεὰς καὶ τὰ χαρίσματα καὶ τὰς ἐνεργείας τοῦ Πνεύματος, εἶτα φησί, «πάντα ταῦτα ἀϊδίως ἔχει τὸ Πνεῦμα τὸ ἅγιον, ἀλλὰ τὸ μὲν ἐκ Θεοῦ πηγάζον ἐνυπόστατόν ἐστι, τὰ δὲ ἐξ αὐτοῦ πηγάζοντα ἐνέργειαι αὐτοῦ εἰσιν». Ἆρ' οὖν καὶ ἐξ ἑαυτοῦ τὸ Πνεῦμα τὸ ἅγιον ἐκπορεύεται, ἐπεὶ ἐξ αὐτοῦ τε καὶ δι' αὐτοῦ πᾶσα ἡ τῶν ἀγαθῶν χορηγία, ἐν ᾗ πάντως καὶ ἡ τοῦ λύειν καὶ δεσμεῖν ἐξουσία, ἣν ὁ Κύριος δι' ἐμφυσήματος τοῖς μαθηταῖς παρέσχεν; Ἄπαγε τῆς ἀτοπίας· ἀλλὰ τὸ μὲν διδόναι τῶν τριῶν ἐστιν ὑποστάσεων κοινόν, ὡς καὶ ὁ ἀπόστολος συμμαρτυρεῖ· «διαιρέσεις γάρ», φησί, «χαρισμάτων εἰσί, τὸ δὲ αὐτὸ Πνεῦμα· καὶ διαρέσεις διακονιῶν, ὁ δὲ αὐτὸς Κύριος· καὶ διαιρέσεις ἐνεργημάτων, ὁ δὲ αὐτὸς Θεός».

12

Κοιναὶ μὲν οὖν τῇ μόνῃ ἁγίᾳ καὶ προσκυνητῇ Τριάδι αἵ τε θεῖαι δυνάμεις καὶ αἱ ἐνέργειαι, δι' ὧν ὁ Θεὸς ἐνοικεῖ καὶ ἐμπεριπατεῖ τοῖς ἀξίοις κατὰ τὴν ἐπαγγελίαν, δι' αὐτῶν ἐνεργῶν τε καὶ γνωριζόμενος. Ὧνπερ θείων ἐνεργειῶν καὶ πηγὴ θεολογεῖται μὴ μόνον ὁ Πατὴρ καὶ ὁ Υἱός, ἀλλὰ καὶ τὸ Πνεῦμα τὸ ἅγιον, ὡς καὶ ὁ μέγας φησὶ Βασίλειος ἐν τοῖς Περὶ τοῦ ἁγίου Πνεύματος ἀντιρρητικοῖς αὐτοῦ κεφαλαίοις γράφων· «αἱ δὲ ἐνέργειαι τοῦ Πνεύματος τίνες; Ἄρρητοι μὲν διὰ τὸ μέγεθος, ἀνεξαρίθμητοι δὲ διὰ τὸ πλῆθος». Καὶ πάλιν· «παρὰ τῷ ἁγίῳ Πνεύματι πάντα τέλεια· ἀγάπη, χαρά, εἰρήνη, μακροθυμία, χρηστότης, σοφία, σύνεσις, βουλή, ἀσφάλεια, εὐσέβεια, γνῶσις, ἁγιασμός, ἀπολύτρωσις, πίστις, ἐνεργήματα δυνάμεων, χαρίσματα ἰαμάτων, καὶ ὅσα τούτοις παραπλήσια, οὐδὲν ἔχον τι ἐν ἑαυτῷ ἐπίκτητον ἀλλ' ἀϊδίως πάντα ἔχον, ὡς Πνεῦμα Θεοῦ καὶ ἐξ αὐτοῦ πεφηνός, αἴτιον ἑαυτῷ ἔχον ὡς πηγὴν ἑαυτοῦ κἀκεῖθεν πηγάζον. Πηγὴ δὲ καὶ αὐτὸ τῶν προειρημένων ἀγαθῶν. Ἀλλὰ τὸ μὲν ἐκ Θεοῦ πηγάζον ἐνυπόστατόν ἐστι, τὰ δὲ ἐξ αὐτοῦ πηγάζοντα ἐνέργειαι αὐτοῦ εἰσι». Ταῦτα δέ εἰσι τὰ γνωριστικὰ τῆς θείας φύσεως αὐχήματα.

Holy Spirit."[58] This man, after he also enumerated all things, both the gifts and the charisms and the energies of the Spirit, then says, "The Holy Spirit eternally has all these things, but what springs from God is enhypostatic, while the things which spring from Him are His energies."[59] So then, does the Holy Spirit also proceed from His own self, since all the supply of good things is both from Him and through Him, in which supply is also entirely the authority to lose and bind, which the Lord granted to His disciples by breathing upon them? Away with the absurdity. But the bestowing is common for the three hypostases, as the Apostle also testifies. For he says, "There are diversities of gifts, but the same Spirit. And there are differences of administrations, but the same Lord. And there are diversities of operations, but it is the same God."[60]

12

Therefore, both the divine powers and the energies are truly common to the only holy and worshipful Trinity, whereby God indwells and walks among those who are worthy, according to the promise.[61] By them He acts and is known. Not only the Father and the Son but also the Holy Spirit are theologized as the fount of these divine energies, as Basil the Great also says in his Rebuttal Chapters *Concerning the Holy Spirit*, when he writes, "Now what are the energies of the Spirit? They actually cannot be described on account of their magnitude, but also on account of their multitude they cannot be reckoned." And again: "All things are perfect in the Holy Spirit: love, joy, peace, longsuffering, kindness,[62] wisdom, understanding, counsel, security,[63] piety, knowledge, sanctification, redemption,[64] faith, workings of spiritual powers, charisms of healing, and whatever things resembling these. He has no acquired thing in Himself. Instead, He possesses all things eternally, since He is the Spirit of God and has shone forth from Him, having the cause in Himself as His own fount from whence He springs forth. He too is the fount of the previously mentioned good things; but what springs from God is enhypostatic, while the things which spring from Him are His energies." These same things are the characteristic boasts of the divine nature.

Θέλων οὖν ὁ Κύριος ἡμῶν Ἰησοῦς Χριστὸς ὁμοούσιον ἑαυτὸν δεῖξαι κατὰ τὴν θεότητα τῷ Πατρὶ καὶ τῷ Πνεύματι, τοῖς μαθηταῖς αὐτὸς ταύτην κατὰ χάριν δίδωσι τὴν φυσικὴν τῆς θεότητος ἐνέργειαν, ὡς καὶ ὁ Πατὴρ πρότερον ἐνίας τῶν τοιούτων ἐνεργειῶν τοῖς προφήταις παρέσχε· καὶ τὸ Πνεῦμα δὲ τὸ ἅγιον κατελθὸν μετὰ τὴν τοῦ Σωτῆρος ἄνοδον, καὶ αὐτὸ τὰς τοιαύτας ἐνεργείας ἔδωκε τοῖς μαθηταῖς, δι᾽ αὐτῶν καὶ αὐτὸ δεικνύμενον ὁμοούσιον τῷ Πατρὶ καὶ τῷ Υἱῷ. Κοινὰ μὲν οὖν καὶ πολλὰ τῇ μόνῃ ἁγίᾳ καὶ προσκυνητῇ Τριάδι τὰ πρὸς ἡμᾶς ἐξ αὐτῆς θεῖα δόματα καὶ ἡ τούτων δόσις, ἡ δέ τοῦ ἁγίου Πνεύματος ἐκπόρευσις μία καὶ τοῦ Πατρὸς ἰδία καὶ προαιώνιος.

13

Ἀλλ᾽ ἵνα καὶ τὴν ἀπολογίαν ἐπισφραγίσωμαι καὶ «πᾶν στόμα τὸ ἀντιτεῖνον φραγῇ», αὐτὸν τὸν τῆς ἀληθείας λόγον τοῦ νυνὶ λόγου κατὰ τοὺς πρὸ ἡμῶν συμφθεγγόμενον ἡμῖν δείξας προβαλοῦμαι μάρτυρα τῆς ἀληθείας. Αὐτὸς δὲ ὁ μηδαμόθεν χωριζόμενος, γῆθεν πρὸς τὸν ἐπουράνιον Πατέρα ἀνιών, τοῖς διαμεμενηκόσιν εἰς τέλος μετ᾽ αὐτοῦ «παρήγγειλεν ἀπὸ Ἱεροσολύμων μὴ χωρίζεσθαι, ἀλλὰ περιμένειν τὴν ἐπαγγελίαν τοῦ Πατρὸς ἣν ἠκούσατέ μου», φησίν. Ἀλλὰ τίς ἡ ἐπαγγελία; Ὅτι «βαπτισθήσεσθε», φησίν, «ἐν Πνεύματι ἁγίῳ, οὐ μετὰ πολλὰς ταύτας ἡμέρας». Οὐκοῦν πρὸ τῆς τοῦ Σωτῆρος ἀναλήψεως οὔπω τῆς ἐπαγγελίας ἔτυχον· οὐκ ἄρα διὰ τοῦ ἐμφυσήματος τὸ Πνεῦμα τὸ ἅγιον ἐδόθη, τοῦτο γάρ ἡ ἐπαγγελία. Πότε δὴ τοῦ Σωτῆρος ἐπαγγειλαμένου ταῦτ᾽ ἤκουσαν οἱ μαθηταί; Ὅτε μέλλων ἑκὼν ὑπὲρ ἡμῶν ἀποθνήσκειν – βαβαὶ τοῦ μεγέθους τῆς πρὸς ἡμᾶς διαθέσεως – οὐχ ἑαυτὸν μόνον ὑπὲρ ἡμῶν παρεδίδου τῇ σφαγῇ, ἀλλὰ καὶ κληρονόμους ἐνδιαθήκως ἐποιεῖτο τῶν ὑπαρχόντων αὐτῷ καὶ τοὺς θησαυροὺς ἡμῖν ἀνεώγνυ τε καὶ παρεδίδου καὶ αὐτὸν τὸν συμφυᾶ καὶ πᾶσαν κτίσιν ὑπεραναβεβηκότα, τὸν ἀκένωτον πλοῦτον τοῦ Πνεύματος· «ἐγὼ γάρ», φησίν, «ἐρωτήσω τὸν Πατέρα καὶ ἄλλον παράκλητον δώσει ὑμῖν, ἵνα μένῃ μεθ᾽ ὑμῶν εἰς τὸν αἰῶνα». Εἶτα μετ᾽ ὀλίγα, «ὁ δὲ παράκλητος, τὸ Πνεῦμα τὸ ἅγιον, ὃ πέμψει ὁ Πατὴρ ἐν τῷ

Willing, therefore, to show Himself consubstantial with the Father
and the Spirit with respect to His divinity, our Lord Jesus Christ
Himself gives to the disciples by grace this same natural energy of
the divinity, just like the Father also previously provided some such
energies to the prophets. And when the Holy Spirit descended after
the ascent of the Savior, He too gave to the disciples these energies,
whereby showing Himself to be also consubstantial with the Father
and the Son. So, the divine gifts to us from the Trinity as well as
the bestowal of them are actually many and common to the only
holy and worshipful Trinity. In contrast, the procession of the Holy
Spirit is one and eternal and specifically from the Father.

13

But so that I may seal up the defense and that "every opposing
mouth may be stopped," I shall put forth a witness of the truth, the
very Word of truth Himself, whom, as regards the present discourse,
I had shown for us that He resounds in harmony with those who
were before us. When He that is separated from nowhere[65] was
ascending from earth to the heavenly Father, "He commanded"
those who had endured steadfastly to the end with Him "not to
depart from Jerusalem, but to wait for the promise of the Father you
heard from Me," as He said.[66] But what exactly was the promise? It
is that "Ye shall be baptized," as He said, "in the Holy Spirit, in not
many days."[67] So they had not yet attained the promised before the
Ascension of the Savior. Therefore the Holy Spirit was not given
through the breathing-upon — since this was the promise. On this
point, when did the disciples hear these things promised by the
Savior? When He was about to willingly die for us. O the magnitude
of His disposition toward us! Not only was He delivering Himself to
the slaughter for us, but He was also making us covenantally heirs of
His belongings and opening to us His treasures and delivering even
the inexhaustible wealth of the Spirit, which is of the same nature
and transcends all creation. And so He says, "I will pray the Father,
and He shall give you another Comforter, that He may abide with
you for ever."[68] Then, after a little while, "But the Comforter, the

ὀνόματί μου, ἐκεῖνος ὑμᾶς διδάξει πάντα». Εἶτ᾿ αὖθις μετὰ τὰς γλυκείας ὑποθήκας ἐκείνας, μετὰ τοὺς ψυχαγωγοῦντας λόγους, μετὰ τὰς πρὸς φυλακὴν τοῦ πλούτου προτροπάς, «ὅταν ἔλθῃ», φησίν, «ὁ παράκλητος, ὃν ἐγὼ πέμψω ὑμῖν παρὰ τοῦ Πατρός, τὸ Πνεῦμα τῆς ἀληθείας, ὃ παρὰ τοῦ Πατρὸς ἐκπορεύεται, ἐκεῖνος μαρτυρήσει περὶ ἐμοῦ». Εἶδες τοῦ ὄντος θησαυροῦ τὰ κατὰ μέρος κλεῖθρα διανοιγόμενα; Μᾶλλον δ᾿, ἵν᾿ εἴπω θεολογικώτερον, ὁρᾷς φωτισμοὺς ἡμῖν κατὰ μέρος ἐλλάμποντας;

14

Ἀλλ᾿ ὑπὲρ οὗ νῦν ὁ λόγος, ἴδωμεν τὴν ἐπαγγελίαν· τὸ δ᾿ «οὐ μετὰ πολλὰς ταύτας ἡμέρας» ποῦ; Αὐτοῦ τῶν λόγων μικρὸν προελθὼν καὶ τοῦτο τότε προείρηκεν ἐκ τῶν μεγίστων τοὺς οἰκείους φιλανθρώπως παραμυθούμενος· «συμφέρει γάρ», φησίν, «ὑμῖν, ἵνα ἐγὼ ἀπέλθω· ἐὰν γὰρ ἐγὼ μὴ ἀπέλθω, ὁ παράκλητος οὐκ ἐλεύσεται πρὸς ὑμᾶς». Πῶς οὖν τις τολμᾷ λέγειν, ὅτι διὰ τοῦ ἐμφυσήματος ἦλθε πρὸς τοὺς μαθητὰς τοῦ Κυρίου πρὶν ἀναληφθῆναι αὐτόν; Ἀλλ᾿ ἔστω, φησίν· οὐ γὰρ ἐδόθη πρὸ τῆς ἀναλήψεως τοῦ Σωτῆρος ὁ ἄλλος παράκλητος. Ἔχεις καὶ τοῦτο λέγειν, ὡς οὐκ αὐτὸς σαφῶς τοῖς μαθηταῖς ἐπηγγείλατο λέγων, «ὃν ἐγὼ πέμψω ὑμῖν», καὶ «ἐὰν ἐγὼ πορευθῶ, πέμψω αὐτὸν πρὸς ὑμᾶς»;

Εὖγέ σοι τοῦτο μετ᾿ ἐκεῖνο προήχθη, πρὸς τὸν εἰπόντα φαίη τις ἄν· ὑποβέβηκε γὰρ καὶ τῇ δυνάμει τοῦ δοκοῦντος ὑμῖν παρὰ τῶν Γραφῶν βοηθήματος. Εἰ γὰρ καὶ τοῦτο λόγος τοῦ Λόγου τῆς ἀληθείας, ἀλλ᾿ οὐχ ὁμοίως τὸ ἐμφυσᾶν καὶ τὸ πέμπειν τὸ παρ᾿ ἑαυτοῦ δείκνυσιν· ὁ μὲν γὰρ ἐμφυσῶν κατὰ πᾶσαν ἀνάγκην ἐξ ἑαυτοῦ ἐμφυσᾷ τῷ παρ᾿ ἑαυτοῦ πνεύματι· ταὐτὸν δ᾿ εἰπεῖν τῷ παρ᾿ ἑαυτοῦ ἐκπορευομένῳ ἐμφυσήματι. Οὐ μὴν δὲ καὶ πᾶς ὁ πέμπων τὸ παρ᾿ ἑαυτοῦ ὄν τε καὶ ἐκπορευόμενον πέμπει, ἀλλὰ καὶ τὸ παρ᾿ ἑτέρου πρὸς αὐτὸν ἧκον. Διὸ καὶ σπουδὴν ὁ Κύριος θέμενος τοῦ μηδένα παραχθέντα δοξάζειν,

Holy Spirit, whom the Father will send in my name, He shall teach you all things."[69] Then again, after those sweet admonitions, after those words given to guide their souls, after the exhortations to the preservation of the wealth, He says, "When the Comforter is come, whom I will send unto you from the Father, even the Spirit of truth, which proceedeth from the Father, he shall testify of me."[70] Did you see the bars of the true treasury being successively opened? Or better yet, to express it more theologically, do you see illuminations successively illuminating us?

14

But for the sake of our present argument, let us look at the promise. The expression "not many days after," when was it? Shortly after stating these words of His, He also then foretold this, with the greatest of things comforting His own out of His love for mankind. For he says: "It is to your advantage that I go away; for if I go not away, the Comforter will not come to you."[71] So how can one dare say that He came to the disciples of the Lord through His breathing-upon before His Ascension? 'Alright, granted,' [the other man] says, 'since the other Comforter was not given before the Ascension of the Savior. [But] are you able to say this too, that He Himself did not clearly promise to His disciples saying, "Whom I will send to you,"[72] and "if I depart, I will send Him to you"?'[73]

You did well in presenting this one after that one (one could say to the questioner), since it is also inferior in power than what you consider to be aid from the Scriptures. For although this, too, is a word of the Word of truth, yet 'to breathe upon' and 'to send' do not prove in the same way that it is from Himself. For certainly one who breathes upon something breathes with absolute necessity from His own self by His own spirit, which is the same as saying, by the breathing-upon that proceeds from himself. Not everyone who sends, however, sends only what both is and proceeds from himself, but also what has come to him from another. On account of this also the Lord, taking pains lest anyone be misled into thinking that

ὅτι τὸ Πνεῦμα τὸ ἅγιον καὶ ἐξ αὐτοῦ ἐκπορεύεται, τὸ μὲν ἐμφύσημα, ὃ τοῦτ᾽ ἐδόκει μᾶλλον παριστᾶν, τότ᾽ ἔδωκεν, ὅτε ἀπείρηκε καὶ ὑπερέθετο τὴν ἐπιδημίαν τοῦ Πνεύματος· τὸ δὲ «πέμψω» προειπών, προσέηκε τὸ «παρὰ τοῦ Πατρός». Εἰ γὰρ καὶ «πέμψω», φησίν, ἀλλ᾽ οὐ παρ᾽ ἐμαυτοῦ ἀλλὰ παρὰ τοῦ Πατρὸς λαβών, ἀφ᾽ οὗ ἐκπορεύεται· ἐκεῖνος γὰρ μόνος πέμπει παρ᾽ ἑαυτοῦ, ὡς παρ᾽ ἑαυτοῦ τοῦτ᾽ ἔχων ἐκπορευόμενον, καὶ ἀεὶ τοῦτ᾽ ἔχων ἐκπορευόμενον, οὐ τότε μόνον ἐκπορευθησόμενον ὅτε καὶ αὐτὸς ἐγὼ «πέμψω», οὐδὲ παρ᾽ ἐμοῦ ἀδιαστάτως πεμπόμενον, ὥσπερ παρ᾽ ἐκείνου ἐκπορευόμενον· οὐ γὰρ εἰπὼν «πέμψω» τό "παρ᾽ ἐκείνου ἐκπορευθὲν" προσεπήγαγον, ἵνα μὴ ἐπὶ τοῦ Πατρὸς προσεπινοηθῇ τὸ "ποτέ". Καὶ ἐπιφέρειν μέλλων «ὃ παρὰ τοῦ Πατρὸς ἐκπορεύεται», φθάσας εἶπον, οὐχ "ὃ ἐγὼ πέμπω", ἀλλ᾽ «ὃ ἐγὼ πέμψω», ἵνα μὴ συνεπινοηθῇ καὶ ἐπ᾽ ἐμοῦ τὸ ἀεί. Τὸ μὲν γὰρ πέμπειν ἔχειν τὸ Πνεῦμα τὸ ἅγιον πρὸς τοὺς ἀξίους κοινόν ἐστιν ἐξ ἀϊδίου τῷ Πατρὶ καὶ τῷ Υἱῷ· πέμπει δὲ χρονικῶς ἑκάτερος, ἀμφότεροι δὲ μᾶλλον, ὁπότε δέοι.

15

Ταῦτ᾽ ἄρα καὶ τὴν προθεσμίαν καὶ τὸν μέλλοντα χρόνον ἐπιδέχεσθαι δύναται· τοῦ δὲ ἐκπορεύειν τὸ ἐκπορεύειν ἔχειν οὐδαμῶς προηγεῖται, οὐδ᾽ ἐν ἐπαγγελίας μοίρᾳ κείσεταί ποτε, οὐδὲ τὸ μέλλειν ἐπιδέξαιτ᾽ ἄν, ἄπαγε τῆς βλασφημίας, ἢ συμβαίνει τοῖς οἰομένοις ἀΐδιον εἶναι τὴν παρὰ τοῦ Υἱοῦ ἔκπεμψιν τοῦ Πνεύματος. Ἐπέμφθη γάρ τισι καὶ ἐδόθη πρὸς τοὺς μαθητὰς ἐκ τοῦ Υἱοῦ, λαβόντος παρὰ τοῦ Πατρὸς χρονικῶς καὶ αὐτῶν τῶν λαμβανόντων ὑστερογενεστέρας οὔσης τῆς ἀποστολῆς, καὶ δι᾽ αἰτίαν, μᾶλλον δὲ διὰ πολλὰς αἰτίας· «ἵνα μένῃ», φησί, «μεθ᾽ ὑμῶν εἰς τὸν αἰῶνα», «ἵνα ὑμᾶς διδάξῃ καὶ ὑπομνήσῃ πάντα ἃ εἶπον ὑμῖν», «ἵνα μαρτυρήσῃ περὶ ἐμοῦ» καὶ ὑμῖν συμμαρτυρήσῃ τὰ κατ᾽ ἐμέ, ἀπ᾽ ἀρχῆς μέχρι τέλους μαρτυροῦσιν,

the Holy Spirit also proceeds from Him, gave the breathing-upon, which seemed more to represent this, at that time at which He denied the coming of the Spirit and placed it in the future; and after He had previously said, "I will send," He appropriately added, "from the Father." "For although 'I shall send,'" He says, "yet not from Myself, but having received from the Father, from whom He proceeds. And that is because only that one, the Father, sends from Himself, as He possesses Him proceeding from Himself, in fact always having Him proceeding, not going to proceed at that time only when I myself 'will send,' neither being sent from Me without distance even as proceeding from the Father. For when I said 'I shall send,' I did not add, 'what has proceeded from the Father,' lest the notion of 'once' be conceived in relation to the Father. And when I was about to add 'which proceedeth from the Father,' once I came to it, I did not say 'whom I send' but 'whom I will send,' so that the notion of 'always' might not be conceived in relation to Me."[74] For the ability to send the Holy Spirit to the worthy ones is common from eternity to the Father and to the Son, and within time each sends, or rather both, whenever it becomes necessary.

15

So, these can be accepted as applying both to the appointed time [of the promise] and to the future time. The ability to cause procession, however, does not in any way precede the causing of procession, nor will it ever be attributed as part of the promise, nor could it possibly be accepted as applying to the future. Away with the blasphemy, which happens to those who think that the sending forth of the Spirit from the Son is eternal. For He was sent to certain individuals and given to the disciples from the Son, who temporally received Him from the Father. The sending was generated even later than the recipients themselves, and for a cause, or rather for many causes. He says, "'That He may abide with you forever,"[75] "That He may teach you and bring all things which I spoke to you to remembrance,"[76] "That He may testify of Me"[77] and that He may testify to what pertains to Me along with you, who bear witness

«ἵνα ἐλέγξῃ τὸν κόσμον» ὑπεύθυνον τῇ ἁμαρτίᾳ, τὸν ἁμαρτίαν
ὀνομάσαντα τὴν ἐμὴν δικαιοσύνην· δικαιοσύνην ἣ καὶ αὐτὸν τὸν
ἄρχοντα τῆς ἁμαρτίας καὶ αὐτῆς τῆς τῶν ἁμαρτωλῶν ἐξέβαλεν
ἀρχῆς κατακρίνασα δικαίως, ὅτι τὸν ὄντως δίκαιον ἀδίκως ὑπὸ τὴν
αὐτὴν τοῖς ἁμαρτωλοῖς ἤγαγεν εὐθύνην, ἵν᾽ ἐμὲ δοξάσῃ, ὁδηγῆσαν
ὑμᾶς πρὸς πᾶσαν τὴν ἀλήθειαν. Καὶ γὰρ «Πνεῦμα ἀληθείας» ἐστί,
καὶ «οὐκ ἀφ᾽ ἑαυτοῦ λαλεῖ, ἀλλ᾽ ὅσα ἂν ἀκούῃ παρὰ τοῦ Πατρός»,
«ὥσπερ κἀγὼ οὐδὲν ἐλάλησα ἀπ᾽ ἐμαυτοῦ»· ἐπεὶ δὲ ὁ Πατὴρ ἐμὸς
καὶ «πάντα ὅσα ἔχει ὁ Πατὴρ ἐμά», «ἐκ τοῦ ἐμοῦ λαμβάνει καὶ
ἀναγγέλλει»· κοινὰ γὰρ ἡμῖν καὶ ὁ πλοῦτος καὶ τὰ δόματα.

Ἐπέμφθη τοίνυν ἐκ τοῦ Πατρὸς καὶ τοῦ Υἱοῦ χρονικῶς καὶ πρός
τινας καὶ δι᾽ αἰτίαν· παρ᾽ αὐτοῦ δὲ μόνου τοῦ Πατρός ἐκπορεύεται
ἀχρόνως καὶ ἀναιτίως, αὐτὸν μόνον ἔχον αἰτίαν ἑαυτοῦ, τὸν μόνον
ἀγέννητον Πατέρα, τὸν ποιοῦντα τὰ πάντα ἐκ μὴ ὄντων διὰ μόνην
τὴν κοινὴν ἑαυτοῦ τε κἀκείνων ἀγαθότητα, τὸν δ᾽ Υἱὸν ἐξ ἀρχῆς
ἔχοντα γεγεννημένον καὶ τὸ Πνεῦμα τὸ ἅγιον ἐκπορευόμενον.

16

Ἆρα νοῦν ἔλαβες ὁ δι᾽ ἐναντίας καὶ φῶς γνώσεως ἐπέλαμψέ σοι
παρὰ τοῦ τῆς ἀληθείας λόγου; Μᾶλλον δὲ σύ γε αὐτὸς ἆρα διαίρειν
ἤρξω τὰ βλέφαρα καὶ διαβλέπειν πρὸς τὸ φῶς, εἰ καὶ μὴ τελέως,
ἀλλ᾽ ἀμυδρῶς γοῦν ἀντιλαμβανόμενος τῆς διαπρυσίου καὶ μὴ
ἀμυδρᾶς αὐγῆς, ὥστε ψηλαφῆσαι καὶ ἰδεῖν ὅτι τὸ «δώσει» τε καὶ
τὸ «πέμψει» τοσαυτάκις εἰρημένον οὐδαμοῦ χωρὶς αἰτίας εἴρηκεν,
οὐδ᾽ ἄνευ προσώπου τοῦ λαμβάνοντος δι᾽ ὃν καὶ πέμπεται, ἀλλ᾽
ἀεὶ συνεζευγμένον ταῖς αἰτίαις ἀποδέδωκεν ὁ μόνος καὶ Θεὸς καὶ
θεολόγος, τὸ δὲ ἐκπορευόμενον ἀπολύτως ἔθηκε χωρὶς ἡστινοσοῦν
αἰτίας; Τὴν μὲν γὰρ συνδιαιωνίζουσαν καὶ χωρὶς αἰτίας οὖσαν
ἔκπεμψιν μόνῳ τῷ Πατρὶ προσένειμε, τὴν δ᾽ ὑπὸ χρόνον οὖσαν
καὶ ἀεὶ μετὰ τῆς αἰτίας συνημμένην κοινὴν οὖσαν, ἐξεκάλυψεν

from the beginning to the end, "That He may reprove the world"[78] as responsible for sin, which called my own righteousness sin—a righteousness which cast the very Prince of sin out of his dominion over sinners and justly condemned him, because he unrighteously brought Him that was truly righteous under the same chastisement with sinners—"That He many glorify Me," having led you to all the truth. For He is "the Spirit of truth" and does "not speak of Himself but whatsoever He hears from the Father,"[79] just as I also have "spoken nothing of Myself."[80] And seeing that the Father is Mine and "all things that the Father hath are Mine,"[81] "He receives from Mine and proclaims it."[82] For both the wealth and the gifts are common to us.'

Accordingly, He was sent from the Father and the Son temporally to certain people and for a cause, yet He proceeds only from the Father timelessly and causelessly[83], having as His own cause only Him, the only unbegotten Father, who makes all things from non-being only for the common good of Himself and of them while from the beginning He has had the Son who has been begotten and the Holy Spirit who proceeds.

16

So have you grasped the point, you opposer, and has the light of knowledge shined upon you from the word of truth? Or rather, at the very least, have you yourself begun to open your eyelids and look with steadfastness at the light, even if not perfectly but at any rate indistinctly sharing in the piercing and not indistinct dawn, so that you may handle and see that both the phrase "He will give" and the phrase "He will send," which have been said so many times, have nowhere been said without a cause nor without a person as recipient, because of whom He is sent, but the only God and theologian has rendered [these phrases] always yoked to the causes, while He has placed What proceeds absolutely independent of any cause whatsoever? For while He attributed the sending forth that is eternal and independent of cause only to the Father, yet He

ἑαυτῷ καὶ τῷ Πατρί, ὡς ἂν τοῦτο συνιδών, μηκέτι βλασφημῇς τῇ ἐκπορεύσει φρονῶν καὶ λέγων τὴν ἀποστολὴν ταὐτόν ἢ ἐκ ταύτης ἐκείνην στοχαζόμενος καὶ διὰ τοῦτο λέγων ἐκ τοῦ Πατρὸς καὶ ἐξ Υἱοῦ τὸ θεῖον Πνεῦμα τὴν ὑπόστασιν ἔχειν. Ὥσπερ γὰρ Θεὸς ἀναίτιος, οὕτω καὶ Θεοῦ ὕπαρξις ἀναίτιος, αὐτὸν αἰτίαν ἔχων τὸν ἐξ οὗ ὑπάρχει ἀναιτίως, ἀλλ' οὐκ ἐξ αὐτοῦ ὑπάρχων δι' αἰτίαν. Ὥσπερ δὲ Θεὸς καὶ Θεοῦ ὕπαρξις ἀναίτιος, οὕτω τὸ δι' αἰτίαν γεγονὸς κοινὸν αὐτῷ τε τῷ ἀναιτίῳ καὶ τοῖς ἀναιτίοις ἐξ αὐτοῦ ὑπάρχουσιν. Ὁ δ' αὐτοῖς κοινόν, θείας ὑποστάσεως οὐκ ἴδιον. Διὸ τὸ μὲν ἀποστέλλεσθαι καὶ τῷ Υἱῷ καὶ τῷ Πνεύματι ὑπάρχει, ὥσπερ καὶ τὸ ἀποστέλλειν τοῖς τρισί· δι' αἰτίαν γάρ. Τὸ δὲ ἐκπορεύεσθαι ἢ καὶ ἐκπορεύειν οὐχὶ καὶ τοῦ Υἱοῦ· καὶ γὰρ οὐ δι' αἰτίαν. Ὅταν οὖν ἀκούσῃς ἐκ τοῦ Υἱοῦ ἢ καὶ δι' Υἱοῦ ἢ καὶ ἐξ ἀμφοῖν πρός τινας πεμπόμενον τὸ Πνεῦμα τὸ ἅγιον, τὴν ὑπὸ χρόνον καὶ δι' αἰτίαν ἐπὶ νοῦν λάμβανέ μοι πρόοδον, ἀλλὰ μὴ τὴν ἐκ Πατρὸς ἄσχετον ἐκείνην καὶ ὑπὲρ αἰτίαν καὶ προαιώνιον.

17

Τί οὖν; Ἤδη πείθομεν καὶ διετρανώθη σοι τὸ φῶς, ἢ ἔτι προσμενοῦμεν συνείροντες τὰς ἀποδείξεις καὶ διαρριπίζοντες τὸ τῆς σῆς ἀγνοίας σκότος; Ὡς πολὺ τοῦτο καὶ βαθὺ τὰ τῆς σῆς ἐπηλυγάζον διανοίας κόρας ἔχεις, εἰ μηδὲ νῦν πρὸς τὴν ἀλήθειαν διέβλεψάς πω, καίτοι τὸ «δώσω» ταὐτόν ἐστι τῷ «πέμψω». Ἐπεὶ γὰρ μήτε τὸ πεμπόμενον τοπικῶς μετάγεται μήτ' αὐτὸς ὁ πέμπων διῖσταται τοῦ πεμπομένου (καὶ γὰρ ἀεί τε ἅμα καὶ ἁπανταχοῦ καὶ ὁ πέμπων καὶ τὸ δι' αὐτοῦ πεμπόμενον, εἰ δὲ βούλει καὶ ἐξ αὐτοῦ· οὐ γὰρ ἐπὶ τῶν συλλαβῶν ἡμῖν ἡ εὐσέβεια)· ἐπεὶ τοίνυν οὐ διαιρεῖται τόπῳ, οὐδὲ τόπῳ περιλαμβάνεται τὸ πέμπον καὶ τὸ πεμπόμενον, οὐκ

unveiled the other sending, which is subject to time and always joined with the cause, since it is common, as belonging to His own self and to the Father, so that being aware of this you may no longer blaspheme with respect to the procession, thinking and saying that the sending is identical to the procession or conjecturing the one from the other and saying, on account of this, that the divine Spirit has His hypostasis from the Father and from the Son. For just as God is causeless, so also the existence of God is causeless, possessing as His own cause Him from whom He exists causelessly, not existing from Him on account of a cause. But just as God and the existence of God are causeless, in the same way what came to be for a cause is common both to the uncaused Himself and to those causeless who exist from Him. But what is common to them is not an idiom of a divine hypostasis. Consequently, "to be sent" does actually exist both for the Son and the Spirit, just like "to send" exists for the three, since it is for a cause. But "to proceed" or "to make proceed" is not the Son's as well, since it is not for a cause. So, whenever you hear that the Holy Spirit is sent from the Son or also through the Son or also from both to certain ones, take it to mean the progression which is temporal and for a cause, not that unrelated procession from the Father, which is both transcendent of cause and eternal.

17

What then? Have we finally persuaded you and disclosed to you the light, or do we still need to continue stringing together demonstrations and breaking up the darkness of your ignorance? How great and deep is this darkness which you have covering the eyes of your understanding, if even now you have not somehow seen through to the truth, although the "I will give" is identical to the "I will send". For neither is the Sent transferred in relation to space, nor is the Sender Himself separated from the Sent, since both the Sender and He that is sent by Him (or, if you prefer, "from Him", since our piety does not rest in words) are ever contemporaneous and everywhere. Accordingly, since the Sender and the Sent are not divided by location and are not circumscribed locally, does the

ἆρα δίδωσιν ὁ πέμπων; Τοῦτο καὶ αὐτὸς ὁ Κύριος ἡμᾶς φωτίζων νῦν
μὲν εἴρηκεν, «ὃ δώσει ὁ Πατήρ», νῦν δ᾽ αὖθις, «ὃ πέμψει ὁ Πατήρ»,
ἐπὶ τῆς ἀμφοτέροις διανοίας χρησάμενος. Ἀλλὰ καὶ αὐτός, νῦν μὲν
ὅτι ἐπέμφη παρὰ τοῦ Πατρός, νῦν δ᾽ ὅτι ἐδόθη, ἀναγέγραπται, ὡς
ταυτοῦ ὄντος ἐπὶ τούτων τοῦ πέμπειν τε καὶ τοῦ διδόναι.

Ἀλλὰ μὴν «ὁ πανταχοῦ ὢν καὶ τὰ πάντα πληρῶν» καὶ διὰ πάντων
χωρῶν πῶς ἥξει καὶ δοθήσεται; Δηλαδὴ φανερούμενος καὶ ἐνεργῶν
τὴν τῶν χαρίτων ἐνέργειαν. Οὐκοῦν οὐδὲν ἄλλο τὸ πέμπεσθαί τε
καὶ δίδοσθαι ἐπὶ Θεοῦ ἢ τὸ φανεροῦσθαι. Λατίνοις οὖν ἀΐδιον τὴν
παρὰ τοῦ Υἱοῦ τοιαύτην ἔκπεμψιν δογματίζουσι καὶ φανέρωσιν τοῦ
Πνεύματος ἀΐδιον δοξάζειν ἀκόλουθον· ἀνάγκη δὲ συναϊδίους εἶναι
καὶ τοὺς πρὸς οὓς ἡ φανέρωσις καὶ πρόσεστι τὸ μηδ᾽ οὕτω τὴν
ὕπαρξιν τοῦ θείου Πνεύματος ἐκ τοῦ Υἱοῦ δείκνυσθαι.

18

Εἰ δ᾽ ἐκ τῆς φανερώσεως στοχάζεσθαί φασιν ἐκεῖνοι τὴν ὕπαρξιν,
ἀλλ᾽ ἡμεῖς οὐ στοχασμοῖς ἀκολουθοῦντες, ἀλλὰ θεολέκτοις λογίοις
τὴν ὁμολογίαν τῆς πίστεως πεπλουτήκαμεν. Ἴσμεν δὲ καὶ αὐτὸ
παρ᾽ ἑαυτοῦ τὸ Πνεῦμα τὸ ἅγιον ἐρχόμενόν τε καὶ φανερούμενον,
ἀλλ᾽ οὐ διὰ τοῦτο καὶ παρ᾽ ἑαυτοῦ δώσομεν ἐκπορεύεσθαι· ὁ διδοὺς
τοίνυν ἢ πέμπων τὸ Πνεῦμα τὸ ἅγιον οὐκ ἐκπορεύει διὰ τὸ πέμπειν,
ἀλλὰ φανερὸν καθίστησιν αὐτό. Τοῦτο γὰρ καὶ ὁ Κύριος ἐποίησε
πρὸ μὲν τῆς οἰκείας ἀναλήψεως φανερώσας μετρίως τοῖς οἰκείοις
μαθηταῖς τὸ Πνεῦμα διὰ τῆς κοινῆς αὐτῶν καὶ παρ᾽ αὐτῶν μετρίας
τηνικαῦτα δεδομένης χάριτος· ὃ καὶ τὴν ἀρχὴν αἴτιον, ὡς ἔγωγ᾽
ἂν φαίην, τοῦ δι᾽ ἐμφυσήματος δεδημιουργεῖσθαι τὴν ἀνθρώπου
ψυχήν.

Sender then not bestow? The Lord Himself enlightening us said just now, "whom the Father will give" and now again, "whom the Father will send", employing the same meaning for both. But also concerning the Lord Himself it is written at one time that He was sent from the Father while at another time that He was given, since in these examples 'to send' and 'to give' are the same.

But of course, how could He that is "everywhere present and filling all things"[84] and permeating through all come or be given? Namely, by manifesting and actualizing the energy of His graces. Consequently, to be sent and to be given is nothing other than to be made manifest. So, since the Latins dogmatize that such a sending from the Son is eternal, they must consequently also believe that the manifestation of the Spirit is eternal. Furthermore, those to whom the manifestation occurs must also be necessarily co-eternal. And it follows that neither in this way can the existence of the divine Spirit from the Son be proved.

18

Now if the Latins state that the existence is conjectured on the basis of His manifestation, we nevertheless have been enriched in the confession of faith not by following conjectures but utterances spoken by God. And we know that the Spirit Himself also comes and is manifested from His own self, but we will not grant that He proceeds from Himself because of this. Accordingly, one who bestows or sends the Holy Spirit does not cause procession because of sending; rather, He makes Him manifest. For the Lord also did this before His own Ascension, when He manifested the Spirit moderately to His own disciples through Their common grace, which had been moderately bestowed by Them at that time. This, at least as I personally would say, is also the cause why in the beginning the soul of man was fashioned through a breathing-upon.

Ἐπεὶ γὰρ ὅ τε λέγων Πατὴρ καὶ ὁ τούτου παντοδύναμος Λόγος πάντων κτιζομένων ἐκηρύττοντο, ἔκφανσις δὲ Πνεύματος οὐ γέγονέ πω, ἔδει δὲ τοῦ ἀνθρώπου γενομένου μηδὲν τῶν τῆς Τριάδος προσώπων ἀνεπίγνωστον εἶναι, ἧς ἐπλάττετο μύστης καὶ προσκυνητὴς ἐπίγειος, διὰ τοῦτο τῷ τε λόγῳ καὶ τῷ λέγοντι, ταὐτὸν δὲ εἰπεῖν τῷ Υἱῷ καὶ τῷ γεννήτορι, προσεπιφέρεται τὸ «ἐνεφύσησεν», ἀνακαλύπτον τὴν τοῦ Πνεύματος ὑπόστασιν· ὃ καὶ ὁ Κύριος ἀνανεῶν ἡμᾶς ἐποίησεν· Υἱοῦ γὰρ ὄντος, αὐτόθεν ὁ Πατὴρ ἐδείκνυτο καὶ δι᾽ ἐμφυσήματος τὸ Πνεῦμα ἐκηρύττετο· ὧν κοινὸν ἔργον ἥ τε τὴν ἀρχὴν ἡμῶν πλάσις, ἥ τ᾽ ἐς ὕστερον χάρις τῆς ἀναπλάσεως.

Οὕτως οὖν δι᾽ ἡμᾶς καθ᾽ ἡμᾶς ἐπὶ γῆς ὀφθεὶς ὁ τοῦ Πατρὸς μονογενὴς Υἱός, πρὸ μὲν τῆς ἑαυτοῦ ἀναλήψεως τὴν τοῦ ἁγίου Πνεύματος ὑπόστασιν ἐφανέρωσε μετρίως διὰ τοῦ πρὸς τοὺς μαθητὰς δι᾽ ἐμφυσήματος δώρου τοῦτο ὑπαινιττόμενος καὶ τῇ τῶν δεχομένων δυνάμει τὴν διδασκαλίαν παραμετρούμενος· μετὰ δὲ τὴν οἰκείαν ἀνάληψιν ἔπεμψε τὸν ἐρχόμενον, αὐτός τε αὐτὸ φανερῶν τελεώτατα τὸ καὶ ἀφ᾽ ἑαυτοῦ φανερούμενον, καὶ αὐτὸ ἐφ᾽ ἑαυτοῦ δεικνύμενον κατ᾽ ἰδίαν ὑπόστασιν. Τοῦτο γὰρ δὴ καὶ τὸ τῆς οἰκονομίας μυστήριον, ἓν καὶ τρία τὸν Θεὸν πιστευθῆναι καὶ κοινὸν αἴτιον μόνον τῶν δύο τὸ ἕν. Διὰ τοῦτο κοινὴ μὲν αὐτοῖς πᾶσα δόσις καὶ δύναμις, μερίζονται δὲ ἑαυτοῖς τὸν καιρὸν ἰδίᾳ φανερούμενον ἕκαστον καὶ σὺν ἑαυτῷ φανεροῦν ἀεὶ τὰ ὑπόλοιπα.

19

Πρῶτον πεφανέρωται ὁ Πατήρ, τῆς θείας φύσεως αὐχήματα, τὰ τῆς θεότητος ἰδιώματα, τὰς φυσικὰς καὶ οὐσιώδεις αὐτῆς ἐνεργείας τοῖς προφήταις κατὰ χάριν διδούς, ὡς ἂν ἅμα τε δείξῃ καθ᾽ ἑαυτὸν ὑφεστὼς καὶ οὐκ αὐτὸν ὢν ἐξ ἄλλου, ἀλλ᾽ αὐτὸς ὢν ἀρχὴ τῆς θεότητος· καὶ δὴ καὶ τ᾽ ἄλλα δεικνὺς ἐξ αὐτοῦ τε ὄντα καὶ

For since, when all things were being created, both the speaking Father and the All-Powerful Word of His were being proclaimed while a manifestation of the Spirit still had not occurred (yet when man was made it was needful that none of the persons of the Trinity should remain unknown, of which he was being formed as a mystic initiate and an earthly worshipper), for this reason the phrase "He breathed in" is further added both by the Word and by the Speaker, (which is to say by the Son and the Begetter), thus revealing the hypostasis of the Spirit. The Lord did this as well when He was renewing us; for since He was the Son, from this the Father was being indicated and by an breathing-upon the Spirit was being proclaimed. Their common work is both our fashioning in the beginning and the latter grace of our refashioning.

In this way then, when the Only-Begotten Son of the Father appeared for us like us upon the earth, before His own Ascension He moderately manifested the hypostasis of the Holy Spirit, hinting at it through the gift given to His disciples through the breathing-upon, measuring out the teaching according to the capacity of those who were receiving it. After His own Ascension, however, He sent the coming one, perfectly manifesting Him who is also made manifest by His own self and who shows Himself by Himself in His own hypostasis. For this here is the mystery of the *economia*, that God be believed in as one and Three and that the one be believed in as the only common cause of the Two. Because of this, every gift and power is common to them, yet they divide the time among Themselves, Each one being made manifest by Himself and always manifesting along with Himself the rest.

19

First the Father has been manifested,[85] bestowing by grace the boasts of the divine nature, the idiomatic properties of the divinity, its natural and essential energies, to the prophets, so that He might at the same time show that He is subsistent by Himself and is not from another, but that He is the Origin of divinity. And what is more,

αὐτῷ συνημμένα, πρὸ πάντων ἐμφυσήματι καὶ λόγῳ δημιουργῶν καταγγέλλεται.

Μετ' αὐτὸν ὁ Υἱὸς πεφανέρωται, τὰ αὐτὰ τῆς αὐτῆς φύσεως αὐχήματα, τὰ τῆς θεότητος ἰδιώματα, τὰς φυσικὰς καὶ οὐσιώδεις αὐτῆς ἐνεργείας, παρ' ὧν τὰ χαρίσματα τῶν ἰαμάτων, τὰ ἐνεργήματα δυνάμεων καὶ τὰ παραπλήσια τούτοις τοῖς οἰκείοις μαθηταῖς κατὰ χάριν διδούς, ὡς ἂν καὶ αὐτὸς ἅμα τε δείξῃ καθ' ἑαυτὸν ὑφεστὼς (τὸ γὰρ μὴ καθ' ἑαυτὸ ὑφεστὼς ἐνεργείας ἔχειν ἢ παρέχειν ἀδύνατον) καὶ οὐκ αὐτὸς ὢν ἀρχή, ἀλλ' αὐτὸς ἐξ ἀρχῆς. Καὶ οὕτω δι' ἑαυτοῦ μὲν τὸν Πατέρα δεικνύς, Υἱὸς γάρ, ἐμφυσήματι δὲ διδοὺς τὰ πνευματικὰ χαρίσματα καὶ Πνεῦμα θεῖον αὐτὰ καλῶν, συνημμένον ἑαυτῷ προσεπεδείκνυ τὸ Πνεῦμα τὸ ἅγιον. Ὃς ἐπεὶ καὶ τὴν ἡμετέραν ἀνειληφὼς φύσιν ἐφανερώθη, οὐκ ἐδείκνυ μόνον διὰ τῶν ἔργων, ἀλλὰ καὶ διὰ γλώττης ἐκήρυττε τοῦ Πατρὸς καὶ τοῦ Πνεύματος τὴν θεότητα καὶ τί τὸ μόνον αἴτιον καὶ τί τὰ ἐξ αὐτοῦ.

20

Μετ' αὐτὸν τὸ ἅγιον πεφανέρωται Πνεῦμα, τὰ αὐτὰ τῆς αὐτῆς φύσεως αὐχήματα καὶ αὐτὸ τοῖς ἀποστόλοις κατὰ χάριν παρέχον, τὰ τῆς θεότητος ἰδιώματα, τὰς φυσικὰς καὶ οὐσιώδεις αὐτοῦ ἐνεργείας. Ἡ γὰρ τοῦ Θεοῦ βασιλεία, ἧς τοὺς ἀρραβῶνας οἱ ἅγιοι ἐνταῦθα κομίζονται, καθάπερ ὁ θεῖος Μάξιμος ἐν τοῖς Πρός Θαλάσσιον σχολίοις φησί, «τῶν προσόντων τῷ Θεῷ φυσικῶς κατὰ χάριν ἐστὶ μετάδοσις· ἃ καὶ τὴν ἀρχὴν εὐθὺς παρὰ Θεοῦ πλασθεὶς ὁ ἄνθρωπος κατὰ χάριν εἴληφεν»· ὡς καὶ ὁ θεῖος Κύριλλος ἐν τῇ Πρός Σόϊμον ἐπιστολῇ φησι γράφων ὅτι, «πλάσας ὁ Θεὸς τὸν ἄνθρωπον, ψυχωθέντα παρήγαγεν, ἔχοντα τὰς πνευματικὰς δωρεάς, σοφίαν, δικαιοσύνην καὶ ὅσα ἔνεστιν οὐσιωδῶς ἐν τῷ Θεῷ· ὁμοῦ γὰρ καὶ ζωὴν ἐνετίθει τὸ Πνεῦμα τῷ πλάσματι καὶ τοὺς ἑαυτοῦ χαρακτῆρας

since He also shows that the others are from Him and are united to Him, He is proclaimed as creating before all by an breathing-upon and by a Word.

After Him, the Son has been manifested, bestowing by grace the same boasts of this same nature, the idiomatic properties of the divinity, Its natural and essential energies, from whence issue the charisms of healing, the operations of powers, and the things that are related to them, to His own disciples, so that He also might show at the same time that He is both subsistent by Himself (for what is not subsistent by itself cannot possess or provide energies) and that He Himself is not an origin but that He is from an origin. And in this way, through Himself He was indicating the Father (since He is a Son), while by breathing-upon He was bestowing the spiritual charisms and calling them a divine Spirit, thus showing in addition that the Holy Spirit is united to Himself. Since this one was manifested once He had assumed our nature, He did not only show through works but also verbally proclaimed the divinity of the Father and the Spirit and what is the only cause and what Others are from Him.

20

After Him the Holy Spirit has been manifested, likewise providing by grace to the Apostles the same boastings of the same nature, the properties of the divinity, His natural and essential energies. For the kingdom of God, the betrothal pledges of which the saints acquire in this [life], just as the divine Maximus says in his scholia *To Thalassios:* "There is a communication by grace of what are attributes naturally to God; which man also immediately received from God in the beginning when he was fashioned;"[86] as also the divine Cyril says in his epistle *To Soimos*, writing that "Once God had formed man, He brought him forth with a soul, having the spiritual gifts, wisdom, righteousness, and whatever else is essentially present in God. For at the same time the Spirit was placing life within His formation and stamping the impressions of His own self as befits

θεοπρεπῶς ἐνεσήμαινεν». Ὅταν οὖν ἀκούσῃς αὐτὸν ἐξ ἀμφοῖν, ὡς
ἐκ Πατρὸς οὐσιωδῶς δι' Υἱοῦ προχεόμενον, τὸ Πνεῦμα τὸ ἅγιον
λέγοντα, τὴν τῶν φυσικῶν τούτων δυνάμεών τε καὶ ἐνεργειῶν τοῦ
Θεοῦ μετάδοσιν, ἀλλὰ μὴ τὴν θείαν τοῦ Πνεύματος ὑπόστασιν
προχεῖσθαι διδάσκειν, εὐσεβῶς νόμισον.

Μετὰ τὸν Υἱὸν τοίνυν διὰ τοῦ τὰς αὐτὰς δυνάμεις καὶ ἐνεργείας
τοῖς ἀξίοις παρέχειν τὸ ἅγιον πεφανέρωται Πνεῦμα· ὡς ἂν ἅμα τε
δείξῃ καὶ αὐτὸ καθ' ἑαυτὸ ὑφεστώς, καὶ τοὺς μαθητὰς σοφίσαν καὶ
πνευματικὴν δύναμιν ἐνδύσαν, αὐτούς τε συνιέναι ποιήσῃ καὶ τοῖς
πᾶσι δι' αὐτῶν κηρύξῃ τὰ τοῦ Σωτῆρος κηρύγματα, δι' ὧν καὶ αὐτό,
οὐ μετὰ τὸν Υἱὸν κατὰ τὴν ὕπαρξιν, ἀλλὰ μετὰ τοῦ Υἱοῦ, οὐδὲ ὡς ὁ
Υἱός, ἀλλ' ἰδιοτρόπως ἐκ τοῦ μόνου Πατρὸς ὑφεστηκὸς κηρύττεται,
συνημμένον ὂν φυσικῶς αὐτῷ καὶ τῷ Υἱῷ ἀδιαστάτως τε καὶ
ἀϊδίως. Δι' ὃ δὲ οὐκ εὐθὺς τὸ Πνεῦμα μετὰ τὸν Πατέρα, καίτοι καὶ
αὐτὸ ἀμέσως ὂν ἐκ τοῦ Πατρός, ἀλλ' ὁ Υἱὸς πρότερος τῷ κόσμῳ
πεφανέρωται, καὶ δι' ὃ ἐκ τοῦ Υἱοῦ τὰ τοῦ Πνεύματος οἱ θεολόγοι
παριστῶσιν, ἐν τῷ προτέρῳ λόγῳ τὰς αἰτίας ἀποδεδώκαμεν.

21

Ἐπεὶ δὲ τῆς τρισυποστάτου θεότητος τὰ ἔργα κοινά, ἓν δὲ τῶν
ἔργων καὶ ἡ φανέρωσις, διὰ τοῦτο παρ' ἑαυτοῦ τε πρὸς ἡμᾶς ἥκει
καὶ παρὰ τοῦ Πατρὸς καὶ τοῦ Υἱοῦ πέμπεται, δι' ὧν καὶ φανεροῦται
τὸ καὶ παρ' ἑαυτοῦ φανερούμενον, καθάπερ καὶ ὁ Υἱὸς πρὸ αὐτοῦ.
Φανεροῦται τοιγαροῦν καὶ ἐκ τοῦ Υἱοῦ πεμπόμενον τὸ Πνεῦμα τὸ
ἅγιον, ἀλλ' οὐκ ἐκπορεύεται. Εἰ δὲ μὴ τοῦτο, μηδὲ φανέρωσις ἡ
ἀποστολὴ καὶ ἡ κατ' αὐτὴν ἔκπεμψις, ἀλλ' ἐκπόρευσις· ἐπεὶ καὶ ὁ
Υἱὸς ἐπέμφθη πρότερον παρ' αὐτοῦ, τοῦ ἁγίου λέγω Πνεύματος
καὶ τοῦ Πατρός· «Κύριος γάρ», φησίν, «ἀπέσταλκέ με καὶ τὸ
Πνεῦμα αὐτοῦ». Ἆρ' ἐκ τοῦ Πατρὸς καὶ τοῦ Πνεύματος ὁ Υἱὸς ἢ

God."[87] So, whenever you hear Him saying that the Holy Spirit is from both, as being poured forth through the Son from the Father essentially, piously consider that He is teaching the communication of these natural powers and energies of God, not the pouring forth of the Hypostasis of the Spirit.

After the Son, accordingly, through granting the very same powers and energies to those who are worthy, the Holy Spirit has been made manifest, so that He might show at the same time both that He too is subsistent by Himself and that He made the disciples wise and endued them with spiritual power, and so that He might make them understand the proclamations of the Savior and that through them He might proclaim these proclamations unto all. By them He, too, is proclaimed as being not after the Son existentially but with the Son, nor in the manner of the Son but in His own manner, to have been substantiated from the only Father, being joined naturally to Him and to the Son, without distance and eternally. In the previous discourse[88] we have given the causes why the Spirit has not been manifested to the world straightway after the Father, even though He also is immediately from the Father, why instead the Son has been manifested previously, and why the theologians present the things of the Spirit from the Son.

21

But since the works of the trihypostatic divinity are common, and since manifestation also is one of the works, for this reason He both came to us from Himself and is sent from the Father and the Son, who make manifest Him that is also manifested from Himself, exactly like the Son before Him. Consequently, the Holy Spirit is manifested as sent also from the Son, but He does not proceed. If this is not so, neither can the mission and its related sending-forth be a manifestation but rather a procession; since earlier the Son was also sent from Him (I am speaking of the Holy Spirit and of the Father). For He says: "the Lord and his Spirit hath sent me."[89] Is the Son then either begotten or proceeding from the Father and the

γεννᾶται ἢ ἐκπορεύεται; Ἄπαγε τῆς ἀσεβείας. Εἰ δὲ λέγει τις ὡς ἄνθρωπον ἀπεστάλθαι τὸν Υἱόν, ἐγγὺς ἡ ἀπάντησις· ἀπεστάλη μὲν γὰρ ὡς ἄνθρωπος· «εἰ δὲ καὶ ὡς Θεός, τί τοῦτο; Τὴν εὐδοκίαν τοῦ Πατρὸς ἀποστολὴν εἶναι νόμισον», Γρηγόριός σοι διακελεύεται ὁ τῆς θεολογίας ἐπώνυμος, κἀγὼ τὴν τοῦ Υἱοῦ καὶ τοῦ Πνεύματος, ἐκείνῳ καὶ τῇ ἀληθείᾳ πειθόμενος.

Ἐπεὶ οὖν καὶ ὡς Θεὸς ὁ Υἱὸς ἀποστέλλεται καὶ παρ᾽ ἀμφοτέρων, Πατρὸς καὶ Πνεύματος, παρ᾽ ἀμφοτέρων τούτων λοιπὸν κατὰ Λατίνους ἔχει καὶ οὗτος τὴν γέννησιν, εἴπερ, ὅτι καὶ τὸ Πνεῦμα παρ᾽ ἀμφοτέρων ἀποστέλλεται, Πατρός τε καὶ Υἱοῦ, παρ᾽ ἀμφοτέρων ἐκπορεύεται τούτων. Κἄν, εἰ λέγοιεν μὴ τὴν ἀποστολὴν νομίζειν ἐκπόρευσιν, ἀλλ᾽ ἐκ ταύτης ἐκείνην τεκμείρεσθαι, καὶ τῆς τοῦ Υἱοῦ γεννήσεως αὐτὴ δήπουθεν ὑπάρξει τεκμήριον.

Τί δὲ καὶ διενήνοχε τοῦ τὴν ἀποστολὴν νομίζειν γέννησιν ἢ ἐκπόρευσιν τὸ λέγειν ὡς ἀϊδίως ἔχον πέμπειν τό τε τὸ Πνεῦμα τὸν Υἱὸν καὶ ὁ Υἱὸς τὸ Πνεῦμα; Τὸ μὲν καὶ νῦν αὐτὸν ὕστερον εἰς τὸν κόσμον ἀπέστειλεν· ὁ δὲ τὸ Πνεῦμα τοῖς οἰκείοις μαθηταῖς ἔπεμψεν, ἐπανελθὼν ὅθεν κατῆλθε. Ἀλλ᾽ ὁ μὲν Υἱὸς καὶ Θεός ἐστι καὶ ἄνθρωπος γέγονεν· ἀπεστάλη γοῦν καὶ ὡς ἄνθρωπος· τὸ Πνεῦμα οὐκ ἐνηνθρώπησεν.

22

Ἐπεὶ γοῦν Θεὸς ὄν ἀπεστάλη τοῦτο παρὰ τοῦ Πατρός, εὐδοκίαν δὲ χρὴ τὴν ἀποστολὴν ἡγεῖσθαι ταύτην κατὰ τοὺς θεολόγους, εὐδοκία δὲ ἡ ἀγαθὴ θέλησίς ἐστι, Λατῖνοι δὲ τῇ ἐκπορεύσει ταὐτὸν ἡγοῦνται τὴν ἀποστολήν, θέλησις οὐκοῦν ἐστι κατ᾽ αὐτοὺς ἡ ἐκπόρευσις· κἀπειδήπερ ἐκπορεύσει τὴν ὕπαρξιν ἔχει τὸ Πνεῦμα τὸ ἅγιον, θελήσει τοῦτο λοιπὸν ἔχει κατ᾽ αὐτοὺς τὴν ὕπαρξιν. Ὢ τῆς δυσσεβείας· οὐκέτι γὰρ ἄκτιστον· τῷ γὰρ θέλειν, ἀλλ᾽ οὐ τῷ πεφυκέναι τοῦτο προήγαγεν ὁ Θεὸς καὶ Πατήρ, καθὰ καὶ τὴν κτίσιν, εἴπερ ἡ ἐκπόρευσίς ἐστιν εὐδοκία καὶ θέλησις· τὰ κτίσματα

Spirit? Away with this impiety! And if someone says that the Son was sent as a Man, the answer is close. For He really was sent as a man. "And if He is also sent as God, what does this mean? Consider the good pleasure of the Father to be a sending,"[90] as Gregory, the namesake of theology, bids you. And I bid you consider it to be the good pleasure of the Son and of the Spirit, since I am persuaded by him and by the truth.

Therefore, since the Son is sent also as God and from both, from Father and Spirit, He too must have, according to the Latins, His generation from both of them, if the Spirit really proceeds from both, from both Father and Son, because He is sent by both of them. And if they say that they do not consider the sending to be a procession but are simply conjecturing the latter from the former, then I suppose this sending will also be a sure sign of the generation of the Son.

Besides, what is the difference between considering the sending to be a generation or a procession and saying that the Spirit eternally sends the Son and the Son the Spirit? The former just now sent the Son later into the world, while the latter sent the Spirit to His own disciples, having returned thither whence he descended. The Son, however, both is God and has become man; therefore he was sent also as a man. The Spirit did not become man.

22

Therefore, since He, being God, was sent from the Father, and since we need to think that the sending is good pleasure, according to the Theologians, and since good pleasure is good will, and since the Latins think that the sending is identical to the procession, therefore, according to them [the Latins], the procession is will. And forasmuch as the Holy Spirit has existence by procession, therefore according to them He has His existence by will. Oh the impiety! He is no longer uncreated! For it was by will, not by nature, that the God and Father brought Him forth, just as with creation, if it

γὰρ κατὰ τοὺς θεολόγους οὐ τῷ πεφυκέναι, ἀλλὰ τῷ θέλειν ὁ Θεὸς προήγαγεν. Ἔργον μὲν γὰρ φύσεως κατ' αὐτοὺς ἡ προαιώνιος καὶ ἀΐδιος γέννησις· ἔργον δὲ θείας θελήσεως ἡ κτίσις.

Ἀρειανοὶ μὲν οὖν τὸν Υἱὸν ἔλεγον θελήσει τοῦ Πατρὸς εἰς τὸ εἶναι προελθεῖν ἐκ τοῦ μὴ ἀθελήτως ἐκ Πατρὸς τὸ εἶναι λαβεῖν τοῦτο δῆθεν κατασκευάζοντες. Λατῖνοι δὲ θελήσει τοῦ Πατρὸς ἢ καὶ τοῦ Υἱοῦ προελθεῖν εἰς τὸ εἶναι δεικνύουσι τὸ Πνεῦμα τὸ ἅγιον ἐκ τοῦ τὴν ἐκπόρευσιν εἶναι νομίζειν ἀποστολὴν κατ' εὐδοκίαν καὶ θέλησιν. Ἐροῦμεν οὖν καὶ ἡμεῖς πρὸς αὐτούς, ὅπερ καὶ ὁ μέγας Ἀθανάσιος πρὸς τοὺς Ἀρειανούς, ὅτι «τοῦ βούλεσθαι τὸ κατὰ φύσιν ὑπέρκειται· καὶ ἡ φύσις οὐχ ὑπόκειται βουλήσει». Ὡς οὖν ἡ γέννησις εὐδοκία καὶ θέλησις οὐκ ἔστιν, ἀλλ' ὑπὲρ εὐδοκίαν καὶ θέλησιν (φύσει γὰρ δείκνυσιν ἐκ Πατρὸς ὄντα τὸν Υἱὸν ὡς αὐτῷ γνήσιον καὶ ὁμοούσιον, ἀλλ' οὐ θελήσει καθὰ τὰ κτίσματα) οὕτως οὐδὲ τοῦ Πνεύματος ἡ ἐκπόρευσις ἀποστολὴ καὶ εὐδοκία καὶ θέλησίς ἐστι· φύσει γὰρ ἡ ἐκπόρευσις δείκνυσι τὸ Πνεῦμα τὸ ἅγιον ἐκ τοῦ Πατρός, ὡς αὐτῷ γνήσιον καὶ ὁμοούσιον, ἀλλ' οὐ θελήσει κατὰ τὰ κτίσματα.

Λατῖνοι γοῦν λέγοντες ταὐτὸν εἶναι τῇ ἀποστολῇ τοῦ θείου Πνεύματος τὴν ἐκπόρευσιν κατὰ πᾶσαν ἀνάγκην κτιστὸν εἶναι τὸ Πνεῦμα κατασκευάζουσι. Καὶ μὴν ἐπειδήπερ εὐδοκία τοῦ Πατρός ἐστιν, ὡς ἐδιδάχθημεν, ἥ τε τοῦ Υἱοῦ ὡς Θεοῦ παρὰ Πατρός τε καὶ Πνεύματος ἀποστολὴ καὶ ἡ τοῦ Πνεύματος παρὰ Πατρός τε καὶ Υἱοῦ (θελήσαντος γὰρ ἑκατέρου τούτων κατὰ καιρὸν ἀφικέσθαι πρὸς ἡμᾶς καὶ ὁ Πατὴρ εὐδόκησε) δι' οὐδὲν ἄλλο πάντως ἢ διὰ φιλανθρωπίαν ἡ εὐδοκία γέγονεν αὕτη. Τοιγαροῦν, εἰ κατὰ Λατίνους τῇ ἀποστολῇ τοῦ Πνεύματος ταὐτὸν ἡ ἐκπόρευσις, ἡ δὲ ἀποστολὴ διὰ φιλανθρωπίαν, κατ' αὐτοὺς οὐκοῦν καὶ ἡ πρὸ αἰώνων ἐκ Πατρὸς ἐκπόρευσίς τε καὶ ὕπαρξις τοῦ Πνεύματος οὐχ ὑπὲρ αἰτίαν, ἀλλὰ διὰ φιλανθρωπίαν. Οὗ τί ἂν ἀκουσθείη δυσσεβέστερόν τε καὶ καινότερον;

is granted that the procession is God's good pleasure and will. For, according to the theologians, God brought forth the creatures not by nature but by will. The pre-eternal and everlasting begetting is a work of nature, while creation, in contrast, is a work of divine will.

On the one hand, the Arians were saying that the Son came forth into being by the will of the Father, pretentiously constructing this from the claim that He did not receive being from the Father without His will. The Latins, on the other hand, demonstrate that the Holy Spirit came forth into being by the will of the Father or of the Son as well, from the basis of the thought that the procession is a sending by good pleasure and by will. So we shall say to them exactly what Athanasius the Great said to the Arians, that "what is according to nature transcends willing, and nature is not subject to will."[91] Therefore, as the begetting is not good pleasure and will but transcends good pleasure and will (for it shows that the Son is from the Father by nature, as   being genuine and consubstantial with Him, not by will like created things), similarly neither is the procession of the Spirit a sending or good pleasure or will; for the procession shows that the Holy Spirit is from the Father by nature, as being genuine and consubstantial with Him, not by will like created things.

Of course, since the Latins say that the procession is identical to the sending of the divine Spirit, by all necessity they represent the Spirit as being created. Of course, inasmuch as both the sending of the Son as God from both Father and Spirit and the sending of the Spirit from both Father and Son is the good pleasure of the Father, as we have been taught (for, when each of them willed in due time to approach us, the Father also was well-pleased), this good pleasure occurred entirely for no other reason than because of His love for mankind. Therefore, if, according to the Latins, the procession is identical to the sending of the Spirit, and the sending was because of love for mankind, then also, according to them, both the Spirit's pre-eternal procession from the Father and His existence are not beyond cause, but occur because of love for mankind. What thing more irreverent and innovative than this could be heard?

23

Πρὸς δὲ τούτοις, εἰ ταὐτὸν ἀποστολὴ καὶ ἐκπόρευσις, δι' ἐμὲ
λοιπὸν τὸ Πνεῦμα (βαβαὶ τῆς κακοδοξίας· οὐ γὰρ ἔχω ταῦτα λέγειν
ἄνευ φρίκης καὶ θαύματος) ἐκ τοῦ Πατρός ἐκπορεύεται· δι' ἐμὲ
γὰρ ἀπέσταλται· εἰ δὲ δ' ἐμὲ, καὶ μετ' ἐμὲ πάντως ἢ οὐ πολὺ πρὸ
ἐμοῦ ἀλλ' ὑπὸ χρόνον ὥσπερ ἐγώ, καὶ οὐχὶ τῷ Πατρὶ καὶ τῷ Υἱῷ
συναΐδιον. Καὶ οὐ τοῦτο μόνον, ἀλλὰ καὶ ὑπείκει τῇ δεσποτείᾳ.
Φεῦ, ποῦ κατάγεται παρὰ τῶν ἀγνωμόνων δούλων τὸ τῇ φύσει
τὴν δεσποτείαν ἔχον ἁπάσης τῆς κτίσεως· «τὸ γὰρ Σάββατον»,
φησί, «διὰ τὸν ἄνθρωπον, οὐχὶ ὁ ἄνθρωπος διὰ τὸ Σάββατον·
ὥστε Κύριός ἐστι τοῦ Σαββάτου ὁ Υἱὸς τοῦ ἀνθρώπου». Ὁρᾷς
πόσον ἀπέχει ἀποστολὴ ἐκπορεύσεως; Ὅσον χρόνων ἀϊδιότης
καὶ κτισμάτων Θεὸς καὶ τῶν φύσει δούλων ὁ φύσει δεσπότης τῆς
κτίσεως.

24

Ὁ τοίνυν παρὰ Θεοῦ καὶ τῶν ὡς ἀληθῶς θεολόγων μεμυημένος
ἐμφυσώμενον μὲν ἀκούων τὸ Πνεῦμα δι' ἐμφυσήματος παρὸν καὶ
συμφυὲς ὂν τῷ ἐμφυσῶντι νοεῖ σημαινόμενον, ἀλλ' οὐκ αὐτὸ ὑπάρχον
ἐμφύσημα, ὡς ἐξ ἀνάγκης ἔχειν τὴν ὕπαρξιν ἐξ οὗ τὸ ἐμφύσημα·
ἂν δὲ καὶ πεμπόμενον, φανερούμενον· ἂν δὲ καὶ διδόμενον, καὶ τὸ
συνημμένον ἐπιγινώσκει τοῦ πεμπομένου τε καὶ τοῦ πέμποντος· ἂν
δὲ παρ' ἡμῶν λαμβανόμενον, οἶδε μὲν ᾗ Θεόν, ἄληπτον, ληπτὰ δὲ
ἡμῖν τὰ παρ' ἐκείνου χαρίσματα· ἂν δὲ καὶ παρὰ τοῦ Υἱοῦ ἀκούσῃ
πεμπόμενον, διδόμενον, ἐμφυσώμενον, εὐθὺς καὶ τοῦτο πρὸς τοῖς
ἄλλοις συνήσιν, ὡς ἐκ τοῦ Πατρὸς ἐκπορεύεται, καθὰ καὶ Γρηγόριος
ἐκλαμβάνειν ἀξιοῖ σοφῶς ὁ ἐν θεολογίᾳ πολύς· «ὅσα γάρ», φησί,

23

Now in addition to these things, if sending and procession are identical, then it is on my account that the Spirit (I am amazed at this cacodoxy! I cannot speak it without fear and amazement) — the Spirit proceeds from the Father. For He has been sent because of me. But if He was sent because of me, He must also be in every sense after me, or not very much prior to me, but subject to time just as I am, not co-eternal with the Father and the Son. And not only this, but He is also subject to dominion. Oh, where do the senseless servants drag down Him that by nature possesses the lordship of every creature! For He says, "The Sabbath was made for man, and not man for the Sabbath: therefore the Son of Man is Lord also of the Sabbath."[92] Do you see how far removed the sending is from the procession? As much as eternity is removed from time and God from created things and the Master of creation by nature from those who are servants by nature.

24

Accordingly, one who has been initiated by God and by those who are truly theologians, when he hears that the Spirit is breathed in, considers that through the breathing-upon it is signified that He is both present and con-natural with Him who breathed in, but not that He Himself is an breathing-upon so as necessarily to have existence from Him from whom came the breathing-upon. And if he hears Him being sent, he considers Him being manifested; and if he hears Him being bestowed, he also acknowledges the junction of both Sent and Sender. And if he hears that He is received by us, he knows that in the manner of God He is unreceivable, although the charisms which are from Him are receivable by us. And should he hear that He is sent, bestowed, breathed in, from the Son, he immediately understands along with the other things this as well, that He proceeds from the Father, as Gregory, great in theology, wisely demands we understand. For he says, "whatever is

«περὶ τοῦ ἁγίου Πνεύματος ταπεινότερα λέγεται, τὸ δίδοσθαι, τὸ στέλλεσθαι, τὸ μερίζεσθαι, τὸ χάρισμα, τὸ δώρημα, τὸ ἐμφύσημα, εἴτε τι ἄλλο τοιοῦτον, ἐπὶ τὴν πρώτην αἰτίαν ἀνακτέον, ἵνα τὸ ἐξ οὗ δειχθῇ», (δηλαδὴ τοῦ Πατρός· αὐτὸς γὰρ ἡ πρώτη αἰτία) καὶ μὴ τρεῖς, φησίν, ἀρχαὶ μεμερισμέναι πολυθέως παραδεχθῶσιν», ὅπερ αὐτὸς ἔπαθες, μὴ πρὸς τὴν πρώτην αἰτίαν διὰ τούτων τῶν φωνῶν ἀναγόμενος.

25

Καὶ δύο μὲν σαφῶς κηρύττων οὐκ αἰσχύνῃ ἀρχὰς ἐκ τοῦ Πατρὸς καὶ τοῦ Υἱοῦ τὸ Πνεῦμα δογματίζων ἔχειν τὴν ὕπαρξιν, τὴν δὲ τρίτην ἀφ' ὧν λέγεις διδοὺς συνάγεσθαι. Εἰ γὰρ διὰ τὸ πέμπεσθαι παρὰ τοῦ Υἱοῦ καὶ ἐξ αὐτοῦ ἐκπορεύεται, πέμπει δὲ καὶ τὸ Πνεῦμα τὸν Υἱόν, οὐχ ὡς ἄνθρωπον μόνον ἀλλὰ καὶ ὡς Θεόν, καθάπερ ἀνωτέρω δέδεικται, ἀλλὰ καὶ τὸν Πατέρα ὁ Υἱός τε καὶ τὸ Πνεῦμα, ὡς ὁ χρυσοῦς θεολόγος Ἰωάννης ἐξηγούμενος τὸ προφητικὸν ἐκεῖνο, «Κύριος ἀπέσταλκέ με καὶ τὸ Πνεῦμα αὐτοῦ, ἐξεδέξατο, ἰδού σοι καὶ τὸ Πνεῦμα ἀρχή, καὶ ἐκ τοῦ Πατρὸς καὶ τοῦ Πνεύματος ὁ Υἱὸς ἢ γεννᾶται ἢ ἐκπορεύεται.

Παρίημι γὰρ τὸν Πατέρα λέγειν, κἂν ἐκ τῆς λατινικῆς καινοφωνίας καὶ τοῦτ' ἐκβαίνῃ, τὸ περιὸν τῆς ὑπερβολῆς εὐλαβούμενος. Ἴδοι δ' ἄν τις οὐδὲ τ' ἄλλα τῶν ἐκβαινόντων ἀτόπων τὴν ἐπὶ τὸ χεῖρον ὑπερβολὴν ἀπολείποντα· καὶ γὰρ δι' ἀλλήλων ἀναιρούμενα δείκνυται, εἰ διὰ τῆς ἀποστολῆς νοήσαιμεν τὴν ἐκπόρευσιν ἢ τὴν γέννησιν. Εἰ γὰρ ταῦτα κατὰ τὴν ἀποστολήν, ἑκάτερον λοιπὸν τούτων οὐχ ὑπάρξεώς ἐστι τρόπος, κἂν προαιώνια ᾖ· εἰ δὲ κατὰ τὴν πρὸ αἰώνων ἐκπόρευσίν τε καὶ γέννησιν τὴν πρὸς ἡμᾶς ἀποστολὴν νοήσαιμεν, ἀποστολή τις πρὸς ἡμᾶς ἄχρονος καὶ ἀΐδιος ἢ χρονική τις ὕπαρξις ἔσται τοῦ Υἱοῦ καὶ τοῦ Πνεύματος.

Ἐπιστῆσαι δὲ καὶ τοῦτο χρὴ τὸν συνετὸν ἀκροατήν, ὡς ὁ

said concerning the Holy Spirit in more lowly fashion, as that He is given, sent, divided, that He is the charism, the gift, the breathing-upon, or any other expression of the sort, is to be referred back to the First Cause, so that the source-from-which may be shown,"[93] (namely, the Father: for He is the first cause),"and lest three divided principles be accepted in a polytheistic way," which, in fact, you yourself have suffered by not being led up to the first cause through these expressions.

25

And you are not embarrassed to preach clearly that there are two origins, by dogmatizing that the Spirit has existence from the Father and the Son, while letting the third origin be deduced from the things which you say. For if, by being sent from the Son, the Spirit also proceeds from Him (and considering that the Spirit also sends the Son, not as a man only but also as God, just as it has been shown above, but also that both the Son and the Spirit send the Father, as John the Golden Theologian accepted while interpret that prophetic passage, "The Lord and His Spirit hath sent Me"[94]), behold! For you the Spirit is an origin as well, and the Son is either begotten or proceeds from the Father and the Spirit.

For I avoid speaking of the Father, reverencing the magnitude of the excessiveness, even if this too would result from the Latin innovation. And one could see that neither do the rest of the absurd conclusions fall behind in excessiveness for the worse. For they are shown to be refuted by each other, if by the sending we consider the procession or the begetting. For if we consider these things in terms of the sending, then each of them is not a mode of existence, even if they be pre-eternal; but if we were to consider the sending to us in terms of the pre-eternal procession and begetting, there will be some type of timeless and eternal sending to us or some temporal existence of the Son and of the Spirit.

Now the understanding listener must also know this, that Gregory,

τῆς θεολογίας ἐπώνυμος Γρηγόριος τοῖς περὶ τοῦ Πνεύματος ταπεινότερον λεγομένοις καὶ τὸ ἀποστέλλεσθαι συνηρίθμησε· τὸ δὲ ἐκπορεύεσθαι μέγα καὶ ὑπὲρ τὸ μέγα ἐστίν. «Εἰ γὰρ μέγα τῷ Πατρὶ τὸ μηδαμόθεν ὁρμᾶσθαι, οὐκ ἔλαττον τῷ Πνεύματι τὸ ἐκ τοιούτου Πατρὸς ἐκπορεύεσθαι». Οὐκ ἄρα ταὐτὸν ἀποστολὴ καὶ ἐκπόρευσις. Ἡ μὲν γὰρ ἀποστολὴ τῆς πρὸς ἡμᾶς συγκαταβάσεως ἐκφαίνει τὴν πρόθεσιν· ἡ δὲ ἐκπόρευσις τῆς καθ᾽ ἑαυτὸ παρὰ Πατρὸς ὑπάρξεως τοῦ Πνεύματός ἐστιν ὄνομα. Καὶ ἡ μὲν ἔστι, καθ᾽ ἣν ἡμεῖς τοῦ εὖ εἶναι μετέσχομεν· ἡ δὲ παρίστησι τὸ φύσει συνημμένον ὁμοτίμως πρὸς τὸν Πατέρα, τὸ κατὰ μόνην ὑπόστασιν διαφέρον αὐτοῦ καὶ τοῦ Υἱοῦ Πνεῦμα ἅγιον.

26

Σὺ δὲ τὸ μεμερισμένον ἐκ τῶν λόγων σοι συμβαῖνον βλέπων διὰ τὰς σὰς καινοτομίας καὶ ἤδη σε μερίζον Θεοῦ (τί γὰρ τὸ προσεχὲς καὶ πόρρω ἢ ἐγγὺς μερισμοῦ;) ἵν᾽ οὖν ὃ κατασκευάζεις αὖθις ἐκφύγῃς, πολὺ τὸ μέσον ἐντίκτεις ταῖς θεολογίαις ταῖς σαῖς. Ἡμεῖς δὲ καὶ ἑωράκαμεν ἐν τοῖς Πνεύματι γράφουσι Θεοῦ μυστήρια καὶ πιστεύομεν καὶ κηρύττομεν ἐν ἀλλήλοις τε ὄντα δι᾽ ἀλλήλων ἀμιγῶς χωροῦντα καὶ οὐ μᾶλλον πρὸς ἑαυτὸ ἕκαστον ἢ πρὸς ἄλληλα ἔχοντα. Εἰ δὲ πρὸς ἑαυτὸ ἕκαστον ἔχει ἀδιαστάτως τε καὶ ἀμέσως – πῶς γὰρ οὔ; - πῶς ἐμμέσως ἕξει πρὸς ἄλληλα; Ὅταν δὲ τὴν αἰτίαν ζητῶμεν τῆς ἀρρήτου ἐκείνης καὶ ὑπὲρ πάντα νοῦν πρὸς ἄλληλα σχέσεως καὶ τῆς ὑπερβαλλούσης συμφυΐας καὶ τῆς ἀπερινοήτου τε καὶ ἀφθέγκτου περιχωρήσεως, αὐτὸν αὖθις εὑρίσκομεν καὶ κηρύττομεν τὸν Πατέρα, αὐτὸν ἕνωσιν, αὐτὸν σύνδεσμον, αὐτὸν καὶ Πατέρα καὶ προβολέα καὶ συνοχέα γινώσκοντες τοῦ γεννήματός τε καὶ τοῦ προβλήματος· καὶ οὕτω μέσον καὶ ἀρχὴν αὐτῶν ἐκεῖνον τιθέμεθα.

Παρ᾽ ὅτου δ᾽ ἂν αὐτῶν, Υἱοῦ λέγω καὶ Πνεύματος, οἰκονομικῶς ἡμῖν ἴδωμεν τὸν ἕτερον παράκλητον φανερούμενον, αὐτίκα διὰ

the namesake of theology, also enumerated "to be sent" along with the things which are said more lowly concerning the Holy Spirit. In contrast, to proceed is great and more than great. "If the Father's greatness lies in not being moved into being from anywhere, it is not lesser for the Spirit to proceed from such a Father."[95] So sending and procession are not identical. For the sending expresses His purpose of condescension to us, while the procession is the name of the existence of the Spirit by Himself from the Father. And the one is that according to which we participated in well being, while the other presents the Holy Spirit, being with the same honour united by nature with the Father, differing from Him and from the Son only with respect to His hypostasis.

26

But as you see that division is resulting from your arguments because of your innovations and is already dividing you from God (for what is proximity and distance other than close to division?), therefore, so as to escape once more from what you are constructing, you create a very great gap in your theologies. We, however, have both seen mysteries of God in those who write by the Spirit and we believe and proclaim that they are in each other, are contained through each other without mingling, and each one does not relate more to itself than to each other. And if each relates to itself without distance and immediately (for how could this not be?), how can they relate mediately to each other? But whenever we seek to determine the cause of that ineffable relation to each another which transcends every intellect and the cause of the exceeding great connaturality and of the ungraspable and unspeakable interpenetration, again we find and proclaim the Father Himself, knowing that He is the union, He is the bond, He is both Father and Generator and the embracing Sustainer both of the Begotten and of the Emanation, and thus we assert that He is their midpoint and origin.

But from whichever one of them (I refer to the Son and Spirit) we see the other Paraclete being manifested economically to us, because of

τούτου πρὸς τὴν πρώτην καὶ μόνην ἀρχὴν ἀναγόμεθα· πέμπων
γὰρ ἢ διδοὺς τὸ Πνεῦμα ὁ Υἱός, πόθεν τοῦτ' ἔχει, ὅτι μὴ παρὰ τῆς
πρώτης καὶ μόνης ἀρχῆς; Οὐκοῦν οὕτω πέμπει τε καὶ δίδωσιν, ὡς
ἔχων ὑφιστάμενον ἐκ τοῦ Πατρός, ἀλλ' οὐκ αὐτὸς συνεκπορεύων
καὶ συνυφιστῶν· καὶ πέμπων καὶ διδούς, τοῦτ' αὐτὸ δείκνυσιν ἡμῖν,
ὡς ἐμοῦ μέν ἐστιν, ἀλλ' ἐκ τοῦ Πατρός, οὐκ ἐξ ἐμοῦ.

27

Τοῦτο δὲ καὶ ὁ πολὺς ἐν θεολογίᾳ καὶ ὄντως μέγας Ἀθανάσιος
ἐννοήσας, μᾶλλον δὲ φωτισθείς, καὶ ἡμῖν τῷ λόγῳ διαπορθμεύσας
τὸ φῶς, ἐν μιᾷ τῶν Πρὸς Σεραπίωνα ἐπιστολῶν· «ἑνὸς ὄντος»,
φησί, «τοῦ Υἱοῦ, τοῦ ζῶντος Λόγου, μίαν εἶναι δεῖ καὶ πλήρη τὴν
ἁγιαστικὴν καὶ φωτιστικὴν ζωήν, οὖσαν ἐνέργειαν καὶ δωρεὰν
αὐτοῦ· ἥτις γε ἐκ τοῦ Πατρὸς λέγεται ἐκπορεύεσθαι, ἐπειδὴ παρὰ
τοῦ Λόγου τοῦ ἐκ Πατρὸς ἐκλάμπει καὶ ἀποστέλλεται. "Οὕτω γὰρ
ὁ Θεὸς ἠγάπησε τὸν κόσμον, ὥστε τὸν Υἱὸν αὐτοῦ τὸν μονογενῆ
ἔδωκεν", ὁ δὲ Υἱὸς τὸ Πνεῦμα ἀποστέλλει». Τοῦτο γὰρ αὐτό ἐστιν
ἐκεῖνο, τὸ παρὰ τοῦ τῆς θεολογίας ἐπωνύμου Γρηγορίου μικρὸν
καὶ ἀνωτέρω εἰρημένον, ὡς ὅ τι ἂν περὶ τοῦ θείου Πνεύματος
ταπεινότερον λέγηται, τὸ χάρισμα, τὸ δώρημα, καὶ εἴ τι ἄλλο
τοιοῦτον, ἐπὶ τὴν πρώτην αἰτίαν ἀνακτέον, ἵνα τὸ ἐξ οὗ δειχθῇ. Εἰπὼν
γὰρ ὁ μέγας ἐνταυθοῖ τὸ Πνεῦμα τὸ ἅγιον ταπεινότερον δωρεὰν καὶ
ἐνέργειαν τοῦ Λόγου, καὶ δείξας ὡς οὐχὶ περὶ τῆς ὑπάρξεως οὐδὲ
περὶ τῆς ὑποστάσεως αὐτῷ τοῦ Πνεύματος ὁ Λόγος (ἡ γὰρ ἐνέργεια
ἐνεργεῖται μᾶλλον ἢ ἐνεργεῖ, τὸ δὲ Πνεῦμα τὸ ἅγιον παρεκτικὸν καὶ
μεταδοτικὸν ὑπάρχει τῶν αὐτοῦ δωρεῶν) σαφῶς οὖν ἐμφήνας ὡς
οὐχὶ περὶ τῆς προαιωνίου λέγει ἐκπορεύσεως, ἐπήγαγεν, ὅτι «παρὰ
τοῦ Λόγου τοῦ ἐκ τοῦ Πατρὸς ἐκλάμπει καὶ ἀποστέλλεται».

28

Τί δή, διά τοῦ ἐκλάμπειν καὶ ἀποστέλλεσθαι παρὰ τοῦ Λόγου

this we are at once led back to the first and only Origin. For when
the Son sends or gives the Spirit, from where does He have Him,
except from the first and only Origin? So this is how He sends and
gives, as having Him been given substance from the Father, but He
Himself does not jointly cause procession or jointly give substance.
And by sending and giving, He shows this same thing to us, that
while He is Mine, He is from the Father, not from Me.

27

Now Athanasius, who was truly very great in theology, noted this,
or, rather, was enlightened, and so transmitted the light to us by his
word. In one of the epistles to Serapion he says, "Since the Son, the
Living Word, is one, the sanctifying and enlightening life must be
one and complete, being His energy and gift. This of course is said
to proceed from the Father, since it shines forth and is sent from the
Word which is from the Father.[96] 'For God so loved the world, that
He gave His only begotten Son',[97] while the Son sends the Spirit."[98]
For this is the exact same thing, which was said a little further up by
Gregory, the namesake of theology, that whatever may be spoken in
a more lowly way concerning the divine Spirit, the charism, the gift,
and if there is some other such thing, it must be referred back to
the first cause, that the source-from-which may be shown. For once
Athanasius the Great had said in this passage that the Holy Spirit is
a more lowly gift and energy of the Word, and once he had showed
that his treatise about the Spirit does not concern the existence nor
the hypostasis of the Spirit (for, while the energy is actualized rather
than effectually acts, the Holy Spirit, in contrast, is able to provide
and transmit His gifts), so after he clearly made it plain that he
speaks not concerning the procession which was before the ages, he
brought forth that He "shines forth and is sent from the Word which
is from the Father."

28

What exactly? Because He shines forth and is sent from the Word

νοοῦμεν ὅτι ἐξ αὐτοῦ ἐκπορεύεται; Ἄπαγε, φησίν, ὡς πορρωτάτω βάλλεις τοῦ σκοποῦ· ἀλλ᾽ ὅτι ἐκ τοῦ Πατρὸς ἐκπορεύεται νοοῦμεν καὶ λέγομεν, ἐπεὶ παρὰ τοῦ Υἱοῦ δίδοταί τε καὶ ἀποστέλλεται. Ἔχων γὰρ ἐκεῖθεν πρὸ αἰώνων συνυφεστὼς ὁ Υἱὸς τὸ Πνεῦμα τὸ ἅγιον, νῦν πρὸς ἡμᾶς καὶ ἀποστέλλει καὶ δίδωσιν. Ἐπεὶ δὲ ἡ δόσις ἔλλαμψις (καὶ τοῦτ᾽ ἴσασιν οἱ μεμυημένοι, ὅσοι λαμπρότητα Θεοῦ καὶ εἶδον καὶ ἔπαθον, ὅσοι τὴν δόξαν τοῦ Κυρίου εἶδον «ὡς μονογενοῦς παρὰ Πατρός», ὅσοι τῷ φωτὶ τῆς θεότητος ἐπὶ τοῦ ὄρους περιηυγάσθησαν, πρὸς δὲ τούτοις καὶ οἱ τούτοις ἀσφαλῶς πιστεύσαντες) ἐπεὶ οὖν ἡ δόσις ἔλλαμψις, ἀντὶ τοῦ παρὰ τοῦ Υἱοῦ δίδοσθαί τε καὶ ἀποστέλλεσθαι, παρά τοῦ Υἱοῦ ἐκλάμπειν ἔφη καὶ ἀποστέλλεσθαι. Καὶ τοῦτ᾽ ἔτι σαφέστερον δείκνυσιν ἐκ τῆς κατασκευῆς τοῦ λόγου· «ὁ μὲν γὰρ Θεὸς καὶ Πατήρ», φησί, «τὸν Υἱὸν ἔδωκεν ὑπὲρ ἡμῶν· ὁ δὲ Υἱός, τὸ Πνεῦμα».

Ἀλλὰ γὰρ ὥσπερ ἡ τοῦ Υἱοῦ παρὰ τοῦ Πατρὸς ὑπὲρ τῆς τοῦ κόσμου σωτηρίας δόσις ἢ ἀποστολὴ γέννησις οὐκ ἔστι, πολλοῦ γε ἂν δήπου δέοι καὶ ἀπείρου εἶναι ἡ προαιώνιος, οὕτως οὐδ᾽ ἡ παρὰ τοῦ Υἱοῦ δόσις τοῦ ἁγίου Πνεύματος ἢ ἀποστολὴ ἐκπόρευσίς ἐστι, πόσῳ γε μᾶλλον καὶ ὑπὲρ τὸ πόσῳ ἢ πρὸ τῶν αἰώνων παρὰ τοῦ Πατρὸς οὐ γενομένη, ἄπαγε, ἀλλὰ καὶ πρὸ τούτων οὖσα καὶ τῷ Πατρὶ συνάναρχος.

Ἔτ᾽ ἔχει τις λέγειν διὰ τὴν ἀποστολὴν ὡς ἐκ τοῦ Πατρὸς καὶ τοῦ Υἱοῦ ἐκπορεύεται τὸ Πνεῦμα τὸ ἅγιον; Οὐκ ἔγωγε οἶμαι, εἰ μὴ σαφῶς ἐθέλει θεομαχεῖν. Ἀλλὰ καὶ αὐτοῦ, φησί, τοῦ Υἱοῦ τὸ Πνεῦμα καὶ ἴδιον αὐτοῦ λέγεται. «Ἐξαπέστειλε γὰρ ὁ Θεός», φησὶν ὁ ἀπόστολος, «τὸ Πνεῦμα τοῦ Υἱοῦ αὐτοῦ ἐν ταῖς καρδίαις ἡμῶν, κρᾶζον· ἀββά, ὁ Πατήρ».

29

Ὑπέρευγε· τὴν "ἐξ" γὰρ ἀφείς, σύγε ὃς τίς ποτ᾽ εἶ ὁ πρόσφατος

do we consider that He proceeds from Him? 'Banish the thought!' he says; 'you are throwing as far as possible from the mark.' But we consider and say that He proceeds from the Father, since He is both given and sent from the Son. For since the Son has the Holy Spirit as having been substantiated together with Him from that source from before the ages, He now both sends and gives Him to us. And since the gift is illumination (and those that have been initiated know this, as many as have seen and experienced the brightness of God, as many as beheld the glory of the Lord 'as of the only begotten of the Father,'[99] as many as have been utterly engulfed by the light of divinity on the mountain, and in addition who have safely believed in them) — therefore, since the gift is illumination, instead of saying that He is both given and sent from the Son, he says that He shines forth and is sent from the Son. And he shows this still more clearly from the construction of the saying: he says, "While the God and Father has given His Son on our behalf, the Son has given the Spirit."[100]

But certainly, just as the giving or sending of the Son from the Father for the salvation of the world is not a begetting (it would of course be far and infinitely far from being the pre-eternal begetting), in this way neither is the giving or sending of the Holy Spirit from the Son a procession, how much more so and immeasurably more so [not] the procession from the Father, which did not come to be before the ages — away with this! — but which was even before them and is cobeginningless with the Father.

Is someone still able to say that the Holy Spirit proceeds from the Father and the Son because of the sending? I myself at least do not think so, unless he clearly wanted to fight God. "But," he rejoins, "the Spirit is also of the Son Himself and is said to be His own. For, the Apostle says: "God sent forth the Spirit of His Son in our hearts crying, Abba, Father."[101]

29

Well done! For you have abandoned the preposition "from", you

ἀντικείμενος, τὸ αὐτοῦ νῦν ἡμῖν προβάλλῃ ταύτης χωρίς· ἤ σοι κἀκ τοῦ αὐτοῦ τὸ ἐξ αὐτοῦ νοεῖταί τε καὶ κατασκευάζεται, τῷ διαλεκτικῷ τῶν ἀπερινοήτων; Εἰπὲ δή μοι, καὶ σὺ αὐτὸς οὐ σαυτοῦ; Τοῦτό γε, οἶμαι, ἀποδράσεις ἡμῶν. Οὐ γὰρ ἔοικάς μοι ἀκοῦσαι τοῦ λέγοντος, «γενοῦ σεαυτοῦ ἄνθρωπε». Εἰ γὰρ ἤκουσας καὶ ὑπήκουσας, ἔστεργες ἂν τὰ παραδεδομένα περὶ Θεοῦ καὶ τοῖς ὑπὲρ ἄνθρωπον καὶ λόγοις καὶ πράγμασι, καὶ ταῦτα καινοτομῶν, ἥκιστα ἐπεχείρησας. Ἀλλ᾽ εἰ ὁ ἄνθρωπος ἑαυτοῦ, οὐκοῦν ὁ ἄνθρωπος ἐξ ἑαυτοῦ κατὰ σέ. Τὸν Υἱὸν δὲ τοῦ Πνεύματος πῶς οὐ λέγομεν, φησίν, εἰκότως· δόξαι γὰρ ἂν Πατὴρ τὸ Πνεῦμα, τοῦ Υἱοῦ συνεισάγοντος τῇ διανοίᾳ τὸν Πατέρα· διὰ τοῦτο τοίνυν Υἱὸν μὲν Πνεύματος οὐ λέγομεν, ἵνα μὴ δόξῃ ἐκ τοῦ Πνεύματος, Υἱοῦ δὲ Πνεῦμα λέγομεν, ἀλλ᾽ οὐ παρὰ τοῦτο καὶ ἐκ τοῦ Υἱοῦ· Πνεῦμα γὰρ αὐτοῦ λέγεται, οὐχ ὡς ἐξ αὐτοῦ, ἀλλ᾽ ὡς ἐν αὐτῷ ὄν.

Καὶ τοῦτο διδάσκου παρὰ τοῦ ἀποστόλου, «οὐδεὶς οἶδε, λέγοντος, τὰ τοῦ ἀνθρώπου, εἰ μὴ τὸ Πνεῦμα τοῦ ἀνθρώπου τὸ ἐν αὐτῷ»· ὡς οὖν Πνεῦμα μὲν ἀνθρώπου λέγεται, ἀλλ᾽ οὐχ ὡς ἐκ τοῦ ἀνθρώπου, ἀλλ᾽ ὡς ἐν τῷ ἀνθρώπῳ ὄν, οὕτω καὶ τὸ θεῖον Πνεῦμα καλεῖται τοῦ Υἱοῦ, ἀλλ᾽ οὐχ ὡς ἐκ τοῦ Υἱοῦ, ἀλλ᾽ ὡς ἐν τῷ Υἱῷ φυσικῶς ἐξ ἀϊδίου ὂν καὶ τὰς ἀφύκτους δοκούσας σοι τῶν συλλογισμῶν ἀνάγκας διαφεῦγον.

Ἐκ διαιρέσεως γὰρ ὁ λατινικῶς φρονῶν συλλογιζόμενός φησι· «ἐπεὶ τοῦ Υἱοῦ ἐστι τὸ Πνεῦμα, ἢ ὡς δι᾽ αὐτοῦ χορηγούμενόν ἐστιν ἢ ὡς ὁμοούσιον ἢ ὡς ἐξ αὐτοῦ ἐκπορευόμενον. Καὶ ὡς μὲν χορηγούμενον οὐκ ἔστι· προαιωνίως μὲν γὰρ ὑπάρχει τοῦ Υἱοῦ τὸ Πνεῦμα, τὸ δὲ χορηγεῖσθαι ὑστερογενές. Οὐδ᾽ ὡς ὁμοούσιον· λέγοιτο γὰρ ἂν καὶ ὁ Υἱὸς τοῦ Πνεύματος. Λείπεται τοίνυν τοῦ Υἱοῦ τὸ Πνεῦμα εἶναί τε καὶ λέγεσθαι ὡς ἐξ αὐτοῦ ἐκπορευόμενον». Τί οὖν, ἐάνπερ ἀναφανῇ

at least, whoever you are that were recently opposed, and now you propose "His" without that preposition. Or is the phrase that He is "His" considered and constructed by you, the dialectician of the incomprehensible, so as to mean that He is "from Him"? Tell me, on this point: are you not also of yourself? In this, at any rate, I think you will escape us. For you do not seem to me to have heard the one who says, "Become your own, O man."[102] For, if you had heard and obeyed, you would have fervently loved what has been handed down in tradition concerning God and would not have made any attempt on the words and deeds that surpass man, and innovating at that. But if man is of himself, then according to you, man is from himself. As for why we do not say "Son of the Spirit", that is reasonable, he says. For, we would think that the Spirit is a father, since the Son introduces the Father to the reasoning. For this reason accordingly we do not say "Son of the Spirit", lest you think that the Son is from the Spirit. However, we do say "Spirit of the Son"; but this does not mean that He is "from the Son" as well. For He is called His Spirit, not because He is from Him, but as being in Him.

Be taught this as well from the Apostle, when he is saying, "No one knoweth the things of a man, save the spirit of man which is in him."[103] So, just as it is said to be "the spirit of man", yet not as being from the man but as being in the man, similarly the divine Spirit is called the Spirit of the Son, not as being "from the Son" but as being in the Son naturally from eternity, and thus He completely evades the apparently ineluctable conclusions from your syllogisms.

For, on the basis of a division [a disjunctive syllogism] the Latin-minded syllogises and says, "since the Spirit is 'of the Son', it is either as being supplied through Him, or as consubstantial, or as proceeding from Him. And it is certainly not as being supplied, since the Spirit of the Son exists before the ages, while to be supplied is a later occurrence. Neither is it as consubstantial, for in that case 'Son of the Spirit' would also be said. Accordingly, what remains is that He is and is called the Spirit of the Son as proceeding from

τι ταύτης τῆς διαιρέσεως ἐκτός, καθ' ὃ τοῦ Υἱοῦ τὸ Πνεῦμα λέγοιτ'
ἄν, οὐχ ὁ ἐκ διαιρέσεως οὗτός σοι καθ' ὑπόθεσιν συλλογισμὸς
ἀσυλλόγιστος τὸ παράπαν γένοιτ' ἄν;

Ἔστι γὰρ τοῦ Υἱοῦ τὸ Πνεῦμα ὡς ἐξ αἰώνων καὶ εἰς αἰῶνας ἐκ
τοῦ Πατρὸς ἐκπορευόμενον καὶ ἐν Υἱῷ φυσικῶς ὑπάρχον καὶ
ἀναπαυόμενον· καὶ διὰ τοῦτο Πνεῦμα μὲν Υἱοῦ λέγεται, ἐκ δὲ τοῦ
Υἱοῦ οὐ λέγεται. Καὶ ὁ νοῦς γὰρ τοῦ ἀνθρώπου ἐκ τοῦ Θεοῦ ἐστι
γενόμενος καὶ ἐν αὐτῷ ὑπάρχων, δηλονότι τῷ ἀνθρώπῳ· καὶ νοῦς
μὲν ἀνθρώπου λέγεται, ἄνθρωπος δὲ τοῦ νοῦ οὐ λέγεται· ἀλλ'
οὐδ' ἐξ ἀνθρώπου λέγεται ὁ νοῦς, ὅ γε κατ' οὐσίαν· οὐ γὰρ δὴ περὶ
ἐνεργείας νῦν ὁ λόγος. Οὐκ ἄρα ἐκ τοῦ Υἱοῦ ἐστι τὸ Πνεῦμα, εἰ μὴ
τὴν χάριν εἴπῃς Πνεῦμα καὶ τὴν ἐνέργειαν· καὶ τὸν νοῦν γάρ, ὅταν
τὴν ἐνέργειαν σημαίνῃ τοὔνομα, φαίης ἂν ἐκ τοῦ ἀνθρώπου, ὡς
ἐκφαινόμενόν τε καὶ μεταδιδόμενον.

30

Ἴδοι δ' ἄν τις τοὺς θεολόγους καὶ νοῦν λέγοντας εἶναι Χριστοῦ τὸ
Πνεῦμα τὸ ἅγιον· ὁ γὰρ θεῖος Κύριλλος ἐν τετάρτῳ κεφαλαίῳ τῶν
Θησαυρῶν φησιν, «ὅτι νοῦς ὑπάρχον τοῦ Χριστοῦ, πάντα τὰ ἐν
αὐτῷ διαλέγεται τοῖς μαθηταῖς». Καθάπερ οὖν ἐφ' ἡμῶν ὁ νοῦς τοῦ
ἀνθρώπου ἐστὶ καὶ κατ' οὐσίαν καὶ κατ' ἐνέργειαν, καὶ κατ' οὐσίαν
μέν αὐτοῦ ἐστιν ὁ νοῦς, ἀλλ' οὐκ ἐξ αὐτοῦ, κατ' ἐνέργειαν δὲ καὶ
αὐτοῦ ἐστι καὶ ἐξ αὐτοῦ, οὕτω καὶ τὸ Πνεῦμα τὸ ἅγιον τοῦ Χριστοῦ
ἐστιν ὡς Θεοῦ καὶ κατ' οὐσίαν καὶ κατ' ἐνέργειαν. Ἀλλὰ κατὰ μὲν
τὴν οὐσίαν καὶ τὴν ὑπόστασιν αὐτοῦ ἐστιν, ἀλλ' οὐκ ἐξ αὐτοῦ· κατὰ
δὲ τὴν ἐνέργειαν καὶ αὐτοῦ ἐστιν καὶ ἐξ αὐτοῦ. Λατῖνοι δὲ τοῦ Υἱοῦ
τὸ Πνεῦμα λέγοντες, ἀλλ' οὐχὶ καὶ τοῦ Υἱοῦ μέν, οὐκ ἐκ τοῦ Υἱοῦ δέ,
αὐτὴν ἀναιροῦσί τε καὶ ἀθετοῦσι τὴν οὐσίαν καὶ τὴν ὑπόστασιν τοῦ
παναγίου Πνεύματος.

Him." What does this mean then? If, in fact, something should appear outside of this same analysis, according to which thing the Spirit could be said to be "of the Son", would not this hypothetical syllogism of yours, based on this analysis, become absolutely logically incoherent?

For the Spirit is "of the Son" since from eternity and unto the ages He proceeds from the Father and exists naturally in the Son and rests in Him, and because of this He is called the Spirit of the Son, but He is not said to be "from the Son". The intellect of man also originates from God and exists in him, that is, in the man. And while "the intellect of man" is said, "man of the intellect" is not said. Neither is the intellect said to be "from the man", at least as pertains to the essence. For, here the present explanation does not concern energy. So, the Spirit is not "from the Son", unless you call the grace and the energy "Spirit". For, you would say that the intellect also is from the man (whenever "intellect" indicates the energy), in the sense that is being expressed and transmitted.

30

But one could see that the theologians say that the Holy Spirit is the intellect of Christ as well. For the divine Cyril says in the [thirty-] fourth chapter of *The Treasuries*: "Since He is the mind [nous][104] of Christ, He has converse with His disciples [about] everything which is in Him."[105] So, precisely as for us the intellect is of a man with respect both to essence and to energy (and while the intellect is indeed His with respect to essence, yet it is not from him, whereas with respect to energy it is both his and from him), in this way also the Holy Spirit is of Christ as of God according to both essence and energy. But on the one hand, according to the essence and the hypostasis He is His but not "from Him." On the other hand, according to energy He is both His and "from Him". But when the Latins are saying, "the Spirit is of the Son," but not also "of the Son, yet not from the Son," they annul and despise the very essence and hypostasis of the all-holy Spirit.

31

Τὸ μὲν οὖν ἐκ διαιρέσεως συμπέρασμα τοῦ λατινικοῦ καθ᾽ ὑπόθεσιν συλλογισμοῦ διαλέλυται τελέως καὶ πρὸς τὸ μὴ ὂν κεχώρηκε· μᾶλλον δὲ πρὸς ἅπαν τοὐναντίον. Ἂν δέ τις ἴδῃ καὶ τὰ παρ᾽ αὐτοῦ τοῦ Λατίνου ἀναιρούμενα, ἵνα ἐξ ἀνάγκης τὸ ἓν ἀπερίτρεπτον δειχθῇ, τοῖς ἁγίοις τοῦτον ὄψεται φανερῶς ἀντίθετον· «τοῦ γὰρ Υἱοῦ», φησίν, «ἔστι τε καὶ λέγεται τὸ Πνεῦμα, οὐχ ὡς δι᾽ αὐτοῦ χορηγούμενον ἢ φαινόμενον (ἐπειδήπερ ἀνάρχως μὲν τὸ Πνεῦμα τοῦ Υἱοῦ, τὸ δὲ χορηγεῖν οὐκ ἄναρχον) οὐδ᾽ ὡς ὁμοούσιον· λέγοιτο γὰρ ἂν καὶ ὁ Υἱὸς τοῦ Πνεύματος».

Ἀλλ᾽ ὁ μέγας Βασίλειος, οὗ καὶ ἀκατάσκευος ἡ ῥῆσις διαφερόντως ἐστὶν ἰσχυροτέρα τῶν λατινικῶν συλλογισμῶν τε καὶ διαιρέσεων, οὗτος οὖν ἐν τῷ Περὶ τοῦ ἁγίου Πνεύματος λόγῳ, «τὸ δι᾽ Υἱοῦ», φησί, «πεφηνέναι τὸ Πνεῦμα σαφὲς πεποίηκεν ὁ ἀπόστολος, Υἱοῦ Πνεῦμα ὀνομάσας αὐτόν. Ὁρᾷς ὅτι Χριστοῦ τὸ Πνεῦμα λέγεται ὡς παρ᾽ αὐτοῦ χορηγούμενόν τε καὶ φαινόμενον; Πνεῦμα μὲν οὖν Υἱοῦ ἀνάρχως ἐστί τε καὶ λέγεται· ἀλλὰ καὶ αὐτὸ τὸ χορηγεῖν ἔχειν ἀνάρχως ἔχει ὁ Υἱός· οὐδεμία γὰρ πρόσληψις ἢ ἀφαίρεσις ἐκεῖ, ὡς δ᾽ ὑπὸ χρόνον ὄντα τὰ λαμβάνοντα, χρονικῶς ἔλαβον τὴν χορηγίαν.

Ἀλλὰ καὶ ὡς ὁμοφυὲς καὶ ὁμοούσιον λέγοιτ᾽ ἂν τὸ Πνεῦμα τοῦ Υἱοῦ, ὡς ὁ αὐτὸς μέγας Βασίλειος ἐν τῷ Πρὸς Ἀμφιλόχιον ὀκτωκαιδεκάτῳ κεφαλαίῳ «Πνεῦμα Χριστοῦ», φησί, «λέγεται, ὡς κατὰ φύσιν ᾠκειωμένον αὐτῷ». Καὶ ὁ θεῖος Κύριλλος ἐν τῷ Περὶ τοῦ ἁγίου Πνεύματος ἀγωνιστικῷ φησι λόγῳ· «τὸ Πνεῦμα τὸ ἅγιον, ὥσπερ κατ᾽ οὐσίαν ὑπάρχει τοῦ Θεοῦ καὶ Πατρός, οὕτω καὶ τοῦ Υἱοῦ κατ᾽ οὐσίαν ἐστίν, ὡς μετὰ τοῦ Υἱοῦ οὐσιωδῶς γεννηθέντος, ἐκ τοῦ Πατρὸς ἀφράστως ἐκπορευόμενον»· κἂν τῇ τοῦ Κατὰ Λουκᾶν

31

So, the conclusion from the disjunction of the Latin hypothetical syllogism has been completely dissolved and has departed to non-being or rather to the complete opposite. And should someone perceive the things annulled by the Latin himself so that the one option might necessarily be shown to be irrefutable, he would see that the Latin is clearly antithetical to the saints. For he says, "The Spirit both is and is called the Spirit of the Son not because He is supplied or manifested through Him (insofar as He is timelessly the Spirit of the Son, while to supply is not without beginning), nor is it in the sense of being consubstantial. For then the Son also would be called 'Son of the Spirit'."

But Basil the Great, whose mere improvised saying is much stronger than the Latin syllogisms and disjunctions, says, then, in his treatise *Concerning the Holy Spirit*, "The Apostle has made it clear that the Spirit has shone forth through the Son, having named Him the Spirit of the Son."[106] Do you see that "the Spirit of Christ" is said in the sense both of being supplied and of shining forth from Him? So, the Spirit both is and is called "the Son's" timelessly. The Son, however, timelessly has even the ability of supplying itself. For, there is no additional reception or removal there, although since the recipients are under time, they received their supply temporally.

But "the Spirit of the Son" could also be said in the sense of being connatural and consubstantial, as the same Basil the Great says in his eighteenth Chapter *To Amphilochios*: "The Spirit is called 'of Christ' since He is by nature familiar with Him."[107] And Cyril the divine says in his masterfully argumentative treatise *Concerning the Holy Spirit*, "Just as the Holy Spirit, according to essence, is of the God and Father, so also He is the Son's according to essence, as proceeding ineffably from the Father along with the Son, who was begotten essentially."[108] Further, he says in his exegesis of the *Gospel According to Luke*, "as the finger is fastened to the hand, being not alien

εὐαγγελίου ἐξηγήσει, «ὥσπερ», φησίν, «ὁ δάκτυλος ἀπήρτηται τῆς χειρός, οὐκ ἀλλότριος ὢν αὐτῆς, ἀλλ' ἐν αὐτῇ φυσικῶς, οὕτω καὶ τὸ Πνεῦμα τὸ ἅγιον τῷ τῆς ὁμοουσιότητος λόγῳ συνῆπται μὲν πρὸς ἕνωσιν τῷ Υἱῷ, ἐκ τοῦ Θεοῦ δὲ καὶ Πατρὸς ἐκπορεύεται». Πνεῦμα μὲν οὖν Υἱοῦ καὶ ὡς ὁμοφυὲς λέγοιτ' ἄν· οὐ λέγεται δὲ καὶ ὁ Υἱὸς τοῦ Πνεύματος, ὡς ἂν μὴ Πατὴρ τὸ Πνεῦμα δόξῃ.

32

Ἐπεισί μοι τοιγαροῦν θαυμάζειν τὸ τῆς λατινικῆς παρανοίας ὑπερβάλλον, ἀναλογιζομένῳ ὅτι τοῦ Πνεύματος κατὰ τοὺς εἰρημένους πάντας τρόπους λεγομένου τοῦ Υἱοῦ, καθ' ἕνα δὲ μόνον οὐδαμῶς, αὐτοὶ πάντας μὲν ἐκείνους δυσσεβῶς ἠγνόησάν τε καὶ ἠθέτησαν, τῷ δὲ μηδαμῶς εἰρημένῳ προσχόντες καὶ τοῦτο δυσσεβῶς, ἐκ τοῦ Υἱοῦ τὴν ὕπαρξιν ἔχειν τὸ Πνεῦμα ἐδογμάτισαν, ὅτι τοῦ Υἱοῦ ἐστί τε καὶ λέγεται. Ἀλλ' ἵν' ἐπὶ βεβαίαν ἕδραν στηρίξωμεν τοὺς περὶ τούτου λογισμούς, σαφεστάτῳ τε καὶ θεοπνεύστῳ λόγῳ τούτους ἐπισημηνάμενοι, Ἰωάννην οἶσθα τὸν ἐκ Δαμασκοῦ πυρσεύσαντα καὶ τὴν οἰκουμένην ὅλην φωτὶ περιαυγάσαντα θεογνωσίας. Οὐχ οὗτος ἀριδηλότατά φησιν, «ὡς Πνεῦμα μὲν Υἱοῦ λέγομεν, ἐκ δὲ τοῦ Υἱοῦ οὐ λέγομεν»; "Ναί", φησί, "καὶ οὐκ ἔχω λέγειν ὡς οὐχ οὗτος οὕτως εἴρηκεν, ἀλλ' ἔχω λέγειν ὡς πρὸς τὸ πρῶτον αἴτιον ἐκ τοῦ Υἱοῦ οὐ λέγεται."

Βαβαί· ἔστι δέ σοι καὶ ἄλλο αἴτιον ἐπὶ τῆς θεότητος, εἰ μὴ τὸ πρῶτον; Τοῦτο γὰρ ἐφ' ἡμῶν τῶν δεδημιουργημένων τοῖς πατράσιν εἴρηται καὶ οὕτως ἔχει λόγον τὸ πρῶτον ἐπὶ τοῦ αἰτίου, ὡς καὶ τοῦ Υἱοῦ τοῦ Πνεύματος ὄντων συναιτίων. Διὸ καὶ προκαταρκτικὸν τὸν Πατέρα αἴτιον ὁ μέγας εἴρηκε Βασίλειος. Ὥσπερ δὲ Πατὴρ μὲν ἔστι κυρίως τοῦ μονογενοῦς, λέγεται δὲ καὶ ἡμῶν τῶν μὴ γεγεννημένων ἀλλὰ δεδημιουργημένων ὑπ' αὐτοῦ, οὕτω πάλιν πρῶτον αἴτιον δι' ἡμᾶς κυρίως· λέγεται δὲ κἀκεῖ παρὰ τῶν θεολόγων, ὡς δεικτικὸν τῆς τοῦ

to it but in it naturally, so also the Holy Spirit is connected by reason
of His consubstantiality but is in it naturally, so also the Holy Spirit
is, by reason of His consubstantiality, connected toward union with
the Son, although He proceeds from the God and Father."[109] So, the
Spirit could be said to be "of the Son" also in the sense of being of
the same nature, while the Son is not said to be "of the Spirit" lest
you think that the Spirit is a Father.

32

So I am forced to marvel at the extreme excess of the Latin insanity
as I consider that, while the Spirit is said to be "of the Son" in all of
the aforementioned ways but is not at all described thus only in one
sense, they indeed irreverently both ignored and set those all aside,
paid attention to what had not been said at all (and irreverently at
that), and dogmatised that the Spirit has existence from the Son
on the basis that He both is and is said to be the Son's. But let us
buttress our thoughts on this upon a sure foundation, setting our
seal upon them with a most clear and God-breathed argument. You
know the John that kindled a torch from Damascus and completely
enlightened the entire world with the light of divine knowledge.
Does he not clearly say that "while we say the 'Spirit of the Son',
yet we do not say 'the Spirit from the Son'"?[110] "Yes," he responds;
"and I am not able to say that this person has not spoken thus, but I
am able to say that it is with respect to the first cause that 'from the
Son' is not said."

Really! So is there in your eyes another cause in the divinity except
the first? For this has been said by the fathers with reference to
us who have been created, and thus the "first" has a reason [to
be used] regarding the cause, since both the Son and the Spirit
are joint causes. Wherefore, Basil the Great has also said that the
Father is the initial cause.[111] And just as in the proper sense He is
Father of the Only-Begotten yet He is also said to be the Father of
us who have not been begotten but have been created by Him, so
again He is called first cause in the proper sense because of us. This

Πατρὸς ὑποστάσεως, ἀλλ᾽ οὐχ ὡς καὶ τοῦ Υἱοῦ συναιτίου ὄντος ἐπὶ τῆς θεότητος.

33

Οὐκ ἐπὶ τοῦ ἀνάρχου τοίνυν Πνεύματος τὸ προκαταρκτικὸν καὶ πρῶτον αἴτιον, ἄπαγε τῆς βλασφημίας, ἀλλ᾽ ἐπὶ τῶν ἐσχηκότων τὴν χρονικὴν ἀρχήν, ἐφ᾽ ὧν καὶ ὁ Υἱὸς τῷ Πατρὶ συναίτιός ἐστιν. Ἀλλὰ μὴν ἐφ᾽ ὧν πρῶτον κυρίως αἴτιόν ἐστιν ὁ Πατήρ, τῶν κτισμάτων δηλαδή, οὐκ εὐσεβὲς εἰπεῖν, ὡς τοῦ Υἱοῦ μὲν τὴν κτίσην λέγομεν, ἐκ δὲ τοῦ Υἱοῦ οὐ λέγομεν. Εἰ τοίνυν καὶ ἐπὶ τοῦ ἀκτίστου Πνεύματος πρῶτον αἴτιον ὑπῆρχεν ὁ Πατήρ, ὡς καὶ τοῦ Υἱοῦ ὄντος συναιτίου, δυσσεβοῦς ἂν ἦν λέγειν, ὡς ἐκ τοῦ Υἱοῦ οὐ λέγομεν. Ἐπεὶ δὲ ὁ τοῦτο λέγων οὐκ εὐσεβὴς μόνον, ἀλλὰ καὶ τοῖς ἁγίοις ἐνάριθμος, δυσσεβὴς ἄρ᾽ ὁ λέγων συναίτιον τῷ Πατρὶ τὸν Υἱὸν ἐπὶ τοῦ Πνεύματος καὶ διὰ τοῦτο πρῶτον αἴτιον ἐπὶ τῆς ἀνωτάτω Τριάδος τὸν Πατέρα. Τοῦτο γὰρ δι᾽ ἡμᾶς τοὺς διὰ τοῦ Υἱοῦ γεγονότας ἀκούει ὁ Πατήρ, διὸ καὶ ποιητὴς ἡμῶν ἑκάτερος, μενοῦνγε καὶ Πατήρ· κἂν εἷς καὶ ἐφ᾽ ἡμῶν λέγηται ποιητής τε καὶ Πατὴρ ὁ Πατὴρ σὺν τῷ Υἱῷ, ἀλλ᾽ ὡς μίαν καὶ τὴν αὐτὴν δημιουργικὴν δύναμιν πλουτοῦντες. Ἐκεῖ δὲ πάντῃ τε καὶ πάντως εἷς Πατήρ, εἷς αἴτιος· οὐ γάρ ἐστι τὸ γόνιμον ἀμφοῖν, ἀλλὰ μία πηγαία θεότης, ὁ Πατήρ. Ποῦ γοῦν ὅλως ἐκεῖ χώραν ἔχει τὸ πρῶτον αἴτιον; ὡς καὶ τοῦ αἰτιατοῦ ὄντος συναιτίου; Ἀσεβὴς ὁ λόγος· ἐς κόρακας ῥιπτέσθω, μὴ τοῖς νοητοῖς σε κόραζι σύννομον καταστήσῃ.

Πῶς δὲ ἄρα ὁ σοφὸς οὗτος εἴπερ τις τὰ θεῖα Ἰωάννης, καὶ ταῦτα τὴν ἀσφαλῆ δόξαν περὶ Θεοῦ ἠκριβωμένως ἐκτιθείς, ἀπροσδιορίστως ἂν προέθετο τὸ προσδιορισμοῦ δεόμενον; Ποῖον δὲ οὐχ ἕξει χώραν τῶν ἀφρόνως παρὰ τῶν κακοδόξων εἰρημένων, εἰ προσδιορίζειν δοίημεν τά ἀπροσδιορίστως περὶ τῆς τρισυποστάτου θεότητος

term, however, is also used by the theologians in the former case as
being indicative of the Father's hypostasis, but not as if it were an
indication that the Son is a joint cause for the divinity.

33

Therefore the initial, first cause concerns not the beginningless
Spirit (away with that blasphemy!) but those that possess a temporal
beginning, in respect to whom the Son also is a joint cause with the
Father.[112] Yet truly, regarding those whose first cause (in the proper
sense) is the Father, that is the creatures, it is not pious to say, "While
we say that creation is the Son's, yet we do not say it is from the
Son." Therefore, if the Father was a first cause also with respect to
the uncreated Spirit, as with the Son being a joint cause, it would
have been impious to say, "We do not say He is from the Son."
But since he that says this is not only pious but counted among the
saints, therefore impious is he that calls the Son a joint cause to
the Father with respect to the Spirit and who, because of this, calls
the Father a first cause with respect to the supreme Trinity. For the
Father is called by this name because of us who have been made
through the Son, wherefore each one of Them is also a creator and
so also a Father. And if the Father along with the Son is said to be
one creator and Father regarding us as well, yet it is in the sense
that They are rich in the one and the same creative power. There,
however, there is in every way and entirely one Father, one cause;
for the generative power is not in both, but rather there is one fount
of divinity, the Father. Well then, where at all is there room for the
"first cause" there? Is it as if the caused one were a joint cause? This
saying is impious: let it be thrown to the crows, lest it render you
partner of the noetic crows.

How is it then that this man John, who was wise more than anyone
in divine matters, would unqualifiedly propose what requires
qualification, and in fact do this as he was setting forth precisely the
unerring belief concerning God? And will we not be making room
for any of the things that have been foolishly said by the cacodox,

ἐκπεφασμένα; Ἐπεὶ γὰρ Πνεῦμα ὁ Θεός, καὶ τῶν τριῶν ἕκαστον
ἐν μέρει Πνεῦμα λέγεται. Εἴ τις οὖν καινοτομῶν ἔλεγεν ὅτι ἐκ τοῦ
Πνεύματός ἐστιν ὁ Υἱός, ἐπεὶ Θεὸς ὁ Υἱὸς καὶ ἐκ Θεοῦ, Πνεῦμα δὲ
ὑπάρχει ὁ Θεός, εἶθ' ἡμεῖς ἀντεπεφέρωμεν ὅτι Θεὸς μὲν Πνεῦμα
καὶ Θεοῦ Πνεῦμα λέγεται, Θεὸς δὲ ἐκ Πνεύματος οὐ λέγεται, ἆρα
ἂν εἶχε λέγειν, ὡς πρὸς τὸ πρῶτον αἴτιον οὐ λέγεται; Οὔμενοῦν.

34

Τολμήσαντος δέ τινος μὴ δημιουργὸν εἶναι φάναι τὸν Υἱόν, ἆρ' ἂν
ἡμεῖς ἐδικαιώσαμεν αὐτὸν εἰπόντες, ὡς πρὸς τὸν πρῶτον αἴτιον οὐκ
εἶναι φάσκει τὸν Υἱὸν δημιουργόν; Ἄπαγε. Ἡμῶν δ' αὖ λεγόντων
εὐσεβῶς, 'ὡς οὐκ ἦν ὅτε οὐκ ἦν ὁ Υἱός', εἴ τις προσδιορίζων ἔλεγε
μὴ αἰωνίως ἀλλὰ χρονικῶς, ὡς τὸν χρόνον μόνον, ἀλλ' οὐχὶ καὶ
τὸν αἰῶνα συμπεριβαλλούσης τῆς φωνῆς, οὐκ εὐθὺς ἂν παρ'ἡμῶν
ἀκούσειεν ὡς τοῦθ' ὃ λέγεις, ἄνθρωπε, σαφὴς ἀθέτησίς ἐστι τῶν
ὁμολογουμένων καὶ διαστροφὴ τῶν εὐσεβῶς κειμένων; Οὕτω
πάσης δυσσεβείας ἐστὶν ἀφορμὴ καὶ ἀρχὴ καὶ ῥίζα καὶ πηγὴ τὸ
προσδιορίζειν τὰ τεθεολογημένα τοῖς θεοφόροις ἡμῶν πατράσιν
ἀπροσδιορίστως· καὶ σχεδὸν τοῦτο μόνον τῶν ἁπάντων μιγνύει
τὰ ἄμικτα καὶ συγκλώθει, τὸ τοῦ λόγου, τὰ ἀσύγκλωστα καὶ τὰ
πολεμιώτατα πρὸς ἄλληλα, εὐσέβειάν τε καὶ ἀσέβειαν, καὶ τοὺς
ἀντεχομένους ἑκατέρας ὡς μηδὲν ἀντικειμένους πρὸς ἀπάτην
δείκνυσι. Τοσούτῳ δὲ οἱ Λατῖνοι τούτῳ καταχρῶνται, ὡς καὶ
τῶν ἁγίων ἀκούοντες θεολογούντων ἀπροσδιορίστως ὅτι μόνος
ὁ Πατὴρ ἀρχὴ καὶ ῥίζα καὶ πηγὴ θεότητος, αὐτοὶ πάντα ταῦτα
προσδιορίζουσι (μᾶλλον δὲ διὰ τοῦ προσδιορισμοῦ δολίως τούτοις
ἀντιδογματίζουσι) καίτοι πάσαις ἐχρῆν αὐτοὺς ὁμοῦ στοιχεῖν ταῖς
τῶν θεοσόφων θεολόγων φωναῖς, καὶ ποῦ μὲν λεγούσαις ἐκ μόνου
τοῦ Πατρὸς τὸ Πνεῦμα, διὸ καὶ μόνον αἴτιον τὸν Πατέρα καὶ

if we should allow the qualification of what has been unqualifiedly expressed concerning the trihypostatic divinity? For it follows that, as God is Spirit, each of the three is separately called Spirit. So if someone was innovatively saying that the Son is from the Spirit because the Son is God and is from God and God is Spirit, and if we then rejoined that, while God is Spirit and is called the Spirit of God, yet God is not said to be from Spirit, would he be able to say that it is not said in reference to the first cause? Not at all.

34

Now, should someone dare to say that the Son is not a Creator, would we then have excused him saying that it is with reference to the first cause that he does not affirm the Son to be the Creator? Away with the idea! But again we piously say, "There was not a time when the Son was not."[113] If someone was qualifying and saying that it was not in the sense of eternally but rather temporally, that the expression does not encompass also the *eternal* age but only time, would he not immediately hear from us, "This which you say, my friend, is a clear despising of things which have been commonly confessed and a perversion of pious texts"? Thus, the occasion and root and fount for all irreverence is to qualify matters which have already been theologized by our Godbearing Fathers without qualification. And scarcely this alone of all things mixes up what cannot be mixed and spins together, as the saying goes,[114] what cannot be spun together, the most polemically opposed points with each other, piety with impiety, and deceitfully displays those that hold each position as not being opponents at all. And the Latins abuse this so much that when they hear even the saints theologizing without further qualification that only the Father is the origin and root and fount of divinity, they qualify all these things (or rather, through their qualification they deceitfully dogmatize against them), although they ought to walk at the same time by all the expressions of those theologians who were made wise by God. These God-wise theologians say in some passages that the Spirit is only from the Father, wherefore the Father is the only cause and fount of divinity, while elsewhere they

πηγὴν θεότητος, ποῦ δ' αὖ ἐκ τοῦ Υἱοῦ τὸ Πνεῦμα συνάγειν εἰς ἓν καὶ φρονεῖν εὖ ἐκ μόνου τοῦ Πατρός, ἀλλ' οὐχὶ καὶ ἐκ τοῦ Υἱοῦ τὸ Πνεῦμα τὸ ἅγιον.

35

Οἱ δὲ συνείροντες ἢ προφασιζόμενοι τὸ πρῶτον ἀνασκευάζουσιν ἑκάτερον, φάσκοντες, ὅτι καθάπερ μόνος Θεὸς ἀληθινὸς ὁ Πατήρ ἔστιν ὅτε λέγεται, καὶ τοῦ Υἱοῦ ὄντος ἀληθινοῦ Θεοῦ καὶ ἀγαθοῦ, οὕτω καὶ μόνος ὁ Πατὴρ πηγὴ καὶ αἴτιος θεότητος ὡς πρῶτος· καὶ οὐδὲν ἐμπόδιον εἶναι καὶ τὸν Υἱὸν αἴτιον θεότητος. Οὐ συνορῶσι γάρ, ὡς ἐντεῦθεν καὶ τὸν Υἱόν, μάλιστα δὲ τὸ Πνεῦμα τὸ ἅγιον εἰς κτίσμα κατασπῶσιν. Ὅταν γὰρ λέγωμεν ὅτι μόνος ὁ Πατὴρ Θεός ἐστιν ἀληθινός, οὐ τῶν ἀκτίστων πρὸς ἄλληλα τὴν ἀντιδιαστολήν ποιοῦμεν, οὐδ' ἁπλῶς τότε τὸν Πατέρα, ἀλλὰ τὴν μόνην ἐν τρισίν ὑποστάσεσι θεωρουμένην φύσιν τῶν κτισμάτων ἀποδιαστέλλομεν. Εἰ τοίνυν οὕτω λέγομεν καὶ μόνος αἴτιος θεότητος ὁ Πατήρ, ὡς ἐπ' αὐτοῦ λέγομεν ὅτι μόνος ἀγαθός, τὸ Πνεῦμα τὸ ἅγιον καὶ κατ' αὐτοὺς οὐκ ὂν αἴτιον θεότητος ἐναρίθμιον ἔσται τοῖς κτιστοῖς.

Καὶ μὴν ἐφ' ὧν ὡς πρῶτος καὶ ὡς προκαταρκτικὸν αἴτιον ἔσθ' ὅτε λέγεται μόνος ὁ Πατήρ, ὡς καὶ τοῦ Υἱοῦ ὄντος συναιτίου καὶ κοινωνοῦντος κατ' ἐκεῖνα τῷ Πατρί, οὐ μόνον ὁ Πατὴρ ἔσθ' ὅτε μόνος λέγεται Θεὸς ἀληθινὸς καὶ μόνος δημιουργὸς καὶ μόνος ἀγαθὸς καὶ τὰ τοιαῦτα, ἀλλ' ἔσθ' ὅτε καὶ ὁ Υἱὸς μόνος ἂν ρηθείη· καὶ οὐχ ὁ Υἱὸς μόνος, ἀλλὰ καὶ τὸ Πνεῦμα. Ἐπεὶ γὰρ τὸ "μόνος" τοῦτο τὴν ἄκτιστον φύσιν ἀντιδιαστέλλει τῶν κτιστῶν, ἡ δ' ἄκτιστος φύσις τρισυπόστατός ἐστι καὶ ἀμερῶς ἐφ' ἑκάστης τῶν ὑποστάσεων ὅλη θεωρεῖται, ἀφ' ἧς ἂν αὐτὴν τῶν τριῶν ἐμφύτων ὑποστάσεων καλέσῃς, ὅλην λέγεις τὴν τρισυπόστατον φύσιν.

say that from the Son we should sum up the Holy Spirit into one and consider that He is only from the Father, but not that the Holy Spirit is also from the Son.

35

But by making connections and using the first cause as an excuse, they fabricate each, saying that, just as there are times when the Father is said to be the only true God although the Son is also a true and good God, in the same way is the Father said to be the only Fount and cause of divinity, as being first; and so there is no impediment for the Son being a cause of divinity as well. They do not comprehend that by this they drag the Son and especially the Holy Spirit down into being a creature. For, whenever we say that only the Father is the true God, we are not differentiating the Uncreated from one another, neither are we in that case simply separating the Father, but rather the only nature contemplated in three hypostases, from created things. Accordingly, if this is how we explain it and if the Father is the only cause of divinity as we speak of Him that He is the only good one, the Holy Spirit, who even according to them is not a cause of divinity, will be numbered with created things.

However, for those for whom there are times when only the Father is spoken of as the first and as the initial cause, as if the Son were a joint cause and a sharer in those things with the Father, there are not only cases when the Father is said to be "the only true God" and "only creator" and "only Good One" and such titles, but there are also times when only the Son could be said to be these things; and not only the Son, but the Spirit as well. For, since this "only" separates the uncreated nature from created beings, and since the uncreated nature is trihypostatic and its entirety is indivisibly considered in each of the hypostases, with whichever one of the three natural hypostases you call it, you are referring to the entire trihypostatic nature.

36

Ἆρ' οὖν, ὥσπερ λέγομεν εὐσεβῶς ὅτι μόνος ἐστὶ Χριστὸς ὁ ἐπὶ πάντων Θεός, ἔχοι τις ἂν εἰπεῖν, μᾶλλον δὲ ἤκουσταί ποτέ τις καὶ τοῦτο εἰρηκώς, ὡς μόνος ὁ Υἱὸς αἴτιός τε καὶ πηγὴ τῆς θεότητος τοῦ Πνεύματος; Ἢ καὶ αὐτὸ τὸ Πνεῦμα μόνον αἴτιόν τε καὶ πηγὴ θεότητος, ὃ καὶ κατὰ Λατίνους οὐδαμῶς αἴτιόν ἐστι θεότητος; Καίτοι καὶ τοῦτο τῶν εἰκότων ἦν, εἴπερ οὕτως ὁ Πατὴρ αἴτιος μόνος θεότητος ἐλέγετο, ὡς καὶ τοῦ Υἱοῦ ὄντος συναιτίου.

Δῆλον τοίνυν, μᾶλλον δὲ κατάδηλον, ὅτι τὸ «μόνος» ἐπὶ τῶν ὑποστατικῶν λεγόμενον οὐ τὰ κτιστὰ τῶν ἀκτίστων, ἀλλὰ μίαν τινὰ τῶν ἀκτίστων ὑποστάσεων πρὸς τὰς ἄλλας διαστέλλει. Τίς δ' οὐκ οἶδεν, ὡς ὑποστατικὸν ἐπὶ τῆς θεότητος τὸ αἴτιόν ἐστιν; Οὐκοῦν, εἰ μόνος ὁ Πατὴρ αἴτιος καὶ μόνος ἀρχὴ καὶ πηγὴ θεότητος, οὐδεμία ἄρα τῶν θείων ὑποστάσεων ἑτέρα αἰτία καὶ ἀρχὴ καὶ πηγὴ θεότητός ἐστιν. Οὐ μὴν ἀλλ' εἰ τοῦ αἰτίου ἐν δυσὶ προσώποις ἐπὶ τῆς θεότητος θεωρουμένου κατὰ τοὺς Λατίνους, οὐδὲν κωλύει λέγειν μόνον τὸν Πατέρα αἴτιον θεότητος· καὶ τοῦ αἰτιατοῦ θεωρουμένου ἐν δυσὶ προσώποις, οὐδὲν κωλύσει λέγειν μόνον τὸ Πνεῦμα τὸ ἅγιον αἰτιατὸν ὑπάρχειν ἢ μόνον τὸν Υἱόν, ὃ μηδείς ποτε οὐδὲν τῶν αἱρετικῶν ἐτόλμησεν εἰπεῖν.

Καίτοι, εἰ προσδιορίζειν δοίημεν τὰ τεθεολογημένα τοῖς ἁγίοις ἀπροσδιορίστως, καὶ τοῦτ' ἂν εὐχερῶς κατασκευασθείη παντὶ τῷ βουλομένῳ· ἀλλ' εὐθὺς οὗτος, εἰ μὴ μεταμεληθείη, καθυποβληθήσεται τῷ ἀναθέματι· «εἰ γάρ τις», φησίν, «εὐαγγελίζεται παρ' ὃ εὐηγγελισάμεθα, ἀνάθεμα ἔστω». Τί δὲ σὺ φῇς ὁ καὶ ἐκ τοῦ Υἱοῦ τὸ Πνεῦμα λέγων καὶ διὰ τοῦτο προσδιορίζων τὰ ἀπροσδιορίστως τεθεολογημένα τοῖς ἁγίοις καὶ τῷ θεολογοῦντι μὴ καὶ ἐκ τοῦ Υἱοῦ τὸ Πνεῦμα λέγεσθαι τῷ προσδιορισμῷ δολίως

36

Therefore, just as we piously state that Christ only is the God of all, would anyone be able to say (or better, has anyone ever been heard to have said even this) that only the Son is the cause and fount of divinity of the Spirit? Or also be able to say that even the Spirit Himself is the only cause and fount of divinity, who even according to the Latins is not possibly a cause of divinity? And yet this also would be a possibility, assuming this is how the Father was said to be the only cause of divinity, as if the Son were a joint cause.

Accordingly it is clear, or rather completely clear, that when the word "only" is spoken in reference to hypostatic things, it is distinguishing not the created from the uncreated but one particular uncreated hypostasis from the others. And who does not know that for the divinity the cause is hypostatic? So then, if only the Father is a cause and only He is a beginning and a fount of divinity, therefore none other of the divine hypostases is a cause and beginning and fount of divinity. Nevertheless, if, when the cause for the divinity is theorized to be in two persons according to the Latins, there is nothing to prevent us from saying that only the Father is a fount of divinity, then when what has been caused is also theorized to be in two persons, nothing will prevent us from saying that only the Holy Spirit, or only the Son, exists as caused, which no one at any time even from the heretics dared to say.

And yet, if we grant the definition of what has already been theologized by the saints in an undefined manner, even this could easily be arranged by anyone who wanted it. Immediately, however, this man, unless he repent, will completely fall under the anathema. For it is said: "If any man proclaim what has not been proclaimed by us, let him be anathema."[115] But what are you saying, you who say that the Spirit is "also from the Son" and because of this are defining what has been already theologized in an undefined manner by the saints and with your definition are deceitfully contradicting the one

ἀντιλέγων; Ἆρ' ἔχεις δεῖξαι, ὡς οὐ σχεδὸν πάνθ' ὅμοιος τυγχάνεις
ὢν τῷ ὑπευθύνῳ τούτῳ; «Ἔχω σοι», φησί, «δεῖξαι πολλοὺς τῶν
θεολόγων ἐναντιουμένους τῇ τοῦ Δαμασκηνοῦ θεολογίᾳ ταύτῃ καὶ
τὸ ἐκπορεύειν νοεῖν διδόντας εἶναι τοῦ Υἱοῦ».

37

Βαβαί· καὶ ὅλως, ἔστιν ἐν τοῖς θεολόγοις, καὶ ταῦτ' ἐπὶ τῶν
ἀναγκαιοτάτων καὶ ὧν ἡ πίστις ἡμῶν ἅπασα ἐξήρτηται, ἐναντιότης;
Ἔστι δ' ὅλως καὶ θεολογίας εἶναι τὰς ἐναντιουμένας ἢ τοὺς
κατ' αὐτὰς θεολόγους ἀμφοτέρους; Ἥκιστα. Οὐκοῦν τοῦτον ἢ
ἐκείνους διαγράψομεν τοῦ χοροῦ τῶν ὀρθοδόξων κατὰ σέ. Τί δέ,
τῶν εὐαγγελικῶν καὶ ἀποστολικῶν ῥημάτων οὕτως ἐχόντων καὶ
οὕτω διευκρινούντων τὰ τοῦ Πνεύματος, καθὰ προαπεδείξαμεν,
οὐ τῇ δι' αὐτῶν πεφανερωμένῃ τῆς εὐσεβείας ἐννοίᾳ παντὶ τρόπῳ
συμβιβάσομεν τὸ δοκοῦν διαφωνεῖν; Ἂν δέ τι καὶ μὴ δυνηθῶμεν
τῶν πατερικῶν ῥημάτων πρὸς ἐκείνην ἀποκαταστῆσαι τὴν
διάνοιαν, οὐκ αὐτὸ μὲν ἀφῶμεν, ὡς μὴ συνεῖναι δυνηθέντες, τῆς δὲ
ἀνωμολογημένης εὐσεβείας οὐδὲν ἧττον ἀντεχόμενοι διατελέσωμεν;
Παντί που δῆλον, ὡς πᾶσι τρόποις ταῖς ἀνακεκηρυγμέναις ὑπὸ τῶν
εὐαγγελικῶν καὶ ἀποστολικῶν ῥημάτων τῆς εὐσεβείας προσέξομεν
ἐννοίαις.

Φέρε δ' ὅμως ὀρθοδόξους ἀναδεῖξαι πρὸς αὐτὰς ἐπιχειρήσωμεν τὰς
ὑπὸ Λατίνων ὑπὲρ τῶν δοκούντων σφίσι προτεινομένας πατερικὰς
φωνάς. Κἂν μὲν διαρκῶς διαλῦσαι σχῶμεν τὴν πρὸς τὸ φαινόμενον
ἀντίθεσιν, τῷ Θεῷ χάρις τῷ καὶ τοῖς ἐν ἐσχατιαῖς ἡμῖν κειμένοις
τῆς ἀγνοίας καὶ τῆς ἀπαθοῦς ζωῆς ἀπῳκισμένοις γνῶσιν συνήγορον
τῆς ἐν αὐτῷ ἀληθείας παρασχόντι. Εἰ δ' ἄρα μὴ τοιοῦτον ἀποδοῦναι
κατὰ πάντα σχοίημεν τὸν λόγον, εἴ τις ἐν Χριστῷ τέλειος καὶ σοφὸς
τὰ θεῖα καὶ πνευματικά, τῆς προαιρέσεως ἡμᾶς ἀποδεξάμενος,
αὐτὸς παρ' ἑαυτοῦ τὸν κρείττω λόγον διδασκέτω, ποθοῦντας

who theologizes that the Spirit is not said to be also from the Son? Are you, then, able to show that you do not happen to be almost entirely similar to the one the lies under this condemnation? He says, "I am able to show that many of the theologians are opposed to this theology of the Damascene and that they allow us to think that procession is the Son's."

37

Really! Is there in a word among the theologians a contradiction, and in fact upon the absolutely necessary things, on which our entire faith hangs? Or is it entirely possible for the contradictions to be theologies or for their respective supporters to both be theologians? Not at all. So according to you we shall exclude either him or the others from the choir of the Orthodox. But why? Since such are the evangelic and apostolic words and since it is in this way that they clarify the things of the Spirit, as we previously demonstrated, will we not in every way reconcile what seems to disagree with the meaning of piety that has been revealed through them? And if we were not able to conform some one of the Patristic words to that understanding, will we not just leave it, as not having been able to understand it, and will we not nonetheless keep on holding fast to the commonly confessed piety? It is, I suppose, clear to all that we shall be attentive in every way to the meanings of piety that have been proclaimed by the evangelic and apostolic words.

But come now, let us endeavor to display that the patristic voices proposed by the Latins on behalf of their own opinions are orthodox in reference to those meanings. And if, on the one hand, we shall be able to adequately dissolve the apparent contradiction, thanks be to God who has provided even to us, who lie on the borders of ignorance and dwell far from the dispassionate life, knowledge in harmony with the truth that is in Him. On the other hand, in the event that we be not able to provide an explanation for everything, if someone is perfect in Christ and wise in divine and spiritual matters, let this very man accept us from our disposition and teach

καὶ μαθητιῶντας ὅτι μάλιστα καὶ τὸ ἐνδέον ἡμῶν ἀναπληρῶν
ἐντρεπέτω τελεώτερον τοὺς τἀναντία τῇ εὐσεβείᾳ συνάγειν ἐκ
τούτων πειρωμένους.

38

Εἰπὲ δή, τίνες καὶ τί τὰ παρ᾽ ἐκείνων εἰρημένα· τῶν γὰρ ἀδυνάτων
ἐστὶ μὴ ὁμολογεῖν ἀλλήλοις ἅπαντας τοὺς θεοφόρους καὶ Χριστῷ
τῷ Θεῷ τῶν θεοφόρων, μιᾶς αὐτοῖς ἐκ τοῦ ἑνὸς Πνεύματος τοῦ
Χριστοῦ τῆς ἐπιπνοίας οὔσης· πρὸς δὲ τούτῳ καὶ μετ᾽ ἐκείνους
σχεδὸν ἅπαντας οὗτος ὁ Δαμασκηνός ἐστι καὶ ὑπ᾽ ἐκείνων ἁπάντων
ἐδιδάχθη καὶ αὐτὸς ἑαυτῷ μαρτυρεῖ τὴν πρὸς ἐκείνους συμφωνίαν,
οὐ "λέγω" λέγων, ἀλλὰ "λέγομεν", καὶ δι᾽ ἑαυτοῦ κἀκείνους
παρίστησιν ἡμῖν οὐδαμοῦ ἐκ τοῦ Υἱοῦ τὸ Πνεῦμα λέγοντας καθ᾽
ὕπαρξιν. Ὑμεῖς δ᾽ ἐοίκατέ μοι τοῦ τῆς αὐτῶν μεγαλονοίας ὕφους
μὴ ἐφικνούμενοι τοιαῦτ᾽ εἴεσθαι περὶ αὐτῶν. Καὶ γὰρ καὶ πρῶτον
αἴτιον λέγεται παρὰ πάντων ὁ Πατήρ, ἀλλ᾽ ἤκουσας ὡς λέγεται· καὶ
ὁ μέγας Ἀθανάσιος παρὰ τοῦ Λόγου τὸ Πνεῦμα τὸ ἅγιον ἐκλάμπειν
εἶπεν, ἀλλ᾽ ἤκουσας ὡς εἶπε· καὶ εἰκόνα Πατρὸς μὲν Υἱόν, Υἱοῦ δὲ
τὸ Πνεῦμα λέγομεν, ἀλλ᾽ ἤκουσας ὡς λέγομεν· καὶ πλεῖσθ᾽ ἕτερα,
δοκοῦντα πρὸς ὑμῶν, ἡμῖν ἀλλ᾽ οὐχ ὑμῖν συμβαίνοντα καθαρῶς
ἀναπεφήνασι. Δώσει δὲ τὸ Πνεῦμα κἂν τοῖς ἑξῆς λόγον ἐν ἀνοίξει
τοῦ στόματος ἡμῶν.

Ἀλλὰ τίς ὁ λέγων ὡς καὶ τοῦ Υἱοῦ τὸ ἐκπορεύειν ἔνι; Αὐτός, φασί,
Γρηγόριος ὁ τὸ θεολογεῖν ἐπωνυμίαν ἔχων· «πάντα γάρ», φησίν,
«ἔχει ὁ Υἱὸς τὰ τοῦ Πατρός, πλὴν τῆς ἀγεννησίας». Ἐπεὶ τοίνυν
χωρὶς μόνης τῆς ἀγεννησίας ἔχει ἅπαντα τὰ τοῦ Πατρός, πῶς οὐκ ἂν
ἔχοι καὶ τὸ ἐκπορεύειν; Ὄντως οὐκ εἰσὶ τοῦ Πνεύματος τοῦ ἐν αὐτῷ
λαλοῦντος· εἰ γὰρ ἦσαν, οὐκ ἂν τοῦ ἁγίου τοιαῦτα κατεψεύδοντο, ὃς

from himself a better explanation to us who long and wish as much as possible to become disciples, and let him make up for what is lacking on our part and more perfectly turn about those who try to infer from these patristic voices the opposites of piety.

38

Well, now. Tell us who they are and what has been said by them. For, it is not possible for all the God-bearers not to be in agreement with one another and with Christ the God of the God-bearers, seeing there is one inspiration for them from the one Spirit of Christ. In addition to this and after nearly all of them there is this Damascene, and he was also taught by them all and he testifies for himself to his agreement with them when he says not "I say" but "we say", and through himself he presents to us that nowhere at all do these same Fathers say that the Spirit is existentially from the Son. It seems to me, though, that you have not arrived at the lofty greatness of their concepts and for this reason you have such thoughts about them. For, the Father also is said by everyone to be the first cause, but you have heard how it is said;[116] and Athanasius the Great said that the Holy Spirit shines forth from the Word, but you have heard how he said it;[117] and we say that the Son indeed is an image of the Father and the Spirit is an image of the Son, but you have heard how we say it;[118]and they have clearly reasoned very many other things, which appear to be in your favour but are agreeing with us, not with you. Yet at the opening of our mouth the Spirit will give an explanation in what follows.

But who is it that says that the ability to cause procession is also the Son's? They say, Gregory himself, who has the title for theologizing, since he says, "the Son has all things which are the Father's except unbegottenness."[119] Accordingly, since He has all things of the Father's except unbegottenness, how could He not also have the ability to cause procession? Truly, they are not of the Spirit that speaks in Gregory; for if they were, they would not have been uttering such complete lies against the saint, who also says, "whatever is said

262 Apodictic Treatises On the Procession of the Holy Spirit

«καὶ ὅσα περὶ τοῦ ἁγίου Πνεύματος», φησί, «ταπεινότερα παρὰ τοῦ Υἱοῦ λέγεται ἐπὶ τὴν πρώτην αἰτίαν ἀνακτέον, ἵνα τὸ ἐξ οὗ δειχθῇ». Τίς οὖν ἡ πρώτη αἰτία; Οὐχὶ μόνος ὁ Πατήρ; «Ἀλλὰ καὶ πάντα ἔχειν τὸν Υἱὸν τὰ τοῦ Πατρὸς φησὶν ἄνευ τῆς αἰτίας, τοῦ αἴτιον εἶναι δηλονότι καὶ αὐτὸν θεότητος». Ἓν γὰρ οὗτος αἴτιον ἐπὶ Θεοῦ καὶ μίαν ἀρχὴν ἀεὶ κηρύττει, τὸν ἀγέννητον Πατέρα, καὶ θεϊκὸν οἶδε τὸ μοναδικόν. Καὶ διὰ τοῦτό φησιν, «ἡμῖν εἷς Θεός, ὅτι πρὸς ἓν αἴτιον τὰ ἐξ αὐτοῦ τὴν ἀναφορὰν ἔχει», οὐ τὸ ἐξ αὐτῶν λέγων ἐκ Θεοῦ τὸν Υἱόν, καὶ Θεὸν ἐκ Θεοῦ τὸ Πνεῦμα τὸ ἅγιον. Διὰ μέσου δὲ Θεοῦ ἐκ τοῦ Θεοῦ, οὐ Θεὸν ὑφιστάμενον δοξάζει, ἄπαγε τῆς βλασφημίας, ἀλλὰ τὰ κτιστά· καθ' ὃ καὶ πρῶτον αἴτιον τίθεται τὸν Πατέρα λέγων ἐν τῷ δευτέρῳ τῶν Εἰρηνικῶν ὡς, «ὅσῳ τιμιώτερον Θεὸς κτισμάτων, τοσούτῳ μεγαλοπρεπέστερον τῇ πρώτῃ αἰτίᾳ θεότητος εἶναι ἀρχὴν ἢ κτισμάτων καὶ διὰ θεότητος μέσης ἐλθεῖν ἐπὶ τὰ κτίσματα».

39

Σὺ δέ, ὦ τῆς βλασφημίας, ὁ λατινικῶς φρονῶν διὰ μέσου τοῦ Υἱοῦ, ταὐτὸ δ' εἰπεῖν διὰ μέσης τῆς τοῦ Υἱοῦ θεότητος, ἐλθεῖν φῄς τὸν Πατέρα ἐπὶ τὸ προενεγκεῖν τὸ Πνεῦμα τὸ ἅγιον, καὶ οὐδὲ μέχρι τούτου σοι τὰ τῆς καινοφωνίας ἵσταται, ἀλλὰ καὶ ἐκ τοῦ Υἱοῦ τὸ Πνεῦμα λέγεις κοινὸν εἶναι Πατρὸς καὶ Υἱοῦ τὸ ἐκπορεύειν, διὰ τὸ τοῦ τουτονὶ τὸν θεολόγον λέγειν πρὸς τοὺς ἀπ' Αἰγύπτου καταπλεύσαντας ἔχειν τὸν Υἱὸν ἅπαντα τὰ τοῦ Πατρὸς ἄνευ τῆς ἀγεννησίας μόνης. Ἐνταῦθα γὰρ δεκτέον σοι τὸ «μόνης», κἂν μὴ συνεκφωνῆται· καὶ διὰ τοῦτό σοι κἀγὼ τοῦτο προσγράφω φανερῶς.

Ἀλλ' εἰπέ μοι, οὐκ αὐτὸς οὗτος ὁ θεολόγος προσεπάγει γράφων, «πάντα δὲ ὅσα τοῦ Υἱοῦ, καὶ τοῦ Πνεύματος, πλὴν τῆς υἱότητος»; Εἴπερ οὖν καὶ τοῦ Υἱοῦ τὸ ἐκπορεύειν, ἔσται τοῦτο καὶ τοῦ Πνεύματος· οὐ γὰρ υἱότητος τὸ ἐκπορεύειν· ἦν γὰρ ἂν Υἱὸς καὶ

concerning the Holy Spirit in more lowly fashion than the Son is to be referred back to the First Cause, so that the source-from-which may be shown."[120] So, who is the first cause? Is it not the Father only? But he also says, "the Son has all things which are of the Father apart from the cause, that is to say, apart from himself being a cause of divinity."[121] For this man perpetually preaches one cause and one origin, the unbegotten Father, in reference to God and acknowledges the unique as divine. And because of this he says, "For us there is one God, because to one cause those that are from Him have their reference,"[122] not saying "the one that is from them", as the Son is from God and the Holy Spirit is God from God. It is not a God—away with the blasphemy!—but rather the created things that he considers as being substantiated from God through a middle God. In this respect he sets down the Father as the first cause, saying in the second oration of peace that "as much as God is more honorable than creatures, so much is it more majestic for the first cause to be an origin of divinity rather than of creatures and to have come to the creatures through a mediating divinity."[123]

39

But you—O the blasphemy!—who think like the Latins, you say that the Father came to bring forth the Holy Spirit through the mediation of the Son, which is the same as to say through mediation of the divinity of the Son. And your innovation does not even stop at this but you also say that it is common for the Father and the Son to cause the Spirit to proceed also from the Son, on account of this here theologian saying to those who sailed in from Egypt that the Son has all things which are the Father's apart from unbegottenness only. For herein you must accept the word "only", even if it is not expressed; and that is why I am clearly adding it for you.

But tell me, does not this the same theologian himself add, "and all things, as many as are of the Son, are also of the Spirit, apart from sonship"?[124] So, if, per chance, to cause procession is also the Son's, this will also be the Spirit's; for to cause procession is not a

Πατήρ, ἐπεὶ καὶ τὸ ἐκπορεύειν ἔχει. Ὁ αὐτὸς δὲ κἂν τῷ Περὶ τοῦ ἁγίου Πνεύματος οἰκείῳ λόγῳ καὶ περὶ τοῦ ἁγίου Πνεύματος αὐτοῦ φησι· «τί οὐ δύναται τῶν μεγάλων καὶ ὧν Θεός; Τί δὲ οὐ προσηγόρευται ὧν Θεός, πλὴν ἀγεννησίας καὶ γεννήσεως»; Οὐκοῦν καὶ προβολέα ὀνομάσομεν τὸ Πνεῦμα. Καὶ τὸ ἐκπορεύειν δὲ κατὰ σὲ ὁμοίως ἔχει τῷ Υἱῷ κἀντεῦθεν καὶ διπλασίως ἢ ἐκεῖνος· ἕξει γὰρ οὐ τὸ τοῦ Πατρὸς μόνον, ἀλλὰ καὶ τὸ τοῦ Υἱοῦ κατὰ τὴν περὶ τοῦ Υἱοῦ σοι δόξαν. Ὁρᾷς ὅσοις ἀτόποις περιπίπτει ὁ πάντα ἔχειν τὸν Υἱόν τὰ τοῦ Πατρὸς ἀκούων καὶ μὴ μόνα τὰ τῆς φύσεως νοῶν, ἀλλ᾽ ἔστιν ἃ καὶ τῶν ὑποστατικῶν τοῖς φυσικοῖς συνείρων;

40

Προάγειν μὲν οὖν τὸν περὶ τούτου λόγον περαιτέρω οὐκ ἐπάναγκες, σοῦ γε ἐξεληλεγμένου, ἀλλὰ τοῦ καλοῦ γε ἕνεκα καὶ ἵνα μὴ προστρίψαιτό τις μέμψιν τῷ ἀμωμήτῳ, δείξομεν ἑξῆς ὡς ἔχειν μὲν καλῶς ἡ τοῦ ἁγίου ῥῆσις, ἀγνοίᾳ δὲ τῶν λατινικῶς φρονούντων ἐκλαμβάνεται κακῶς. Συντελέσει δ᾽ οἶμαι καὶ πρὸς αὐτὸ τὸ προκείμενον ὁ λόγος οὐκ ἐλάχιστα. Προσεκτέον δ᾽ ὅτι μάλιστα τὸν νοῦν.

Ταὐτὸν εἰπεῖν ἐπὶ Θεοῦ ἀγέννητον καὶ ἀναίτιον· διὸ κἂν πάσας ἀνελίξῃς τὰς θεολογούσας βίβλους, οὐδαμοῦ τὸ Πνεῦμα τὸ ἅγιον ἀγέννητον εὑρήσεις εἰρημένον καὶ ταῦτ᾽ ὂν οὐ γεννητόν. Δαμασκηνὸς δὲ ὁ θεοφόρος εἰπὼν ἐν ὀγδόῳ τῶν Δογματικῶν ὅτι, «πάντα ὅσα ἔχει ὁ Πατὴρ καὶ αὐτοῦ τοῦ Πνεύματός εἰσι, πλὴν τῆς ἀγεννησίας», ἔδειξεν ὡς οὐ μόνον τό ἀγέννητον τῷ ἀναιτίῳ ταὐτόν, ἀλλὰ καὶ τὸ ἀναίτιον τῷ αἰτίῳ ταὐτόν ἐστιν ἐπὶ Θεοῦ· συντρέχει

characteristic of sonship. Otherwise the Father also would be a Son, since He too would be able to cause procession. Yet the same man also says in his treatise *Concerning the Holy Spirit,* speaking of the Holy Spirit Himself, "What can He not do of the great things that God can do? And what was not ascribed to Him of the things that are ascribed to God, apart from unbegottenness and begottenness?"[125] Therefore, we also will not call the Spirit an originator. And according to you, He will have the power to cause procession like the Son, and from this vantage even twice as much as the Son; for He will not only have the Father's power but the Son's as well, according to your belief concerning the Son. Do you see into how many absurd fallacies a person falls when he hears that the Son has all things which are the Father's and does not think they are only things of the nature but instead connects even some of the hypostatic things with the natural?

40

Therefore there is certainly not any compelling reason to produce a further argument concerning this, seeing you, at any rate, have been refuted, but at least for the sake of the good, and lest anyone attribute blame to the blameless, in the following we shall demonstrate that the utterance of the saint is actually sound, yet because of ignorance it is wrongly understood by those who think as the Latins. I believe the argument will considerably contribute to the resolution of the matter before us. We must pay as much attention as possible.

With respect to God, to say "unbegotten" and to say "uncaused" are the same thing. Wherefore, even if you read through all the theological books nowhere will you find the Holy Spirit described as being unbegotten, although He is not begotten. And by saying in the eighth chapter of his dogmatics that "all things, as many as the Father has, also belong to the Spirit Himself, apart from unbegottenness,"[126] Damascene the Godbearer showed that not only is the unbegotten identical to the uncaused but also the uncaused is identical to the cause in the case of God. For with respect to

γὰρ τῷ ἀναιτίῳ τὸ αἴτιον ἐπὶ Θεοῦ, αἴτιον δέ φημι θεότητος Υἱοῦ καὶ Πνεύματος. Θέλων οὖν εἰπεῖν ὅτι τὸ Πνεῦμα πάντα τὰ τοῦ Πατρὸς ἔχει πλὴν τοῦ ἀναίτιον εἶναι καὶ τοῦ αἴτιον εἶναι, κατὰ τὸ γεννᾶν δηλαδὴ καὶ ἐκπορεύειν, χωρὶς μόνης τῆς ἀγεννησίας εἶπεν, ὡς αὐτῆς πάντα συμπεριβαλλούσης, ὅσα τοῦ Πατρός ἐστιν ἴδια.

Θεὸς οὖν ἀγέννητος καὶ ἀναίτιος· Θεὸς δὲ ἀναίτιος θεότητος αἴτιος. Οὕτω δὲ ὢν αἴτιος ἐμφύτου πλούτου, ἑαυτοῦ κατὰ μηδὲν ἀποδέοντος, αὐτεπίβουλος ἂν ἦν, ἑνὸς καὶ μόνου ὑπάρχων αἴτιος καὶ οὕτω πενίαν ἑαυτῷ τὸν πλοῦτον ποιούμενος. Πρὸς δὲ τούτῳ καὶ ἀτελὲς τὸ πάντη καὶ πάντως ἕν· διὸ καὶ χωρητὸν τοῖς πρὸς θεογνωσίαν ἀτελέσιν Ἰουδαίοις ἐγένετο. Ἀλλ᾽ οὐδὲ ὁμοουσίου δυάδος ὑπάρχων αἴτιος καὶ τὸ μὲν γεννῶν, τὸ δὲ ἐκπορευτῶς προβαλλόμενος, ἀπειροκάλως, ἵν᾽ οὕτως εἴπω, ἐπὶ πλεῖον ἐξενεχθείη, καὶ ταῦτ᾽ ἐν ἑαυτῷ τε καὶ τοῖς ἐξ αὐτοῦ πᾶσαν ἀπειρίαν περιορίζων. Πρὸς δὲ τούτοις οὐδὲ τρόπος ἕτερος ἐμφύτου ὑπάρξεως· διὸ καὶ τὸ ὑπὲρ ταῦτα οὐ θεότης, ἀλλὰ θεότητος ἔκπτωσις· ταῦτ᾽ ἄρα καὶ τῶν ἀθέων Ἑλλήνων ἡ πολυθεΐα ἐστίν.

41

Ἀλλὰ μὴν μονάδος πρὸς δυάδα κεκινημένης καὶ περαιτέρω μὴ προηγμένης, δηλαδὴ παντουργοῦ Θεοῦ Πατρὸς πρὸς γέννησίν τε καὶ πρόοδον Υἱοῦ δημιουργοῦ τῶν πάντων καὶ τὰ πάντα τελεσιουργοῦντος, οὔθ᾽ ὁ Υἱὸς διὰ τοῦ Πνεύματος (ἀτελὴς γὰρ ἦν ἐκ τοῦ Πατρός, εἰ διὰ τοῦ τελεσιουργοῦντος ἐγεννᾶτο Πνεύματος) οὔτε τὸ Πνεῦμα δι᾽ Υἱοῦ· πρὸς γὰρ τῷ ἀτελὲς εἶναι ἐκ Πατρός, καὶ ταῦτα τὸ πάντα τελειοῦν, καὶ τῶν δεδημιουργημένων ἦν ἂν ἕν· τὰ γὰρ δι᾽ ἐκείνου γέγονε, δι᾽ Υἱοῦ δὲ τὸ Πνεῦμα ἔγνωσται. Καὶ ἐν φωτὶ τῷ Πνεύματι φῶς ὁρῶμεν τὸν Υἱὸν προφητικῶς ὁμοῦ καὶ πατρικῶς

God, the cause corresponds to the uncaused, and I am referring to the cause of the divinity of the Son and the Spirit. So, wanting to say that the Spirit has all things of the Father apart from being uncaused and apart from being a cause, which, namely, is to beget and to cause procession, he said "apart only from unbegottenness," as this encompasses everything, as many idioms as belong to the Father.

Therefore, God is unbegotten and uncaused. And the uncaused God is the cause of the divinity. Thus, being the cause of innate wealth, as His own self lacks in nothing, He would be plotting against Himself if He were the cause of one and only and thus turned His wealth into poverty. Furthermore, what is in every way and completely one is imperfect, wherefore it was receivable to the Jews who were imperfect in their knowledge of God. Not even, however, by being the cause of a consubstantial dyad, begetting the one while emanating the other by procession, in an infinitely beautiful manner, so to speak, would He be brought forth more, while in fact circumscribing all infinititude within Himself and within those from Him. Furthermore, neither is there any other mode of innate existence; and so what goes beyond this is not divinity but a fall from divinity. This therefore is the polytheism of the godless Hellenes.

41

As the monad, however, has been moved to a dyad and has not proceeded further, that is, when the all-effecting God the Father has been moved to the begetting and progression of His Son, who is the Creator of all things and who brings all things to perfection, neither is the Son through the Spirit (for in that case, if He was begotten through the perfecting Spirit, He would be imperfectly from the Father), nor is the Spirit through the Son. For besides being imperfectly from the Father (He, the Perfecter of all things!), He would also be one of the creatures. For they came into existence through that one, but through the Son the Spirit came to be known. And in the light, in the Spirit, we see light, the Son (to speak

εἰπεῖν· ὡς ἂν εἰδῶμεν μὴ μόνον ἐκ μιᾶς ὑπάρχοντα ἀρχῆς, ἀλλὰ καὶ ἀδιαστάτως ἔχοντα πρὸς ἄλληλα καὶ ἐνυπάρχοντα ἀλλήλοις καὶ ἄλληλα δεικνύντα καὶ δι' ἀλλήλων προφαινόμενα, ἀλλ' οὐ δι' ἀλλήλων ἢ καὶ ἐξ ἀλλήλων ἢ ἀλλήλων ὄντα· ἓν γὰρ τὸ ἐξ οὗ.

Καὶ τοίνυν ὁ θεολογῶν πάντα ἔχειν πλὴν τὸν Υἱὸν τὰ τοῦ Πατρὸς πλὴν ἀγεννησίας πάντα ἔχειν πλὴν αἰτίας εἴρηκεν, ὡς καὶ ἀλλαχοῦ τῶν συγγραμμάτων σαφῶς οὕτω προσδιώρισεν. Εἰ δὲ πάντα ἔχει ὁ Υἱὸς τὰ τοῦ Πατρὸς πλὴν τοῦ εἶναι αἴτιος, δηλαδὴ θεότητος, αἴτιος δὲ ὁ Πατὴρ οὐ γεννῶν μόνον τὸν Υἱόν, ἀλλὰ καὶ τὸ Πνεῦμα ἐκπορεύων, πάντα ἔχει ὁ Υἱὸς τὰ τοῦ Πατρός, πλὴν τοῦ τὸν Υἱὸν γεννᾶν τε καὶ τὸ Πνεῦμα ἐκπορεύειν· ἃ μόνου τοῦ Πατρὸς ὄντα τὸ ἀγέννητον αὐτῷ προσμαρτυρεῖ. Διὸ καὶ ὁ Δαμασκηνὸς θεολόγος ἐν τῷ Περὶ τῆς ἁγίας Τριάδος, «διὰ τὸν Πατέρα», φησί, «τουτέστι διὰ τὸ εἶναι τὸν Πατέρα, ἔχει ὁ Υἱὸς καὸ τὸ Πνεῦμα πάντα ἃ ἔχει, τουτέστι διὰ τὸ τὸν Πατέρα ἔχειν αὐτά, πλὴν τῆς ἀγεννησίας καὶ τῆς γεννήσεως καὶ τῆς ἐκπορεύσεως».

42

Εἰ δὲ ἡ ἀγεννησία τὸ πάντῃ τε καὶ πάντως αἴτιον ἐπὶ Θεοῦ δηλοῖ, ἡ γέννησις τὸ μηδαμῇ μηδαμῶς αἴτιον θεότητος εἶναι τὸ γεννητὸν ἀναγκαιότατα δηλώσει, καθάπερ καὶ ἡ ἐκπόρευσις τὸ ἐκπορευτῶς ἐκ τοῦ Πατρὸς ὑπάρχον. Εἰ δὲ μὴ μηδαμῇ μηδαμῶς αἴτιος ὑπάρχει ὁ Υἱὸς θεότητος, πῶς ἂν εἴη ἐξ αὐτοῦ τὸ Πνεῦμα; Ἢ πῶς πρῶτον αἴτιον ὁ Πατήρ, εἶτα ὁ Υἱὸς τούτῳ, ὡς καὶ ἐξ αὐτοῦ τοῦ ἁγίου ἐκπορευομένου Πνεύματος, καθὼς φρονεῖν δεῖν οἴονται Λατῖνοι, παραφρονοῦντες, ὡς ἐγῷμαι, καὶ τὰς πατρικὰς παρανοοῦντες

prophetically and at the same time patristically), that as a result we might know not only that they exist from a single origin, but also that they relate to each other without intervening distance and exist in each other and display each other and are manifested through each other, but not that they are through each other or even from each other or of each other; for, the source-from-which is one.

And accordingly, the one who theologized that the Son has all things that are the Father's except unbegottenness has said that He has all things except cause, since he also clearly defined it this way in other passages of his writings. Now if the Son has all things which are the Father's apart from being a cause, I mean, apart from being a cause of divinity, and if the Father is a cause not only by begetting the Son but also by causing the Spirit to proceed, then the Son has all things which are the Father's apart from both begetting the Son and causing the Spirit to proceed, which properties, being only the Father's, bear witness to His unbegottenness. Wherefore also the theologian from Damascus says in his treatise *Concerning the Holy Trinity*, "Because of the Father, that is, on account of the Father's being, the Son and the Spirit have all things which They have. That is, because the Father has these same things they also have these things, apart from unbegottenness and begottenness and procession."[127]

42

Now if unbegottenness indicates what is completely and in every way the cause in respect to God, then by all necessity begottenness will indicate that what has been begotten can in no way at all be a cause of divinity, just as procession indicates what exists by procession from the Father. And if the Son cannot in any way exist as a cause of divinity, how would the Spirit be from Him? Or how would the Father be the first cause of the Spirit, followed by the Son, as if the Holy Spirit proceeds from Him as well? That is how the Latins suppose we must believe, becoming delirious, as I see it, and misinterpreting the sense of the patristic sayings. For does not

ῥήσεις; Οὐ γὰρ ὁ φερωνύμως θεολόγος οὗτος οὕτως, «ἀλλὰ πάντα», φησίν, «ἔχει ὁ Υἱὸς τὰ τοῦ Πατρὸς πλὴν ἀγεννησίας», ταὐτὸν δ' εἰπεῖν, ἄνευ τῆς αἰτίας, τούτῳ δὲ ταὐτὸν εἰπεῖν, ἄνευ τοῦ γεννᾶν καὶ ἐκπορεύειν; Κατὰ ταῦτα γὰρ αἴτιον τὸ αἴτιον.

Καὶ πάντα, ὅσα ἔχει ὁ Υἱός, τοῦ Πνεύματος, πλὴν τῆς υἱότητος, εἰ δὲ βούλει τῆς γεννήσεως· οὐ γὰρ φοβησόμεθα μὴ ἀναίτιον, εἰ καὶ αὐτὸ αἴτιον εἶναι φωραθείη, γέννησιν μὴ ἔχον· οὐδὲ γὰρ ἀναίτιον, εἰ καὶ μὴ γεννητόν· τὸ γὰρ ὡς ἀναίτιον γέννησιν μὴ ἔχον, αὐτό τε καθ' ἑαυτὸ παντάπασιν ἀναίτιον, καὶ παντὶ τρόπῳ θεότητος αἴτιον. Οὕτως ἡμεῖς τοῖς ἐν Πνεύματι θεολογοῦσι, συνῳδὰ φθεγγόμεθα· καὶ οὕτω τοὺς ἀπάδοντα φθεγγομένους ἀπελέγχομεν, καθ' ἑαυτῶν δεικνύντες τὰς γραφικὰς μαρτυρίας προτιθέντας.

43

Κἀκεῖνο γάρ, ὃ παρὰ τοῦ αὐτοῦ θεολόγου προάγειν ὑπὲρ τῆς σφῶν αὐτῶν δόξης τῶν Λατίνων οἴονται φῦλον, ὅτι τὸ οἰκεῖον ἀξίωμα ὁ Κύριος ἔδειξε πρὸς τοὺς μύστας εἰπών, «αὐτὸς ὑμῖν ἐγὼ πέμψω τὸ Πνεῦμα» τὸ ἅγιον, καθ' ἑαυτῶν ὡς οὐκ ἴσασι προάγουσιν. Ἐπεὶ γὰρ ὡς ἀληθῶς τὸ πέμπειν τὸ Πνεῦμα μέγα καὶ ὑπὲρ τὸ μέγα καὶ Θεοῦ μόνου (ὁ Πατὴρ γὰρ εἰπὼν πρότερον πέμψειν τὸν παράκλητον, εἶτ' αὐτὸς "ἐγώ", φησί, "πέμψω", τὸ οἰκεῖον ἀξίωμα δεικνύς, ὡς ἂν αὐτό τε τὸ πρᾶγμα φωνὴν ὥσπερ ἀφιὲν κηρύττοι καὶ ὁ τῆς θεολογίας ἐπώνυμος ἐξηγήσαιτο). Εἰ μὴ παρὰ τοῦ Πατρὸς ὁ Κύριος μόνου, ἀλλὰ καὶ παρ' ἑαυτοῦ ᾔδει ἐκπορευόμενον καὶ τὴν ὕπαρξιν ἔχον, πῶς οὐ προσθεὶς εἶπεν, «ὃ παρὰ τοῦ Πατρὸς καὶ παρ' ἐμοῦ ἐκπορεύεται»; Οὐ γὰρ ἦν ταπεινότερον τηνικαῦτα περὶ ἑαυτοῦ φθεγγόμενος, δι' ὅπερ ἂν τοῦτο μόνον καὶ παρῆκεν ἐπικρυψάμενος. Δῆλον οὖν καὶ τυφλῷ, φασίν, ὡς οὐχὶ καὶ ἐκ τοῦ Υἱοῦ ἐκπορεύεται τὸ Πνεῦμα τὸ ἅγιον.

this man, worthily named the Theologian, say that "the Son has all things of the Father apart from unbegottenness," which is the same as to say, apart from the cause, which is the same as to say, apart from begetting and causing procession? For it is with respect to these things that the cause is a cause.

And all things, whatever the Son has, are the Spirit's, apart from sonship, or (if you prefer) apart from begottenness. For, we will not fear lest the Holy Spirit be uncaused, if it is discovered that He Himself is also a cause inasmuch as He does not have begottenness. He is not uncaused either, although He is not begotten. For what does not have begottenness as being uncaused, that is itself by itself in every way uncaused and is in every way a cause of divinity. This is how we speak in harmony with those who theologize in the Spirit, and this is how we refute those who do not speak harmoniously, demonstrating that the scriptural witnesses they have proposed are against their own selves.

43

For that argument—from the same theologian [John], which the tribe of the Latins thinks advances their own belief—that the Lord was indicating His own dignity to His initiates when He said, "I myself will send the Holy Spirit,"[128] this they advance against their own selves without knowing it. Since sending the Spirit is truly great and transcends greatness and belongs to God alone (for having previously said that the Father will send the Paraclete,[129] then He Himself says "I will send,"[130] indicating His very own dignity, so that the fact itself proclaims it with a loud voice and the namesake of theology exegetes it), if the Lord knew that the Holy Spirit proceeded and had existence not only from the Father but also from His own self, why did He not add and say, "the Spirit which proceedeth from the Father and from Myself"? For He was not speaking at that time more humbly about Himself to explain why He would have concealed and omitted this thing only. So it is clear even to a blind man, as they say, that the Holy Spirit does not proceed from the Son.

Μέγα μὲν οὖν ἀξίωμα τὸ πέμπειν ἔχειν τὸ θεῖον Πνεῦμα, καὶ τοσοῦτο μέγα, ὡς ὁμοφυᾶ καὶ ἴσον καὶ ὁμότιμον δεικνύναι τῷ Πατρὶ τὸν Υἱόν, καθάπερ καὶ τὸ Πνεῦμα ὁμοούσιόν τε καὶ ὁμότιμον τῷ Πατρὶ συνίστησι τὸ μὴ παρὰ τοῦ Πατρὸς μόνου, ἀλλὰ καὶ παρ' αὐτοῦ τοῦ Πνεύματος τὸν Υἱὸν ἀποστέλλεσθαι. Θεϊκόν γε μὴν καὶ φυσικόν ἐστι τουτὶ τὸ ἀξίωμα, ἀλλ' οὐχ ὑποστατικόν· εἰ γὰρ ὑποστατικὸν ἦν τὸ ἀποστέλλειν, οὐκ ἂν ἦν κοινὸν Πατρός, Υἱοῦ καὶ Πνεύματος. Θεὸς οὖν ἀληθινὸς ὁ ἄλλος παράκλητος· ὁ δὴ τοῦτον ἀποστέλλων πῶς οὐχὶ Θεὸς ἀληθινός; Εἰ δὲ καὶ παρ' ἑαυτοῦ ἐρχόμενον ὡς αὐτοκέλευστον ἀποστέλλει τὸν παράκλητον ὁ Υἱός, πῶς οὐ μιᾶς ἂν εἴη σὺν αὐτῷ θελήσεως καὶ ἐξουσίας; Εἰ δὲ μιᾶς ἐστιν ἐξουσίας καὶ θελήσεως, πῶς οὐχὶ καὶ μιᾶς ἂν εἶεν φύσεως;

44

Ὁρᾷς ὡς ἡ ἀποστολὴ τοῦ θείου Πνεύματος τὴν τοῦ ἀποστέλλοντος πρὸς τὸν ἀποστελλόμενον ὁμοβουλίαν καὶ ὁμουσιότητα παρίστησιν, ὃ μέγιστόν ἐστιν ἀξίωμα, προσὸν μέντοι τοῖς τρισὶ καλῶς τε καὶ θεοπρεπῶς, ὡς καὶ τὴν αὐτεξουσιότητα δεικνῦον τῶν ἀποστελλομένων οὕτως; Ὁ δὲ λέγων μὴ θεϊκὸν εἶναι τὸ ἀξίωμα τοῦτο, ἀλλὰ προβλητικόν, πρῶτον μὲν οὐ τὸν Υἱὸν μόνον αἴτιον δείκνυσι τοῦ θείου Πνεύματος, ἀλλὰ καὶ τοῦ Υἱοῦ τὸ Πνεῦμα. Πρὸς δὲ τούτῳ καὶ τῆς πρὸς ἡμᾶς ἐλευθέρως τὴν ἑκατέρου τούτων αὐτοβουλίαν ἄλλοτε ἄλλην ἀθετεῖ κακῶς, μὴ θελήσεως ἀλλὰ φύσεως δογματίζων εἶναι τὴν πρὸς ἡμᾶς ἀποστολήν, τοιγαροῦν καὶ ἄναρχον. Ἃ γὰρ μὴ τῷ θέλειν ἀλλὰ τῷ πεφυκέναι ἐκ Θεοῦ, προάναρχά ἐστιν, ἀλλ' οὐκ ἀρκτά.

Καὶ μὴν ὁ τῆς θεολογίας ἐπώνυμος πρὸς τοὺς ἐλάττω νομίσαντας τὸν Υἱόν, ὅτι ἀπεστάλη παρὰ τοῦ Πατρός, τεκμήριον εἶναί φησι τὴν ἀποστολὴν τῆς πατρικῆς εὐδοκίας, ἀλλ' οὐχὶ τῆς αὐτοῦ προαιωνίου ὑπάρξεως. Φρενοβλαβῶς οὐκοῦν οἱ Λατῖνοι τεκμήριον ἡγοῦνται τὴν ἐκ τοῦ Υἱοῦ τοῦ Πνεύματος ἀποστολὴν τῆς παρ'

So the ability to send the divine Spirit is indeed a great dignity, and is so great that it shows the Son to be co-natural and equal and of the same honor with the Father, just as also the fact that the Son is sent not only by the Father but also by the Spirit Himself proves the Spirit consubstantial and of the same honor with the Father. In any case, this very dignity is most definitely natural, not hypostatic. For if the ability to send were hypostatic, it would not be common to the Father, Son, and Spirit. So, the other Paraclete is true God. How then can He who sends Him not be true God? And if the Son sends the Paraclete, who comes also by Himself as it were self-called, how could He not be of one will and authority with Him? And if they are of one authority and will, how would they not also be of one nature?

44

Do you see that the sending of the divine Spirit proves the oneness of will and the consubstantiality of the one sending with the one sent? This sending is an exceedingly great dignity, being nevertheless properly and God-befittingly attributed to the three, as showing the free will[131] of those who are thus sent. But whoever says that this dignity [of sending] is not divine but emanative,[132] such a man first of all actually shows not only that the Son is a cause of the divine Spirit, but also that the Spirit is a cause of the Son. Besides this, he also unwarrantedly rejects the self-will of each one of them (sometimes the Son's, sometimes the Spirit's) in coming to us when dogmatizing that the sending to us is not from will but from nature and so, consequently, it is also beginningless. For things which are from God not by the will but by nature, such things are prebeginningless [προάναρχα], not having a beginning.

Besides, the namesake of theology says to those who thought that the Son is lesser on account of being sent from the Father that this sending is a certain proof of the good pleasure of the Father but not of His pre-eternal existence.[133] So it is in madness that the Latins consider the sending of the Spirit from the Son as proof that He

αὐτοῦ προαιωνίου ὑπάρξεως. Ἀλλὰ καὶ ἐγήγερθαι γέγραπται, φησί, καὶ ἀνειλῆφθαι παρὰ τοῦ Πατρός, ἀλλὰ καὶ ἑαυτὸν ἀνεστακέναι καὶ ἀνεληλυθέναι πάλιν· ἐκεῖνα τῆς εὐδοκίας, ταῦτα τῆς ἐξουσίας. Ἐπεὶ γοῦν καὶ τὸ Πνεῦμα τὸ ἅγιον εἰ καὶ παρὰ τοῦ Υἱοῦ ἀπεστάλη, ἀλλὰ καὶ παρ' ἑαυτοῦ πρὸς ἡμᾶς ἀφίκετο, ἐκεῖνο τῆς εὐδοκίας χρὴ λέγειν, τοῦτο τῆς ἐξουσίας· ἀλλὰ μὴ καινοτομεῖν ἐντεῦθεν ἀλόγως τὸν τῆς ὑπάρξεως τρόπον τοῦ θείου Πνεύματος.

45

Πρὸς μὲν δὴ τῷ τῆς θεολογίας ἐπωνύμῳ τούτῳ οὐδ' ὁ μέγας Βασίλειος εὕρηταί που λέγων καὶ ἐκ τοῦ Υἱοῦ τὸ Πνεῦμα· εἰ δ' ἐκ τοῦ Πατρὸς τοῦτο διὰ τοῦ Υἱοῦ ἐν τοῖς Πρὸς Εὐνομιανοὺς περὶ τοῦ θείου Πνεύματος εἰρήκει κεφαλαίοις, ἀλλ' αὐτὸς ἑαυτοῦ ἐν τοῖς αὐτοῖς κεφαλαίοις ἑρμηνεὺς γενόμενος, ἐπὶ τῆς μεταδόσεως τοῦτο φάναι διεσάφησε γράφων· «τὸ μὲν ἐκ Θεοῦ τὸ Πνεῦμα εἶναι τρανῶς ἀνεκήρυξεν ὁ ἀπόστολος, λέγων ὅτι τὸ Πνεῦμα τὸ ἐκ τοῦ Θεοῦ ἐλάβομεν, καὶ τὸ διὰ τοῦ Υἱοῦ πεφηνέναι σαφὲς πεποίηκεν, Υἱοῦ Πνεῦμα ὀνομάσας αὐτό, καθάπερ Θεοῦ, καὶ νοῦν Χριστοῦ προσειπών, καθάπερ καὶ Θεοῦ Πνεῦμα ὡς τοῦ ἀνθρώπου.

Ὁρᾷς ὅτι ἐκ Θεοῦ μέν, δηλονότι τοῦ Πατρός, ἔχει τὸ εἶναι, διὰ δὲ τοῦ Υἱοῦ τὸ μεταδιδόσθαι καὶ φανεροῦσθαι; Καὶ ὡς Υἱοῦ Πνεῦμα ὀνομάζεται καὶ νοῦς, ἀλλ' οὐκ ἐκ τοῦ Υἱοῦ, καθάπερ καὶ τοῦ ἀνθρώπου; Καὶ τούτου γὰρ τὸ οἰκεῖον πνεῦμα καὶ ὁ νοῦς αὐτοῦ ἐστιν, ἀλλ' οὐκ ἐξ αὐτοῦ, εἰ μὴ ἄρα κατ' ἐνέργειαν. Τοῦτο δὴ καὶ ἀλλαχοῦ ποιῶν ἀριδηλότερον ὁ μέγας οὗτος, «τὸ Πνεῦμα», φησί, «τοῦ Υἱοῦ μὲν ἤρτηται, ᾧ ἀδιαστάτως συγκαταλαμβάνεται, ἐκ δὲ τῆς τοῦ Πατρὸς αἰτίας ἐξημμένον ἔχει τὸ εἶναι, ὅθεν καὶ ἐκπορεύεται, τοῦτο γνωριστικὸν τῆς κατὰ τὴν ὑπόστασιν ὑπάρξεως σημεῖον

exists from Him pre-eternally. Furthermore, it is written He has been raised up and taken up by the Father, but it is also written that He has raised up Himself and assumed Himself again to heaven. The former are of His good pleasure: the latter, of His authority. So too, although the Holy Spirit was sent from the Son, yet He also came to us of His own self, and therefore we should say that the former is of His good pleasure while the latter is of His authority. Nevertheless we should not recklessly innovate in this regard about the mode of existence of the divine Spirit.

45

Besides Gregory, who was titled for his theology, neither was Basil the Great found anywhere saying that the Spirit is from the Son; and if He has said in his chapters *To the Eunomians Concerning the Holy Spirit*[134] that He is from the Father "through" the Son, yet he personally became his own interpreter in these same chapters and thoroughly clarified the matter saying that this speaks about the transmission of the Spirit and writing: "The apostle distinctly proclaimed that the Spirit is from God when he says that we have received the Spirit that is from God;[135] and he made it clear that the Spirit was manifested through the Son since he named Him the Spirit of the Son just as he named Him the Spirit of God. He also named Him the mind of Christ, just as he also named Him the Spirit of God, as is the case with the spirit of man."[136]

Do you see that He has being from God, that is, from the Father, but through the Son He is transmitted and manifested? And that He is named the Spirit and mind of the Son, yet He is still not from the Son, just as with man? For man's own spirit and mind are his but not from him, except in the sense of activity [energeia]. This great theologian elsewhere makes this point clearer, saying: "While the Spirit depends upon the Son, with whom He is understood together inseparably, yet He has existence dependent on the cause of the Father, from whom He also proceeds, having this as a sign that distinguishes His own hypostatic existence, namely to be

ἔχον, τὸ μετὰ τὸν Υἱὸν καὶ σὺν αὐτῷ γνωρίζεσθαι καὶ ἐκ τοῦ Πατρὸς ὑφεστάναι. Ὁ δὲ Υἱός, τὸ ἐκ τοῦ Πατρός ἐκπορευόμενον Πνεῦμα δι᾽ ἑαυτοῦ καὶ μεθ᾽ ἑαυτοῦ γνωρίζων, μόνος μονογενῶς ἐκ τοῦ ἀγεννήτου φωτὸς ἐκλάμψας, οὐδεμίαν κατὰ τὸ ἰδιάζον τῶν γνωρισμάτων τὴν κοινωνίαν ἔχει πρὸς τὸν πατέρα ἢ τὸ Πνεῦμα τὸ ἅγιον».

Ἀκούεις τὸ γνωριστικόν σημεῖον τῆς τοῦ θείου Πνεύματος ὑποστάσεως, ὅτι τὸ γνωρίζεσθαι διὰ τοῦ Υἱοῦ ἐστιν, ἀλλ᾽ οὐχὶ τὸ τὴν ὑπόστασιν ἔχειν ἐξ αὐτοῦ ἀλλ᾽ ἐκ τοῦ Πατρός ὑφεστάναι; Λέγων δὲ καὶ αὐτὸς ὁ Κύριος ἐν τοῖς εὐαγγελίοις, «ὅταν ἔλθῃ ὁ Παράκλητος ὃν ἐγὼ πέμψω ὑμῖν παρὰ τοῦ Πατρός, τὸ Πνεῦμα τῆς ἀληθείας, ὃ παρὰ τοῦ Πατρὸς ἐκπορεύεται», οὐχὶ τοῦ Πνεύματος μὲν ἔδειξεν ἰδιάζον ὑπάρχον γνώρισμα τὸ ἐκπορεύεσθαι, τὸ δὲ ἐκπορεύειν τοῦ Πατρός, ἐπεὶ καὶ ὑποστατικὸν τούτων ἑκάτερόν ἐστιν, ἰδιάζοντα δέ ἐστι τὰ ὑποστατικά; Μηδεμίαν οὖν κατὰ τὸν μέγαν Βασίλειον πρὸς τὰ ἰδιάζοντα τῶν γνωρισμάτων τοῦ Πατρὸς τὴν κοινωνίαν ἔχων ὁ Υἱός, οὐδὲ τὸ ἐκπορεύειν ἕξει.

46

Διὰ τοῦτο πάλιν ὁ αὐτὸς Πρὸς τοὺς Εὐνομιανοὺς περὶ τοῦ Πνεύματός φησιν· «Υἱὸς Θεοῦ, καρπὸς ἅγιος ἐξ ἁγίου, ἀΐδιος ἐξ ἀϊδίου, Πνεύματος ἁγίου χορηγὸς εἰς ὑπόστασιν καὶ μόρφωσιν κτίσεως». Ὁρᾷς ὅτι χορηγὸς τοῦ Πνεύματος, ἀλλ᾽ οὐχ ὑποστάτης ὁ Υἱός; Καὶ ὡς ἡ ἐκ τοῦ Υἱοῦ χορηγία δι᾽ αἰτίαν, ἵν᾽ ὑποστήσῃ καὶ μορφώσῃ τὴν κτίσιν τῷ Πνεύματι; Πρόσεχε δὴ καὶ τοῖς ἑξῆς· «ὁ γὰρ τὸν Υἱόν», φησίν, «ἀναιρῶν, τὴν ἀρχὴν τῆς τῶν ὅλων δημιουργίας ἀνεῖλεν· ἄρχει γὰρ τῆς ἁπάντων ὑποστάσεως ὁ τοῦ Θεοῦ Λόγος, δι᾽ οὗ τὰ πάντα γέγονεν». Ὁρᾷς; Τῆς ἁπάντων ὑποστάσεως ὁ τοῦ Θεοῦ Λόγος, ἀλλ᾽ οὐχὶ τῆς τοῦ θείου Πνεύματος ὑποστάσεως ἄρχει· καὶ ἀρχή ἐστι τῆς τῶν ὅλων δημιουργίας, ἀλλ᾽ οὐχὶ τῆς ὑπάρξεως τοῦ Πνεύματος. Πῶς δ᾽ ἂν ἐνταῦθα τὸν Υἱὸν ὑπερυψοῦν

acknowledged after the Son and together with Him and to receive His substance from the Father. Yet while the Son makes known the Spirit, Which proceeds from the Father, through Himself and with Himself, being the only one that shone forth as only-begotten from the unbegotten Light, He the Son has no communion with the Father or the Holy Spirit regarding the individuating characteristics."[137]

Do you hear that the characteristic sign of the hypostasis of the divine Spirit is for Him to become known through the Son, but it is not for Him to have His hypostasis from Him, which instead is substantiated from the Father? When even the Lord Himself says in the Gospels, "When the Comforter is come, whom I will send unto you from the Father, even the Spirit of truth, which proceedeth from the Father,"[138] does He not actually show that the individuating characteristic of the Spirit is to proceed, while the individuating characteristic of the Father is to cause procession, since each of these properties is hypostatic, and the hypostatic are what individuate? And so, according to Basil the Great, the Son will not be able to cause procession, since He has no communion at all with the individuating characteristics of the Father.

46

On account of this, the same man says again *To the Eunomians Concerning the Holy Spirit:* "Son of God, holy fruit from the Holy, eternal from eternal, provider of the Holy Spirit for the existence[139] and shaping of creation."[140] Do you see that the Son is a provider of the Spirit but not a bestower of His existence?[141] And that the supply from the Son is done for a cause, that He might give existence and shape to creation by the Spirit? At this point, note also the following wherein he says: "Whoever takes out the Son takes out the origin of the creation of all things, for the Word of God is the origin of the existence of all things, through whom they have come into being."[142] Do you see? The Word of God is the origin of the existence of all things, but is not the origin of the existence of the Holy Spirit. For He is the origin of the creation of all things, but not of the existence

βουλόμενος ὁ μέγας Βασίλειος, εἴπερ εἶχε λέγειν ἀρχὴν τοῦτον τοῦ θείου Πνεύματος, ὡς δι᾽ αὐτοῦ τὸ εἶναι σχόντος, οὐκ ἂν εἶπεν, ἀλλὰ χορηγὸν μὲν αὐτοῦ μόνον, ἀρχὴν δὲ μόνης τῆς δι᾽ αὐτοῦ τὸ εἶναι λαβούσης κτίσεως;

47

Ἀλλ᾽ ὁ Χρυσόστομος, φασί, θεολόγος, «ἦλθε», φησὶν «ὁ Χριστὸς πρὸς ἡμᾶς, ἔδωκεν ἡμῖν τὸ ἐξ αὐτοῦ Πνεῦμα καὶ ἀνέλαβε τὸ ἡμέτερον σῶμα»· καὶ πάλιν, «διὰ τὸ γενέσθαι ναὸν τῆς θείας δυνάμεως ἐπὶ γῆς τὸ σῶμα τοῦ Χριστοῦ, γίνῃ καὶ σὺ ναὸς καθ᾽ ὁμοίωσιν αὐτοῦ· δέχῃ γὰρ ἐκπεμπόμενον παρ᾽ αὐτοῦ τὸ Πνεῦμα· ὥσπερ οὖν Χριστὸν ἐπιγνοὺς ἐπέγνως Θεόν, οὕτω δὴ καὶ Πνεῦμα Χριστοῦ ἐδέξω Θεόν».

Περὶ μὲν οὖν τῆς ἐπιγνώσεως αὐτόθεν δῆλον· περὶ δὲ τῆς ἀποστολῆς καὶ τῆς δόσεως καὶ πρότερον εἰρήκαμεν. Δεῖ δ᾽ ὅμως κανταῦθα πρῶτον συνιδεῖν, τί ποτ᾽ ἄρα Πνεῦμά φησιν ὁ Χρυσόστομος Πατὴρ λαμβανόμενόν τε καὶ διδασκόμενον, αὐτὴν τὴν οὐσίαν καὶ τὴν ὑπόστασιν τοῦ Πνεύματος ἢ τὴν χάριν καὶ τὴν ἐνέργειαν; Ἀλλ᾽ ἵνα μὴ κάμνωμεν ἀνερευνῶντες, αὐτὸν τοῦτον τὸν χρυσοῦν θεολόγον ἑρμηνέα προβαλώμεθα καὶ τοῦ νῦν ζητουμένου παρ᾽ ἡμῶν· οὗτος γὰρ ἐν μὲν τῷ Περὶ τοῦ Πνεύματος λόγῳ, «ἡ δωρεά», φησί, «πέμπεται, τὸ Πνεῦμα οὐκ ἀποστέλλεται». Ἰωάννου δὲ τοῦ προδρόμου καὶ βαπτιστοῦ λέγοντος ἀκηκοὼς περὶ Χριστοῦ, ὡς οὐκ ἐκ τοῦ μέτρου παρὰ τοῦ Πατρὸς ἔλαβε τὸ Πνεῦμα, «οὐ γὰρ ἐκ μέτρου», φησί, «δίδωσι τὸ Πνεῦμα ὁ Πατήρ», ἀλλὰ «πάντα δέδωκεν ἐν τῇ χειρὶ αὐτοῦ», ἐξηγούμενος αὐτός φησι· «Πνεῦμα ἐνταῦθα τὴν ἐνέργειαν λέγει· αὕτη γάρ ἐστιν ἡ μεριζομένη. Πάντες γὰρ ἡμεῖς μέτρῳ τὴν ἐνέργειαν τοῦ Πνεύματος ἐλάβομεν, ἐκεῖνος δὲ ὁλόκληρον ἔλαβε πᾶσαν τὴν ἐνέργειαν· εἰ δὲ ἡ ἐνέργεια αὐτοῦ ἀμέτρητος, πολλῷ μᾶλλον ἡ οὐσία». Καὶ ἀλλαχοῦ πάλιν ἐκεῖνο τὸ ψαλμικὸν εἰς ἐξήγησιν προθείς, «ἐξεχύθη χάρις ἐν χείλεσί σου»,

of the Holy Spirit. In this regard, since Basil the Great wanted to exalt the Son, if in fact he had been able to say that the Son is the origin of the divine Spirit (in the sense that the Spirit took being through Him), why did he not say it? Why did he say instead that He is only a provider of the Spirit, that He is an origin only of the creation which took being through Him?

47

But, they say, the golden-mouthed theologian says, "Christ came to us, He gave to us the Spirit that is from Him and assumed our body."[143] And again: "Because the body of Christ became a temple of the divine power upon the earth, you also may become a temple in His likeness; For you receive the Spirit sent from Him. So then, just as in coming to know Christ you have come to know God, in the same way you also received the Spirit of Christ as God."[144]

So, concerning [the last part about] the "coming to know." the matter is self-evident.[145] As for the sending and the transmission, we have also spoken about that previously. Nevertheless, here, too, we need to understand, first, what does our Father Chrysostom mean when he says that the Spirit is taught and received? Is it the very essence and hypostasis of the Spirit, or is it His grace and energy? But that we may not exhaust ourselves searching, let us again put forth this golden theologian himself as an interpreter of what we are now discussing. On one hand, in his treatise *Concerning the Spirit* he says: "The gift is sent; the Spirit is not sent forth."[146] On the other hand, having heard John the Forerunner and Baptist speaking about Christ, that He received not the Spirit by measure from the Father (for he says, "the Father gives the Spirit not by measure," but "has given all things into His hand"[147]), he exegetes and says, "By 'Spirit' here he means energy; for this is what is divisible. For we have all received the energy of the Spirit in measure, but He received all the energy in its entirety. But if His energy is measureless, much more the essence."[148] And elsewhere, putting forth that psalmic passage for exegesis, "grace hath been poured forth on Thy lips,"[149] he says, "Do

«ὁρᾷς», φησίν, «ὅτι περὶ τῆς οἰκονομίας ὁ λόγος»; Καὶ μετ᾽ ὀλίγα·
τὴν χάριν γάρ φησιν ἐνταῦθα τὴν ἐλθοῦσαν ἐπὶ τὴν σάρκα· πᾶσα
γὰρ ἡ χάρις ἐξεχύθη εἰς τὸν ναὸν ἐκεῖνον· "οὐ γὰρ ἐκ μέτρου
δίδωσιν ἐκείνῳ τὸ Πνεῦμα ὁ Πατήρ". Ἡμεῖς δέ, μικρόν τι καὶ
ρανίδα ἀπὸ τῆς χάριτος ἐκείνης ἔχομεν· "ἐκ τοῦ πληρώματος γάρ,
φησίν", "αὐτοῦ ἡμεῖς πάντες ἐλάβομεν", ὡς ἂν εἴποι τις, ἐκ τοῦ
ὑπερβλύζοντος, ἐκ τοῦ περιττεύοντος. Καὶ πάλιν, οὐκ εἶπε "δίδωμι
τὸ Πνεῦμα", ἀλλ᾽ ἐκχεῶ ἀπὸ τοῦ Πνεύματός μου ἐπὶ πᾶσαν σάρκα".
Καὶ ἡ ἐν τοσούτοις τοῦ κόσμου κλίμασι διδομένη χάρις μέρος τι τῆς
δωρεᾶς ἐστι καὶ ἀρραβών· "δοὺς γάρ", φησί, "τὸν ἀρραβῶνα τοῦ
Πνεύματος ἐν ταῖς καρδίαις ἡμῶν". Τὸ μέρος λέγει τῆς ἐνεργείας,
οὐ γὰρ δὴ ὁ παράκλητος μερίζεται».

48

Τὴν γοῦν ἐνέργειαν ταύτην καὶ ὁ ναὸς ἐκεῖνος ἔλαβε καὶ τοῖς ἀξίοις
παρ᾽ ἑαυτοῦ παρέχει ὁ Χριστός. Σὺ δ᾽ ἐνταῦθα νῦν ἀκούων τοῦ
χρυσορρήμονος λέγοντος, «ὁ Χριστὸς ἔδωκεν ἡμῖν», ἀναμνήσθητι
καὶ τῶν λόγων ἐκείνων, οὓς φθάσαντες εἰρήκαμεν, ὅτι Θεὸς καὶ
Θεοῦ ὕπαρξις πρὸς ἕτερον οὐκ ἔστιν, οὐδὲ δίδοταί τινι· ἀλλὰ καὶ
ἀναίτιός ἐστιν, αὐτὸν αἰτίαν ἔχων τὸν ἐξ οὗ ὑπάρχει ἀναιτίως, ἀλλ᾽
οὐκ ἐξ αὐτοῦ ὑπάρχων δι᾽ αἰτίαν. Ὥσπερ δὲ Θεὸς καὶ Θεοῦ ὕπαρξις
ἀναίτιος, οὕτω τὸ δι᾽ αἰτίαν γεγονὸς κοινὸν αὐτῷ τε τῷ ἀναιτίῳ
καὶ τοῖς ἀναιτίως ἐξ αὐτοῦ ὑπάρχουσι. Διὸ πολλάκις εἰρημένον καὶ
παρὰ τοῦ θεανθρώπου Λόγου καὶ καθεξῆς παρὰ τῶν θεοφόρων
πέμπεσθαί τε καὶ δίδοσθαι παρὰ τοῦ Υἱοῦ τὸ Πνεῦμα, οὐδαμοῦ
χωρὶς αἰτίας εἴρηται, οὐδ᾽ ἄνευ προσώπου τοῦ λαμβάνοντος, δι᾽
ὃν καὶ πέμπεται· ἀλλ᾽ ἀεὶ συνεζευγμένον ταῖς αἰτίαις ἀποδέδωκε
πρῶτον μὲν ὁ μόνος καὶ Θεὸς καὶ θεολόγος, ὃς καὶ τὸ ἐκπορευόμενον
ἀπολύτως ἔθηκε χωρὶς ἡστινοσοῦν αἰτίας, ἔπειτα δὲ καὶ οἱ δι᾽ αὐτοῦ
λαλοῦντες ἅπαντες, παρ᾽ ὧν ἡμεῖς διδασκόμεθα μὴ τὴν ὑπόστασιν
τοῦ παναγίου Πνεύματος εἶναι καὶ ἐκ τοῦ Υἱοῦ, μηδὲ δίδοσθαι
ταύτην, μηδὲ λαμβάνεσθαι παρ᾽ οὐδενός, ἀλλὰ τὴν θείαν χάριν καὶ
τὴν ἐνέργειαν. Εἰ δ᾽ ἄρα καὶ μὴ πάντες, μηδ᾽ ἀεὶ μέμνηνται τῶν

you see that he is speaking of His *economia*?"[150] And a bit later, "Here he is referring to the grace that came upon the flesh, since all the grace was poured forth upon that temple: 'For the Father giveth not the Spirit by measure unto him.'[151] But we have a small portion, even a drop, from that grace: 'for of his fulness have we all received,'[152] as one might say, 'from the overflowing, from the excess'. And again, He did not say, 'I give the Spirit', but 'I will pour out of my Spirit upon all flesh.'[153] And the grace which is given in so many regions of the world is some part of the gift and an earnest [engagement]. For he says, 'He hath given the earnest of the Spirit in our hearts.'[154] He means the part of the energy, for, of course, the Paraclete is not divided."[155]

48

Therefore, as that Temple received this same energy, so Christ then bestows it from Himself to those who are worthy. And so you now, when you hear the golden speaker saying, "Christ has given to us," remember those words which we have said earlier,[156] that God and the existence of God is not for another, nor is it given to anyone. Rather He is causeless, having as a cause Him from whom He exists causelessly, not existing from Him on account of a cause. Now just as God and the existence of God are causeless, so what came to be for a cause is common both to Him who is uncaused and to those who exist causelessly from Him. And so, although it has been said many times both by the theanthropic Word and by the God-bearers that the Spirit is sent and given from the Son, yet nowhere is it said without a cause, nor without a person as recipient, on account of whom He is also sent. On the contrary, the only God and Theologian has always rendered [these phrases] yoked to the causes, while He has also laid down that what proceeds is absolutely independent of any cause whatsoever, and afterward so did also all those speaking through Him, by whom we are taught that it is not the hypostasis of the All-Holy Spirit that is from the Son, neither is it given nor received by anyone, but that rather the divine grace and energy are received. Now, if not everyone nor always mentions the

προσώπων ἢ τῶν αἰτιῶν, οὐχ ὡς μὴ οὕτω φρονοῦντες, ἀλλ᾽ ὡς πολλάκις εἰρημένων καὶ ὡς ἐντεῦθεν ὁμολογουμένων ὄντων. Καὶ τοῦτο μὴ προσχόντες μηδ᾽ ἐπιστήσαντες οἱ λατινικῶς φρονοῦντες, πολλὰ τῶν τοῦ μεγάλου Ἀθανασίου καὶ τῶν τοῦ θείου Κυρίλλου παρενόησαν καὶ περιέτρεψαν κακῶς.

49

Ἀλλὰ τί ἄν τις εἴποι, πάλιν οἱ τοιοῦτοι λέγουσιν, τοῦ Νύσσης θεηγόρου ἀκούων Γρηγορίου λέγοντος, «προθεωρεῖσθαι τὸν Υἱὸν κατὰ τὸν τῆς αἰτίας λόγον τῆς τοῦ Πνεύματος ὑποστάσεως»; Τί δ᾽ ἄν τις φαίη, ἕτερον ἡμεῖς ἐροῦμεν ἀνθυπενεγκόντες ἢ τὸ ἀληθὲς καὶ τοῖς μικρὸν ἐφιστᾶσι γνωριμώτατον, ὅτι προθεωρεῖται ἡ τοῦ Υἱοῦ ὑπόστασις ἐκ τοῦ Πατρὸς κατὰ τὸν τῆς αἰτίας λόγον τῆς τοῦ Πνεύματος ὑποστάσεως, οὐ κατὰ τὸν τῆς αἰτίας λόγον τῆς τοῦ Πνεύματος, ἀλλὰ κατὰ τὸν λόγον τῆς ἑαυτοῦ ἐκ τοῦ Πατρὸς ὑποστάσεως, ὅς ἐστι τὸ γεννητῶς ὑπάρχειν ἐκ Πατρός; Πατέρα γάρ τις ἀκούων, γεννήματος εὐθὺς αὐτὸν ἐννοεῖ Πατέρα· ἡνίκα δ᾽ ἄν ὄντα καὶ λόγον ἀκούσῃ τὸ γέννημα, τότε καὶ τοῦ θείου Πνεύματος εἰς ἔννοιαν ἔρχεται. Καὶ διὰ τοῦτο ὁ Υἱὸς πρὸ τοῦ Πνεύματός ἐστι καθ᾽ ὕπαρξιν οὐδαμῶς. Διὸ φησιν ὁ Νύσσης θεῖος οὗτος πρόεδρος ἐν τῷ πρώτῳ τῶν Πρὸς Εὐνόμιον ἀντιρρητικῶν· «ὡς συνάπτεται τῷ Πατρὶ ὁ Υἱὸς καὶ τὸ ἐξ αὐτοῦ εἶναι ἔχων οὐχ ὑστερίζει κατὰ τὴν ὕπαρξιν, οὕτω πάλιν καὶ τοῦ μονογενοῦς ἔχεται τὸ Πνεῦμα τὸ ἅγιον, ἐπινοίᾳ μόνον κατὰ τὸν τῆς αἰτίας λόγον προθεωρουμένου τῆς τοῦ Πνεύματος ὑποστάσεως».

Τί οὖν ἐστι τὸ ἐντεῦθεν τῷ ἁγίῳ δεικνύμενον; Οὐδὲν ἄλλο πάντως ἢ ὅτι ἅμα ἐστὶν ὁ Πατὴρ καὶ ὁ Υἱὸς καὶ τὸ Πνεῦμα τὸ ἅγιον· καὶ οὔτε τὸ ἐκ τοῦ Πατρὸς εἶναι τὸν Υἱὸν προσίσταταί τι κωλῦον ἅμα τῷ Πατρὶ ἐξ ἀϊδίου εἶναι τὸν Υἱόν, οὔτε τὸ ἐπινοίᾳ μόνῃ κατὰ τὸν τῆς οἰκείας αἰτίας λόγον, τουτέστιν ὡς Υἱὸν προθεωρεῖσθαι ἀπὸ

persons or the causes, it is not because they do not think this way but because these things have already been said many times and they are therefore agreed upon. And because the Latin-minded did not pore over this or give attention to it, they have misinterpreted and wrongly and completely twisted many sayings of the great Athanasius and of the divine Cyril.

49

"But what could one say," such men retort once more, "when hearing the instructor on God, Gregory of Nyssa, saying: 'The Son is conceived of as before the Spirit's hypostasis by reason of the cause'?"[157] What actually *would* someone say? Will we in rejoinder say something other than what is true and most familiar to those who pay but a little attention, that is, that the hypostasis of the Son is considered to be from the Father prior than the hypostasis of the Spirit by reason of the cause, not by reason of the cause of the Spirit but by reason of His own hypostasis from the Father, which is to exist by begetting from the Father. For when someone hears "Father", immediately he considers Him to be Father of an offspring; and whenever he hears that the offspring is a Word, then he enters into the conceptual understanding of the divine Spirit.[158] So on account of this, the Son is in no way at all existentially prior to the Spirit. Wherefore this divine president of Nyssa in the first of his disputations *Against Eunomius* says: "As the Son is bound to the Father, and, while deriving existence from Him, is not existentially after Him, so again the Holy Spirit clings closely to the Only-begotten, who is conceived of as before the Spirit's hypostasis only notionally, by reason of the cause."[159]

What then is being shown by the saint in this passage? Entirely nothing other than that the Father and the Son and the Holy Spirit are contemporaneous; and neither does the Son's being from the Father in any way prevent the Son from being contemporaneously with the Father from eternity, nor does the fact that the Son is considered prior (only notionally, by reason of His own cause, namely, as a Son

τοῦ Πατρός, προσίσταταί τι κωλῦον τοῦ Υἱοῦ ἔχεσθαι τὸ Πνεῦμα καὶ σὺν αὐτῷ ἅμα εἶναι ἀπὸ τοῦ Πατρός. Σκεπτέον δὲ καὶ τοῦτο φανερῶς προσκείμενον, ὡς οὐδ' ἁπλῶς ἐπινοίᾳ, ἀλλ' ἐπινοίᾳ μόνον ἔφη προθεωρεῖσθαι τὸν Υἱὸν τοῦ Πνεύματος· καὶ ὅτι τὸν μὲν Υἱὸν εἶπεν ἐκ Πατρός, τὸ δὲ Πνεῦμα τὸ ἅγιον ἔχεσθαί φησι τοῦ Υἱοῦ, τουτέστιν ἅμα σὺν τῷ Υἱῷ ἐκ τοῦ Πατρὸς ὑπάρχειν, ἀλλ' οὐκ ἐξ αὐτοῦ τὸ εἶναι ἔχειν.

50

Ἀλλ' ὁ αὐτός, φασί, Νύσσης θεηγόρος, ἀλλαχοῦ σαφῶς μέσον τίθησι τὸν Υἱὸν τοῦ Πατρὸς καὶ τοῦ Πνεύματος, καὶ δι' αὐτοῦ προσεχῶς ὄντος τῷ Πατρὶ καὶ τὸ Πνεῦμα παραδίδωσιν· οὕτω γάρ, φησίν, ἔσται καὶ μονογενής. Τί γοῦν, ἂν ἡμεῖς δείξωμεν αὐτὸν τὴν ἐκπορευτικὴν ἰδιότητα μόνῳ τῷ Πατρὶ προσμαρτυροῦντα καὶ μόνον αἴτιον Υἱοῦ καὶ Πνεύματος τὸν Πατέρα λέγοντα καὶ ἐξ ἑνὸς καὶ τοῦ αὐτοῦ προσώπου τὸν Υἱόν τε καὶ τὸ Πνεῦμα τὸ ἅγιον καὶ προσεχῶς ἄμφω ἐξ αὐτοῦ καὶ τὸν μὴ οὕτω φρονοῦντα πολύθεον δεικνύντα; Διδάσκων γάρ, πῶς ἐν τρισὶ προσώποις εἷς ἐστι Θεὸς «τὰ τοῦ ἀνθρώπου», φησί, «πρόσωπα πάντα, οὐκ ἀπὸ τοῦ αὐτοῦ προσώπου κατὰ τὸ προσεχὲς ἔχει τὸ εἶναι, ὡς πολλὰ καὶ διάφορα εἶναι πρὸς τοῖς αἰτιατοῖς καὶ τὰ αἴτια. Ἐπὶ δὲ τῆς ἁγίας Τριάδος οὐχ οὕτως· ἓν γὰρ πρόσωπον καὶ τὸ αὐτὸ τοῦ Πατρός, ἐξ οὗπερ ὁ Υἱὸς γεννᾶται καὶ τὸ Πνεῦμα τὸ ἅγιον ἐκπορεύεται. Διὸ καὶ κυρίως τὸν ἕνα αἴτιον μετὰ τῶν αὐτοῦ αἰτιατῶν ἕνα Θεόν φαμεν τεθαρρηκότως». Τὴν δὲ ἐκπορευτικὴν ἰδιότητα μόνῳ προσεῖναι δεῖξαι τῷ Πατρὶ διὰ τοσαύτης ἐποιήσατο σπουδῆς, ὡς καὶ μάρτυρα παραγαγεῖν τὸν ἐν βασιλεῦσι θεῖον ᾠδικὸν Δαβίδ, οὐ μόνον ἐκ τοῦ Πατρὸς ἐκπορευόμενον λέγοντα τὸ Πνεῦμα τὸ ἅγιον, ἀλλ' ἐξ αὐτῆς αὐτοῦ τῆς ὑποστάσεως. Φησὶ γὰρ ἐν τῷ Περὶ θεογνωσίας λόγῳ προφιλοσοφήσας οὐκ ὀλίγα περὶ Πατρὸς καὶ Υἱοῦ, ὡς «Πνεῦμα δὲ

from the Father) in any way prevent the Spirit from clinging close to the Son and being with Him contemporaneously from the Father. We must also consider this, which the saint clearly added, namely, that he did not simply say, "notionally" but "only notionally is the Son conceived of as before to the Spirit." Furthermore, he said that the Son is from the Father, while for the Holy Spirit he said that He clings closely to the Son, that is, that He exists contemporaneously with the Son from the Father, not that He has His being from Him.

50

They say, "But the same instructor on God from Nyssa in another passage clearly places the Son in the middle position between the Father and the Spirit, and he hands down[160] the Spirit through the Son being immediately with the Father.[161] For this, he says, is how He will also be only-begotten. And what if we proved that he testifies that the property to cause procession belongs only to the Father and that he says the Father is the only cause of the Son and Spirit and that the Son and Holy Spirit are from the one and same person and that both are immediately from Him, and that he shows that a person not minded this way is polytheistic, what would they say then? For when he was teaching how God is one in three persons he says, "All the persons of mankind do not have being from the same person with an immediate connection, since the causes as well as the caused are many and diverse. But in the case of the Holy Trinity, it is not like this, for there is one and the same Person, the Father's, from whom precisely the Son is begotten and the Holy Spirit proceeds. It is principally for this reason that we boldly say that the one cause along with those caused by Him is one God."[162] Now he tried with such diligence to point out that the property to cause procession is attributed to the Father only that he even brought forth a witness, David the divine musician among the kings, who said not only that the Holy Spirit proceeds from the Father but that He proceeds from His very hypostasis. For he says in his treatise *Concerning the Knowledge of God*, after he had philosophized not a little about the Father and the Son, that "the Spirit is the

τὸ τῆς πατρικῆς ἐκπορευόμενον ὑποστάσεως· τούτου γὰρ ἕνεκα καὶ πνεῦμα στόματος ὁ Δαβὶδ εἴρηκεν, ἵνα τὴν ἐκπορευτικὴν ἰδιότητα τῷ Πατρὶ μόνῳ προσοῦσαν πιστώσηται». Τί τούτων τῶν ῥημάτων σαφέστερον ἢ βεβαιότερον ἢ ἀλειπτότερον ἢ δεικτικώτερον, ὡς οὐχὶ καὶ ἐκ τοῦ Υἱοῦ ἐκπορεύεται τὸ Πνεῦμα;

Εἰ γὰρ καὶ ἐξ αὐτοῦ, οὐκ ἂν ἦν ἐξ ἑνὸς προσώπου κατὰ τὸ προσεχὲς ἑκάτερον, οὐδ᾽ ἂν εἴχομεν θαρρεῖν μίαν λέγειν σέβειν θεότητος ἀρχὴν καὶ ἕνα Θεὸν ἰσχυρίζεσθαι τὰ τρία εἶναι πρόσωπα. Εἰ καθάπερ τὸ αἰτιατόν, οὕτω καὶ τὸ αἴτιον ἐν δυσὶ προσώποις ἦν ὡς καὶ ἐφ᾽ ἡμῶν ὁρᾶται, οὐδ᾽ ἂν ἦν ἡ ἐκπορευτικὴ ἰδιότης μόνου τοῦ Πατρός, εἰ καὶ ὁ Υἱὸς τὸ ἐκπορεύειν εἶχε· νῦν δὲ μόνῳ τῷ Πατρὶ προσοῦσαν αὐτός τε ὁ Νυσσαέων Γρηγόριος πιστοῦται καὶ τὸν θεοπάτορα Δαβὶδ προάγει προσπιστούμενον, μᾶλλον δὲ τὸ Πνεῦμα τὸ ἅγιον τὸ διὰ τῶν προφητῶν λαλῆσαν.

51

Ὁρᾷς τἀναντία σαφῶς τοῦ Πνεύματος φρονῶν καὶ ἀπεναντίας ἐκείνου δογματίζων καὶ μαχόμενος, ἀλλ᾽ οὐ θεολογῶν τὸ Πνεῦμα, πονηρὸς διαιτητὴς θεογόνου θεότητος γενόμενος καὶ τῶν τοῦ Θεοῦ Πατρὸς ἰδίων ἀποστερητής, κινῶν καὶ μεταφέρων τὰς ἀκινήτους ἰδιότητας καὶ τὸ σαυτοῦ μέρος κυκῶν καὶ συνταράσσων τὴν ὑπὲρ πάντα νοῦν καὶ αὐτόχρημα εἰρήνην; Τί οὖν, οὐ φρίττεις ταῦτ᾽ ἀκούων καὶ ἀφίστασαι πρὸς τάχος τῆς δεινῆς κακοδοξίας καὶ θρηνεῖς τὸν πρῴην βίον ὡς μὴ εὐσεβῶς ἀνύσας;

Ἀλλ᾽ ἴδωμεν καὶ τὴν προτεινομένην ὑπ᾽ αὐτῶν ἀρτίως τοῦ Νύσσης μαρτυρίαν καὶ πρὸς δύναμιν ἀναθεωρήσαντες αὐτὴν ἀνακαθάρωμεν τοῖς πᾶσι τὸ ἐν ταύτῃ δύσληπτον, ὃ αὐτοῖς καὶ τὴν πλάνην ὡς ἐπίπαν ἀπειργάσατο· εἴθε δ᾽ ἦν καὶ αὐτοὺς καθάραντας, ἐξελέσθαι τῆς ἀπάτης. Ἀλλὰ συντείνατε παρακαλῶ τὸν νοῦν οἱ νῦν τε καὶ

one who proceeds from the paternal hypostasis; for this reason has David said 'Spirit of His mouth', that he may give assurance that the property to cause procession is attributed only to the Father."[163] What could be clearer or more certain, or more invincible, or more indicative than these words, that the Spirit does not proceed also from the Son?

For if He was also from the Son, then each would not be from one person immediately, nor would we have the boldness to say that we revere one origin of divinity and affirm that the three persons are one God. If (as is the case with what is caused) that which causes were likewise in two persons, as it is seen in our case; if the Son also had the ability to cause procession, then the property of causing procession would not be only the Father's. But now Gregory of the Nyssans himself assures us that it is attributed only to the Father, and he brings forward David, the ancestor of God, or better yet, the Holy Spirit, who spoke through the prophets, as also affirming this.

51

Do you see that you are clearly holding positions contrary to the Spirit, dogmatizing opposite to Him, even warring against Him? That instead of theologizing about the Spirit you have become a wicked arbitrator of the divinity-generating divinity and a robber of the Father's characteristic idioms, moving and transferring the immovable properties and for your own part stirring up and all at once disturbing the very peace which transcends every intellect?[164] Do you not tremble at hearing these things? Do you not run as fast as possible away from the terrible cacodoxy and then bewail your previous life since you did not traverse it piously?

Let us nevertheless look at the testimony of the Nyssan which has recently been proposed by them and once we have looked at it again let us clarify for all, as much as possible, what is herein hard to understand, which in general has also effected their error. If only we could purify and deliver them from deceit! But direct all your

αὖθις ἐντευξόμενοι. Πάντα μὲν γὰρ τ᾿ ἀνδρὸς τουτουὶ τὰ ῥήματα βαθείας ἔχεται φρενός, τὰ δὲ περὶ Θεοῦ ὡς μάλιστα καὶ τούτων μᾶλλον τὸ νῦν προτεθησόμενον ἡμῖν· γράφων γὰρ Πρὸς Ἀβλάβιον, διὰ τί, μίαν θεότητα ἐπὶ Πατρὸς καὶ Υἱοῦ καὶ Πνεύματος ἁγίου λέγοντες, τρεῖς θεοὺς λέγειν ἀπαγορεύομεν, τὸ παντάπασιν ἑνιαῖον παραστήσας τῆς θείας φύσεως, «εἰ δέ τις», φησί, «συκοφαντοίη τὸν Λόγον ὡς ἐκ τοῦ μὴ δέχεσθαι τὴν κατὰ φύσιν διαφορὰν μίξίν τινα τῶν ὑποστάσεων καὶ ἀνακύκλησιν κατασκευάζοντα, τοῦτο περὶ τῆς τοιαύτης ἀπολογησόμεθα μέμψεως· ὅτι τὸ ἀπαράλλακτον τῆς θείας φύσεως ὁμολογοῦντες τὴν κατὰ τὸ αἴτιον καὶ αἰτιατὸν διαφορὰν οὐκ ἀρνούμεθα, ἐν ᾧ μόνῳ διακρίνεσθαι τὸ ἕτερον τοῦ ἑτέρου καταλαμβάνομεν, τῷ μὲν αἴτιον πιστεύειν εἶναι, τὸ δὲ ἐκ τοῦ αἰτίου. Καὶ τοῦ ἐξ αἰτίας ὄντος πάλιν ἄλλην διαφορὰν ἐννοοῦμεν. Τὸ μὲν γὰρ προσεχῶς ἐκ τοῦ πρώτου, τὸ δὲ διὰ τοῦ προσεχῶς ἐκ τοῦ πρώτου· ὥστε καὶ τὸ μονογενὲς ἀναμφίβολον ἐπὶ τοῦ Υἱοῦ μένειν καὶ τὸ ἐκ τοῦ Πατρὸς εἶναι τὸ Πνεῦμα μὴ ἀμφιβάλλειν, τῆς τοῦ Υἱοῦ μεσιτείας καὶ ἑαυτῷ τὸ μονογενὲς φυλαττούσης καὶ τὸ Πνεῦμα τῆς φυσικῆς πρὸς τὸν Πατέρα σχέσεως μὴ ἀπειργούσης».

52

Τοῦτο δὴ πρῶτον ἐνταῦθα λεκτέον ἂν εἴη πρὸς Λατίνους· ἐπειδήπερ ὑμεῖς οὐ τὸ ἐξ αἰτίας μόνον, ἀλλὰ καὶ τὸ αἴτιον ἐν δυσὶν οἴεσθε προσώποις (ἐν γὰρ δυσὶ προσώποις τίθεσθε τὴν αἰτίαν τοῦ θείου Πνεύματος καὶ ἐν ἑκατέρῳ τούτων διαφόρως), εἴπερ ἐφρόνει καθ᾿ ὑμᾶς ὁ τῆς Νύσσης οὗτος φανότατος φωστήρ, διεῖλεν ἂν πρὸ τοῦ αἰτιατοῦ τὸ αἴτιον. Τοῦτο δὲ ποιήσας οὐδαμῶς δῆλός ἐστι μηδ᾿ εἰς νοῦν λαβών, ὅπερ ὑμεῖς ἐκ τῶν ἐκείνου συνάγειν πειρᾶσθε λόγων, ἀφ᾿ ὧν τῷ καλῶς σκοπουμένῳ καὶ τἀναντία τῶν ὑμετέρων ἀναφαίνεται δογμάτων. Τοῦτο γάρ ἐστιν ὅ φησιν, ὡς ὁ Υἱὸς οὐκ ἀπείργει τὴν ἄμεσον τοῦ Πνεύματος πρὸς τὸν Πατέρα σχέσιν, εἰ καὶ μόνος αὐτός ἐστιν Υἱός. Ἔπειτα μηδὲ τοῦτο παραλειπτέον

attention, I beg you, who are now and will be dealing with this. Indeed all the words of this man have such depth of understanding, but especially the words that concern God and of these particularly that which will be now set before you. For in writing *To Ablabios* regarding why, although we name one divinity with regard to Father and Son and Holy Spirit, we forbid from saying there are three gods, having presented the complete oneness of the divine nature he says, "If, however, any one cavils at our argument, on the ground that by not admitting the difference of nature it leads to a mixture and confusion of the persons, we shall make to such a charge this answer; — that while we confess the invariable character of the nature, we do not deny the difference with respect to cause and caused, by which alone we apprehend that one person is distinguished from another; — by our belief, that is, that one is the cause, and another is of the cause; and again in that which is of the cause we recognize another distinction. For one is directly from the first cause, and another is through that which is directly from the first cause; so that the attribute of being Only-begotten abides without doubt in the Son, and the interposition of the Son, while it guards His attribute of being Only-begotten, does not shut out the Spirit from His relation by way of nature to the Father."[165]

52

About this point the following must be said to the Latins: forasmuch as you think that not only the caused but also the cause is in two persons (for you place the cause of the divine Spirit in two persons and in each of them in a different way), if it were assumed that this most brilliant luminary of Nyssa really was thinking like you, he would have divided the cause before the caused. But since he did not do this at all, it is clear that he had not even consider that which you are trying to draw from his arguments. From his arguments even the opposite of your dogmas becomes apparent to the one that looks at them correctly. For this is what he says, that the Son does not prevent the immediate relationship of the Spirit to the Father, even though only He is a Son. And then, neither should we neglect

συνιδεῖν, ὡς μετὰ τὸ εἰπεῖν ὅτι «τὴν κατὰ τὸ αἴτιον καὶ αἰτιατὸν διαφορὰν οὐκ ἀρνούμεθα», αἰτιατὸν ὁμοῦ μετὰ τοῦ Πνεύματος καὶ τὸν Υἱὸν εἰπών, ἐπήνεγκεν, «ἐν ᾧ μόνῳ διακρίνεσθαι τὸ ἕτερον τοῦ ἑτέρου καταλαμβάνομεν», φανερῶς ἀπαγορεύων τὴν λατινικὴν καινοτομίαν, ὡς οὐ μόνον αἰτιατός, ἀλλὰ καὶ αἴτιός ἐστιν ὁ Υἱός, καὶ πάσας τούτων ἐν βραχεῖ τὰς ἐπινενοημένας διαφορὰς ἀποσειόμενος, ὅτι πρῶτον μὲν ὁ Πατὴρ αἴτιόν ἐστιν ἐπὶ τοῦ Πνεύματος, δεύτερον δὲ ὁ Υἱός, καὶ ὅσα τούτοις παραπλήσια· ἐν μόνῳ γάρ, φησί, τῷ αἰτίῳ καὶ τῷ αἰτιατῷ τὴν θείαν φύσιν κατανοοῦμεν, καὶ τὸ μὲν αἴτιον οὐκ ἐν δυσὶ προσώποις θεωροῦμεν, τοῦ δὲ αἰτιατοῦ μόνου ταύτην τὴν ἐν δυσὶ προσώποις διαφορὰν ἐννοοῦμεν, ἥτις ἐστὶν οὐχ ὅτι τὸ μὲν τούτων καὶ αἴτιόν ἐστι, τὸ δὲ μόνον αἰτιατόν, ὡς Ἰταλοὶ φρονοῦσι, μᾶλλον δὲ παραφρονοῦσιν, ἀλλ᾽ ὅτι τὸ μὲν Υἱός ἐστι, τὸ δὲ οὐχ Υἱός. Καὶ οὐκ ἀπείργεται τοῦτο παρὰ τῆς τοῦ Υἱοῦ πρὸς τὸν Πατέρα κατὰ φύσιν ἑνώσεως. Εἰπὼν γὰρ ἀνωτέρω τοῦ λόγου, τί ἐστι τὰ τρία ταῦτα, ὁ Πατήρ, ὁ Υἱὸς καὶ τὸ Πνεῦμα τὸ ἅγιον, ὅτι μία ὑπερούσιος οὐσία, δεικνὺς ἔπειτα πῶς ἐστι τὰ τρία ταῦτα, ἆρα αἰτιατῶς ὡς ἔχοντά τι καὶ αἴτιον, ἢ ἀναιτίως πάντῃ, φησὶν ὅτι τὸ μὲν αὐτῶν ἐστιν αἴτιον, τὸ δὲ αἰτιατῶς ἔχει τὸ εἶναι, αἰτιατῶς δέ φησιν ἔχει τὸ εἶναι ὁ Υἱός τε καὶ τὸ Πνεῦμα τὸ ἅγιον.

53

Ἆρ᾽ οὐκ ἐντεῦθεν ἔδειξεν ἐνταῦθα, ἓν εἶναι μόνον αἴτιον τὸ ληφθὲν ἐκ τῶν τριῶν, δηλονότι τὸν Πατέρα μόνον; Εἶτα θέλων δεῖξαι πῶς τῶν δύο τούτων προσώπων ἑκάτερον αἰτιατῶς ἐστιν, ἵνα μή τις νομίσῃ, καθάπερ οἱ Λατῖνοι, πάλιν ἐκείνην τὴν τοῦ αἰτίου καὶ αἰτιατοῦ διαφορὰν καὶ ἐπὶ Υἱοῦ καὶ Πνεύματος εἰσάγειν, φησὶ σαφῶς, ὅτι ἐπὶ τούτων ἄλλην διαφορὰν ἐννοοῦμεν. Λατῖνοι δὲ ἀντιθετικῶς τούτῳ φασὶν οὐκ ἄλλην, ἀλλὰ τὴν αὐτήν· καὶ τοῦ ἁγίου πάλιν, πῶς αἰτιατῶς ἔχει τὸ εἶναι ὁ Υἱὸς φάναι προθεμένου, αὐτοὶ πῶς αἴτιός ἐστι φάναι συκοφαντοῦσιν αὐτόν. Τὸ μὲν γὰρ εἶναι τὸν Υἱὸν ὁπωσοῦν αἴτιον, οὐδαμῇ δείκνυται λέγων ἢ φρονῶν ὁ

to observe that he said, "We do not deny the difference with respect to cause and caused," naming the Son together with the Spirit as "caused". Then he added: "by which alone we apprehend that one person is distinguished from another," clearly forbidding the Latin innovation that the Son is not only caused but also a cause, and quickly shaking off all invented differences of theirs, such as that while the Father is the first cause of the Spirit, yet the Son is the second cause, and many other things like this. He says that only in the cause and the caused do we apprehend the divine nature, and while we indeed theorize that the cause is not in two persons, we consider that this very difference in the two persons belongs only to the caused. This difference is not that the one of them is also a cause while the other is only a caused (as the Italians opine, or rather, are out of their mind), but that the one indeed is a Son while the other is not a Son. And further, this is not prevented by the natural union of the Son with the Father. For having said earlier in his treatise what these three are, the Father, the Son, and the Holy Spirit (that they are one superessential essence), and then having shown how these three exist (whether they are caused at all, and have a cause, or are rather completely uncaused), he says that one of them is the cause while the other has existence by being caused, and he says that it is the Son and the Holy Spirit that have being by being caused.

53

So did he not prove in this argument here that there is only one cause, the one which was taken out from the three, clearly the Father only? Then, wanting to show how each of the two persons is caused, lest someone might think, like the Latins, that he introduces again that difference of cause and caused for the Son and Spirit as well, he clearly says that we note another difference in their respect. The Latins, however, in opposition say that it is not different but the same; and again, when the saint intended to say how the Son has being by being caused, these men mischaracterize him as saying how the Son is a cause. For this God-bearer is nowhere shown to

θεοφόρος οὗτος, καὶ μάλιστα ἐν τοῖς ἀρτίως προκειμένοις ῥήμασιν αὐτοῦ. Ἀλλὰ τὸ αἰτιατῶς μὲν καὶ τοῦτον ὑπάρχειν, καθάπερ καὶ τὸ Πνεῦμα τὸ ἅγιον, αἰτιατῶς μέντοι γεννητῶς, αἰτιατῶς δὲ καὶ τὸ Πνεῦμα τὸ ἅγιον ὑπάρχειν, οὐ γεννητῶς δέ.

Ἀμφοτέρων γὰρ λεγομένων, τοῦ Πατρὸς καὶ ἐκ Πατρός, Υἱοῦ δηλονότι καὶ Πνεύματος, τῷ Πατρὶ προσεχὲς ὁ μεγαλόνους εἶπε τὸν Υἱόν, διὰ μέσου δὲ αὐτοῦ, προσεχοῦς ὄντος τῷ πατρί, ἐκ Πατρὸς εἴρηκε τὸ Πνεῦμα νοούμενον, ἀλλ᾽ οὐκ ἐκπορευόμενον διὰ μέσου τοῦ Υἱοῦ, πάλιν οἷον ἐκεῖνο λέγων, ὅτι τοῦ αἰτίου καὶ πρώτου ὡς αἰτίου Πατρὸς φώτων ὄντος τε καὶ λεγομένου, τουτέστιν Υἱοῦ καὶ Πνεύματος (ἄμφω γάρ, ἀλλ᾽ οὐχ ὁ Υἱὸς μόνος δευτερεύει τοῦ Πατρός, ὡς καὶ Γρηγόριος ὁ θεολόγος ἐν τοῖς Ἔπεσί φησι) τοῦ γοῦν πρώτου πρὸς ἀμφότερα ταῦτα Πατρὸς τῶν φώτων λεγομένου (ἐκ γὰρ τῶν λογίων οὐκ ἂν εὕροις ἑτέραν αὐτοῦ ἐπωνυμίαν) τῶν ἐξ αἰτίου τούτου ὄντων, τὸ γεννητῶς ἐκ φωτὸς προερχόμενον φῶς προσεχῶς τῷ Πατρὶ νοεῖται πάραυτα, καθάπερ καὶ αὐτὸς ὁ Νύσσης ἐν τῷ δευτέρῳ τῶν Πρὸς Εὐνόμιον διατείνεται γράφων, «ὡς οὐκ ἂν Πατὴρ κεχωρισμένος ἀφ᾽ ἑαυτοῦ νοηθείη μὴ υἱοῦ συνημμένου διὰ τῆς τοῦ Πατρὸς ἐκφωνήσεως», καὶ πάλιν, «εἰς τὸν Πατέρα τὴν πίστιν ἔχοντες, ὁμοῦ τῷ ἀκοῦσαι τὸν Πατέρα συμπαραδεξόμεθα τῇ διανοίᾳ καὶ τὸν Υἱόν».

54

Ὁ μὲν οὖν Υἱὸς ἐκ τοῦ Πατρὸς καὶ ἔστι καὶ νοεῖται, τὸ δὲ Πνεῦμα τὸ ἅγιον δι᾽ ἑαυτὸ μὲν ἐκ προβολέως εἴη ἂν καὶ νοηθείη, ἀλλ᾽ οὐκ ἐκ Πατρός, διὰ δὲ τοῦ προσεχῶς νοουμένου ἐκ Πατρὸς Υἱοῦ, καὶ ἐκ Πατρὸς εἴη ἂν τὸ Πνεῦμα, ἐκπορεύοντος μὲν αὐτὸ τὸ

speak or think that the Son is actually a cause in any way whatsoever, and least of all in the recently articulated expressions of his texts. To the contrary he is shown to believe that, while the Son (just like the Holy Spirit) exists by being caused, yet it is caused by being begotten, while the Holy Spirit exists also by being caused, but not by being begotten.

For since both are said [to be] "of the Father" and "from the Father", I mean the Son and the Spirit, this great intellect said that the Son is immediately related to the Father, and he said that through the interposition of Him who is immediately related to the Father the Spirit is considered from the Father, not that He proceeds through the mediation of the Son. Thus he is repeating, as it were, the position that since He who is the cause and (as the cause) is first both is and is called the Father of Lights,[166] that is, of the Son and Spirit (since both, not only the Son, take second place to the Father, as Gregory the Theologian says in his odes[167])—so since He who is first toward both of them is said to be the Father of Lights, which are from this Cause (for among the [inspired] sayings you would not find any other designation for Him), then the Light that comes by begetting from the Light is considered immediately with the Father. In the same way the Nyssan himself asserts, writing in his second chapter *To Eunomius*, "A Father separated from Himself could not be conceived, if the Son were not united together with Him by the expression of 'Father';"[168] and again, "having our faith in the Father, as soon as we hear 'Father' we also accept the Son in our understanding."[169]

54

Therefore, the Son indeed is from the Father, and is considered so. The Holy Spirit, however, would be (and be considered to be) from an Originator, not from a Father, on account of His own self;[170] but through the Son being considered immediately from a Father, the Spirit would also be from a Father, who, on one hand, causes the Spirit Himself to proceed while, on the other hand, begetting

Πνεῦμα, γεννῶντος δὲ τὸν Υἱόν. Ἐκ γοῦν τοῦ γεννῶντος τὸ μὴ γεννητὸν Πνεῦμα πῶς ἂν ῥηθείη; Οὐ διὰ τὸν Υἱὸν μονογενῆ τε ὄντα καὶ διὰ τοῦτο προσεχῶς εὐθὺς τῷ γεννῶντι συνοούμενον καὶ τὸ γεννητὸν ἑαυτοῦ ποιοῦντα μόνον ἴδιον καὶ συντηροῦντα, τὸ δὲ Πνεῦμα δεικνύντα οὐ γεννητῶς ὂν ἐκ τοῦ Πατρός; Διὰ τοῦ Υἱοῦ ἆρ' ἔχει τὸ εἶναι καὶ νοεῖσθαι ἐκ Πατρὸς τὸ Πνεῦμα· δι' ἑαυτοῦ δὲ ἐκ προβολέως ἀμέσως καὶ αὐτὸ προβαλλομένου. Διό, καθάπερ ἔφημεν, οὐδ' αἴτιον, ἀλλ' αἰτιατὸν εἶπε μόνον τὸν Υἱὸν καὶ ἐπίσης τῷ Πνεύματι αἰτιατόν· καὶ ὁμοίως κατὰ τὸ αἴτιον ταῦτα διέστειλεν ἀπὸ Πατρός, καίτοι κατὰ τὴν τῶν Λατίνων ἐκδοχὴν οὐχ οὕτως ἔδει φάναι.

Ἀλλά, καθάπερ ἔφημεν, τὸ αἴτιον πρῶτον διελεῖν διὰ τοῦ κατ' αὐτοὺς ἐμμέσου καὶ ἀμέσου, ὡς ἐν δυσὶν οὕτω κατ' αὐτοὺς καὶ τὸ αἴτιον ὑποστάσεσιν ὁρώμενον, εἶτα τῷ λόγῳ προϊὼν καὶ ἐκ τοῦ Πατρὸς εὐθὺς νοεῖσθαι τὸν Υἱὸν εἰπὼν καὶ τὴν αἰτίαν προστιθείς, ἐχρῆν εἰπεῖν, εἰ κατὰ Λατίνους ἦν φρονῶν, ἵνα μὴ μόνον αἰτιατὸς ὁ Υἱός, ἀλλὰ καὶ αἴτιος ἀναφανῇ· ὁ δέ, τοῦτο μὲν οὐδαμῶς φησιν, ἀλλ' "ἵνα", φησί, "μόνος ὢν γεννητὸς ἀναφανῇ" ταὐτὸ δ' εἰπεῖν αἰτιατὸς τὸν τρόπον τοῦτον. Ποῦ τοίνυν ἐνταῦθ' ὁρᾶτε τὸν Υἱόν, οὗ μόνον αἰτιατὸς ὢν ἀνακηρύττεται;

55

Καὶ τοῦτο δέ μοι λάβε κατὰ νοῦν, ὅτι μηδὲ συνεργοῦσαν εἴρηκε ὁ μέγας οὗτος τὴν μεσιτείαν τοῦ Υἱοῦ, ἀλλὰ μὴ ἀπείργουσαν, τουτέστι μὴ κωλύουσαν ἀμέσως ἐκ τοῦ Πατρὸς καὶ τὸ Πνεῦμα ἐκπορεύεσθαι. Ποιήσωμεν δ' ὡς ἔνι φανερὰν καὶ διὰ παραδειγμάτων τὴν διάνοιαν. Ἐκ τοῦ πυρὸς ἀμέσως καὶ τὸ φῶς καὶ ὁ ἀτμὸς προέρχεται· οὐ γὰρ ἕτερον διὰ θατέρου. Τὸ τοίνυν πῦρ ἐπειλημμένον ὕλης ἀτμίζειν ἅμα καὶ φωτίζειν πέφυκε, τὸ μὲν φῶς οἷα δὴ γεννῶν, τὸν ἀτμὸν

the Son. Therefore how could the non-begotten Spirit be said to
be from the Begetter? Would it not be because of the Son, who is
only-begotten and as a result of this is immediately directly thought
of along with Him who begets, who also makes begottenness his
only idiom and preserves it so, while also showing that the Spirit
is not from the Father by being begotten? So it is through the Son
that the Spirit has the ability to be (and be considered to be) from
a Father — but by Himself He, too, is from an Originator who
originates Him immediately. That is why, just as we said, He did
not call the Son a cause but only a caused and equally caused with
the Spirit, and in a similar way it was with respect to the cause that
he distinguished them from the Father, although, according to the
received understanding of the Latins, he should not have spoken
thus.

But, just as we have said, if he was thinking like the Latins he should
have first divided the cause between the indirect one and the direct
one, according to them, since the cause is also witnessed thus in two
hypostases according to them; then, proceeding in his treatise and
having said that the Son is considered immediately from the Father
and having added the cause, he should have said, "so that the Son
may be shown to be not only caused but also a cause." But he does
not in any way actually say this. Instead, he says, "so that He may
be shown to be the only begotten one," which is the same as to say,
"caused, in this particular manner." Where, then, in this passage do
you see the Son being proclaimed as not only caused?

55

Now consider this for me. This great man has not said that the
interposition of the Son collaborates but rather that it does not
exclude, that is, that it does not hinder the Spirit from proceeding
immediately from the Father. But let us make the rationale as clear
as possible through model examples as well. Both light and smoke
proceed immediately from fire. For one is not through the other. So
when fire has received fuel it naturally both smokes and enlightens

δὲ ἐκπορεῦον. Ἐκ μὲν οὖν τοῦ φωτίζοντος τὸ φῶς προσεχῶς καὶ ἔστι καὶ δι' ἑαυτοῦ νοεῖται ἐξ αὐτοῦ· ὡσαύτως καὶ ὁ ἀτμὸς ἐκ τοῦ ἀτμίζοντος. Εἰ δὲ τὸν ἀτμὸν φαίη τις ἐκ τοῦ φωτίζοντος, διὰ τὸ φῶς ἐρεῖ, διὰ τοῦ φωτὸς νοήσας τὸν ἀτμὸν ἐκ τοῦ φωτίζοντος, τῆς μεσιτείας τοῦ φωτὸς καὶ ἑαυτῷ τὸ μονογενὲς φυλαττούσης καὶ τὸν ἀτμὸν μὴ ἀπειργούσης τῆς πρὸς τὸ φωτίζον σχέσεως, τουτέστι μὴ ἐμποδιζούσης ἀμέσως εἶναι ἐξ αὐτοῦ.

Ἀλλ', εἰ βούλεσθε, καὶ ἕτερον παράδειγμα προσθῶμεν, οὐ καινὸν οὐδ' ἄηθες τοῖς θεολόγοις, σαφηνείας χάριν πλείονος. Ὁ Κάϊν υἱὸς ὑπῆρχε τοῦ Ἀδὰμ καὶ μονογενὴς αὐτῷ πρὸ τοῦ τεκεῖν τοὺς ἄλλους, ἡ δὲ Εὔα τμῆμα τοῦ Ἀδάμ. Πατρὸς τοίνυν γενομένου τοῦ Ἀδάμ, Πατρὸς ἦν ἡ Εὔα τμῆμα· καὶ ἐγένετο ἂν καὶ ἐνοεῖτο τότε τμῆμα Πατρὸς ἐπ' ἀληθείας πάσης διὰ τοῦ Κάϊν καὶ εἶναι καὶ νοεῖσθαι καὶ λέγεσθαι πατρὸς τμῆμα κτησαμένη, τῆς τοῦ υἱοῦ τούτου μεσιτείας καὶ τὸ μονογενὲς ἑαυτῷ τότε φυλαττούσης καὶ τὴν Εὔαν πατρὸς εἶναι τμῆμα μὴ κωλυούσης· ἀλλ' οὐ διὰ τοῦτο ἐμμέσως τε καὶ οὐκ ἀμέσως ἡ Εὔα τὴν ἀρχὴν ἐκ τοῦ Ἀδὰμ ἐτμήθη. Ἀφεὶς τοίνυν τὴν χρονικὴν ἀρχήν τε καὶ διάστασιν καὶ τὴν ἐκ συζυγίας γέννησιν καὶ τ' ἄλλ' ὅσα μὴ θεότητι κατάλληλα, σκόπει πρὸς τοὺς τοῦ ἁγίου λόγους τὸ παράδειγμα καὶ συνήσεις τἀληθές.

56

Ἀλλ' μὲν οὕτω δι' Υἱοῦ νοοῦμεν ἐκ γεννητικοῦ, ταὐτὸν δ' εἰπεῖν ἀπὸ Πατρός, τὸ μὴ γεννητὸν ὑπάρχον Πνεῦμα· διὰ τὸν Υἱὸν γάρ ἐστί τε καὶ λέγεται Πατήρ. Δι' αὐτοῦ δὲ τοῦ Πνεύματος, οὐ γεννητοῦ ὄντος ἀλλ' ἐκπορευτοῦ, ἀμέσως ἐκ τοῦ ἐκπορεύοντος αὐτὸ νοοῦμεν, ταὐτὸν δ' εἰπεῖν ἐκ προβολέως. Διὰ τί γὰρ καὶ ὁ φερώνυμος θεολόγος

at the same time. The light, on the one hand, is like begetting, while the smoke is like causing procession. Thus while the light is immediately from the light source and is also by itself considered to be from it, likewise also the smoke is from the source of the smoke. Now if someone were to say that the smoke is from the source of the light, he would be saying this because of the light, because through the light he considered the smoke as being from the light source; and the interposition of the light preserves its only-begottenness and does not exclude the smoke from its relation to the source of the light, I mean, it does not impede it from being immediately from it.

But if you prefer, for the sake of greater clarity, let us add another model example, neither new nor unfamiliar to the theologians. Cain was Adam's son and was his only begotten, before the others were born, while Eve was a part of Adam. Therefore when Adam became a father, Eve was a part of the father; and in all truth she then became and was considered to be a part of the father, having acquired the ability to be and to be considered and to be called a part of the father through Cain. The interposition of this son Cain at that time also kept intact his own only-begottenness without preventing Eve from being a part of the father. But this does not mean that in the beginning Eve was taken from Adam indirectly and not immediately. So leaving behind the temporal beginning and the distance and the birth from a union and all other matters that are not the most appropriate for the divinity, compare this example to the words of the saint and you will understand the truth.

56

So through the Son we consider the Spirit, which does not exist as begotten, to be from the Begetter, which is the same as to say from the Father. For He is and is called a Father on account of the Son. But through the Spirit Himself, as He is not begotten but proceeding, we consider Him to be immediately from the Causer of procession, that is to say, from an originator. For to what other

Γρηγόριος ὁ μέγας οὐ Πατέρα μόνον, ἀλλὰ καὶ προβολέα τὴν μόνην πηγαίαν θεότητα καλεῖ; Οὐ Πατέρα μὲν γεννήματος, προβολέα δὲ προβλήματος; Ὥσπερ οὖν ἔχει τὸ γέννημα πρὸς τὸν γεννήσαντα, οὕτως ἔχει καὶ τὸ πρόβλημα πρὸς τὸν προβολέα ἑαυτοῦ, ἀμέσως δηλαδὴ ἑκάτερον. Ἐὰν δὲ τὸ πρόβλημα Πατρὸς λέγῃς, διὰ τὸν Υἱὸν ἐρεῖς.

57

Ἐβουλόμην δὲ καὶ περὶ τῆς "διὰ" διὰ πλειόνων δεῖξαι, ἀλλὰ τίς ἔτι χρεία λόγων, δι' αὐτοῦ τοῦ ἁγίου Πνεύματος ἡμῖν ἑρμηνευθείσης; Ἐγὼ γὰρ ἐξετάζων τίς ὁ πρῶτος εἰρηκὼς τὸ ἅγιον Πνεῦμα δι' Υἱοῦ, μᾶλλον δὲ τίς ὁ δι' ἐπιπνοίας θείας τοῦτο παραδοὺς ἡμῖν (οὐδεμίαν γὰρ λέξιν ἡ καθ' ἡμᾶς θεολογία φέρει μὴ διὰ θείας ἀποκαλύψεως τὴν ἀρχὴν ἐκπεφασμένην) ἐξετάζων οὖν ἐγὼ τίς ὁ πρῶτος οὗτος εἰρηκώς, τοῦτ' αὐτὸ περὶ ἑαυτοῦ τὸ Πνεῦμα τὸ ἅγιον διὰ τοῦ θεολογικωτάτου ἐν ἀποστόλοις Ἰωάννου, Γρηγορίῳ τῷ θαυματουργῷ τῆς τοῦ Θεοῦ μητρὸς προτρεψαμένης, ἀποκαλύφαν τε ὁμοῦ καὶ ἑρμηνεῦσαν εὗρον· καὶ ὁ συγγραφεὺς τοῦ Γρηγορίου θαυμασίου Βίου καὶ τῆς ἐν αὐτῷ ἀποκαλύψεως, ὁμώνυμός τε καὶ ἀξιόλογος οὐχ ἧττον, Γρηγόριος γάρ ἐστιν ὁ Νυσσαέων οὗτος, οὗ μικρὸν ἀνωτέρω διευκρινήσαντες τὴν ῥῆσιν ἐκ Πατρὸς δι' Υἱοῦ τὸ Πνεῦμα νοούμενον εὑρήκαμεν, ἀλλ' οὐκ ἐκπορευόμενον· ὃς εὖ ὅτι μάλιστα ποιῶν, αὐτοῖς ῥήμασι προΰθηκεν ἡμῖν τὴν ἀποκάλυψιν ἐκείνην οὕτω πως ἐν βραχεῖ διατρανοῦσαν τὰ τοῦ Πνεύματος· «ἓν γάρ», φησί, Πνεῦμα ἅγιον ἐκ Πατρὸς καὶ αὐτὸ τὴν ὕπαρξιν ἔχον καὶ δι' Υἱοῦ πεφηνός, δηλαδὴ τοῖς ἀνθρώποις». Ὁρᾷς πῶς χρὴ τὸ Πνεῦμα νοεῖν καὶ λέγειν δι' Υἱοῦ; Δηλονότι φανερωθὲν τοῖς ἀνθρώποις δι' αὐτοῦ. Οὕτω τοίνυν νόει καὶ αὐτὸς ὅπουπερ ἂν εὕρῃς διὰ τοῦ Υἱοῦ ἐκ τοῦ Πατρὸς τὸ Πνεῦμα διδόμενόν τε καὶ

purpose does Gregory the great, who is named after theology, name the sole source of divinity not 'Father' only, but also 'Originator'? Is He not, on the one hand, the Father of His Offspring, but on the other hand, the Originator of the Emanation? For just as the offspring relates to the begetter, in the same way will the emanation also relate to its originator,; that is, each one is immediately related. So if you say, "the Emanation of the Father", you will say it on account of the Son.

57

Now I wanted to demonstrate the meaning of the preposition "through" through more examples, yet what further need of arguments is there, as this has been interpreted for us through the Holy Spirit Himself? Because I, for my part, when examining who was the first to have said that the Holy Spirit is "through" the Son, or rather, who it was that has handed this tradition down to us through divine inspiration (for our theology bears no single word which has not been expressed at the very start through divine revelation)—so when I was examining who it was, the first man to have said this, I found the Holy Spirit Himself revealed and at the same time interpreted this very thing regarding His own self through John the most theological among the Apostles to Gregory the Wonderworker, following the exhortation of the Mother of God. The author of Gregory's wonderful biography and of the revelation therein, who shares the name and is no less worthy of mention, is Gregory of the Nyssans, whose saying we elucidated a short while ago and we found that the Spirit is considered but does not proceed from the Father through the Son. Doing it exceptionally well, he laid before us words for word that revelation, which thus very briefly explained the things of the Spirit. For he says, "One is the Holy Spirit, He too having His existence from the Father and manifested through the Son, that is to say, to men."[171] Do you see how it is that we must consider and say that the Spirit is through the Son? In other words, that He was manifested to men through Him. This is how you yourself should consider it, whenever you find that the Holy Spirit is given and sent from the Father through the Son.

πεμπόμενον, εἴγε μὴ ἀντίθεος ἐθέλεις εἶναι, ἀλλ᾿ ὁμοῦ καὶ θεοσεβὴς καὶ θεοδίδακτος.

58

Εἰ δὲ καὶ ἀντὶ τῆς "διὰ" τὴν "ἐκ" πρόθεσιν τιθέναι βούλοιο, μεμφόμεθά σε οὐδαμῶς, μόνον τἀληθὲς καὶ φρονῶν καὶ προστιθείς, ἐκ τοῦ Υἱοῦ φανερωθὲν ἡμῖν τὸ Πνεῦμα λέγε· ἂν δὲ τὴν τοῦ ἁγίου Πνεύματος ὕπαρξιν λέγῃς δι᾿ Υἱοῦ, ὡς ἐκ τοῦ Υἱοῦ ὑπάρχουσαν, ὡς ἐκτὸς ὑπάρχοντα τῆς εὐσεβείας καὶ τῆς ἐκκλησίας ἔξω στήσομεν· ἐπεὶ γὰρ «καὶ μεμαθήκαμεν Πνεῦμα θεῖον συμπαρομαρτοῦν τῷ λόγῳ, δύναμιν ὂν αὐτὴν ἐφ᾿ ἑαυτῆς ἐν ἰδιαζούσῃ ὑποστάσει θεωρουμένην, ἐκφαντικὴν τοῦ Λόγου, μὴ χωρισθῆναι τοῦ Θεοῦ ἐν ᾧ ἐστι καὶ τοῦ Λόγου, ᾧ παρομαρτεῖ δυναμένην», ὡς συνακολουθούσης ἀδιαστάτως τε καὶ ἀχρόνως τῇ γεννήσει τῆς ἐκπορεύσεως, πῶς τὴν "διὰ" ἐπὶ τῆς ἐκπορεύσεως εἰς τὴν "ἐκ" μεταλαμβάνοντες οὐχ ἁμαρτήσομεν; Εὐσεβῶς οὖν εἴπουπερ εὑρεθείη διὰ τοῦ Υἱοῦ ἐκπορευόμενον τὸ Πνεῦμα τὸ ἅγιον, οὐκ εἰς τὴν "ἐκ", ἀλλ᾿ εἰς τὴν "σὺν" πρόθεσιν τὴν "διὰ" νοήσομέν τε καὶ μεταληψόμεθα, μετὰ τοῦ τῆς θεολογίας ἐπωνύμου Γρηγορίου λέγοντος, «εἷς ἡμῖν Θεός, ὁ ἄναρχος Πατήρ· ἡ ἀρχὴ τῶν πάντων, ὁ Υἱὸς καὶ τὸ οὐκ ἐκ τῆς ἀρχῆς, ἀλλὰ σὺν τῇ ἀρχῇ καὶ μετὰ τῆς ἀρχῆς ἐκ τοῦ Πατρὸς Πνεῦμα ἅγιον». Διὸ καὶ αὐτὸς ὁ θεῖος Κύριλλος ἐν Θησαυροῖς ἐν Υἱῷ παρὰ Πατρὸς φυσικῶς ὑπάρχειν διὰ πολλῶν τὸ Πνεῦμα συμπεραίνει καὶ παρὰ Πατρὸς φυσικῶς τε καὶ οὐσιωδῶς διήκειν ἐν Υἱῷ τὸ Πνεῦμα γράφει, δι᾿ οὗ πάντα χρίων οὗτος ἁγιάζει· ἐκ μέν οὖν τοῦ Πατρὸς ἐν τῷ Υἱῷ διήκει ἀϊδίως, ἐκ δὲ τοῦ Πατρὸς διὰ τοῦ Υἱοῦ τοῖς ἁγιαζομένοις ἐγγίνεται, ἡνίκ᾿ ἂν δέοι.

That is, of course, if in fact you do not want to be against God, but rather desire to be God-fearing and God-instructed.

58

But should you prefer the preposition "from" to be inserted instead of "through", we shall not censure you at all. Only be mindful of the truth and insert it, and say that the Spirit has been manifested to us from the Son. But if you say that the Holy Spirit has existence through the Son, as though His existence exists from the Son, in this case, inasmuch as you exist outside of the pious understanding we shall also set you outside the church. For since "we have been taught that the divine Spirit accompanies the Word, being a power which is perceived individually in its own hypostasis, expressive of the Word, unable to be separated from God, in whom He is, or from the Word, whom He accompanies,"[172] inasmuch as the Son's begetting is accompanied by His own procession without distance and timelessly, how will we not sin if, regarding the procession, we convert the preposition "through" into "from"? So if in any place it should be found that the Holy Spirit proceeds through the Son, we shall devoutly understand and convert the preposition "through" not into the preposition "from" but into the preposition "with", along with Gregory, the namesake of theology, who says, "for us there is one God, the unoriginate Father; the Origin of all things, the Son, and He who is not from the Origin but is along with the Origin and together with the Origin from the Father, the Holy Spirit."[173] Wherefore the divine Cyril personally concludes through many examples in his Treasuries[174] that the Spirit naturally exists from the Father in the Son, and writes that the Spirit, naturally and essentially from the Father, pervades the Son, through whom He anoints and sanctifies all things. So while from the Father in the Son He pervades eternally, yet into those who are being sanctified He comes from the Father through the Son, whenever this should be demanded.

59

Καὶ τοῦτο δὲ σκοπεῖν τῶν ἀναγκαιοτάτων, ὡς ὅταν μηδὲν διαφέρῃ φάναι ἐκ τοῦ Πατρὸς διὰ τοῦ Υἱοῦ, καὶ ἐκ τοῦ Πατρὸς καὶ ἐκ τοῦ Υἱοῦ, καὶ τοῦτον τὸν τρόπον ἐπὶ τῆς θεολογίας ἰσοδυναμῶσιν ἀλλήλαις ἡ "ἐκ" καὶ ἡ "διά", οὐ τὴν διαίρεσιν οὐδὲ τὴν διαφορὰν παριστῶσι τῆς ἁγίας Τριάδος, ἀλλὰ τὴν ἕνωσιν καὶ τὴν ἀπαραλλαξίαν, ἥτις ἐστὶ κατὰ τὰ φυσικὰ ἰδιώματα, δεικνῦσα μιᾶς καὶ τῆς αὐτῆς ἐνεργείας καὶ θελήσεως εἶναι τὸν Πατέρα καὶ τὸν Υἱὸν καὶ τὸ Πνεῦμα τὸ ἅγιον.

Λατῖνοι δὲ τὴν διαφορὰν τῶν θείων ὑποστάσεων ἐκ τούτων ἐπιχειροῦσι δεικνύναι τῶν προθέσεων, καὶ ὡς ἐκ τῶν δύο ὑποστάσεων καὶ παρ᾽ ἑκατέρας τούτων διαφόρως ἔχει τὴν ὑπόστασιν τὸ Πνεῦμα. Φανερὸν οὖν ὡς ἐν μὲν τοῖς ἁγίοις αἱ προθέσεις ἔχουσιν εὐσεβῶς τε καὶ καλῶς, ἐκλαμβάνονται δ᾽ αὗται παρὰ τῶν Λατίνων κακῶς καὶ δυσσεβῶς. Ὅτι δὲ τὴν ἕνωσιν καὶ τὸ ἀπαράλλακτον ἡ τοιαύτη δείκνυσι "διά", παρίστησι σαφῶς ὁ μέγας Βασίλειος γράφων ἐν ὀγδόῳ τῶν Πρὸς Ἀμφιλόχιον· «τὸ διὰ τοῦ Υἱοῦ δημιουργεῖν τὸν Πατέρα οὔτε ἀτελῆ τοῦ Πατρὸς τὴν δημιουργίαν συνίστησιν, οὔτε ἄτονον τοῦ Υἱοῦ παραδηλοῖ τὴν ἐνέργειαν, ἀλλὰ τὸ ἡνωμένον τοῦ θελήματος παρίστησιν·»

60

Ὁ γοῦν λέγων διὰ τοῦ Υἱοῦ καὶ ἐκ τοῦ Υἱοῦ τὸ Πνεῦμα προϊέναι κατὰ τὴν χορηγίαν, τὴν ὁμοβουλίαν τοῦ Πατρὸς καὶ τοῦ Υἱοῦ παρέστησε καλῶς· εὐδοκίᾳ γὰρ τοῦ Πατρὸς καὶ τοῦ Υἱοῦ καὶ αὐτὸ συνευδοκοῦν, τοῖς ἀξίοις χορηγεῖται τὸ Πνεῦμα τὸ ἅγιον. Ὁ δὲ λέγων διὰ τοῦ Υἱοῦ καὶ ἐκ τοῦ Υἱοῦ τὴν ὕπαρξιν τὸ Πνεῦμα ἔχειν, θελήσεως ἔργον καὶ κτίσμα ἐξ ἀνάγκης, ἀλλ᾽ οὐ θείας φύσεως καρπὸν ὑπάρχειν δυσσεβῶς παρίστησι τὸ Πνεῦμα τὸ ἅγιον. Κατὰ γὰρ τὸν ἱερὸν Δαμασκηνόν, ἔργον θείας θελήσεως ἡ κτίσις, ἀλλ᾽ οὐχ ἡ θεότης, ἄπαγε· οὐδὲ γὰρ τῆς θελήσεως, ἀλλὰ τῆς θείας φύσεως ἔργον, αὖθις κατὰ τὸν αὐτόν, ἡ προαιώνιος καὶ ἀΐδιος γέννησίς τε καὶ ἐκπόρευσις.

59

This also is one the things most needful to examine, that whenever it makes no difference to say "from the Father through the Son" and "from the Father and from the Son" and when in theology, in this way, the "from" and the "through" are equal to each other, this does not prove the division or difference of the Holy Trinity but rather the union and the indistinguishability, which pertains to the natural characteristics and which thus shows that the Father and the Son and the Holy Spirit are of one and the same energy and will.

But from these prepositions the Latins endeavor to show the difference of the divine hypostases, and that the Spirit has His hypostasis from two hypostases and from each of them differently. It is clear, then, that while the prepositions stand fast piously and soundly with the saints, yet they are understood unsoundly and irreverently by the Latins. And Basil the Great clearly proves that a word like "through" displays the union and the immutability, when he writes in his eighth chapter *To Amphilochius*, "The fact that the Father creates through the Son neither causes the Father's creation to be imperfect nor implies that the Son's activity is weak; rather it presents the union of their will."[175]

60

So whoever says that the Holy Spirit comes forth through the Son and from the Son according to the supply has soundly presented the mutual will of the Father and the Son; for the Holy Spirit is supplied to those who are worthy by the good will of the Father and of the Son and by His own joint good will. But one who says that the Spirit has existence through the Son and from the Son irreverently presents the Spirit as a work of will and a creature by necessity, not as the fruit of the divine nature. According to the sacred Damascene,[176] the creation is a work of divine will, but not the divinity, away with the thought! For, again according to the same Father, neither is the pre-eternal and ever-lasting begetting and procession a work of will but rather of the divine nature.

Πῶς δὲ καὶ φῂς αὐτὸς ἐκ τοῦ Πατρὸς εἶναι τὸ Πνεῦμα δι' Υἱοῦ καὶ ἐξ Υἱοῦ ὁ λατινικῶς φρονῶν; Ἡμεῖς μὲν γὰρ τὴν φανέρωσιν ὑπὸ χρόνον οὖσαν ἴσμεν, πάντα δὲ τὰ ὑπὸ χρόνον ὄντα διὰ τοῦ Υἱοῦ γενόμενα· διὸ καί φανεροῦσθαι μὲν ἐξ αὐτοῦ καὶ δι' αὐτοῦ φαμεν τὸ Πνεῦμα, ἀλλ' οὐκ ἐκπορεύεσθαι. Σὺ δὲ πῶς λέγεις τὸ Πνεῦμα δι' αὐτοῦ; Εἰ μὲν διαβατικῶς τε καὶ παροδικῶς, βαβαὶ τῆς ἀσεβείας· ὡς γὰρ διὰ σωλῆνος οἴει τοῦ Υἱοῦ διέρχεσθαι τὸ Πνεῦμα καὶ κενὸν ἑαυτοῦ τοίνυν ἕξει μεταξὺ ὁ πληρῶν τὰ πάντα καὶ πλήρης ὢν ἀεί· καὶ ὡς ἐν τόπῳ τῷ Υἱῷ περιληφθήσεται τὸ Πνεῦμα καὶ πέρας ἔσται τοῦ Υἱοῦ, καθ' ὃ τὸ Πνεῦμα περιλήψεται (πέρας γὰρ τοῦ περιέχοντος ὁ τόπος), καὶ φύσεως δὲ οὐκ ἔσται τῆς αὐτῆς τῷ Πνεύματι· καὶ γὰρ οὐχ ἡ αὐτὴ τόπου φύσις καὶ τοῦ ἐν αὐτῷ. Πῶς δὲ καὶ αὐτὸς ὁ Υἱός ἐστιν ἐν τῷ παροδικῶς δι' αὐτοῦ διερχομένῳ Πνεύματι;

61

Εἰ δ' ὡς δι ὀργάνου, καὶ τοῦτο ἀσεβές· ἄλλη γὰρ ὀργάνου φύσις καὶ τοῦ δι' ἐκείνου ἄλλη· καὶ αὖθις ἑτέρα τοῦ δι' αὐτοῦ τὸ τελούμενον τελοῦντος. Οὐκοῦν τοῦτό σοι λέγειν ἔτι λείπεται, ὅτι καθάπερ δι' αὐτοῦ τὰ πάντα ἐκ Πατρός, οὐ διαβατικῶς ἀλλὰ δημιουργικῶς, οὐχ ὡς δι' ὀργάνου ἀλλ' ὡς συνδημιουργοῦντος, οὕτω καὶ τὸ Πνεῦμα δι' αὐτοῦ. Ὁρᾷς ποῦ κατάγεις, ὦ οὗτος, τὸ ἀνωτάτω Πνεῦμα καὶ τίσι συντάττεις τὸν ἐπὶ πάντων Θεόν; Ἀλλ' οὐχ ὡς συνδημιουργοῦντος λέγω, φησίν, ἀλλ' ὡς συνεκπορεύοντος. Οὐκοῦν συνεκπορεῦον καὶ τὸ Πνεῦμα τελειώσει ἑαυτὸ ὥσπερ κἀκεῖ συνδημιουργοῦν τελεσιουργεῖ τὰ πάντα· μᾶλλον δὲ οὐχ ἑαυτό, ἀλλ' ἕτερον ἀπαράλλακτον αὐτοῦ ἐν ἰδίᾳ ὑποστάσει θεωρούμενον· καὶ τοῦ Πατρὸς γὰρ δι' Υἱοῦ ἐν

But how do you yourself, O Latin-minded, say that the Spirit is from the Father through the Son and from the Son? For we know that the manifestation is temporal, but we also know that all temporal things came to be through the Son. And so while we say that the Spirit is manifested from Him and through Him, we do not say that He proceeds from or through Him. So how is it you say the Spirit is through Him? If you mean it transitively, in the sense of crossing through or passing by, what impiety! For you think that the Spirit passes through the Son as through a channel. But then He who fills all things and is ever complete will be empty of Himself in between, and the Spirit will be circumscribed as in a location in the Son, and the area in which the Spirit will be circumscribed will be the boundary of the Son (for a place is the boundary of its container[177]), and the Son will not be of the same nature as the Spirit, for the nature of a place is not the same as the nature of what is in it. Furthermore, how can the Son Himself be in the Spirit that passes through Him transiently?

61

But if He is as it were through an instrument, this also is irreverent. For the nature of an instrument is one thing and the nature of what is done through it is something different; and again the nature of him that executes what is done through it is also different. So what still is left for you to say is this, that just as all things are from the Father through Him, not transitively but creatively, not as through an instrument but as through a co-creator, this is also how the Spirit is through Him. Do you see, O man, to where you degrade the most high Spirit and with what things you classify the God over all? Nevertheless, he says, "I am referring to Him not as co-creator but as co-processor." Consequently if the Spirit also jointly causes procession, He will also in effect complete Himself, just as in jointly creating He brings all things to completion. Rather He will not complete Himself but some other spirit, indistinguishable from Himself and contemplated in his own hypostasis. Besides, what has been given substance is something altogether different from the

ἁγίῳ Πνεύματι δημιουργοῦντος ἕτερον παντάπασι τὸ ὑφιστάμενον, καὶ τοῦ Πατρὸς πρὸ τῶν αἰώνων γεννῶντός τε καὶ ἐκπορεύοντος, εἰ καὶ ὁμοούσια τὰ παρ' ἑαυτοῦ, ἀλλ' ἑκάτερον ἕτερον αὐτοῦ τε καὶ ἀλλήλων καθ' ὑπόστασιν.

62

Εἰ δέ τις εὕρηται μείζω λέγων τὸν Υἱὸν τοῦ Πνεύματος, ἀλλὰ καὶ τὸ Πνεῦμα τοῦ Υἱοῦ, ὡς καὶ ὁ θεῖος Κύριλλος ἐν Θησαυροῖς φησι· προθεὶς γὰρ ἐκεῖνο τὸ παρὰ τοῦ Σωτῆρος εἰρημένον, «εἰ δὲ ἐγὼ ἐν Πνεύματι Θεοῦ ἐκβάλλω τὰ δαιμόνια», ἐπήνεγκεν, «εἰ διὰ τῆς ἐνεργείας τοῦ Πνεύματος Θεὸς ἐξελαύνων τὰ δαιμόνια δοξάζεται, πῶς οὐ μεῖζόν ἐστι αὐτοῦ, τὸ ἐν ᾧ δοξάζεται»; Κατασκευάζων ἐντεῦθεν ἄκτιστον εἶναι τὸ Πνεῦμα τό ἅγιον. Πῶς γὰρ ἂν ἐπὶ κτίσματος ἔμφασιν ἐξ ὧν εἶπεν ὁ Κύριος παρεῖχε τοῦ τοιούτου μείζονος; Λέγεται δὲ τὰ τοιαῦτα ἐπί τε τοῦ Υἱοῦ καὶ τοῦ Πνεύματος οὐ διὰ τὸ ἀλλήλων αἴτια ὑπάρχειν, ἄπαγε, ἀλλὰ διὰ τὸ ποικίλον καὶ πολυειδὲς τῆς κατὰ τὴν πρὸς ἡμᾶς οἰκονομίαν σοφίας τοῦ Θεοῦ δι' ἀλλήλων τὸ ἴσον ἐν πᾶσι δεικνύσης ἀμφοτέρων, τοῦ Υἱοῦ λέγω καὶ τοῦ Πνεύματος.

Ἀλλ' ὁ τῆς Ἀλεξανδρείας, φασί, Κύριλλος, ἔχειν φησὶ τὸν Υἱὸν φυσικῶς ἐν ἑαυτῷ τὰ τοῦ Πατρὸς ἴδια καὶ ἐξαίρετα, διαβαινούσης εἰς αὐτὸν φυσικῶς τῆς τοῦ γεννήσαντος ἰδιότητος, καὶ ἐκ τῆς οὐσίας τοῦ Υἱοῦ τὸ Πνεῦμα λέγει καὶ προχεόμενον ἐκ Πατρὸς δι' Υἱοῦ τὴν κτίσιν ἁγιάζειν, καὶ ἐξ ἀμφοῖν προχεόμενον οὐσιωδῶς. Καὶ αὖθις ἐν ἑβδόμῳ τῶν Πρὸς Ἑρμείαν ἐξενηνεγμένων λόγων περὶ τοῦ Υἱοῦ ταῦθ' ἡμῖν διατρανοῖ· «ἀπολύων γάρ», φησίν, «ἁμαρτίας τὸν αὐτῷ προσκείμενον, τῷ ἰδίῳ λοιπὸν καταχρίει Πνεύματι, ὅπερ ἐνίησι μὲν αὐτὸς ὡς ἐκ Θεοῦ Πατρὸς Λόγος καὶ ἐξ ἰδίας ἡμῖν ἀναπηγάζει φύσεως. Καὶ οὐκ ἐκ μέτρου ἔχων δίδωσι τὸ Πνεῦμα κατὰ τὴν Ἰωάννου φωνήν, ἀλλ' αὐτὸς ἐνίησιν ἐξ ἑαυτοῦ, καθάπερ ἀμέλει καὶ ὁ Πατήρ».

Father who creates through the Son in the Holy Spirit, and, when the Father both begets and causes processes before the ages, although the two that issues from His own self are consubstantial, yet each is different from Him and from each other in respect to hypostasis.

62

But if someone may be found saying that the Son is greater than the Spirit, yet another is found saying that the Spirit is greater than the Son, as Cyril the divine says in his *Treasuries*. For after he quoted the saying spoken by the Savior, "but if I cast out devils by the Spirit of God,"[178] he made a further inference: "If God is glorified in driving demons out by the energy of the Spirit, how is that by which He is glorified not greater than Him?" From this premise he argues that the Holy Spirit is uncreated. For how could the Lord, with what He said, have bestowed the distinction of being in this way greater to a creature? Such things are said about both the Son and the Spirit not because they are each other's causes — away with the thought! — but because of the variety and many forms of the wisdom of God in His dispensation toward us, showing by each other the equality of both in all things — I am speaking of the Son and the Spirit.

"But," they say, "Cyril of Alexandria says that the Son naturally has in Himself the properties and exceptional characteristics of the Father, that the particular property of the one who begat is naturally communicated to Him, that the Spirit is from the substance of the Son, that being poured forth from the Father through the Son He sanctifies the creation, and that He is essentially[179] poured forth from both.[180] And once again in the seventh chapter of his published treatises *To Hermias* concerning the Son He makes the same point thoroughly clear, saying, 'In releasing from sin the one attached to Him, He anoints him by His own Spirit, which He Himself indeed infuses, as being the Word from God the Father, and which from His own nature He springs forth to us. And He gives the Spirit not as having Him by measure, according to the declaration of John,[181] but He Himself infuses from Himself, as the Father also does.'"[182]

63

Καιρὸς δὴ ἡμῖν εἰπεῖν πρὸς τὸν τὰ τοιαῦτα προβαλλόμενον· ἔτ᾽ ἀσύνετος εἶ καὶ οὐδ᾽ ἀκηκοὼς πάνυ πολλάκις ἀνωτέρω παρ᾽ ἡμῶν συνῆκας, ὅτι Θεὸς καὶ ἐκ Θεοῦ ὕπαρξις ἀναίτιός τε καὶ ὑπέρχρονος; Ἐνταῦθα γὰρ προχεόμενόν φησι καὶ τὴν κτίσιν ἁγιάζον. Χρονικὸν τοίνυν καὶ δι᾽ αἰτίαν ἀκούων τὸ προχεῖσθαι (καὶ γὰρ μετ᾽ αὐτὴν καὶ δι᾽ αὐτὴν προκέχυται τὴν ἁγιαζομένην· πῶς γὰρ οὔ;), πρὸς δὲ καὶ εἰς ἄφεσιν ἁμαρτιῶν διδόμενον παρὰ τοῦ Υἱοῦ, ὥσπερ ἀμέλει καὶ παρὰ τοῦ Πατρός, καὶ οὐκ ἀπολύτως πηγαζόμενον ἀλλὰ τισὶν ἀκούων, οὐκ ἀναμιμνήσκῃ ὃ διδαχθεὶς ἔχεις παρ᾽ ἡμῶν τε καὶ τῆς ἀληθείας, ὡς ἡ παρὰ τοῦ Πατρὸς προαιώνιος τοῦ ἁγίου Πνεύματος ἐκπόρευσις οὐ διά τι οὐδὲ πρός τινας οὔτε ὑπὸ χρόνον ὅλως; Εἰ δὲ καὶ οὐσιωδῶς ἐξ ἀμφοῖν εἶπε προχεόμενον, οὐδὲν καινόν. Ὡς γὰρ ἐπιδημοῦν τοῖς ἀποστόλοις καὶ ἐνεργοῦν τελεώτερον, καὶ ὡς Γρηγόριος ὁ θεολόγος λέγει, «οὐσιωδῶς ὡς ἂν εἴποι τις παρὸν καὶ συμπολιτευόμενον». Τί δέ, οὐκ οὐσιώδης ἦν καὶ ἡ πρὸς ἡμᾶς ἀποστολὴ τοῦ Λόγου, ἐξ ἀμφοῖν τοῦ Πατρὸς γενομένη καὶ τοῦ Πνεύματος; Ἀλλ᾽ ἡ ἀποστολὴ γέννησις οὐκ ἦν· οὐ γὰρ ἐξ ἀμφοῖν ὁ Υἱὸς γεγέννηται, οὐδὲ δι᾽ ἡμᾶς, ἀλλ᾽ οὐδὲ μεθ᾽ ἡμᾶς, εἰ καὶ μεθ᾽ ἡμᾶς δι᾽ ἡμᾶς οὐσιωδῶς κατῆλθεν ἑνωθεὶς τῇ καθ᾽ ἡμᾶς φύσει καθ᾽ ὑπόστασιν καὶ γεγονὼς καθ᾽ ἡμᾶς ὑπὲρ ἡμῶν, μὴ πρὸ ἡμῶν μόνον, ἀλλὰ καὶ πρὸ τῶν αἰώνων, ἐκ μόνου τοῦ Πατρὸς γεγεννημένος ὤν. Καὶ τὸ Πνεῦμα τοίνυν τὸ ἅγιον οὐσιωδῶς ἐπέμφθη ἐξ ἀμφοῖν ἀρτίως, εἰ δὲ βούλει, καὶ ἐκκέχυται παρ᾽ ἀμφοτέρων· ὕδωρ γὰρ ἐκλήθη ζῶν. Καὶ «Ἰωάννης μὲν ἐβάπτισεν ὕδατι· ὑμεῖς δέ, φησὶν ὁ Κύριος, βαπτισθήσεσθε ἐν Πνεύματι ἁγίῳ». Πῶς ἂν οὖν ἐβαπτίσθησαν, μὴ τοῦ ζῶντος ἐκχυθέντος ὕδατος;

64

Ἐκκέχυται τοίνυν οὐσιωδῶς δι᾽ ἡμᾶς καὶ μεθ᾽ ἡμᾶς· αὐτὸ γὰρ

63

At this point, it is time for us to address the individual who advances such ideas: are you still without understanding and have not understood very well what has been said many times by us further up, that God and the existence from God is without cause and transcends time? For in this passage Cyril says that He is poured forth and sanctifies creation. Therefore when you hear that the pouring forth is temporal and for a cause (since He is poured forth after and because of the creation that is being sanctified, for how could it be otherwise?), and furthermore that He is given from the Son for the remission of sins (just as He is also given from the Father of course), and when you hear that He springs forth not absolutely but to certain individuals, do you not remember what you have been taught from us and from the truth, namely that the pre-eternal procession of the Holy Spirit from the Father is not for a cause nor to certain people nor temporal at all? Now if he said that He is poured forth from both essentially, this is no innovation. For He is poured forth as sojourning with the Apostles and working more perfectly in them, as Gregory the Theologian also says: "One could say He is essentially present and residing with us".[183] Why, was the sending of the Word to us not essential? Was it not from both the Father and the Spirit? The sending, however, was not a begetting. For the Son has not been begotten from both. He was begotten only from the Father, not on account of us, nor after us, but before the ages. Then, after us, because of us, He descended essentially, when He became united to our nature hypostatically and had become like us for our sake. So the Holy Spirit was also sent essentially, perfectly, from both, or, if you prefer, has been poured forth from both; for He has been called living water.[184] "John indeed baptized with water," says the Lord, "but you will be baptized with the Holy Spirit."[185] How else would they have been baptized, unless living water had been poured forth?

64

So He has been poured forth essentially for us and after us. For

ἐφανερώθη δι' ἑαυτοῦ τὴν θείαν δύναμιν παρέχον, ἀλλὰ καὶ
πάρεστιν ἀεὶ οὐσιωδῶς ἡμῖν, πάντως δὲ καὶ καθ' ὑπόστασιν, κἂν
ἡμεῖς τῆς οὐσίας ἢ τῆς ὑποστάσεως ἥκιστα μετέχωμεν, ἀλλὰ τῆς
χάριτος. Ἐκπορεύεται δὲ οὐ πρὸ ἡμῶν μόνον, ἀλλὰ καὶ πρὸ τῶν
αἰώνων ἀναιτίως ἐκ μόνου τοῦ Πατρός. Ὁ δὲ τῆς ἐκκλησίας ἐν
ταὐτῷ καὶ θεμέλιος καὶ κορυφαῖος Πέτρος καὶ αὐτῆς τῆς παρ'
ἀμφοτέρων ἐκχύσεως τοῦ ἁγίου Πνεύματος διαφορὰν ἐγνώρισεν
ἡμῖν· «τὴν γὰρ ἐπαγγελίαν τοῦ Πνεύματος ὁ Υἱὸς λαβών, φησί,
παρὰ τοῦ Πατρός, ἐξέχεε τοῦτο ὃ νῦν ὑμεῖς βλέπετε καὶ ἀκούετε»,
ἄντικρυς ἐκείνην λέγων τοῦ Κυρίου καὶ διδασκάλου τὴν φωνήν,
«ὅταν δὲ ἔλθῃ ὁ παράκλητος, ὃν ἐγὼ πέμψω παρὰ τοῦ Πατρός».

Ἐκχεῖται τοιγαροῦν ἡμῖν τὸ Πνεῦμα παρὰ τοῦ Πατρὸς ὡς καὶ
ἑαυτοῦ, παρὰ δὲ τοῦ Υἱοῦ ὡς παρὰ τοῦ Πατρὸς λαμβάνοντος.
Ὥστε, οὐκ ἐξ ἑαυτοῦ μὲν ἔχει τὸ Πνεῦμα ὁ Υἱός, οὐδὲ διὰ τοῦ
Υἱοῦ τὴν ὕπαρξιν τὸ Πνεῦμα ἔχει, ἀλλ' ἐξ ἑαυτοῦ ἔχει ὁ Πατήρ, ἐξ
ἑαυτοῦ ἀμέσως ἐκπορευόμενον ἀναιτίως καὶ προαιωνίως· ἀλλὰ καὶ
ἐκ τῆς ἰδίας ἡμῖν, φησί, ὁ Υἱὸς τοῦτ' ἀναπηγάζει φύσεως, εἰκότως
καὶ παναληθῶς· μία γὰρ φύσις τοῖς τρισὶ καὶ φυσικῶς ἔνεισιν
ἀλλήλοις. Καὶ ὁσάκις ὁ θεόφρων οὗτος Κύριλλος ἐκ τῆς οὐσίας τοῦ
Υἱοῦ τό Πνεῦμα λέγει, τὸ ὁμοούσιον παρίστησιν, ἀλλ' οὐκ αἴτιον
εἶναι τὸν Υἱὸν τοῦ Πνεύματος. Ἐπεὶ καὶ πρὸς τοὺς ἀντιλέγοντας
τῷ ὁμοουσίῳ τὰ τοιαῦτα γέγραφεν· ὕδωρ μὲν γὰρ ζῶν καλεῖται τὸ
Πνεῦμα τὸ ἅγιον καὶ πηγή ἐστι τούτου τοῦ ὕδατος ὁ Πατήρ, ὃς διὰ
τοῦ προφήτου περὶ τῶν Ἰουδαίων λέγει· «ἐμὲ ἐγκατέλιπον πηγὴν
ὕδατος ζῶντος καὶ ὤρυξαν ἑαυτοῖς λάκκους συντετριμμένους».

65

Πηγή ἐστι τούτου τοῦ ὕδατος καὶ ὁ Υἱός, καθὰ καὶ ὁ Χρυσόστομος
περὶ τοῦ βαπτίσματος γράφων, «δείκνυσι», φησίν, «ἑαυτὸν ὁ σωτὴρ
πηγὴν ζωῆς καὶ ὕδωρ ζῶν τὸ Πνεῦμα τὸ ἅγιον». Ἀλλὰ τοῦ ὕδατος

He was manifested through Himself, providing the divine power; but He is also always present with us essentially, certainly in His hypostasis as well, even though we do not partake in the least of His essence or hypostasis, but of His grace. In contrast, He proceeds not only before us but also before the ages causelessly from only the Father. Peter, simultaneously both the foundation and the pinnacle of the Church, made known to us the distinction of the pouring forth of the Holy Spirit from both. For, he says, "Having received the promise of the Spirit from the Father, the Son poured forth this which ye now see and hear,"[186] boldly repeating the statement of the Lord and Teacher, that "when the Comforter is come, whom I will send unto you from the Father."[187]

And so the Spirit is poured forth to us from the Father as also from Himself, and from the Son since the Son receives Him from the Father. As a result, the Son does not possess the Spirit of Himself, neither does the Spirit have existence through the Son; the Father, however, does have the Spirit of Himself, proceeding from Himself immediately, causelessly, and pre-eternally. But he also says that the Son springs Him forth to us as from a well from His own nature. This makes sense and is completely truly, for the nature of the three is one and they naturally inhere in one another. Further, as many times as this God-bearer Cyril says that the Spirit is from the Son, he is presenting Him as consubstantial, not that the Son is the cause of the Spirit. This follows, as he has written things like this to those who were disputing the consubstantiality. Consequently the Holy Spirit indeed is called living water, and the Father is the fount of this water,[188] who says through the prophets concerning the Jews, "they have forsaken me the fountain of living waters, and hewed them out broken cisterns."[189]

65

The Son is a fount of this water as well, as when Chrysostom writes about baptism, "the Savior points to His own self as the fount of life and to the Holy Spirit as the living water."[190] But Christ shows that

τούτου πηγὴν εἶναι δείκνυσιν ὁ Χριστὸς καὶ αὐτὸ τὸ Πνεῦμα τὸ ἅγιον· «ὁ πιὼν γάρ», φησίν, «ἐκ τοῦ ὕδατος οὗ ἐγὼ δώσω αὐτῷ, οὐ μὴ διψήσῃ εἰς τὸν αἰῶνα· ἀλλὰ τὸ ὕδωρ ὃ ἐγὼ δώσω, δηλαδὴ τὸ Πνεῦμα τὸ ἅγιον, γενήσεται αὐτῷ πηγὴ ὕδατος ἁλλομένου εἰς ζωὴν αἰώνιον».

Ἔστιν οὖν καὶ ὁ Πατὴρ καὶ ὁ Υἱὸς καὶ τὸ Πνεῦμα τὸ ἅγιον ὁμοῦ πηγὴ τοῦ ζῶντος ὕδατος, τουτέστι τῆς θείας χάριτος καὶ ἐνεργείας τοῦ Πνεύματος. Τὴν χάριν γὰρ τοῦ Πνεύματος ἡ Γραφή, ὁ Χρυσόστομός φησι πατήρ, ποτὲ μὲν πῦρ, ποτὲ δὲ ὕδωρ καλεῖ δεικνῦσα ὅτι οὐ οὐσίας ἐστὶ ταῦτα ὀνόματα, ἀλλ’ ἐνεργείας». Οὐ γὰρ ἐκ διαφόρων οὐσιῶν συνέστηκε τὸ Πνεῦμα τὸ ἅγιον, ἀόρατόν τε καὶ μονοειδὲς ὄν. «Ἀλλ’ ἐκ τῆς θείας φύσεως», φασί, «καὶ αὐτῆς τῆς τοῦ Υἱοῦ ἀναπηγάζει τὸ Πνεῦμα τὸ ἅγιον». Ἔστω δή, εἰ βούλεσθε, καὶ κατὰ τὴν ἀΐδιον ὕπαρξιν· πηγάζει γοῦν ἐκ τῆς θείας φύσεως, ἀλλὰ καθ’ ὑπόστασιν μόνην τὴν πατρικήν. Διὸ οὐδεὶς οὐδέποτε τῶν ἀπ’ αἰῶνος εὐσεβῶν θεολόγων ἐκ τῆς ὑποστάσεως εἶναι τοῦ Υἱοῦ τὸ Πνεῦμα εἶπεν, ἀλλ’ ἐκ τῆς τοῦ Πατρὸς ὑποστάσεως· ἐκ δὲ τῆς φύσεως τοῦ Υἱοῦ καὶ φυσικῶς εἶναι ἐξ αὐτοῦ εἴπερ τις φαίη, ἀλλ’ ὡς μιᾶς καὶ τῆς αὐτῆς φύσεως οὔσης τοῦ Πατρὸς καὶ τοῦ Υἱοῦ.

Ἵνα γὰρ κατ’ αὐτὸν εἴπω τὸν θεῖον Κύριλλον, ὡς αὐτὸς Πρὸς Ἑρμείαν γράφει, «οὐχ ἕτερος ἂν ὁ Υἱὸς εἶναι νοοῖτο παρὰ τὸν Πατέρα, ὅσον εἰς ταὐτότητα φυσικήν, πάντως δὲ καὶ τὸ Πνεῦμα τὸ ἅγιον», ὡς καὶ περὶ τούτου ὁ αὐτὸς ἐξηγούμενος ἐκεῖνο τὸ εὐαγγελικόν, «οὐ γὰρ λαλήσει ἀφ’ ἑαυτοῦ», φησίν, «οὐδὲν ἕτερον παρὰ τὸν Υἱὸν ὑπάρχει τὸ Πνεῦμα τὸ ἅγιον, ὅσον εἰς ταὐτότητα φύσεως». «Πηγὴ δέ ἐστι ζωῆς, κατὰ τὸν μέγαν Διονύσιον, ἡ θεία φύσις εἰς ἑαυτὴν χεομένη καὶ ἐφ’ ἑαυτῆς ἑστῶσα καὶ ἀεὶ δι’ ἑαυτῆς θεωμένη».

the Holy Spirit Himself is a fount of this water as well, for he says, "whosoever drinketh from the water that I shall give him shall never thirst; but the water that I shall give, namely, the Holy Spirit, shall become in him a well of water springing up into everlasting life."[191]

Therefore, the Father, and the Son, and the Holy Spirit, are at the same time a fount of living water, that is, of the divine grace and energy of the Spirit. For the golden-mouthed father says that the Scripture calls the grace of the Spirit sometimes fire, sometimes water, showing that these names are not referring to the essence but to the energy.[192] For the Holy Spirit is not comprised of different essences, since it is invisible and of one form. "But," they counter, "the Holy Spirit springs forth from the divine nature, and this is the Son's, as well)." Let it be referring even to His eternal existence, if you so prefer. So, He springs forth from the divine nature, but only from the paternal hypostasis. For this reason no one among the devout theologians at any time since time began said that the Spirit is from the hypostasis of the Son, but rather said that He is from the hypostasis of the Father. And if by chance someone might say that He is from the nature of the Son and naturally from Him, yet he would say this insofar as the nature of the Father and of the Son is one and the same.

Let me speak in accord with Cyril the divine himself, as he writes *To Hermias*: "The Son would not be considered to be different from the Father, insofar as natural identity, and certainly not different from the Holy Spirit."[193] About this matter, when exegeting that passage in the Gospel, "for He shall not speak of Himself,"[194] this same man says, "The Holy Spirit does not exist as something different from the Son, insofar as identity of nature."[195] And according to the great Dionysius, "A fount of life is the divine nature, diffused into Itself, and resting in Itself, and ever contemplated through Itself."[196]

66

Ἀλλ' οὐκ ἔστι, φησίν, ἐκ τῆς οὐσίας τοῦ Υἱοῦ εἶναι τὸ Πνεῦμα καὶ ἐκ τῆς ὑποστάσεως αὐτοῦ μὴ εἶναι· οὐ γὰρ συνορῶσιν, ὡς, ὅταν τι μιᾶς μὲν οὐσίας ᾖ καὶ ὑποστάσεως, τὸ ἐξ ἐκείνης τῆς οὐσίας ἔχον ὁπωσδήποτε τὴν ὕπαρξιν καὶ ἐκ τῆς ὑποστάσεως ἐκείνης ταύτην ἔχει, καὶ ἀντιστρόφως· ὃ γὰρ ἂν ἐκ τῆς ὑποστάσεως ἐκείνης ᾖ καὶ ἐκ τῆς οὐσίας ἐκείνης ἐστίν. Ὅταν δέ τι μιᾶς μὲν οὐσίας ᾖ, οὐ μιᾶς δὲ ὑποστάσεως, ἀλλὰ πλειόνων, τὸ ἐκ τῆς μιᾶς ἐκείνης οὐσίας οὐκ ἐκ τῶν λοιπῶν αὐτῆς ὑποστάσεών ἐστιν, ἀλλ' ἐκ μιᾶς τινος αὐτῶν. Ἐπεὶ γοῦν ἡ ἀνωτάτω καὶ προσκυνητὴ Τριὰς ἡμῖν μία φύσις ἐστὶν ἐν ὑποστάσεσι τρισίν, οὐχὶ τὸ ἐκ τῆς οὐσίας τὴν ὑπόστασιν ἔχον ἐκ τῶν ὑπολοίπων ὑποστάσεών ἐστιν, ἀλλ' ἐκ μιᾶς τινος αὐτῶν, δηλαδὴ τῆς πατρικῆς· ἐκ ταύτης γὰρ μὴ εἶναι οὐκ ἐνδέχεται, οὐκοῦν οὐχὶ καὶ ἐξ ἑτέρας, ἀλλ' ἐκ μόνης, εἴπερ ἐκ μιᾶς.

Καὶ τοῦτο δῆλον ἀπὸ τῶν ἀνθρώπων· ἕκαστος γὰρ ἡμῶν ἐκ τῆς οὐσίας μὲν ἔστι τοῦ Ἀδάμ, οὐκ ἔστι δὲ καὶ ἐκ τῆς ὑποστάσεως αὐτοῦ, διότι μία μὲν οὐσία τῶν ἀνθρώπων νῦν, πολλαὶ δὲ ὑποστάσεις. Ἀνθρωπίνης δὲ τὴν ἀρχὴν μιᾶς οὔσης οὐσίας τε καὶ ὑποστάσεως, τῆς τοῦ Ἀδάμ, ἐκ τῆς οὐσίας τοῦ Ἀδὰμ ἡ Εὔα οὖσα, καὶ ἐκ τῆς ὑποστάσεως ἐκείνου ἦν. Ἀλλὰ καὶ πρὶν τὸν Κάϊν εἶναι, μιᾶς οὔσης ἀνδρικῆς οὐσίας τε καὶ ὑποστάσεως, ἐκ μιᾶς καὶ τῆς αὐτῆς ὁ Κάϊν ἀνδρικῆς οὐσίας τε καὶ ὑποστάσεως ὑπῆρχε, τοῦ Ἀδάμ· δυοῖν δὲ ἀνδρῶν ἤδη καθ' ὑπόστασιν τελούντων, ὁ τοῦ Κάϊν Ἐνὼχ ἐκ τῆς οὐσίας μὲν ὑπῆρχε τοῦ Ἀδάμ, ἀλλ' οὐχὶ καὶ ἐκ τῆς ὑποστάσεως αὐτοῦ, ἀλλ' ἐκ μόνης τῆς τοῦ Κάϊν.

Οἱ γοῦν λατινικῶς φρονοῦντες διατεινόμενοι καὶ ἐκ τῆς ὑποστάσεως εἶναι τοῦ Υἱοῦ τὸ Πνεῦμα, εἴπερ εἶναι θεολογεῖται ἐκ τῆς φύσεως, πλὴν τοῦ θείου Πνεύματος, μίαν εἶναι δείκνυνται φρονοῦντες ὥσπερ οὐσίαν οὕτω καὶ ὑπόστασιν ἐπὶ Θεοῦ, τὸν Πατέρα τελέως ἀθετοῦντες καὶ τὸν Υἱὸν εἶναι μόνον καθ' ὑπόστασιν δεικνύντες

66

"But it is impossible," they counter, "for the Spirit to be from the essence of the Son and not be from His hypostasis." For they do not comprehend that, whenever something is of one essence and hypostasis, that which has existence in whatever way from that essence also has existence from that hypostasis; and conversely, whatever happens to be from that hypostasis is also from that essence. But whenever something happens to be of one essence but not of one hypostasis but of many, then what is from that one essence is not from the remaining hypostases of that nature, but from one of them in particular. Therefore, since our most high and worshipful Trinity is one nature in three hypostases, what has its existence from the essence is not from the remaining hypostases but from one of them in particular, namely, from the Father's, since it is impossible for it not to be from this hypostasis. Consequently, it cannot be from another, but, insofar as it is from one, it shall be only from one.

This is clear in the example of men; for while each one of us is from the essence of Adam, yet each of us is not also from his hypostasis, because while the essence of men at this time is one, yet there are many hypostases. But in the beginning when there was one human essence and hypostasis, that of Adam, Eve was from the essence of Adam, and was also from his hypostasis. But also before Cain came into being, when there was one male essence and hypostasis, Cain existed from the one and same male essence and hypostasis, that of Adam. When, however, there were already two complete men in regard to hypostasis, Cain's son Enoch indeed existed from the essence of Adam but not also from his hypostasis, since instead he existed only from the hypostasis of Cain.

So, when the Latin-minded maintain to the uttermost that the Spirit is also from the hypostasis of the Son inasmuch as it is theologized that He is from the nature, except for the divine Spirit's, they are shown to think that, just as there is one essence, so also there is one hypostasis in God, completely setting at naught the Father, and

καὶ τὸ Πνεῦμα τὸ ἅγιον ἐκ μόνου τοῦ Υἱοῦ τὴν ὕπαρξιν ἔχειν παριστῶντες.

67

Εἴ τις οὖν ἐκ τῆς φύσεως ἀκούων τοῦ Υἱοῦ τὸ Πνεῦμα, ἐκ τῆς ὑποστάσεως νοεῖ, ὁμοϋπόστατον ποιεῖ τῷ Πατρὶ τὸν Υἱόν, ἐπειδήπερ ὁμοούσιος· ἢ καὶ τὴν διαφορὰν καὶ τὴν διάκρισιν κἂν τῇ θείᾳ φύσει, ἀλλ᾽ οὐκ ἐν μόναις ταῖς τρισὶ θείαις ὑποστάσεσι νοεῖ, μὴ πρὸς τοῖς ἄλλοις καὶ τοῦ Χρυσοστόμου θεολόγου διδάσκοντος ἀκούων, «ὡς ἡ μὲν τῶν θείων ὑποστάσεων διακριτικὴ τάξις, τοῖς ἁγίοις καθέστηκε γνώριμος, ἡ δὲ φύσεως διακριτικὴ ἐπὶ τῆς ἁγίας Τριάδος ἀπόβλητος». «Οὐ γὰρ ἐμερίσθη ἡ οὐσία ἀπὸ τοῦ Πατρὸς εἰς Υἱόν, πρὸς τὰς κανονικάς φησιν ὁ μέγας Βασίλειος, οὐδὲ ῥυεῖσα ἐγέννησεν».

Τοιγαροῦν εὖ ἂν ἔχοι λέγειν οὐκ ἐκ τῆς ὑποστάσεως τοῦ Υἱοῦ, ἀλλ᾽ ἐξ αὐτοῦ φυσικῶς κἀκ τῆς οὐσίας τοῦ Υἱοῦ τὸ Πνεῦμα, διὰ τὸ τοῦ Υἱοῦ πρὸς τὸν Πατέρα ὁμοούσιον, καὶ τῆς τοῦ θείου Πνεύματος πρὸς τὸν Πατέρα καὶ τὸν Υἱὸν ὁμοουσιότητος ἐντεῦθεν δεικνυμένης, ἀλλ᾽ οὐχὶ τῆς διαφόρου ἐκ τοῦ Πατρὸς ὑπάρξεως τοῦ Πνεύματος, ἴσον δέ ἐστιν εἰπεῖν καὶ ἐκ τῆς οὐσίας τοῦ Υἱοῦ τὸ Πνεῦμα διὰ τὴν ὁμοουσιότητα, καὶ ὅτι τῆς αὐτῆς ἐστιν οὐσίας τῷ Υἱῷ τὸ Πνεῦμα. Ἐκ δὲ τῆς τοῦ Υἱοῦ ἡ ὁμοουσιότης δείκνυται τοῦ Πνεύματος ὡς φανερωτέρας καὶ προκατηγγελμένης καὶ προπεπιστωμένης· «ἔχει τε ὁ Υἱὸς φυσικῶς ἐν ἑαυτῷ τὰ τοῦ Πατρὸς ἴδια καὶ ἐξαίρετα, διαβαινούσης εἰς αὐτὸν φυσικῶς τῆς τοῦ γεννήσαντος ἰδιότητος»· οὐ τὰ ὑποστατικὰ ἴδια τοῦ Πατρὸς καὶ ἐξαίρετα – οὐδὲ γὰρ τὸ ἄναρχον ἔχει καὶ ἀγέννητον ἢ τὸ γόνιμον - ἀλλὰ τὰ φυσικὰ καὶ ἴδια τῆς τοῦ Πατρὸς φύσεως αὐχήματα, ἅπερ ἔχει φυσικῶς καὶ τὸ Πνεῦμα τὸ ἅγιον.

showing only the Son as existing in His hypostasis, and presenting the Holy Spirit as having existence only from the Son.

67

So, if someone considers the Spirit to be from Son's hypostasis because he hears that the Spirit is from the Son's nature, he makes the Son be of the same hypostasis with the Father, on the basis that He is consubstantial. Alternatively, he considers that there is both a difference and a distinction even in the divine nature, not only in the three divine hypostases. He listens neither to the others nor particularly to Chrysostom the theologian, who teaches "that the distinguishing order of the divine hypostases has been set down as known to the saints, yet distinction of natures in the holy Trinity is rejected."[197] For, as Basil the Great says to the consecrated virgins, "the essence was not divided from the Father into a Son, nor did it beget having flowed."[198]

So a man could soundly say that the Spirit is not from the hypostasis of the Son but is instead from Him naturally and from the essence of the Son, because of the Son's consubstantiality with the Father. And herein is seen the divine Spirit's consubstantiality with the Father and the Son, not the different existence of the Spirit from the Father. It is equivalent to saying that the Spirit is also from the essence of the Son because of the consubstantiality, and that the Spirit is of the same essence with the Son. Now, the consubstantiality of the Spirit is shown on the basis of the consubstantiality of the Son because the latter is more evident and foretold and previously believed on: "The Son naturally has in Himself the properties and exceptional characteristics of the Father, since the particular property of the one who begat is naturally communicated to Him."[199] It is not the hypostatic properties and exceptional characteristics of the Father that are communicated, since the Son has neither beginninglessness nor unbegottenness nor the capability to generate. Rather it is the natural and characteristic boasts of the Father's nature, which the Holy Spirit also naturally possesses.

68

Καὶ τοῦτο διὰ πολλῆς ποιούμενος σπουδῆς ὁ θεῖος Κύριλλος, τὸ μηδένα παραχθέντα δοξάζειν ἐκ τῆς ὑποστάσεως τοῦ Υἱοῦ τὸ Πνεῦμα τὸ ἅγιον, ἐκ τῆς φύσεως αὐτοῦ καὶ φυσικῶς καὶ κατὰ φύσιν ὁσάκις λέγει, τὸ Πνεῦμά φησι τὸ ἅγιον καὶ ἐκ τῆς φύσεως αὐτοῦ πηγάζειν, καθ᾽ ἣν ὁ αὐτός ἐστι μετὰ Πατρός, ἀλλ᾽ οὐδαμοῦ τῶν λόγων ἐκ τῆς ὑποστάσεως· καὶ τὰ ἴδια τοῦ Πατρὸς ἔχειν αὐτὸν φυσικῶς τε καὶ οὐσιωδῶς καὶ κατὰ φύσιν ἀεὶ θεολογεῖ.

Καὶ συκοφαντηθεὶς γὰρ ὡς καὶ ἐκ τῆς ὑποστάσεως τοῦ Υἱοῦ δοξάζων τὴν ὕπαρξιν τὸ Πνεῦμα ἔχειν, τοῦτ᾽ αὐτὸ ὅτι συκοφαντεῖται ἰσχυρίσατο, ἴδιον τοῦ Υἱοῦ καὶ οὐκ ἀλλότριον εἶναι τὸ Πνεῦμα διατεινάμενος, ἀλλ᾽ οὐκ ἐκ τοῦ Υἱοῦ. Καὶ τοῦτ᾽ ἀνάγραπτον κεῖται πρὸς Λατίνων περιφανῆ τε καὶ λαμπρὸν ἔλεγχον· οἳ παρ᾽ ὧν ἔδει μᾶλλον ἀποσχέσθαι τῆς κακονοίας, ἐκ τούτων ἐνάγεσθαι δικαιοῦσιν εἰς τὸ μὴ τὸν Πατέρα μόνον, ἀλλὰ καὶ τὴν τοῦ Υἱοῦ ὑπόστασιν αἰτίαν εἶναι κακῶς νομίζειν τῆς τοῦ θείου Πνεύματος ὑποστάσεως. Ὁ δὲ λέγων εἶναι ἐκ τῆς τοῦ Υἱοῦ ὑποστάσεως τὸ Πνεῦμα, διὰ τὸ εἰπεῖν τὸν θεῖον Κύριλλον διαβαίνειν φυσικῶς εἰς τὸν Υἱὸν τὴν τοῦ γεννήσαντος ἰδιότητα παρ᾽ αὐτοῦ τοῦ θείου Κυρίλλου ἐντρεπέσθω, γράφοντος ἐν Θησαυροῖς· «πῶς οὐκ ἔσται τὸ Πνεῦμα ὁ Θεός, ὅλην ἔχον ἐν ἑαυτῷ οὐσιωδῶς τὴν ἰδιότητα τοῦ Πατρὸς καὶ τοῦ Υἱοῦ, οὗ καὶ Πνεῦμά ἐστι, δι᾽ Υἱοῦ τῇ κτίσει χορηγούμενον»; Κατὰ γὰρ τὴν αὐτῶν σύνεσιν, ἣν ἐν ταῖς τῶν θεοφόρων κέκτηνται θεολογίαις, τὸ Πνεῦμα γεννητόν τε ἅμα καὶ γεννήτωρ ἔσται· οὗ τί ἂν ἀκουσθείη καινότερον;

69

Ἀλλὰ ταῦτα μὲν ὥσπερ ἐκ περιουσίας ἡμῖν ἀρτίως εἴρηται πρὸς

68

Cyril the divine was diligently making this point, that no one should believe that the Holy Spirit is from the hypostasis of the Son. And so, as often as he says "from His nature" and "naturally" and "in accordance with nature," he says that the Holy Spirit springs also from His nature, with respect to which the Son Himself is with the Father; but nowhere at all in his treatises does he say that He is from His hypostasis. And he always theologizes that He has the particular characteristics of the Father both naturally and essentially and according to nature.

In fact, when Cyril was falsely accused of believing that the Holy Spirit has existence from the hypostasis of the Son, he asserted this very thing, that he was being falsely accused, strenuously maintaining that the Spirit is the Son's own, and not different, yet not from the Son. And this lies inscribed unto the manifest and outstanding accusation of the Latins. They, from the arguments from which they ought all the more to turn from their unsound conjecture, from these very arguments they justify themselves in being lead to think wrongly that not only the Father but also the hypostasis of the Son is the cause of the hypostasis of the divine Spirit. But whoever says that the Spirit is from the hypostasis of the Son because Cyril the divine said that the particular characteristic of Him who begat is communicated naturally to the Son, let him be put to flight by the same Cyril, who writes in his *Treasuries:* "How can the Spirit not be God, as He possesses in Himself, by essence, the entire particular characteristic belonging to the Father and to the Son, whose Spirit He also is, as He is suppplied to creation through the Son"?[200] For, according to the Latins' understanding, which they possess in the theological writings of the God-bearers, the Spirit will at the same time be both generated and Generator. What thing more innovative than this could ever be heard?

69

But we have spoken these things as it were superabundantly just

τοὺς διατεινομένους ἐκ τῆς ὑποστάσεως εἶναι τοῦ Υἱοῦ τὸ Πνεῦμα, ἐπειδήπερ ἐκ τῆς φύσεως εἴρηται. Ὁ γὰρ θεῖος Κύριλλος ἐνταῦθ᾽ ἡμῖν ἀναπηγάζειν ἐκ τῆς φύσεως οὐ τὴν φύσιν φησὶ τοῦ Πνεύματος, οὐδὲ τὴν ὑπόστασιν, ἀλλὰ τὴν ἐνέργειαν, ἥτις ἀναπηγάζει, κατὰ τὸν Δαμασκηνὸν θεολόγον, ἐκ μιᾶς τρισυποστάτου φύσεως. Ὅτι μὲν γὰρ ἄκτιστός ἐστι καὶ ἡ τῆς θείας φύσεως ἐνέργεια καὶ ὅτι φυσικὴ καὶ οὐσιώδης λέγεται, παραστήσει δι᾽ ὀλίγων καὶ ὁ μέγας Ἀθανάσιος ἐν τοῖς Κατὰ Μακεδονίου γράφων· «οὐ κατὰ ἄλλην καὶ ἄλλην πρόνοιαν ὁ Πατὴρ καὶ ὁ Υἱὸς ἐργάζεται, ἀλλὰ κατὰ μίαν καὶ τὴν αὐτὴν οὐσιώδη τῆς θεότητος ἐνέργειαν».

Ὅτι δὲ οὐκ ἐκ μιᾶς τινος τῶν ὑποστάσεων, ἀλλ᾽ ἐκ τῆς τρισυποστάτου φύσεως ἡ τοιαύτη ἐνέργεια πηγάζει προσμαρτυρείτω καὶ ὁ μέγας Διονύσιος γράφων ἐν κεφαλαίῳ τετάρτῳ τῆς Περὶ τῆς οὐρανίου ἱεραρχίας βίβλου· «πάντα μετέχει προνοίας ἐκ τῆς παναιτίου θεότητος ἐκβλυζομένης». Ὅτι δὲ Πνεῦμα ἐνταῦθα ὁ θεῖος Κύριλλος ἐκ τοῦ Πατρὸς καὶ τοῦ Υἱοῦ διδόμενον ἡμῖν οὐ τὴν φύσιν φησὶν οὐδὲ τὴν ὑπόστασιν τοῦ Πνεύματος, ἀλλὰ τὴν ἄκτιστον αὐτοῦ καὶ φυσικὴν χάριν καὶ ἐνέργειαν, σαφὲς δεῖγμα πρὸς τοῖς ἄλλοις καὶ τὸ μνησθῆναι τῆς ἐν τῷ εὐαγγελίῳ τοῦ προδρόμου καὶ βαπτιστοῦ περὶ τοῦ Χριστοῦ φωνῆς, τῆς οὐκ ἐκ μέτρου δίδοσθαι λεγούσης παρὰ τοῦ Πατρὸς τὸ Πνεῦμα τῷ Υἱῷ. Ἰωάννης γὰρ ὁ χρυσορρήμων, τὸ χωρίον τοῦτο τοῦ κατὰ τὸν θεολόγον Ἰωάννην εὐαγγελίου ἐξηγούμενος, «Πνεῦμα», φησίν, «ἐνταῦθα τὴν ἐνέργειαν λέγει· πάντες γὰρ ἡμεῖς μέτρῳ τὴν ἐνέργειαν τοῦ Πνεύματος ἐλάβομεν, ἐκεῖνος δὲ ὁλόκληρον· εἰ δὲ ἡ ἐνέργεια αὐτοῦ ἀμέτρητος, πολλῷ μᾶλλον ἡ οὐσία».

Οὕτω πάντα νικᾷ τῆς τῶν παρ᾽ ἡμῶν εἰρημένων ἀληθείας ἡ δύναμις, εὐπορίας ἀφορμὴν ποιουμένη τὰς ὑμῶν ἀπορίας καὶ δι᾽ ἑαυτῆς ὡς διὰ μιᾶς τινος εὐθείας πλῆθος σκολιῶν, ἑτεροκλινεῖς ἀπελέγχουσα γραμμάς.

Ταύτῃ τοι τῶν μὲν γραφικῶς προβαλλομένων ἅλις.

now to those who strenuously maintain that the Spirit is from the hypostasis of the Son since He is said to be from the nature. For in this regard, Cyril the divine says that from the nature springs not the nature nor the hypostasis, but the energy,[201] which, according to the Damascene theologian, springs forth from one hypostatic nature.[202] As for that the energy of the divine nature is certainly uncreated and is called natural and essential, Athanasius the Great will also present this briefly in his treatises *Against Macedonius* writing, "The Father and the Son do not act each one by a different providence, but by the one and same essential activity of the divinity."[203]

But that an energy like this springs from the trihypostatic nature and not from a particular one of the hypostases, let Dionysius the Great bear witness to it, when he writes in the fourth chapter of his book *On the Celestial Hierarchy,* "All things participate in the providence which wells forth from the divinity which is the cause of all."[204] As for that when the divine Cyril says in this passage that the Spirit is given us from the Father and the Son he means neither the nature nor the hypostasis of the Spirit but rather His uncreated and natural grace and energy, a clear sign of this is, among other things, to also remember the saying of the Forerunner and Baptist concerning Christ in the Gospel, which says that the Spirit is not given by measure from the Father to the Son. For John Chrysostom when exegeting this passage from the Gospel according to John the Theologian says: "In this passage, he calls the energy Spirit; for we all have received in measure the energy of the Spirit, but He received the entirety. Now if His energy is without measure, much more so His essence."[205]

Thus the force of the truth of our interpretations conquers everything, making your doubtful disputations an opportunity for solutions and by itself thoroughly refuting the deviating lines as a multitude of crooked lines [of argumentation] are refuted by one straight one.

Thus there are indeed enough Scriptural arguments in regard to this.

70

Ἐπεὶ δὲ οὐ μόνον τοῖς λογίοις οἱ Λατῖνοι χρῶνται καθ' ἡμῶν, μᾶλλον δὲ καθ' ἑαυτῶν, ἀλλὰ καὶ διανοήμασιν οἰκείοις, φέρ' ἴδωμεν τὸ ἀναμφίλεκτον αὐτοῖς δοκοῦν, ᾧ καὶ τ' ἄλλα συνδιαρρυήσεται λυθέντα, μᾶλλον δὲ καὶ τὸ παρωνύμως ἀπὸ τῆς διανοίας λέγεσθαι στερήσεται, ἀδιανόητα δειχθέντα· κατὰ μέρος γὰρ ταῦτ' ἐπαξιέναι οὐκ ἀνάγκη. Καὶ ταῦθ' ἡμῖν ἀρτίως οἷς πέρα τοῦ μετρίου μηκύνειν ἥκιστα προῃρημένοις, ὅμως εἰς μῆκος ἐκτέταται ὁ λόγος, ταῖς αὐτῶν ἐξ ἀγνοίας ἀπορίαις συμπαρεκτεινόμενος.

Ἀλλὰ τί τὸ δοκοῦν αὐτοῖς ἀκράδαντον τῆς δυσσεβείας ἔρεισμα; Πᾶν, φησί, τὸ ἐκπορευόμενον ἔκ τινος, διά τινος ἐκπορεύεται καὶ οὕτως ἐπὶ πάντων ἐστί, κἂν μὴ ῥήματι ὁ λέγων ἐπισημαίνηται· τὸ δ' αὖ διά τινος, καὶ ἐξ ἐκείνου δι' οὗ ἐστι λέγεται· διὰ τίνος οὖν ἑτέρου, εἰ μὴ διὰ τοῦ Υἱοῦ τὸ Πνεῦμα; Σαφὲς οὐκοῦν τὸ περαινόμενον, ὅτι διὰ τοῦ Υἱοῦ καὶ ἐκ τοῦ Υἱοῦ τὸ Πνεῦμα ἐκπορεύεται.

Τί οὖν ἡμεῖς πρὸς ταῦτα; Οὐ τὴν "διὰ" μὲν αὐτοῖς δώσομεν, τὴν δὲ "ἐκ" ἀπαγορεύσομεν, ὃ πολλοὶ πεπόνθασιν, ἀγνοοῦντες ὃ πεπόνθασι. Τὸ γὰρ διὰ στόματος, καὶ ἐκ στόματος σαφῶς προφέρεται. Καὶ τῷ Ἰὼβ «διὰ νεφέλης» γέγραπται λαλήσας ὁ Θεὸς καὶ αὖθις «ἐκ τοῦ νέφους». Ἀλλ' οὐδ' ἐπὶ τῶν κτιστῶν καὶ κατὰ φύσιν ἐκπορευομένων τὸ διά τινος οὐ συννοήσομεν καὶ μὴ λεγόμενον. Οὐ μὴν διὰ τοῦτο τοῖς κατὰ φύσιν τὰ ὑπὲρ φύσιν ὁμοιώσομεν. Ἀπόκριναι γὰρ δή μοι ὁ ἐμβατεύων ἃ μὴ ἑώρακας· οὐχὶ καὶ πᾶς υἱὸς ἔκ τινος γεννώμενος διά τινος γεννᾶται καὶ οὕτως ἐπὶ πάντων ἔχει, κἂν μὴ ῥήματι ὁ λέγων ἐπισημαίνηται; Ἆρ' οὖν διὰ τοῦτο καὶ

70

Since, however, the Latins employ not only scriptural passages but also their own reasonings against us, or rather, against their own selves, let us see what seems indisputable to them, along with which all the rest will be brought down, having been dissolved, or better, these reasonings will even be deprived of their name which comes from the word "reason", since they will be shown to be irrational. It is not necessary to pass through these reasonings individually, especially since, though we had no purpose to lengthen our treatise beyond the average, it has just now been extended to a great length, stretching out alongside their doubtful disputations sprung from their ignorance.

But what seems to them to be the unshakeable support for their irreverence? They say that everything that proceeds from something proceeds through something, and so it is for all things, even if the speaker does not indicate it verbally. But, again, when a thing is through something, it is also said to be from that through which it is; so through whom else could the Spirit be, if not through the Son? Therefore the conclusion is clear: the Spirit proceeds through the Son and from the Son.

What do we say then to these arguments? We certainly will not grant them the "through" while forbidding the "from", which many have suffered, not knowing what they have suffered. For what is spoken "through" a mouth is clearly also expressed "from" a mouth. And it has been written that God spoke to Job "through a cloud" and again "from the cloud".[206] Yet even in the case of things created and proceeding according to nature we will not take the "through something" as implied, even when it is not said. Yet we certainly shall not, on account of this, liken what transcends nature to things which are according to nature. For at this point, answer me, you who intrude into things which you have not seen: is not also every son that is begotten from someone begotten through someone, and

τὴν κάτω καὶ χρονικὴν τοῦ μονογενοῦς ὑπὲρ φύσιν οὖσαν ἐκ μόνης παρθένου μητρὸς ἀθετήσομεν γέννησιν καὶ τὴν ἄνω ἐκ μόνου παρθένου Πατρὸς προαιώνιον, ζητοῦντες τὸ διὰ τίνος τε καὶ ἐκ τίνος κατὰ τὰς ἀπολουμένας σὰς ὑποθήκας καὶ τοὺς ἀσυλλογίστους συλλογισμούς; Οὔμενουν, ἀλλὰ δι' αὐτῆς κἀπὶ γῆς φανερωθείσης καὶ τὴν τοῦ ἁγίου Πνεύματος ἐκπόρευσιν ἀμέσως οὖσαν ἐκ Πατρὸς ἐπιγνωσόμεθα καὶ τὴν σὴν ἀποποιησόμεθα προσθήκην, ὡς τοῖς φυσικῶς διοικουμένοις τὰ ὑπερφυῆ συντάττουσαν.

71

Καὶ τοῦτο δὲ οὐ σύννοεῖς ὁ τῶν ἀνεξερευνήτων ἐξεταστής, ὅτι τὸ ἐκπορευόμενον ἅπαν οὐ διά τινος μόνο, ἀλλὰ καὶ εἴς τι ἀεὶ ἐκπορεῦεται; Ἡ τοίνυν δώσεις ἡμῖν εἰς τί πρὸ τῶν αἰώνων τὸ Πνεῦμα τὸ ἅγιον ἐκπορεύεται, καὶ ἀντὶ τῆς μόνης προαιωνίου καὶ σεπτῆς διὰ τοῦτο Τριάδος τετράδα σεβόμενος ἀποδειχθήσῃ, τὸ ἐξ οὗ, τὸ δι' οὗ, τὸ εἰς ὃ καὶ αὐτὸ τὸ ἐκπορευόμενον, ἢ τοῦτο σοῦ μὴ διδόντος οὐδ' ἐκεῖνο δεξόμεθα. Τίς γὰρ ὁ λόγος καθ' ὅν, ἀμφοτέρων ἑπομένων τῷ ἐκπορευομένῳ παντί, τὸ μὲν προσίεσθαι, τὸ δὲ μή;

Καίτοι τὸ μὲν ἐκ Πατρὸς ἐκπορεύεσθαι τὸ Πνεῦμα τὸ ἅγιον καὶ ἐν τῷ Υἱῷ ἀναπαύεσθαι, καὶ γέγραπται παρὰ τῶν θεολόγων καὶ πεφανέρωται ἐν Ἰορδάνῃ τοῦ Σωτῆρος βαπτιζομένου καὶ τοῦθ' οὕτως ἔχον ὁμολογοῦμεν, οὐκ ἐκ τῶν ὄντων τὰ ὑπὲρ πάντα τὰ ὄντα στοχαζόμενοι, ἀλλ' ἐκ τῶν ἀρρήτως τελουμένων τὰ ὑπὲρ ἔννοιαν διδασκόμενοι. Ποῦ δή σοι τὸ δι' Υἱοῦ καὶ ἐξ Υἱοῦ ἐπὶ τῆς τοῦ θείου Πνεύματος ὑπάρξεως, εἰ ἐκ Πατρὸς ἐκπορευόμενον τὸ Πνεῦμα πρὸς τὸν Υἱὸν σαφῶς ἔρχεται καὶ ἐν αὐτῷ ἀναπαύεσθαι θεολογεῖται; Καθάπερ ὁ ἱερὸς Δαμασκηνὸς ἐπὶ λέξεώς φησι καὶ Γρηγόριος ὁ θεολόγος τοῦτ' αὐτὸ δεικνὺς ταμίαν εἶναι τοῦ θείου

does this not hold true for all created things, whether the speaker indicates this verbally or not? So will we because of this set at naught the earthly and temporal generation of the Only Begotten, which was above nature from only a Virgin Mother, and the heavenly and eternal generation from only a virgin Father, searching what it means to be through something and from something, in a way befitting your destructive counsels and your unsyllogistic syllogisms? Not at all, but through this generation which was manifested even upon the earth we shall also acknowledge the procession of the Holy Spirit as immediately from the Father and will undo your addition, which subordinates what transcends nature to what properly belonging to nature.

71

But you who are an examiner of things unexaminable, do you not understand this, that everything that proceeds is not only through something but also forever into something? Therefore, either you grant to us into what the Holy Spirit proceeds before the ages (and thereby it will be proven that instead of the only pre-eternal and revered Trinity you revere a tetrad, the from-which, the through-which, the to-which, and the proceeding Spirit Himself), or, if you will not grant this, neither will we accept your argument.[207] Since both [prepositions] accompany every proceeding thing, for what reason should the one be accepted and the other not?

And yet, that the Holy Spirit proceeds from the Father and rests in the Son has been both written by the theologians and revealed when the Savior was baptized in the Jordan, and we confess that this is so, not using the beings to conjecture on what transcends all beings, but being taught what transcends conception from things ineffably performed. Where then in your eyes is the "through the Son" and "from the Son" with reference to the existence of the divine Spirit, if in fact in proceeding from the Father the Spirit clearly comes to the Son and it is theologized that He rests in Him?—just as the sacred Damascene says word for word[208] and as Gregory the theologian,[209]

Πνεύματος ὡς Θεοῦ Υἱὸν καταγγέλλει τὸν Χριστόν. Καὶ ὁ θεῖος Κύριλλος ἐν Θησαυροῖς ἐν Υἱῷ παρὰ Πατρὸς φυσικῶς ὑπάρχειν τὸ Πνεῦμα συμπεραίνει καὶ παρὰ Πατρὸς φυσικῶς τε καὶ οὐσιωδῶς διήκειν ἐν Υἱῷ τὸ Πνεῦμα λέγει, δι' οὗ πάντα χρίων ἁγιάζει ὁ Υἱός. Ἐκ γοῦν τοῦ Πατρὸς ἐν τῷ Υἱῷ ὑπάρχον φυσικῶς καὶ ἀϊδίως, ἐκ τοῦ Υἱοῦ πρὸς τοὺς ἀξίους, ὅπως καὶ ἡνίκα δέοι, πρόεισι καὶ φανεροῦται τὸ Πνεῦμα τὸ ἅγιον.

72

Οὐ μήν, ἀλλ' ἐπιεικέστερον τὸν προκείμενον μεταχειρίζων λόγον, μάλιστα διὰ τοὺς μετ' εὐγνωμοσύνης ἐντυγχάνειν μέλλοντας καθολικωτέραν ἔκφανσιν ἐν βραχεῖ ποιήσομαι τῆς ἀληθείας, ὡς ἐν ἐπιλόγῳ τὸ πᾶν διαλαμβάνουσαν. Ὁ δ' ἔχων ὦτα πρὸς διάκρισιν ὀρθοῦ καὶ μὴ τοιούτου μυείσθω κατὰ τὸ ἐγχωροῦν τὸ τοῦ μυστηρίου βάθος· πύλας δ' ἐπίθεσθε τοῖς ἑαυτῶν ὠσίν, ὅσοι μὴ κριτικωτάτην κέκτησθε διάνοιαν, εἰ μὴ τοῖς εὖ λέγειν δυναμένοις, μᾶλλον δὲ παρὰ Θεοῦ δυναμουμένοις, πειθηνίους ἑαυτοὺς παρέχετε, ὡς ἂν μὴ τὸ ὑπὲρ τὴν ὑμετέραν γνῶσιν ἀφροσύνην τῶν εὖ εἰδότων ὀνομάσητε. Τί δέ ἐστιν ὃ λέγω; Καὶ συντείνατε παρακαλῶ τὸν νοῦν.

73

Τὸ Πνεῦμα τὸ ἅγιον πρὸ αἰώνων καὶ ἀπ' αἰῶνας καὶ ἔτι ἰδιαίτατον μὲν ἔχει τῆς ἰδιοτρόπου ὑπάρξεως τὸ ἐκ τοῦ Πατρός, τῆς μόνης πηγαίας θεότητος, ἐκπορεύεσθαι, τουτέστιν ἐκ τῆς ὑπερθέου ἐκείνης οὐσίας καθ' ὑπόστασιν μόνην τὴν πατρικήν, ὑπέρθεος ὂν καὶ αὐτοουσία καὶ κατ' αὐτὴν τοῦ προσενεγκότος κατ' οὐδὲν ἀποδέον, μᾶλλον δὲ μηδαμῶς διαφέρον ἢ διαιρούμενον, ἑτεροϋπόστατον δ' ὅμως καὶ αὐθυπόστατον. Οὕτω δὲ ὂν ἐκ τοῦ Πατρός, οὔτ' αὐτοῦ διΐσταταί ποτε, καὶ τῷ Υἱῷ οὐχ ἧττον ἥνωται οὐσιωδῶς τε καὶ ἀδιαστάτως, αὐτῷ τε ἐπαναπαυόμενον καὶ ἴδιον αὐτοῦ ὑπάρχον καὶ

showing this very thing, announces that, as the Son of God, Christ
is the treasurer of the divine Spirit. And the divine Cyril in his
Treasuries concludes that the Spirit naturally exists from the Father
in the Son and says the Spirit naturally and essentially extends from
the Father in the Son, through whom the Son anoints and sanctifies
all things. Thus, while the Holy Spirit exists naturally and eternally
from the Father in the Son, He proceeds and is manifested from
the Son to those who are worthy, in the way and at the time that is
necessary.[210]

72

Nevertheless, handling the present argument more gently, and
particularly for the sake of those who will chance upon it with
goodwill in the future, I shall shortly make a more comprehensive
exposition of the truth, grasping the whole as in an epilogue.
Let whoever has ears to discern right from not right be initiated,
according to his capacity, into the depth of this mystery; but set
gates upon your ears, as many of you as have not acquired the most
discerning reason, if you do not make yourselves obedient to those
who have the power, or rather, who are empowered by God, to
articulate it well, in order to keep yourselves from labelling what
transcends your knowledge as foolishness of those who know well.
What is it I am referring to? I beg you, pay attention to the following.

73

The Holy Spirit, before the ages and from the ages and still, has
His most particular characteristic of existence in a particular mode,
which is to proceed from the Father, the only fount of divinity, that
is, from that essence which is beyond divine, by only the paternal
hypostasis, being supremely divine, and self-existence, and not at all
inferior to Him who offered, or rather, in no way differing or being
divided, though He is hypostatically different and self-existent.
Being in this way from the Father, He is not separated from Him
at any time, and He is no less united with the Son essentially and

ἐν αὐτῷ φυσικῶς διατελοῦν ἀεί· αὐτὸς γάρ ἐστιν ὁ τοῦ Πνεύματος ταμίας. Οὐδὲν οὖν καινόν, εἰ καὶ ἐξ αὐτοῦ καὶ ἐκ τῆς φύσεως αὐτοῦ προϊέναι λέγεται, καθ᾽ ὑπόστασιν μέντοι τὴν πατρικήν· καὶ δι᾽ αὐτοῦ καὶ ἐξ αὐτοῦ φυσικῶς καὶ δίδοται καὶ πέμπεται καὶ προχεῖται καὶ προέρχεται, δι᾽ αὐτοῦ διδόμενόν τε καὶ φανερούμενον, εἰ δὲ βούλει καὶ ἐκπορευόμενον πρὸς οὓς ἄξιον. Καὶ ἐκπόρευσιν γὰρ εἴπουπερ ἂν ἐν τοῖς τοιούτοις ἀκροάσῃ, τὴν φανέρωσιν νόει· οὐ γὰρ ἀεὶ τὸ ἐκπορεύεσθαι παρὰ Θεοῦ ὑπάρξεώς ἐστι σημαντικὸν αὐθυποστάτου· «οὐκ ἐπ᾽ ἄρτῳ γάρ», φησί, «μόνῳ ζήσεται ἄνθρωπος, ἀλλ᾽ ἐπὶ παντὶ ῥήματι ἐκπορευομένῳ διὰ στόματος Θεοῦ». Ὁρᾷς ὅτι τὰ μὲν παρὰ Θεοῦ ἐκπορευόμενα πολλά, πλήθους γὰρ συνεκτικὸν τὸ πᾶν, τὸ δὲ Πνεῦμα τὸ ἅγιον ἕν, ὃ καὶ ἰδιοτρόπως παρὰ πάντα ἐκπορεύεται παρὰ Θεοῦ; Καὶ πάλιν· «ἐθαύμαζον», φησί, «οἱ ὄχλοι ἐπὶ τοῖς λόγοις τῆς χάριτος τοῖς ἐκπορευομένοις ἐκ τοῦ στόματος αὐτοῦ». Ἆρ᾽ οὖν ἡ τῶν λόγων χάρις αὐθυπόστατος, ὥσπερ τὸ Πνεῦμα τὸ ἐκπορευόμενον παρὰ μόνου τοῦ Πατρός; Ἄπαγε· καίτοι ταύτην τὴν χάριν ὁ Κύριος Πνεῦμα προσηγόρευσεν εἰπών, «τὰ ῥήματα ἃ ἐγὼ λαλῶ, Πνεῦμά εἰσι καὶ ζωή εἰσιν». Ἀλλ᾽ ὁρᾷς ὅπως ἐξ Υἱοῦ ἡ χάρις καὶ οὐκ αὐτὴ μόνον, ἀλλὰ καὶ πᾶσαι αἱ δωρεαὶ τοῦ ἁγίου Πνεύματος.

74

Εἰ γὰρ ἐκ τῆς τῶν πιστευόντων εἰς Χριστὸν κοιλίας ποταμοὶ ῥέουσιν ὕδατος ζῶντος κατὰ τὴν ἐπαγγελίαν («ὁ πιὼν γάρ», φησὶν ὁ Κύριος «ἐκ τοῦ ὕδατος, οὗ ἐγὼ δώσω αὐτῷ, γενήσεται πηγὴ ὕδατος ἁλλομένου εἰς ζωὴν αἰώνιον», ταὐτὸν δ᾽ εἰπεῖν ἐκπορευομένη, κατὰ τὸ «πηγὴ δὲ ἦν ἐκπορευομένη ἐξ Ἐδὲμ») εἰ οὖν ἐκ τῶν ὡμοιωμένων τῷ Υἱῷ ποταμηδὸν ἅλλεται, ταὐτὸν δ᾽ εἰπεῖν πηγάζεται καὶ ἐκπορεύεται τὸ Πνεῦμα κατὰ χάριν ἐνυπάρχον αὐτοῖς, πολλῷ μᾶλλον ἐκ τοῦ Υἱοῦ τοῦ κατὰ φύσιν προαιωνίως τε καὶ ἀϊδίως ἔχοντος ἑαυτῷ ἐπαναπαυόμενον αὐτὸ καὶ συνημμένον φυσικῶς.

without distance, resting in Him and being His own and forever
continually in Him naturally; for He is the treasurer of the Spirit.
So it is no innovation if He is said to go forth from Him and from
His nature, however, by the paternal hypostasis. He is both given
and sent and poured forth and progressing both through and from
Him naturally. Through Him He is given and made manifest, and,
if you prefer, also proceeds to those whom He deems worthy. And
should you ever hear of procession in this context, consider it to
mean the manifestation. For procession from God is not always
indicative of self-hypostatic existence, since He says "Man shall not
live by bread alone, but by every word that proceedeth through the
mouth of God."[211] Do you see that the things that proceed from
God are certainly many (since the word "every" encompasses many
things), while the Holy Spirit is one, who proceeds from God in His
own mode, differently from all things? And again, he says, "The
multitudes marvelled at the gracious words which proceeded out
of His mouth."[212] Does it mean consequently that the grace of the
words was self-existent, like the Spirit which proceeds only from the
Father? Away with the thought! And yet the Lord called this grace
spirit when He said, "the words that I speak unto you, they are
spirit, and they are life."[213] But do you see how from the Son comes
the grace, and not only this but also all the gifts of the Holy Spirit?

74

For if, according to the promise, rivers of living water[214] flow from the
belly of those who believe in Christ (for the Lord says, "Whosoever
drinketh from the water that I shall give him, it will become a fount
of water springing up into everlasting life,"[215] which is the same
as to say "proceeding", according to the verse, "and a fount was
proceeding out of Eden"[216]) — if, then, the Spirit springs forth like a
river from those that have become like the Son (which is the same as
to say that He wells forth and proceeds from them, since He exists
in them by grace), much more will He do so from the Son, who by
nature before the ages and eternally has the Spirit resting in Him
and united to Him naturally.

Ἀλλ᾽ οὐ διὰ τοῦτο δογματίσομεν ἐκ τοῦ Πατρὸς καὶ ἐκ τοῦ Υἱοῦ καὶ ἐκ τῶν ὡμοιωμένων κατὰ χάριν τῷ Υἱῷ ἐκπορεύεσθαι τὸ Πνεῦμα· ἰδιαίτατα γὰρ ἐκ τοῦ Πατρός, ὡς ἐξ αὐτοῦ μόνου τὴν ὕπαρξιν ἔχον τὴν προαιώνιόν τε καὶ ὁμοούσιον. Ἔστι γὰρ καὶ ἐκ τοῦ Πατρὸς καὶ τοῦ Πατρὸς τὸ Πνεῦμα τὸ ἅγιον, καὶ προηγεῖται τῇ ἐπινοίᾳ τοῦ εἶναι Πατρὸς τὸ ἐκ τοῦ Πατρὸς εἶναι· (τὸ γὰρ εἶναί τι προθεωρεῖται τοῦ τίνος εἶναι, εἰ καὶ μὴ κατὰ χρόνον) καὶ διὰ τοῦτο τοῦ Πατρός, ὅτι ἐκ Πατρός, ὡς καὶ ὁ μέγας Βασίλειος ἐν τοῖς Πρὸς Εὐνομιανούς φησι κεφαλαίοις· «τὴν πρὸς τὸν Πατέρα οἰκειότητα νοῶ τοῦ Πνεύματος, ἐπειδὴ παρὰ τοῦ Πατρὸς ἐκπορεύεται». Ἐκ δὲ τοῦ Υἱοῦ, εἴπου εὑρεθείη καὶ οἷς τισι ῥήμασιν, ὡς αὐτῷ φυσικῶς ἐναναπαυόμενον προαιωνίως τε καὶ ἀϊδίως, ἅτε κατὰ τὴν ἀπόρρητόν τε καὶ ἄχρονον ἐκείνην γέννησιν τέλειον ἐν ἑαυτῷ σχόντι ἐκ Πατρὸς τὸ Πνεῦμα, ἐκ τῆς αὐτῆς ὂν αὐτῷ οὐσίας, καθ᾽ ὑπόστασιν μέντοι τὴν πατρικήν. Οὐκοῦν ἐπὶ τοῦ Υἱοῦ προθεωρεῖται τὸ εἶναι αὐτοῦ Πνεῦμα τοῦ ἐξ αὐτοῦ εἶναι, εἰ καὶ μὴ κατὰ χρόνον· καὶ διὰ τοῦτο ἐκ τοῦ Υἱοῦ, ὅτι τοῦ Υἱοῦ. Τοιγαροῦν οὐκ ἔχει παρ᾽ αὐτοῦ τὴν ὕπαρξιν.

75

Διὰ δὲ τοῦ Υἱοῦ λέγεται τὸ Πνεῦμα τὸ ἅγιον, ἔσθ᾽ ὅτε μὲν ὡς δι᾽ αὐτοῦ νοούμενον Πνεῦμα Πατρὸς καὶ ἐκ Πατρός, ἅτε μὴ γεννητὸν ὑπάρχον ἀλλ᾽ ἐκπορευτόν, καὶ ὡς ἐκπορευτὸν ἀμέσως ἐκ τοῦ ἐκπορεύοντος αὐτὸ νοούμενον· ἔστι δὲ καὶ ὡς συμπαρομαρτοῦν ἀχρόνως αὐτῷ κατὰ τοὺς θεολόγους καὶ σὺν αὐτῷ καὶ μετ᾽ αὐτοῦ, ἀλλ᾽ οὐχὶ καὶ ἐξ αὐτοῦ ἐκ τοῦ Πατρὸς ὑπάρχον, ὡς καὶ αὐτόθεν τοῖς συνετοῖς ἐστι κατάδηλον· οὐδεὶς γὰρ τῶν εὖ φρονούντων λόγον ἀκούσας προαιωνίως ἐκ Πατρὸς γεννώμενον οὐκ εἰς ἔννοιαν εὐθὺς ἔρχεται τοῦ τῷ λόγῳ συμφυῶς καὶ συνανάρχως συμπαρομαρτοῦντος Πνεύματος, καθ᾽ ἣν ἔννοιαν οὐδ᾽ εἰς "ἐκ" τὴν "διὰ" χρὴ μεταλαμβάνειν· ἔστι δὲ καὶ ὡς δι᾽ Υἱοῦ καὶ ἐξ Υἱοῦ

But we will not therefore dogmatize that the Spirit proceeds from the Father and from the Son and from those that have become like the Son by grace; for it is His most particular characteristic to be from the Father, since He has the pre-eternal and consubstantial existence only from Him. For the Holy Spirit is both from the Father and of the Father, and being from the Father notionally precedes being of the Father (for "what it is" comes earlier to mind than "whose it is", although not with respect to time); and this is why He is the Father's, because He is from the Father, as Basil the Great says in his chapters *To the Eunomians*: "I consider the kindred relationship of the Spirit to the Father, since He proceeds from the Father."[217] But wherever it may be found in particular sayings that He is "from the Son", it means that He rests in Him naturally before the ages and eternally, because by that ineffable and timeless begetting the Son received the Spirit from the Father perfect in Himself, being from the same essence as Himself, although He is by the paternal hypostasis. So then, in the case of the Son, that the Spirit is His comes to mind earlier than that the Spirit is from Him, although not in time; and this is why He is from the Son, because He is the Son's. Consequently, He does not have His existence from the Son.

75

Now, the Holy Spirit is said to be through the Son, sometimes because it is through the Son that He is considered the Spirit of the Father and from the Father, seeing that He does not exist as begotten but as proceeding, while as proceeding He is considered immediately from Him who causes processions. On the other hand, it is sometimes said because, according to the theologians,[218] He accompanies the *Son* timelessly and is together with Him and along with Him, but is not from Him and from the Father, as is completely clear from this to those who understand. For nobody from those who believe rightly, when he has heard that the Word has been begotten from the Father before the ages, does not immediately grasp the notion that the Spirit accompanies the Word connaturally and coeternally, and according to this notion one must not change the "through" into

τοῖς ἁγίοις χορηγούμενον, οὐ μὴν προαιωνίως ἐκεῖθεν πεμπόμενον ἢ διδόμενον ἢ πηγάζον, εἰ δὲ βούλει ἐκπορευόμενον, ἀλλ᾽ ἡνίκα ληφθῆναι καὶ φανερωθῆναι εὐδόκησε καὶ ὡς εὐδόκησε διδόμενόν τε καὶ φανερούμενον· οὐ γὰρ αὐτὴ καθ᾽ ἑαυτὴν ἡ οὐσία καὶ ἡ ὑπόστασις φανεροῦταί ποτε τοῦ θείου Πνεύματος. Εἰ δὲ Λατῖνοί φασιν ἐντεῦθεν στοχάζεσθαι τὴν προαιώνιον πρόοδον, ἀκολούθως οὐδ᾽ ἐκεῖ κατὰ τὴν ὕπαρξιν ἔσται. Καὶ τὸ τεκμήριον ὃ φασιν αὐτοὶ τοῦτο, οὐδὲν αὐτοῖς συμβαλεῖται πρὸς τὴν πρόθεσιν.

76

Ἀλλ᾽ ἐκ μὲν τοῦ Υἱοῦ καὶ διὰ τοῦ Υἱοῦ οὕτω προϊὸν θεολογεῖται τὸ Πνεῦμα τὸ ἅγιον· μιᾶς γὰρ καὶ τῆς αὐτῆς οὐσίας, μία καὶ ἡ αὐτὴ καὶ θέλησις καὶ δόσις καὶ φανέρωσις. Ἐκ δὲ τῶν υἱοποιήτων τῷ Θεῷ καὶ διδόμενόν ἐστι καὶ ἁλλόμενον καὶ πηγάζον καὶ ἐνεργοῦν καὶ φαινόμενον, ὡς ἐνυπαρχούσης μὲν αὐτοῖς καὶ ἐνοικούσης τῆς ἐμφύτου χάριτος καὶ δυνάμεως τοῦ Πνεύματος, ἀλλὰ κατὰ χάριν καὶ οὐ φυσικῶς καὶ ὕστερον ἐπιδημησάσης, τουτέστι δι᾽ αὐτῶν ἐνεργησάσης, ἀλλ᾽ οὐ προαιωνίως ἐπαναπαυομένης.

Ὁρᾷς ὅση ἡ διαφορά, ὡς ἀπειρίας ἐπέκεινα; Λατῖνοι δὲ ἐν τῷ συμβόλῳ τῆς πίστεως, ἐκ μὲν τοῦ Πατρὸς λέγοντες γεννηθῆναι τὸν Υἱόν, ἐκ δὲ τοῦ Πατρὸς καὶ τοῦ Υἱοῦ τὸ Πνεῦμα ἐκπορεύεσθαι, οὐ σαφῶς περὶ τῶν προαιωνίων καὶ ὑποστατικῶν φασι προόδων καὶ αὐτῆς τῆς ὑπάρξεως τοῦ Υἱοῦ τε καὶ τοῦ Πνεύματος; Σαφῶς τοιγαροῦν μιγνύουσι τὰ ἄμικτα· τοῖς ὑπὲρ χρόνον τὰ ὑπὸ χρόνον, τοῖς ὑπὲρ αἰτίαν τὰ δι᾽ αἰτίαν. Δι᾽ ἡμᾶς γὰρ ἐκ τοῦ Υἱοῦ πέμπεται· εἰ δὲ δι᾽ ἡμᾶς, καὶ μεθ᾽ ἡμᾶς. Ἐκ δὲ τοῦ Πατρὸς οὐ διά τι, οὐδὲ μετά τι· ἄπαγε τῆς βλασφημίας, εἰ μὴ σὺ καὶ τοῦτ᾽ ἀναπλάσεις ὁ πάντολμος, μᾶλλον δὲ ψευδώνυμος θεολόγος, καὶ τὸν λόγον οἷον ἐγγυτέρω τοῦ Πατρὸς τιθείς, πορρωτέρω δὲ τὸ Πνεῦμα τὸ ἅγιον.

"from". Yet other times it is said because He is supplied through the
Son and from the Son to the Saints. He most certainly is not sent or
bestowed or springing forth or, if you prefer, proceeding from Him
pre-eternally, but rather He is given and manifested when it pleased
Him and as it pleased Him to be received and manifested. For the
divine Spirit's essence and hypostasis per se are not made manifest
at any point in time. But if the Latins say that from this they infer
the pre-eternal progression, then logically neither in that case will
the procession be existential. And this proof which they give will not
help them at all in their purpose.

76

The Holy Spirit on one hand is theologized as proceeding in this
way from the Son and through the Son; for, since the essence is one
and the same, the will and bestowal and manifestation are also one
and the same. On the other hand, He is both given and springs
up and wells forth and acts and is manifested from those who are
adopted by God,[219] since in fact the innate grace and power of the
Spirit exists and dwells within them. Yet this grace came later, by
grace and not naturally, that is, it acted through them but did not
rest upon them before the ages.

Do you see how the difference is so great, that it transcends even
infinity? When the Latins, however, say in the Symbol of Faith that
the Son has been begotten from the Father while the Spirit proceeds
from the Father and the Son, do they not clearly speak concerning
the pre-eternal and hypostatic progressions and of the very existence
of the Son and the Spirit? Consequently, they are clearly mingling
what cannot be mingled, things temporal with things transcending
time, things caused with things transcending cause. For it is on our
behalf that He is sent from the Son; and if on our behalf, then also
after us. But from the Father He is not through something, neither
after something—away with the blasphemy!—unless you were to
invent this too, you who are the epitome of audacity or, better, you
who are a falsely named theologian, since you have placed the Word
as it were nearer to the Father and the Holy Spirit more remote.

Ταῦτ' ἄρα καὶ οἱ θεόσοφοι Πατέρες ἡμῖν μὲν παραδιδόντες τὴν τῆς πίστεως ὁμολογίαν, ὡς ἐκ τοῦ Πατρὸς ἐθεολόγησαν γεννηθέντα τὸν Υἱόν, οὕτω καὶ τὸ Πνεῦμα ἐξ αὐτοῦ τοῦ Πατρὸς ἐκπορευόμενον· δηλονότι ἀμέσως ἑκάτερον αὐτῶν καὶ ἐκ μόνου τοῦ Πατρός, ἐξ αὐτῆς δηλαδὴ τῆς πατρικῆς ὑποστάσεως. Εἰ δὲ διὰ τὴν γενομένην ἐπιφοίτησιν ὕστερον ἡμῖν, καὶ ταῦτα πρὸς τοὺς ἀλλοτριοῦντας τοῦ Υἱοῦ τὸ Πνεῦμα ἐνιστάμενοι, ἐξ ἀμφοῖν εἶπέ τις αὐτό, ἢ ἐκ Πατρός δι' Υἱοῦ ἢ ὅτι τοῦ Υἱοῦ ἐκλάμπει καὶ τὰ ὅμοια τούτοις, ἀλλ' ὡς καὶ ἐν τῷ Υἱῷ ὑπάρχον καὶ ἴδιον αὐτοῦ καὶ κατ' οὐδὲν ἀλλότριον.

77

Πρὸς δὲ τούτοις οὐδ' ἄνευ χρονικῆς προσθήκης ἢ αἰτίας εἴρηκέ τις δι' Υἱοῦ ἢ καὶ ἐξ Υἱοῦ τὸ Πνεῦμα τὸ ἅγιον ἀποστελλόμενον, προσημαίνων δὲ ἀεὶ ἐνέργειαν, καθ' ἣν ἐφ' ἡμᾶς ἐλθεῖν πρὸ ἡμῶν τῶν ἀδυνάτων ἦν. Εἰ δ' ἄρα που καὶ μὴ προσημήναντες εἰρήκεσαν, ἀλλ' ὡς πολλάκις τοῦτο πράξαντες. Ἔπειτα οὐδὲ συνίης τοῦτο, ὦ ὑπερλίαν σὺ καὶ καυχώμενος εἰς τὰ ἄμετρα, ὅτι πολλ' ἄττα τῶν λεγομένων παρὰ τῇ θείᾳ Γραφῇ, τῇ μὲν συνόδῳ τῶν ῥημάτων ἐστὶν ἕν, τῇ δὲ διανοίᾳ καὶ τῷ πράγματι οὐχ ἕν; Ὃ καὶ τοῖς αἱρετικοῖς τὴν πλάνην ὡς ἐπίπαν ἀπειργάσατο, μὴ δυναμένοις διακρίνειν τὸ τῇ συνόδῳ τῶν ῥημάτων ἕν, τοῖς δὲ πράγμασιν οὐχ ἕν, ὡς καὶ Γρηγορίῳ τῷ θεολόγῳ συνδοκεῖ;

Σαφὲς γὰρ τοῦτο τοῖς σοφοῖς τὰ θεῖα καὶ τῷ θείῳ Πνεύματι μεμυημένοις, ὡς ὅταν ἐξ ἀμφοτέρων, Πατρὸς καὶ Υἱοῦ, τὸ Πνεῦμα λέγηται, ἢ ἐκ Πατρὸς δι' αὐτοῦ, εἰ καὶ συνάγεται ῥήματι, ἀλλὰ διέστηκε πράγματι. Καὶ πρὸς μὲν τοὺς ἀλλοτριοῦντας τὸ Πνεῦμα τοῦ Υἱοῦ δεόντως ἂν συνημμένως οὕτως εἴποιμεν ἐν κρίσει τοὺς λόγους οἰκονομοῦντες, οἰκειωθεῖσι δὲ Θεῷ διὰ τοῦ γνῶναι ἴδιον αὐτοῦ τὸ Πνεῦμα ἠκριβωμένως ἐκκαλύψομεν ἑκάτερον, ὡς ἐκ Πατρὸς μὲν ἔχει πρὸ πάντων τῶν αἰώνων τὴν ὑπαρκτικὴν τὸ

That is also why, when the divinely-wise Fathers were passing down to us the Confession of Faith, they theologized that the Son had been begotten from the Father in the same way that the Spirit was proceeding from the same Father; that is, each of them is immediately and only from the Father, namely, from the very paternal hypostasis. But if, because of the visitation that came to us later, and actually addressing himself to those who alienate the Spirit from the Son, if someone said that the Spirit is from both persons, or that He is from the Father through the Son, or that He shines forth from the Son and things similar to these, yet it is in the sense that He exists also in the Son and is His own and is not alienated in any respect.

77

Besides, neither has anyone said that the Holy Spirit is sent through the Son or from the Son without adding some temporal qualification or cause, always indicating an energy beforehand, whereby it was impossible for Him to have come upon us before us. But if in some place they spoke without having indicated the activity beforehand, it is because they had already done this many times. So, you who excessively boast without any limits, do you not understand this either, that even though many of the things spoken by the divine Scripture are one in verbal construction, yet in reality and in meaning they are not one? This in general also caused error for the heretics, who are not able to accurately distinguish what is one in the construction of the words but not one in reality, as Gregory the Theologian also agree.

For this is clear to those who are wise in divine matters and who have been initiated by the Holy Spirit, that whenever the Spirit is said to be from both, from the Father and the Son, or from the Father through the *Son*, although it is implied verbally, yet in actuality it is different. And so, on one hand, we would necessarily speak thus, in this united way, to those who alienate the Spirit from the Son, judiciously managing our words[220] Nevertheless, when they have become familiar with God by having come to know that the Spirit

Πνεῦμα πρόοδον, τῷ Υἱῷ δὲ αἰωνίως ἐνυπάρχον, ἐξ αὐτοῦ εἰς τοὐμφανές προῆλθε δι' ἡμᾶς καὶ μεθ' ἡμᾶς κατ' ἐκφαντικὴν καὶ οὐχ ὑπαρκτικὴν προέλευσιν.

78

Ἀλλὰ καὶ ὁ Υἱός, φησίν, ἐν τῷ Πνεύματί ἐστι. Πάνυ γε, διὸ καὶ ἐκφαντικόν ἐστιν αὐτοῦ τὸ Πνεῦμα, καὶ ἀποστέλλεται καὶ παρ' αὐτοῦ οὐχ ὡς ἄνθρωπος μόνον, ἀλλὰ καὶ ὡς Θεὸς κατὰ τὸν θεολόγον Γρηγόριον, καὶ ἐμμορφοῦται ταῖς καρδίαις τῶν πιστῶν καὶ ἐνοικεῖ καὶ ὁρᾶται δι' αὐτοῦ. Ἐν γὰρ Θησαυροῖς ὁ θεῖος Κύριλλος, «Χριστοῦ», φησί, «τὸ Πνεῦμα, ὡς τοῦ Θεοῦ λόγου διὰ Πνεύματος ἡμῖν ἐνοικιζομένου». Γεννᾶσθαι δὲ οὐ λέγεται, ἐπεὶ τὸ γεννώμενον Υἱὸς ἀεὶ τοῦ γεγεννηκότος ἐστί τε καὶ λέγεται καὶ ὁ γεννῶν ἀεὶ Πατήρ· τὸ δὲ ἐκπορευόμενον ἐπὶ Θεοῦ, καθὰ προέφημεν, οὐχ ἁπλῶς οὐδὲ μόνου τοῦ ἁγίου Πνεύματός ἐστι· ἀλλὰ τὸ μὲν προαιώνιον καὶ ὑπαρκτικὴν πρόοδον δηλοῦν, ἑτερότροπον οὖσαν τῆς τοῦ Υἱοῦ ἐκ τοῦ Πατρὸς γεννήσεως, μόνου τοῦ ἁγίου Πνεύματός ἐστι· τὸ δ' ἐκ τοῦ κρυφίου φανεροῦσθαι καὶ παρρησιάζεσθαι καὶ δημοσιεύειν τὴν οἰκείαν δύναμιν διὰ τῶν ἐπιτελουμένων θαυμασίων οὐ μόνον τοῦ ἁγίου Πνεύματος, ἀλλ' ἔστι καὶ αὐτοῦ· «ὁ Θεὸς» γάρ, φησὶν ὁ προφητικώτατος ἐν βασιλεῦσιν «ἐν τῷ ἐκπορεύεσθαί τε ἐν μέσῳ τοῦ λαοῦ σου, ἐν τῷ διαβαίνειν σε ἐν τῇ ἐρήμῳ γῇ ἐσείσθη».

Καὶ τοῦ Πατρὸς τοίνυν πάλαι ποτὲ φανερουμένου καὶ διὰ Μωσέως θαυματοποιοῦντος, ὁ πρῶτος κατὰ τὸν θεολογικώτατον Γρηγόριον γέγονε σεισμός, μετατιθεμένων τῶν Ἑβραίων ἀπὸ τῆς τῶν εἰδώλων προσκυνήσεως ἐπὶ τὴν ἀμυδρὰν μέν, ἀληθῆ δὲ θεογνωσίαν. Ἀλλὰ καὶ ἐπὶ τοῦ Υἱοῦ καὶ τοῦ ἁγίου Πνεύματος ὁ δεύτερος γέγονε

is the Son's own, we shall then with exactitude make known each procession to them, that on one hand the Spirit has His existential progression from the Father before all the ages, while on the other hand, since He exists in the Son from eternity, He came forth from Him in order to be manifested, for us and after us, according to the revelatory and not the existential procession.

78

"But," he says "the Son is also in the Spirit." That is all true, of course. And so the Spirit is revelatory of Him, and He is sent from the Spirit, not only as a man, but also as God, according to Gregory the Theologian, and He is formed within the hearts of the faithful and indwells and is seen through Him. For the divine Cyril in his *Treasuries* says: "The Spirit is Christ's, as the Word of God dwells within us through the Spirit."[221] But it is not said that He is begotten, since what is begotten is always the Son of Him who has begotten Him and is called so, as also the begetter always is and is called Father. But what proceeds in the case of God, as we previously said, does not absolutely only refer to the Holy Spirit. Rather, the one indicating the pre-eternal existential progression, as it is a mode of being differing from the begetting of the Son from the Father, is only the Holy Spirit's. But the other procession, which is to be made manifest from out of the hidden and to boldly express and make public His inherent power through the miracles which are accomplished, does not pertain only to the Holy Spirit, but is also His. For David, the most prophetic among the kings, says: "O God, when Thou wentest forth[222] in the midst of Thy people, when Thou didst traverse the wilderness, the earth was shaken."[223]

And so, when the Father once in ancient times was being manifested and through Moses was working miracles, then, according to the most theological Gregory, the first seismic shake occurred, when the Hebrews were translated from the worship of idols to the knowledge of God, which, while indistinct, was nevertheless true. But the second seismic shake occurred with the Son and the Holy

σεισμός, τῶν μὲν Ἰουδαίων μεταρρυθμιζομένων ἀπὸ τοῦ νόμου πρὸς τὸ εὐαγγέλιον, παντὸς δὲ ἔθνους καλουμένου πρὸς τὴν εὐαγγελιζομένην κοινωνίαν τῆς θεώσεως. Ἀλλὰ καὶ τοῦ Υἱοῦ μόνου διὰ τοῦ σταυροῦ διαβαίνοντος ἐν τῇ ὡς ἀληθῶς ἐρήμῳ, τῷ θανάτῳ καὶ τῷ ᾅδῃ, καὶ φανερουμένου ἐν μέσῳ τοῦ λαοῦ τῶν Ἰουδαίων, διὰ τῆς ἐκ τῶν οὐρανῶν θεοσημίας καὶ αἰσθητῶς ἡ γῆ ἐσείσθη. Ὁρᾷς ἐπὶ τῆς τοιαύτης σημασίας τὸ ἐκπορευόμενον οὐ μόνον ὂν τοῦ Πνεύματος, ἀλλὰ κοινὸν Πατρός, Υἱοῦ καὶ Πνεύματος; Ἀλλ' ὑστερογενὴς καὶ ὑπὸ χρόνον αὕτη ἡ ἐκπόρευσις· «ἐν τῷ λαῷ» γάρ φησιν. Εἰ δ' ἐν τῷ λαῷ, καὶ μετά τόν λαόν.

79

Καλῶς ἄρ' ἔφημεν, ὡς τὸ ἐκπορευόμενον ἐπὶ τοῦ ἁγίου Πνεύματος οὐκ ἀεὶ τὴν ἐκ τοῦ Πατρὸς προαιώνιον ὕπαρξιν δηλοῖ ἀλλ' ἔστιν ὅτε καὶ τὴν ὕστερον φανέρωσιν, καθ' ἣν καὶ ὁ Υἱὸς κοινωνήσει τῷ Πατρί, ὃ καὶ ὁ θεῖος Κύριλλος δείκνυσι σαφῶς λέγων, «Τὸ Πνεῦμα τὸν Υἱὸν ἐξ ἰδίας ἡμῖν ἀναπηγάζει φύσεως». Προστιθεὶς γὰρ τὸ "ἡμῖν", συνιέναι δίδωσι τὸ χρονικὸν τῆς ἀναδόσεως. Καὶ ὅτι ἐνέργεια καὶ δωρεά ἐστι τοῦ θείου Πνεύματος τὸ ἐκ Πατρὸς καὶ Υἱοῦ πηγαζόμενον ἡμῖν, Ἰωὴλ προκαταγγέλλων, μᾶλλον δὲ διὰ τούτου ὁ Θεός, οὐκ «ἐκχεῶ τὸ Πνεῦμα μου», φησίν, ἀλλ' «ἐκχεῶ ἀπὸ τοῦ Πνεύματός μου». Ὡς γὰρ καὶ ὁ Χρυσόστομός φησι πατήρ, «τὸ μέρος λέγει τῆς ἐνεργείας· οὐ γὰρ ὁ παράκλητος μερίζεται». Ὁ δὲ τῶν ἀποστόλων κορυφαῖος πολλαχοῦ, μᾶλλον δὲ πανταχοῦ, δωρεὰν καλεῖ τὴν ἐκχυθεῖσαν τηνικαῦτα πρὸς αὐτούς. Καὶ ὁ χρυσοῦς πάλιν θεολόγος· «οὐχ ὁ Θεός», φησίν, «ἀλλ' ἡ χάρις ἐκχεῖται».

80

Οὐκ ἄρα διὰ ταῦτα ἐκ τοῦ Πατρὸς καὶ τοῦ Υἱοῦ ἐκπορεύεσθαι δοξάσομεν τὸ Πνεῦμα· ἀτιμάσαιμεν γὰρ ἂν τοῦτο μᾶλλον ἢ δοξάσαιμεν, τοῖς διὰ τοῦ Υἱοῦ εἶναι σχοῦσι συντάττοντες αὐτό.

Spirit, when the Jews were shifted from the law to the gospel, while every nation was called to the promised communion of theosis. But also when the Son only was traversing in the true desert, in death and Hades, and when He was manifested in the midst of the people of the Jews, through the sign from God from the heavens, the earth was perceptibly shaken.[224] Do you see how in this sense the procession is not only of the Spirit, but is common to the Father, Son and Spirit? This procession, however, is temporal and a later occurrence. For he says, "in the people." But if it is in the people, it is also after the people.

79

So we have soundly said that procession as pertaining to the Holy Spirit does not always indicate the eternal existence from the Father before the ages but there are also times when it indicates the later manifestation, in which the Son will also share with the Fathe, which the divine Cyril also shows when he clearly says, "The Spirit springs forth the Son to us from His own nature."[225] For by adding the phrase "to us", he meant for us to understand it as a temporal giving. And when Joel announced beforehand, or, rather, when God announced through him, that what springs forth from the Father and the Son to us is the energy and the gift of the divine Spirit, he does not say, "I will pour out My Spirit", but he says, "I will pour out of My Spirit."[226] For as the golden-mouthed father says, "he means a portion of His energy; for the Paraclete is not divided."[227] And the chief of the Apostles in many passages, or, rather, everywhere, calls what was at that time poured out to them a gift.[228] Again, the golden theologian says: "God is not poured forth, but the grace is."[229]

80

So, because of these things, we will not glorify[230] the Spirit as proceeding from the Father and the Son, because [thus] we would have dishonored Him rather than glorified Him, classifying Him together with those that have their being through the Son. Therefore

Τοιγαροῦν ἐκ τοῦ Πατρὸς μόνου δοξάζομεν ἐκπορευόμενον ἰδιοτρόπως καὶ προαιωνίως, ὡς καὶ ὁ Υἱὸς γεννᾶται· καὶ οὕτω δοξάζοντες, συνδοξάζομεν αὐτὸ καὶ συμπροσκυνοῦμεν τῷ Υἱῷ καὶ τῷ Πατρί.

Καὶ τοῦτο δηλοῦντες οἱ θεόσοφοι πατέρες, ἐπὶ τοῦ συμβόλου τῆς ὀρθοδοξίας τὸ ἐκ τοῦ Πατρὸς ἐκπορεύεσθαι τὸ Πνεῦμα καὶ τὸ συνδοξάζεσθαι τῷ Πατρὶ καὶ τῷ Υἱῷ συνήγαγον εἰς ἕν, συνημμένως ἐκφωνήσαντες καὶ παραδόντες, ὡς τῶν μὴ δοξαζόντων ἐκ μόνου τοῦ Πατρὸς ἐκπορευόμενον τὸ Πνεῦμα τὸ ἅγιον, ὥσπερ ἀμέλει καὶ τὸν Υἱὸν γεγεννημένον, οὐδὲ συμπροσκυνεῖν τὸ Πνεῦμα ἐκείνοις δυναμένων, ἐν ἰδίᾳ ὑποστάσει θεωρούμενον.

81

Εἰ γὰρ κοινὸν ἀεὶ αὐτοῖς ὡς ἐξ αὐτῶν ἡ τοῦ Πνεύματος ἐκπόρευσις, ἐνέργεια ἂν τὸ Πνεῦμα εἴη μόνη καὶ οὐκ ἐν ὑποστάσει· μόνον γὰρ ἐνέργεια, ἥ γε αὐτοῖς κοινή. Κοινὸν μὲν οὖν αὐτοῖς ὡς ὁμοούσιον, ἀλλ' οὐκ ἀεὶ αὐτοῖς κοινὸν ὡς ἐξ ἀμφοῖν εἰ καὶ νῦν ἐπ' ἐσχάτου τῶν αἰώνων ἐξ ἀμφοῖν ἐκκέχυται, προσθήσω δ' ὅτι καὶ παρ' ἑαυτοῦ· καὶ γὰρ αὐτεξουσίως πρὸς ἡμᾶς ἐκχεῖται. Καὶ πρὸς τὸν Υἱὸν γὰρ εἴρηται προφητικῶς εἰπεῖν, «Υἱός μου εἶ σύ, ἐγὼ σήμερον γεγέννηκά σε». Ἀλλ' ἴσμεν ὑπὸ χρόνον ταύτην ὑπάρχουσαν τὴν γέννησιν. Τί δέ, οὐχὶ καὶ τὸ Πνεῦμα ταύτην συνειργάσατο τὴν γέννησιν, ᾧ τὸ καθ' ἡμᾶς ἀνειλημμένον τοῦ Υἱοῦ φύραμα ἐπὶ τοῦ βαπτίσματος ἐχρίσθη καὶ χρισθὲν ἐφανερώθη, ὅτι καὶ πρὸ τοῦ βαπτίσματος γέγονεν ὁμόθεον, ἐπεὶ καὶ τὴν ἀρχὴν ὁ τοῦ Θεοῦ Υἱός, «ἐκ Πνεύματος ἁγίου καὶ Μαρίας ἐσαρκώθη τῆς παρθένου», κατὰ τὸ γεγραμμένον;

Ἆρ' οὖν ἐκ τοῦ Πατρὸς καὶ ἐκ τοῦ Πνεύματος ἐρεῖς γεγεννῆσθαι πρὸ αἰώνων τὸν Υἱὸν διὰ τὴν ὑπὸ χρόνον ταύτην γέννησιν; Σὺ

we glorify Him as proceeding in a unique mode pre-eternally only from the Father, as the Son is also begotten; and so glorifying Him in this way, we glorify and worship Him together with the Son and the Father.

Indicating this, in the Symbol of Orthodoxy the divinely-wise Fathers combined into one the clause that the Spirit proceeds from the Father and the clause that He is glorified together with the Father and the Son; and they pronounced them joined together and handed them down in Tradition together, [in the belief] that those who do not think that the Holy Spirit proceeds only from the Father, just as also that the Son has been begotten thus, these are also not able to worship the Spirit, considered in His own hypostasis, together with the Son and the Father.

81

For if the procession of the Spirit were forever common to the Father and the Son, as if He were from both of them, the Spirit would be only an energy and not in a hypostasis. For what is common to them is only an energy. So while He is common to them as consubstantial, yet He is not always common to them as being from both of them, although now at the end of the ages He has been poured forth from both of them, and I would add, from Himself as well; for He is poured forth to us by His own free will. For He is also said to have prophetically spoken to the Son: "Thou art my Son, this day have I begotten Thee."[231] But we know that this begetting is temporal. Or what, did not the Spirit also help cause this same begetting? He by whom our doughy lump, after it was assumed by the Son, was anointed at His baptism, and after it was anointed, it was revealed that even before the baptism it had become the same as God. For the Son of God in the beginning "was incarnate of the Holy Spirit and the Virgin Mary," as it has been written.[232]

Will you then say, on account of this temporal begetting, that the Son has been begotten from the Father and from the Spirit before

γὲ ἴσως ὁ λογικαῖς ἐφόδοις τὴν περὶ Θεοῦ γνῶσιν ποριζόμενος
καὶ ἐκ τῶν ὕστερον ὡς αὐτὸς φῄς γεγονότων τὰ προαιωνίως
ὄντα στοχαζόμενος· ἀλλὰ καὶ μάρτυρά γε ἀξιολογώτατον ἡμῖν
ἂν ἐπαγάγοις τὸν Υἱὸν αὐτὸν διὰ τοῦ προφήτου λέγοντα, «Κύριος
ἀπέσταλκέ με καὶ τὸ Πνεῦμα αὐτοῦ»· καὶ τοῦτο γὰρ σόν, ταὐτὸν
εἴεσθαι ἀποστολήν τε καὶ τρόπον ὑπάρξως. Πρὸς δὲ τούτῳ καὶ
τῷ τοῦ μεγάλου προσχρήσῃ καὶ παρεξηγήσῃ Παύλου, καὶ τοῦθ᾽
ἑκών καὶ ἐθελοκακῶν ἢ ἀγνοῶν καὶ μὴ ὁμολογῶν. «Ὧι μὲν γὰρ»
φησὶν ἐκεῖνος, «διὰ τοῦ Πνεύματος δίδοται λόγος σοφίας, ἄλλῳ
δὲ λόγος γνώσεως». Ἀλλὰ καὶ ὁ Χριστὸς ἐνοικεῖ ταῖς καρδίαις
τῶν μὴ ἀδοκίμων, πάντως διὰ τοῦ Πνεύματος, καὶ νοερῶς ὁρᾶται
καὶ ἐμμορφοῦται καὶ ἐμφανίζεται, καὶ ταῦτα διὰ τοῦ Πνεύματος.
Οὐκοῦν προσυλλογιζόμενος ἐρεῖς, εἰ διὰ τοῦ Πνεύματος, καὶ
ἐκ τοῦ Πνεύματος. Εἰ δ᾽ ἐκ τοῦ Πατρὸς καὶ ἐκ τοῦ Πνεύματος ὁ
Υἱὸς σαφῶς ἀποστέλλεται καὶ τὸ βάπτισμα δέχεται, καθ᾽ὃ πᾶς
βαπτιζόμενος γεννᾶται ἐκ Πνεύματος, καὶ ταῖς καρδίαις ἐλλάμπει,
καὶ τοῦτο διὰ τοῦ Πνεύματος, καὶ πολλὰ ἕτερα τῶν παραπλησίων
συνείρας, εἶτα κοινῶς κατὰ τὰς σὰς ἐπιστήμας συμπεραίνων, καὶ
ἐκ τοῦ Πνεύματος γεγεννημένον εἶναι τὸν Υἱὸν δοξάσεις τε καὶ
δείξεις. Ἀλλ᾽ οὐχ ἡμεῖς γε, ὦ σοφώτατε ἐπιχθονίων, οἱ τῆς κατὰ
σὲ ταύτης θεολογίας ἄμοιροι παντάπασιν, ἀλλ᾽ ὀρθῶς ἂν καὶ
προσενέγκωμεν καὶ διέλωμεν τὴν τῆς πίστεως ὁμολογίαν, ἐκ τοῦ
Πατρὸς μόνου λέγοντες ἐξ ἀρχῆς ἀμέσως εἶναι τὸν Υἱόν τε καὶ τὸ
Πνεῦμα, ἰδιοτρόπως μέντοι ἑκάτερον αὐτῶν.

82

Καὶ δὴ τὸ ἴδιον δηλοῦντες ἑκατέρου τρόπου, τὴν μὲν ἐκ Πατρὸς
ὕπαρξιν τοῦ Υἱοῦ γέννησιν προσαγορεύομεν, ἐκπόρευσιν δὲ τὴν
τοῦ ἁγίου Πνεύματος. Τὰ δ᾽ ὕστερον ἐν χρόνῳ καὶ μετὰ τὴν κτίσιν
ἐπὶ ταύτης καὶ ὑπὸ τούτων ὑπηργμένα, νοήμασι μὲν ἀεὶ διαιροῦμεν

the ages? You at least might do that, you who go on acquiring the knowledge about God[233] with rational deductions and on the basis of what happened later, as you personally testify, you conjecture on the things that exist before the ages. But you could even produce before us the Son Himself as an absolutely reliable witness, Him who said through the prophet, "The Lord and His Spirit hath sent Me."[234] For this is another characteristic of yours, to think that a sending and a mode of existence are identical. But besides this, you will misuse and improperly exegete the saying of the great Paul, and you would do this voluntarily and willingly mischievously, or else from ignorance and non-agreement. He says: "For to one is given by the Spirit the word of wisdom; to another the word of knowledge."[235] But Christ also dwells in the hearts of those who are not reprobate entirely through the Spirit, and is seen and formed within and manifested noetically, and these things are through the Spirit. So applying your reasoning to this, you would say, if "through the Spirit," then also "from the Spirit." And once you have strung together that if the Son is clearly sent and receives baptism from the Father and from the Spirit, whereby every baptized man is begotten from the Spirit,[236] and shines within the hearts, and this again is through the Spirit, and many other similar arguments, then, drawing a common conclusion according to your sciences, you will believe and prove that the Son has also been begotten from the Spirit. But we do not do this, of course, O wisest of those on earth, we who do not have any part in this theology of yours in any way whatsoever. Instead, let us rightly bring forward and divide the confession of faith, saying that the Son and the Spirit are immediately from the Origin, from the Father only, although each of them in a unique mode.

82

And when we make evident the particular characteristic of each mode, on one hand we call the existence of the Son from the Father by the name "begetting", while on the other hand we call that of the Holy Spirit by the name "procession". As for the benefactions that were done by them upon the creation later in time and after the creation, we always divide them conceptually from those pre-

τῶν προαιωνίων καὶ ἀνάρχων ὑπάρξεων ἐκείνων, ῥήμασι δ᾽ ἔστιν ὅτε καὶ τοῦτο σπανιώτατα συνάπτοντες ἢ καὶ συνημμένα παρά τινων ἀκούοντες, τὴν ἐν τοῖς νοήμασι διαίρεσιν οὐκ ἀποβάλλομεν. Τοιοῦτόν ἐστι καὶ τὸ παρὰ τοῦ Κυρίου λεγόμενον, «ἐγὼ ἐκ τοῦ Θεοῦ ἐξῆλθον καὶ ἥκω», καὶ «ἐξῆλθον παρὰ τοῦ Πατρὸς καὶ ἐλήλυθα εἰς τὸν κόσμον». Κἀνταῦθα γὰρ τὸ "ἐξῆλθον" ἓν ὂν οὐ μιᾶς διακονίας ἐστὶ δηλωτικόν· τήν τε γὰρ ἐφ᾽ ἡμᾶς δι᾽ ἡμᾶς ἐφ᾽ ἡμῶν παρὰ τοῦ Πατρὸς ἀποστολὴν δηλοῖ καὶ τὴν ἐκ τῆς οὐσίας καὶ τῆς τοῦ Πατρὸς ὑποστάσεως προαιώνιον πρόοδον.

Τί οὖν, διὰ τὸ τοῦ ῥήματος ἑνιαῖον συνάψομεν τὰ πλεῖστον καὶ ὑπὲρ τὸ πλεῖστον διεστῶτα; Ἢ διότι τὸ "ἐξῆλθον" καὶ τὴν ἀποστολὴν δηλοῖ, ἡ δὲ τοῦ Υἱοῦ ἀποστολὴ παρὰ τοῦ Πατρὸς ἐγεγόνει καὶ τοῦ Πνεύματος, κατὰ τὸ «Κύριος ἀπέσταλκέ με καὶ τὸ Πνεῦμα αὐτοῦ», ἵν᾽ εἴπω πάλιν τὸ πολλάκις εἰρημένον, προελθεῖν δογματίσομεν ἐκ τοῦ Πατρὸς καὶ ἐκ τοῦ Πνεύματος τὸν Υἱὸν καὶ Λόγον τοῦ Θεοῦ; Οὔμενουν. Οὐκοῦν οὐδὲ διὰ τὴν ἐκ Πατρὸς καὶ Υἱοῦ τοῦ ἁγίου Πνεύματος ἀποστολὴν ἢ ἔκφανσιν ἢ πρόοδον, τὴν ἐκφαντικὴν καὶ ὑπὸ χρόνον λέγω, κἂν εἰς ἓν τῇ προαιωνίῳ ἐνίοτε συνάγηται κατὰ τὴν λέξιν, ἐκ τοῦ Πατρὸς καὶ ἐκ τοῦ Υἱοῦ δογματίσομεν ἐκπορεύεσθαι τὸ Πνεῦμα τὸ ἅγιον, μέχρις ἂν ἐκ Θεοῦ Θεὸν γινώσκωμεν αὐτὸ τῷ προενεγκόντι Πατρὶ ἐπίσης προαιώνιον.

83

Ἀλλ᾽ ὁ μόνος διανοίγων ὀφθαλμοὺς τυφλῶν, καὶ δι᾽ οὗ ὁρῶσιν οἱ ὁρῶντες, εἰ καὶ μὴ ἁπαζαπλῶς τοῖς πᾶσιν, ἀλλὰ τοῖς ἐν ἀληθείᾳ σε ζητοῦσιν ἅπασι, δίδου δι᾽ ἀοράτου θεωρίας ἀνηκούστοις σοῖς ἐν νῷ διδάγμασιν, ἐπιγινώσκειν τὴν ἀλήθειαν. Εἰ δ᾽ οὖν, ἀλλὰ δι᾽ ἀκοῆς πιστεύσαντας πρὸς τὴν ἑνότητα τῆς σῆς ἐπιγνώσεως διὰ πίστεως ἀνάγαγε, καὶ δι᾽ ἔργων ἀγαθῶν βεβαιοπίστους ἀποδείξας ἐν καιρῷ εὐθέτῳ φανέρωσον σαυτὸν αὐτοῖς, ἵν᾽ εἰδῶμεν τὴν σὴν

eternal and beginningless beings, but on the other hand, there are times, albeit they are most rare, when we join them verbally or when we hear them joined together from some other person, yet we do not reject the division in concepts. Something like this is also what has been said by the Lord, "I came forth and have come from God,"[237] and, "I came forth from the Father, and am come into the world."[238] Because here, too, although the phrase "I came forth" is one and the same in both cases, it does not indicate one ministry; for it indicates both the sending upon us, for us, and among us, from the Father, and the pre-eternal procession from the essence and hypostasis of the Father.

What then? Will we join what are separated as far as possible, and even more than what is possible, just because the word is the same? Or will we, because the phrase "I came forth" also indicates the sending (and the sending of the Son was from the Father and the Spirit, in accordance with the phrase, "the Lord and His Spirit hath sent Me,"[239] to repeat what has been often said), will we then dogmatize that the Son and Word of God came forth from the Father and from the Spirit? Not at all. Therefore neither on account of the sending or manifestation or progression of the Holy Spirit from the Father and the Son (I mean the manifestative and temporal one, even if it is sometimes joined together with the pre-eternal one in the wording), will we dogmatize that the Holy Spirit proceeds from the Father and from the Son, until we may know Him as God from God, equally pre-eternal with the Father that brought Him forth.

83

But O Thou who alone openest the eyes of the blind and art the one through whom they see that do see, do Thou grant, even if not to all in general, at least to all them that seek Thee in truth, to acknowledge the truth by an invisible contemplation, through Thine unheard noetic teachings. So, in this way, lead through faith those who have believed through hearing toward the unity which cometh from the acknowledgement of Thee, and, through their good works proving them sound in faith, do Thou manifest Thyself

ἐπ' ἀληθείας δόξαν ἅπαντες καὶ καταπολαύσωμεν ἐν πνευματικῇ καὶ ἀπορρήτῳ θέᾳ τῆς τρισηλίου καὶ μοναρχικωτάτης φαιδρότητος, καὶ δοξάζωμέν σε πρὸς δύναμιν ἀδιαλείπτως, νῦν καὶ ἀεὶ καὶ εἰς τοὺς ἀκαταλήκτους αἰῶνας τῶν αἰώνων. Ἀμήν.

in due time unto them, so that we all may in truth see Thy glory and delight in a spiritual and ineffable vision of the thrice-sunned and absolutely singular gladness, and may unceasingly glorify Thee as much as we are able, now and ever and unto the unending ages of ages. Amen.

NOTES

[1] Gr. φρόνημα, *phronema*.

[2] A play on words, contrasting "ἀνάγωγος", "ill-bred, spoiled", with ἀναγωγός", "leading up, uplifting".

[3] In Greek, "ἐπανόρθωσις". Besides the senses of "correction, amendment", this word also has the literal meaning of "setting upright once more".

[4] Jer. 51:9.

[5] 1 Cor.15:28.

[6] See 1 Cor.15:25.

[7] John.14:28.

[8] Wis.Sir.1:4.

[9] Wis.Sir.23:20.

[10] John.5:19, 30.

[11] John.6:38.

[12] Luke 6:12.

[13] Heb.5:8.

[14] Luke 2:52.

[15] John.3:14 et alibi.

[16] John.7:39 et alibi.

[17] Luke 13:32.

[18] John.1:1.

[19] Pro.8:25.

[20] Ps.71:17.

[21] Baruch 3:36.

[22] Baruch 3:38.

[23] John.10:30.

[24] John.14:10.

[25] John.14:9.

[26] Ps. 109:3. The Greek word 'ἀρχή', here translated as 'dominion', can also mean 'origin' or 'beginning.' The Father is the 'origin' or 'source' (ἀρχή) of the Son and the Holy Spirit.

[27] Ps.71:7-8.

[28] Phil.2:10.

[29] See Ps.144:13.

[30] Dan.2:44.

[31] 2 Cor.3:6.

[32] John 20:22.

[33] The technical term is "insufflation." The Greek ἐμφύσημα, however, denotes not simply the action but the very thing which is imparted in the breathing-upon.

[34] John 20:23.

[35] St. John Chrysostom, *Homily 86 on John* (PG 59:375,5).

[36] John 6:63.

[37] Ps. 118:13.

[38] Or, "can be".

[39] Luke 3:2.

[40] Luke 1:70; 72.

[41] Jon. 1:1.

[42] Is. 2:1.

[43] Gen. 2:7.

[44] Ibid.

[45] 1 Cor. 15:45.

[46] Cf. Ps. 103:2.

[47] 1 Cor. 15:45.

[48] 1 Cor. 2:16.

[49] 1 Cor. 6:17.

[50] I.e. "the anointed one".

[51] See Luke 4:18, Acts 4:27, 10:38, Heb. 1:9.

[52] St. John of Damascus, *Exact Exposition of the Orthodox Faith* 1, 8 (PG 94:833A).

[53] James 1:17.

[54] Joel 3:1 (KJV 2:28).

[55] 1 Cor. 12:8.

[56] 1 Cor. 2:10.

[57] 1 John 2:27, 3:24, 4:13.

[58] St. Basil the Great, *On the Holy Spirit* 24, 55, (PG 32:172B).

[59] St. Basil the Great, *Against Eunomius* 5, (PG 29, 772C).

[60] 1 Cor. 12:4-6.

[61] See 2 Cor. 6:16.

[62] Cf. Gal. 5:22.

[63] Cf. Prov. 8:14.

[64] Cf. 1 Cor. 1:30.

[65] Cf. The kontakion of the Feast of the Ascension.

[66] Acts 1:4.

[67] Acts 1:5.

[68] John 14:16.

[69] John 14:26.

[70] John 15:26.

[71] John 16:7.

[72] John 15:26.

[73] John 16:7.

[74] The crucial difference lies in the aspect of the verbs used here in the Greek: πέμπω ('I send' or 'I am sending') is in the present tense, signifying a continual, ongoing action or process, while πέμψω ('I shall send') is in the future tense, signifying an action that will be done at some point. The same holds true for ἐκπορευόμενον ('proceeding', a present participle) and ἐκπορευθὲν ('having proceeded', an aorist participle) respectively.

[75] John 14:16.

[76] John 14:26.

[77] John 15:26.

[78] John 16:8.

[79] John 16:13.

[80] John 14:10.

[81] John 16:15.

[82] John 16:14.

[83] "Causelessly": Gr. ἀναιτίως. The Greek word ἀναίτιος has a double meaning: 1. not caused, & 2. not for a cause or reason, not for something's sake. Both are true of the Father, the uncaused cause, while the second is true of the Son and Spirit, who are caused but not for something's sake. Henceforth, "uncaused" will be used to render ἀναίτιος in the first sense, while "causeless" will be used for ἀναίτιος in the second sense; nevertheless it should be kept in mind that in Greek this is one and the same word, occasionally bearing both meanings.

[84] Cf. the prayer "O Heavenly King".

[85] Saint Gregory is probably alluding to the 31st Oration of Saint Gregory the Theologian (PG 36:161D), whose sections 25 and 26 detail the economy of God exhaustively.

[86] St. Maximus the Confessor, *To Thalassius* (PG 90:264 B).

[87] St. Cyril of Alexandria, *Commentary on the Gospel of John* 2 (PG 73:204D).

[88] See section 34 of the first treatise.

[89] Is. 48:16.

[90] St. Gregory the Theologian, *Oration* 38, 15 (PG 36:323D).

[91] St. Athanasius the Great, *Against the Arians* 3 (PG 26:435C).

[92] Mark 2:27-28.

[93] St. Gregory the Theologian, *Oration 31*, 30 (PG 26:168D).

[94] Is. 48:16.

[95] St. Gregory the Theologian, *Oration 29*, 11 (PG 36:88C). See also section 21 in the First Treatise of the present volume.

[96] "Sent from [παρὰ] the Word which is from [ἐκ] the Father": more literally, "sent on the part of the Word [or, 'from the side of the Word'] which is from out of the Father".

[97] John 3:16.

[98] St. Athanasius, *Epistle to Serapion*, 1, 20 (PG 26:580B).

[99] John 1:14.

[100] St. Athanasius, *Epistle to Serapion*, 1, 20 (PG 26:580B).

[101] Gal. 4:6.

[102] Sophocles, *Philoctetes* 950.

[103] 1 Cor. 2:11.

[104] In this translation the Greek word νοῦς [nous] has been rendered as "intellect".

[105] St. Cyril of Alexandria, *Treasuries 34* (PG 75:584 C).

[106] He attributed it to the work *On the Holy Spirit*, 18. The text is Basil the Great, *Against Eunomios* (book 5), (PG 29:733,14).

[107] St. Basil the Great, *On the Holy Spirit* 18 (PG 32:150,35C).

[108] This is attributed to St. Cyril, but it is not extant. Gennadius and Barlaam both cite St. Cyril, as well.

[109] St. Cyril of Alexandria, *Commentary on the Gospel of* Luke 11, 20 (PG 72:704 B).

[110] St. John of Damascus, *Exact Exposition of the Orthodox Faith* 1, 8 (PG 96:819-33).

[111] *On the Holy Spirit* 8 and 16.

[112] Cf. footnote 159 on section 32 in the first treatise.

[113] St. Gregory of Nyssa, *On the Divinity of the Son and the Holy Spirit* (PG 46:560).

[114] Cf. John Philoponus the Philosopher, *Commentary on Aristotle's Physics* 34.14.

[115] Gal. 1:8.

[116] See section 32 and hence in this present treatise.

[117] See sections 27 and 28 in this present treatise.

[118] See section 35 of the first treatise.

[119] St. Gregory the Theologian, *On Pentecost* 9 (PG 36:441).

[120] St. Gregory the Theologian, *On the Holy Spirit, Oration 31*, 30 (PG 36:168D)).

[121] St. Gregory the Theologian, *On Those Who Came From Egypt, Oration 34*, 10 (PG 36:252).

[122] St. Gregory the Theologian, *Oration 31*, 14 (PG 36:149).

[123] St. Gregory the Theologian, *Third Oration of Peace* (PG 35:1157 C).

[124] St. Gregory the Theologian, *On Those Who Came From Egypt, Oration 34*,

10 (PG 36:252).

[125] Ibid. *Oration 31*, 29.

[126] St. John of Damascus, *Exact Exposition of the Orthodox Faith* 1, 8 (PG 96:792D).

[127] *Exact Exposition of the Orthodox Faith,* 1, 8.

[128] John 15:26.

[129] John 14:26.

[130] John 15:26.

[131] Lit. 'authority over oneself'.

[132] I.e. regarding the eternal procession.

[133] Cf. St. Gregory the Theologian, Oration 38, 15 (PG 36:329) and 45, 27.

[134] *Against Eunomius* 5 (PG 29:733 AB), which he does not cite verbatim.

[135] Cf. 1 Cor. 2:12.

[136] *Against Eunomius* 5, PG 21, 733 A B. See section 9 of the first treatise.

[137] St. Basil, *Letter 38, To His Brother Gregory*, 4 (PG 32:329C). Cf. section 31 of the first treatise.

[138] Jn. 15:26.

[139] *Existence*: in Greek, ὑπόστασις (*hypostasis*). The same word, of course, is used of the persons of the Trinity.

[140] St. Basil, *Against Eunomius* 5 (PG 29:736 D).

[141] Or, "of His hypostasis". Throughout this paragraph the word ὑπόστασις (*hypostasis*) has been rendered as "existence".

[142] Ibid.

[143] St. John Chrysostom, *On the Incarnation* 5 (PG 59:697).

[144] For relevant passages, see *Against the Jews* 7; *Catechetical* 3, 10 and 4, 2.

[145] Regarding the phrase "the Spirit of Christ" see section 45 above and 9 in the first treatise.

[146] St. John Chrysostom, *Concerning the Holy Spirit* 11 (PG 52:826).

[147] John. 3:34 et seq.

[148] St. John Chrysostom, *Homily on John 30*, 2 (PG 59:174).

[149] Ps. 44:3.

[150] St. John Chrysostom, *Interpretation of Psalm 44*, 3 (PG 55:185-186).

[151] John 3:34.

[152] John. 1:16.

[153] Joel 3:1 (KJV 2:28). See also Acts 2:17. Here the KJV, apparently because it is not based on the Septuagint, is in error and misses the fine distinction, reading, "I will pour out my spirit."

[154] 2 Cor. 1:22.

[155] St. John Chrysostom, *Interpretation of Psalm 44*, 3 (PG 55:185-186).

[156] See section 16 above.

[157] *Against Eunomius* 1 (PG 45:464 BC).

[158] Since in Greek 'spirit' (πνεῦμα) literally means 'breath', 'breeze'.

[159] Or "only in the theoretical light of a cause." *Against Eunomius,* ibid.

[160] "He hands down": Gr. παραδίδωσιν, whence παράδοσις, "tradition". The Saints hand down the teachings, the traditions, that they themselves previously received (παρέλαβον), whether from their predecessors or directly from God Himself (cf. 1 Cor. 15:3). As St. John of Damascus wrote, "I shall say nothing of my own" (*The Fount of Knowledge*, Preface) — and this is what vouches for the truth of their words.

[161] Letter to Ablabius on "Not Three Gods" (PG 45:133 BC).

[162] St. Gregory of Nyssa, 'That When We Speak of Three Persons in the Godhead We Do Not Speak of Three Gods: To the Greeks, From the Common Notions' (PG 45:180 C). Cf. Treatise 1, section 7 herein.

[163] This is a reference to a work by St. Gregory of Nyssa, Περὶ Θεογνωσίας, which has been lost. See also 'On the Holy Spirit' I.19. The Psalmic reference is Ps. 32:6.

[164] Cf. Phil. 4:6-8.

[165] *To Ablabius* (PG 45:133 B).

[166] James 1:17.

[167] Theological Odes 3, On the Holy Spirit 24-28.

[168] *To Eunomius* 2 (PG 45:469B).

[169] *To Eunomius* 2 (PG 45:512 B).

[170] I.e. since He is a Spirit, not a Son.

[171] St. Gregory of Nyssa, *Exposition of Faith* (PG 10:985A).

[172] St. Gregory of Nyssa, *Great Catechetical Homily* 2 (PG 45:17B).

[173] St. Gregory the Theologian, *Oration 42*, 15 (PG 36:476 AB).

[174] St. Cyril of Alexandria, *Treasuries* 34 (PG 75:577 A).

[175] St. Basil, *On the Holy Spirit* 8 (PG 32:96-97)..

[176] Reference not found. Apparently, here Saint Gregory is freely rendering the Damascene's thoughts.

[177] I.e. the container stops where the contained begins, and vice versa.

[178] Luke 11:20. Cf. Matthew 12:28.

[179] I.e. in His essence.

[180] St. Cyril of Alexandria, *Treasuries* 33 (PG 75:568 C) et alibi.

[181] See John 3:34.

[182] This quote is from the Oration on the Incarnation of the Only-Begotten (PG 75:1241A).

[183] Reference not found.

[184] John. 7:38.

[185] Acts 1:5.

[186] Acts 2:33.

[187] John. 15:26.

[188] Cyril of Alexandria, *Commentary on the Gospel of Luke* (11:20), (PG 72:704B).

[189] Jer. 2:13.

[190] *On Psalm 96:1 and on the Mystery of Baptism* (Pseud.) 3 (PG 55:607).

[191] John. 4:14.

[192] St. John Chrysostom, *Homily 32 on John* (PG 59:183).

[193] *Dialogue 3 On the Holy Trinity* (PG 75:726 C).

[194] John. 16:13.

[195] *Commentary on the Gospel of John* (16:13) 10 (PG 74:444 B).

[196] *Letter 9 to the Bishop Titus* 1 (PG 3:1104 BC).

[197] *On the Saying of Abraham* 2 (*In Genesim Sermo 3*, PG 56:535).

[198] Letter 52 *To the Nuns* 3 (PG 32:396A).

[199] St. Cyril of Alexandria, *Treasuries* 33 (PG 75:568C).

[200] *Treasuries* 34 (PG 75:576C).

[201] *On the Incarnation of the Only-Begotten (*PG 75:1241A).

[202] *Exact Exposition of the Orthodox Faith* 3,15; 4,18 (PG 96:1016-64).

[203] Probably *Discourse with Macedonius* (pseud.), (PG 28:1308 B, 1309 A).

[204] *On the Celestial Hierarchy* 4, 1 (PG 3:177C.)

[205] *Homily on the Gospel of John 30*, 2 (PG 59:174).

[206] Job 38:1, 40:6.

[207] Namely, "that everything that proceeds from something proceeds through something".

[208] *Exact Exposition of the Orthodox Faith* 1,8,13 (PG 94:808-9).

[209] Oration 31, 25 (PG 36:160).

[210] *Treasuries* 34 (PG 75:577A).

[211] Mt 4:4.

[212] Cf. Luke 4:22.

[213] John 6:63.

[214] See John. 7:38.

[215] John. 4:14.

[216] Cf. Gen. 2:10.

[217] *Against the Sabellians* 6. (PG 31:612)

[218] See St. Gregory of Nyssa, *Great Catechetical Homily* 2 (PG 45:17B).

[219] Cf. John 1:12.

[220] 'Managing': οἰκονομοῦντες, whence comes also the word οἰκονομία, '*economia*'. The idea is that we speak thus with *economia* to those that are not yet mature enough to hear about this 'with exactitude' (ἠκριβωμένως, akin to *akriveia*, 'exactitude').

[221] *Treasuries* (PG 75:569C).

[222] Literally, "when Thou didst proceed".

[223] Ps. 67:8 et sequ.

[224] St. Gregory the Theologian, *Oration 31*, 25.

[225] *On the Incarnation of the Only-Begotten* (PG 75:1241A).

[226] Joel 3:1.

[227] *Commentary on Psalm 44*, 33 (PG 55:186).

[228] Acts 2:38, 8:20, 10:45.

[229] St. John Chrysostom, *On the Holy Spirit* (PG 52:626).

[230] Or "suppose, think".

[231] Ps. 2:7.

[232] Symbol of Faith (Nicene-Constantinopolitan Creed).

[233] This is the great chasm that separates rational academic theology from the experiential theology of the saints. The former is περὶ Θεοῦ γνῶσις, knowledge about God, as one might know about gravity or his country's history, while the later is θεογνωσία, knowledge of God, as one might know a friend, personally.

[234],Is. 48:16.

[235] 1 Cor. 12:8.

[236] See John. 3:5: "Except a man be born of water and of the Spirit, he cannot enter into the kingdom of God".

[237] John 8:42.

[238] John 16:28.

[239] Is. 48:16.

UNCUT MOUNTAIN PRESS TITLES

Books by Archpriest Peter Heers

Fr. Peter Heers, *The Ecclesiological Renovation of Vatican II: An Orthodox Examination of Rome's Ecumenical Theology Regarding Baptism and the Church*, 2015

Fr. Peter Heers, *The Missionary Origins of Modern Ecumenism: Milestones Leading up to 1920*, 2007

The Works of our Father Among the Saints, Nikodemos the Hagiorite

Vol. 1: *Exomologetarion: A Manual of Confession*
Vol. 2: *Concerning Frequent Communion of the Immaculate Mysteries of Christ*
Vol. 3: *Confession of Faith*

Other Available Titles

Elder Cleopa of Romania, *The Truth of our Faith, Vol. I: Discourses from Holy Scripture on the Tenants of Christian Orthodoxy*

Elder Cleopa of Romania, *The Truth of our Faith, Vol. II: Discourses from Holy Scripture on the Holy Mysteries*

Fr. John Romanides, *Patristic Theology: The University Lectures of Fr. John Romanides*

Demetrios Aslanidis and Monk Damascene Grigoriatis, *Apostle to Zaire: The Life and Legacy of Blessed Father Cosmas of Grigoriou*

Protopresbyter Anastasios Gotsopoulos, *On Common Prayer with the Heterodox According to the Canons of the Church*

Robert Spencer, *The Church and the Pope*

G. M. Davis, *Antichrist: The Fulfillment of Globalization*

Athonite Fathers of the 20th Century, Vol. I

St. Hilarion Troitsky, *On the Dogma of the Church: An Historical Overview of the Sources of Ecclesiology*

Fr. Alexander Webster and Fr. Peter Heers, Editors, *Let No One Fear Death*

Subdeacon Nektarios Harrison, *Metropolitan Philaret of New York: Zealous Confessor for the Faith*

Elder George of Grigoriou, *Catholicism in the Light of Orthodoxy*

Archimandrite Ephraim Triandaphillopoulos, *Noetic Prayer as the Basis of Mission and the Struggle Against Heresy*

Select Forthcoming Titles

Nicholas Baldimtsis, *Life and Witness of St. Iakovos of Evia*
Georgio, *Errors of the Latins*
Fr. Peter Heers, *Going Deeper in the Spiritual Life*
Abbe Guette, *The Papacy*
Athonite Fathers of the 20th Century, Vol. II

This 1ˢᵗ Edition of
APODICTIC TREATISES
ON THE PROCESSION OF THE HOLY SPIRIT
by our Father among the Saints, Gregory Palamas, Archbishop of Thessaloniki, translated by Fr. Christopher Moody and Gregory Heers, with a cover design by George Weis, typeset in Baskerville and printed in this two thousand and twenty second year of our Lord's Holy Incarnation, is one of the many fine titles available from Uncut Mountain Press, translators and publishers of Orthodox Christian theological and spiritual literature. Find the book you are looking for at

uncutmountainpress.com

**GLORY BE TO GOD
FOR ALL THINGS**

AMEN.

Made in United States
Orlando, FL
03 September 2024

51087504R00214